THE

# COMEDY THESAURUS

## 3,241 Quips, Quotes, and Smartass Remarks

**Edited by Judy Brown**

QUIRK BOOKS
PHILADELPHIA

Copyright © 2005 by Judy Brown

Library of Congress Cataloging in Publication Number: 2005922079

ISBN-10: 1-59474-058-5

ISBN-13: 978-1-59474-058-9

Printed in the United States

Typeset in New Baskerville and Futura

Designed by Karen Onorato
Illustrations by Karen Onorato

Distributed in North America by Chronicle Books
85 Second Street
San Francisco, CA 94105

10 9 8 7 6

Quirk Books
215 Church Street
Philadelphia, PA 19106
www.quirkbooks.com

# INTRODUCTION

It's always seemed a shame to me that every book of "humorous quotations" drags out the same tired one-liners from dead white males like Oscar Wilde and Mark Twain. As a comedy critic for more than a dozen years, I'd become aware of the length, breadth, and wit of what stand-up comedians have to say—not all of them Caucasians with a penis, and most still very much alive and quipping.

Stand-up comedy may have started as old-fashioned vaudeville gags, Catskill story jokes ("Two guys walk into a bar . . ."), and jokey jokes ("I just flew in from Miami, and boy are my arms tired!"), in which no one, least of all comedians, pretended to believe that their material had any connection to a personal reality. But after World War II, stand-up went through a sea change—influenced by bohemian poets, the civil rights movement, and jazz riffs—to become a more confrontational and conversational social commentary.

## "The truth is what is, not what should be. What should be is a dirty lie."
### —Lenny Bruce

In the 1950s, Lenny Bruce practically invented stand-up comedy plain-speak, most infamously talking funny about the realities of sex and race, instead of making a dirty joke of either. Dick Gregory, Godfrey Cambridge, and Bill Cosby were among the first black comedians to make a mainstream (read: white) audience laugh while keeping their dignity, and without having to demean themselves. And then a thirty-seven-year-old mother of five named Phyllis Diller stood up and also did something revolutionary: evoked cathartic laughter while examining the assumptions about a woman's place in society. "Housework can't kill you, but why take the chance?"

The 1960s—and Bruce's convictions for obscenity—may have produced a chill on stand-up, until two master commentators named Richard Pryor and George Carlin rejected too-easy setups and punch lines for comedic observational monologue masterpieces.

In the 1970s, Elayne Boosler was one of many new female comedians who refused to rely on self-deprecating humor, and incorporated a new feminist perspective into comedy: "There's no leeway for a woman's looks. You never see a man walking down the street with a woman who has a little potbelly and a bald spot."

The 1980s comedy boom gave top stand-ups the opportunity to reinvent the sitcom: Bill Cosby and Roseanne Barr sucked the goo out of the typically gooey family situation comedy, and *Seinfeld* (introduced in 1989) taught sitcoms the stand-up trick of picking at the nothings of daily life and making something funny out of them.

The 1990s and the turn of the new century saw the arrival of funny alternative-attitude girls like Janeane Garofalo, and the coming out party of Ellen DeGeneres on network TV. The decade saw even more ethnic comedians, like George Lopez and Margaret Cho, telling ethnic jokes from the ethnic's point of view: "I was walking down the street and this man actually calls me a chink! I was so mad: Chinks are Chinese; I'm Korean, I'm a gook. If you're gonna be racist, at least get the terminology correct. Okay, Bubba?"

In this comedy quote book you'll find a full range of stand-up material: from the old-fashioned jokey jokes of the founding great-grandfathers of stand-up, to cutting-edge cutting up from contemporary working comedians, some of whom you may be familiar with, and some who haven't become famous—yet.

## ACKNOWLEDGMENTS

First and foremost, I'd like to thank the stand-up comedians who have had such wonderfully funny and quotable things to say. And then, mucho gracias to David Borgenicht, President of Quirk Books, who agreed that a dictionary of comedian quotes would be a valuable and fun resource. Merci beaucoup to Senior Editor Jason Rekulak, who climbed the Mount Everest of more than three thousand comedy quotes with me, and danke to my sometime assistants Andi Rhoads and Jeanie Dietz, who transcribed comedy tapes when I was joked out.

And thanks to Felix and Oscar, two orange kitties who've made me laugh for eight years: through thick and thin, sitcom writing and comedy book editing, and truly outrageous vet bills. Just keep in mind, boys, that it might be cheaper to have you stuffed, and that would be permanent.

E-mail: judy@judybrown.info
Web site: www.judybrown.info

**ACCIDENTS**

I spilled spot remover on my dog, now he's gone.
—*Steven Wright*

I know a guy who had his nose broken in two places. He ought to stay out of those places.
—*Henny Youngman*

Vehicular

While driving I had an accident with a magician. It wasn't my fault, the guy came out of nowhere.
—*Auggie Cook*

A cement mixer collided with a prison van. Motorists are asked to be on the lookout for sixteen hardened criminals.
—*Ronnie Corbett*

If most auto accidents happen within five miles of home, why not move ten miles away?
—*Michael Davis*

I have a driving tip for you: Never hit the lead car in a funeral. I have never seen that many people in that bad a mood.
—*Phyllis Diller*

When I saw a car get sideswiped by a UPS truck, I had to leave a note. It said, "You have been hit by a UPS truck, but you were not in your car. This truck will return the same time tomorrow. If you are not in your car after a third accident, you can pick up your side-view mirror at the local UPS facility."
—*Steve Hofstetter*

There was a 194-car crash in Los Angeles. Luckily the guy in the first car was still able to complete his cell phone call.
—*Jay Leno*

I think cops cause more accidents than they prevent. When you're driving and see a cop ahead, what do you do? Slam on the brakes and struggle to get your seatbelt on. Next to every accident you always see a police car. Coincidence? I think not.

—*Rob O'Reilly*

## ACTIVISM

### Animal

I get into animal causes. I once came up with a method to change horses into glue painlessly with hypnosis. In my method, you take the horse into a dark room, swing a light-bulb in front of his face while the hypnotist says, "You're starting to feel sticky." Naturally, all glue manufactured this way will come with a warning label that says, "Do not snap your fingers in front of this tube."

—*Ed Bluestone*

A lady came up to me on the street and pointed at my suede jacket. "Did you know a cow was murdered for that jacket?" she sneered. I replied in a psychotic tone, "I didn't know there were any witnesses. Now I'll have to kill you too."

—*Jake Johannsen*

### Picketing

See also: **PRO-LIFE**

I'm against picketing, but I don't know how to show it.

—*Mitch Hedberg*

### Volunteering

Have you ever wondered why Republicans are so interested in encouraging people to volunteer in their communities? It's because volunteers work for no pay. Republicans have been trying to get people to work for no pay for a long time.

—*George Carlin*

### World

I'd love to change the world, but I can't find a big enough diaper.

—*Myq Kaplan*

I once wanted to save the world. Now I just want to leave the room with some dignity.
> —*Lotus Weinstock*

## ADOPTION

### Adoptees

I'm adopted and finally found my parents a few years ago. But my first meeting with my father was weird. What could I say to him? "Thanks for coming"?
> —*Tricia Shore*

### Babies

I adopted a baby. I wanted a highway, but it was a lot of red tape.
> —*Margaret Smith*

### Highways

See also: **MOTHERS** Cleaning

I adopted a highway. I'm trying to teach it to pick up after itself.
> —*Nancy Jo Perdue*

The KKK adopted a highway. The joke is on them: It's black.
> —*Jon Stewart*

## ADVERTISING

Advertising is 85 percent confusion and 15 percent commission.
> —*Fred Allen*

The very first law in advertising is to avoid the concrete promise and cultivate the delightfully vague.
> —*Bill Cosby*

### Automobiles

SUVs are named for exotic places we'll never go, like the Dodge Durango or the MGC Yukon. There should be truth in advertising: like calling them the Dodge Dubuque, or the GMC "I'm Going to 7-Eleven for a Moon Pie."
> —*Daryl Hogue*

Beer

The basic beer ad: big-breasted babes in bikinis. Beer won't get you babes. But if you drink enough, you think they're babes, and if you drink more, you can grow your own breasts.
—*Norman K.*

Beer commercials usually show big men doing manly things, "You just killed a small animal: It's time for a lite beer." Why not a realistic beer commercial? "It's five o'clock in the morning, you've just pissed in a Dumpster: It's Miller time!"
—*Robin Williams*

Cosmetics

I can't stand makeup commercials. "Do you need a lipstick that keeps your lips kissable?" No, I need a lipstick that gets me equal pay for equal work. How about eye shadow that makes me stop thinking I'm too fat?
—*Heidi Joyce*

Hemorrhoids

I saw a TV commercial that said, "Kiss your hemorrhoids goodbye." Not even if I could.
—*John Mendoza*

and Men

A man is paralyzed mentally by a beautiful woman, and advertisers take advantage. Like those ads where a woman in the bikini is next to a 32-piece ratchet set. We're going, "She's right next to the ratchet set, if I had the ratchet set, it would mean that . . . I better just buy the ratchets."
—*Jerry Seinfeld*

Subliminal

I saw a subliminal advertising executive. But only for a second.
—*Steven Wright*

**ADVICE**

See also: **MOONING**

It's a rare person who wants to hear what he doesn't want to hear.
—*Dick Cavett*

**AFFIRMATIVE ACTION**

How come the white male politicians who vote against affirmative action are always so willing to accept a handicap on the golf course?
—*Paul Krassner*

**AFTERLIFE**

See: **HELL, RELIGION**

**AGING**

See also: **SENIOR CITIZENS**

I don't know how you feel about old age, but in my case I didn't even see it coming. It hit me from the rear.
—*Phyllis Diller*

I'm now old enough to personally identify every object in antique stores.
—*Anita Milner*

Changes

When you get older your body changes. I've noticed it myself. Now I groan louder after a meal than I do after an orgasm.
—*Joel Warshaw*

Definition of

Old is always fifteen years from now.
—*Bill Cosby*

Feel

I don't feel old. I don't feel anything until noon. Then it's time for my nap.
—*Bob Hope*

Fifty-Something

I recently turned fifty, which is young for a tree, mid-life for an elephant, and ancient for a quarter miler, whose son now says, "Dad, I just can't run the quarter with you anymore unless I bring something to read."
—*Bill Cosby*

Forty-Something

I'm 482 months old; can you tell I'm a new father?
—*Reno Goodale*

How to Know

You know you're getting older when the first thing you do after you're done eating is look for a place to lie down.

*—Louie Anderson*

You know you're getting old when you stoop to tie your shoelaces and wonder what else you could do while you're down there.

*—George Burns*

I know I'm getting older. I pulled my left shoulder out putting peanut butter on a bagel. It was chunky, though. I pulled out my right shoulder putting Ben Gay on my left shoulder.

*—Jeff Cesario*

You know you're getting old; there are certain signs. I walked past a cemetery, and two guys ran after me with shovels.

*—Rodney Dangerfield*

You know you're getting old when people tell you how good you look.

*—Alan King*

as Kids

Do you realize that the only time in our lives when we like to get old is when we're kids? You're so excited about aging that you think in fractions. You're never thirty-six and a half, you're "four and a half, going on five!" You become twenty-one, you turn thirty, you're pushing forty, you reach fifty, you make it to sixty, you build up so much speed you hit seventy. Then a strange thing happens. If you make it over 100, you become a little kid again, "I'm 101, and a half!"

*—Larry Miller*

When I turned two I was really anxious, because I'd doubled my age in a year. I thought, "If this keeps up, by the time I'm six, I'll be ninety."

*—Steven Wright*

| | |
|---|---|
| Middle Age | Middle age is when your age starts to show around your middle.<br>—*Bob Hope* |
| Obituaries | Like everyone else who makes the mistake of getting older, I begin each day with coffee and obituaries.<br>—*Bill Cosby* |
| Senility | "Don't worry about senility," my grandfather used to say. "When it hits you, you won't know it."<br>—*Bill Cosby* |
| Sensations | I'm a goofy old fart, but I still have fun. Have you ever been on a rollercoaster? I'm so old I get that same sensation just rolling over in bed.<br>—*Old Man Heywood* |
| Sleeping | I'm officially at the age where I see that commercial for the Craftmatic Adjustable Bed and think, "Sweet! Are you kidding me? You mean I can sleep in the shape of a U?"<br>—*John Heffron* |
| Smiling More | I'm getting older so I've started to smile more, because I want the crow's feet to go up.<br>—*Simone Alexander* |
| So Old | He's so old his blood type was discontinued.<br>—*Bill Dana* |
| | That man is so old, he's older than his birthday.<br>—*Moms Mabley* |
| | I'm so old that when I order a three-minute egg they make me pay up front.<br>—*Henny Youngman* |
| Thirty-Something | See also: **MARRIAGE** Maybe |

I just celebrated my thirtieth birthday. Ten years late, but I did it.
    —*Reno Goodale*

I turned thirty, and suddenly I was at that point in your life where you want to eat Fruity Pebbles, but you're concerned about the fiber content.
    —*Paul Provenza*

**Waist Size**

It used to be that my age and waist size were the same size. Unfortunately, they still are.
    —*Reno Goodale*

**Waking up**

I wake up in the morning, it takes me a half hour to find my glasses, just so I can look for my teeth, to tell my wife to find my hair.
    —*Richard Jeni*

**ALCOHOL**

See also: **ALCOHOLISM, BARS, DRINKING, HEALTH** Warnings, **WINE**

**Accessories**

Coffee's a drink that encourages a lot of accessories. Coffee cake, coffee table, coffee table book, clutches of people. Say what you want about alcohol, but not only are there not a lot of optional accessories, alcohol actually helps you get rid of things. Family, home, job, driver's license. In fact, at a certain point, the only thing you have to remember to get is more alcohol. And maybe a rag for your squeegee.
    —*Jerry Seinfeld*

**Definition of**

Is it bad when you refer to all alcohol as "Pain Go Bye-Bye Juice"?
    —*Patton Oswalt*

**Effects**

You rarely meet a wino with perfect pitch.
    —*George Carlin*

Booze makes you loud. It's written on the label: "Alcohol percent by volume."
—*Mark Lundholm*

Alcohol kills brain cells. We take the only organ in our body that won't grow back, and we kill it for fun.
—*Cary Odes*

I hate being around alcoholics because they're either telling you how much they love you or how much they hate you. And those are the two statements that scare me the most.
—*Jerry Seinfeld*

If you enjoy your alcohol, remember this: If you put your old, rotten used-up liver under your pillow, the Beer Fairy will leave you a keg.
—*Paul F. Tomkins*

The first purpose of alcohol is to make English your second language. You may be a Nobel prize physicist, but after nine, ten Heinekens you're speaking fluent Drunken-ese. Next thing you know, you have a friend in a headlock, "I love ya, I love ya, that's the kinda love I have for you, goddamn it."
—*Robin Williams*

Jack Daniels

Jack Daniels, that is a wild man drink. It should come with bail money. Because on Jack you don't know where you're going to end up, but you know when you get there you're not going to be wearing pants.
—*Dave Attell*

Jägermeister

I was drinking tequila, and I was drinking grappa, which is Italian for gasoline. And I was drinking Jägermeister, which I believe is the liquid equivalent of Wonder Woman's golden lasso, because it will make you tell anybody the truth for no reason whatsoever. "You have really bad skin. Thanks for the drink."
—*Margaret Cho*

and Pregnancy

They've put warning labels on liquor. "Caution: Alcohol can be dangerous to pregnant women." Did you read that? That's ironic. If it weren't for alcohol, most women would never be that way.
—*Rita Rudner*

Tequila

One tequila, two tequila, three tequila, floor.
—*George Carlin*

**ALCOHOLISM**

See also: **ALCOHOL**, **BARS**, **DRINKING**

Alcoholism is a disease, but it's the only one you can get yelled at for having. "Goddamn it, Otto, you are an alcoholic." "Goddamn it, Otto, you have Lupus." One of those two doesn't sound right.
—*Mitch Hedberg*

Scientists have located the gene that causes alcoholism. They found it at a party talking too loudly.
—*Conan O'Brien*

Every alcoholic who has stopped drinking can remember the last time he got drunk. For me, it was the night I drank so much Crown Royal my scrotum turned into a purple pouch with a gold-tasseled drawstring.
—*Jeff Shaw*

My dad was the town drunk. A lot of times that's not so bad, but New York City?
—*Henny Youngman*

**ALIVE**

Every day I beat my own previous record for number of consecutive days I've stayed alive.
—*George Carlin*

**AMBITION**

I used to be driven, but I pulled over.
—*Heidi Joyce*

**AMBULANCES**    See: **HEALTH CARE**, **MEDICINE** Ambulances

**AMERICA, UNITED STATES OF**    See also: **HISTORY**, **PATRIOTISM**, **STATES**

America's one of the finest countries anyone ever stole.
—*Bobcat Goldthwait*

If you're black, you got to look at America a little bit different. You got to look at America like the uncle who paid for you to go to college, but molested you.
—*Chris Rock*

Amish Country

My parents took me to Amish country, to see a bunch of people who have no cars, no TV, no phone. Who wants to see a whole community that's been grounded? That's the way they should punish kids after they've seen the Amish. "Get up to your room. That's it, I've had it, you are Amish, young man! And don't come down till you've made some noodles and raised a barn."
—*Jerry Seinfeld*

Eating in

Americans are gluttons. We shop with forklifts. We have a holiday where we stuff food into other food. Our strippers wrestle in Jell-O, where other countries have to use mud.
—*Bill Maher*

People in other countries, they all want to come to America. They say, "You can eat twenty-four hours a day in America." I say yeah, they're right. If you have some money, or a pistol, you can get something to eat.
—*Richard Pryor*

the South

I'm going to write a book about the South. I'm going to call it *When Beautiful Places Happen to Bad People*.
—*Brett Butler*

the West

I like the West. That's where men are men and women are women, and it's hard to beat a combination like that.

—*Milton Berle*

I don't understand people who go to amusement parks. I spend most of my time trying not to be nauseous and dizzy. "Excuse me, could you strap me in upside down? I'd like to be as sick as humanly possible. I feel great today; I think I'll go down to Funland and snap my neck on the back of a ride. Honey, let's bring the kids. I want to give them a spinal cord injury for Christmas."

—*Dom Irrera*

**ANESTHETICS**

See: **MEDICINE** Anesthesia

**ANIMALS**

See also: **BIRDS, CATS, DOGS, PETS, ZOOS**

Cattle

We've all done this, because we're so mature. You see a cow on the side of the road, stick your head out the window and go "Mooo!" Like we expect the cow to think, "Hey, there's another cow, driving that car! How can he afford that?"

—*Garry Shandling*

Coyotes

In LA we get coyotes in our garbage cans. Coyotes are just like my relatives. They go out in pairs, they whine at night, and they go anywhere there's food.

—*Billy Crystal*

Dead

How many of those dead animals you see on the highway are suicides?

—*Dennis Miller*

Endangered Species

See also: Size

What should you do when you see an endangered animal that is eating an endangered plant?

—*George Carlin*

**as Friends**

Animals may be our friends, but they won't pick you up at the airport.
—*Bobcat Goldthwait*

I find that ducks' opinion of me is greatly influenced by whether or not I have bread.
—*Mitch Hedberg*

**Functions**

Animals have two functions in today's society, to be delicious and to fit well.
—*Greg Proops*

**Group Names**

It's so weird all the different names they have for groups of animals. They have pride of lions, school of fish, rack of lamb. . . .
—*Ellen DeGeneres*

**Hyenas**

The Discovery Channel had a fascinating show on the mating habits of hyenas. They said that the male hyena often will get angry at the female hyena while they are having sex. It doesn't help that the female hyena is laughing at you all the time.
—*Jay Leno*

**Kangaroos**

See also: **PREGNANCY** Pondering

Two kangaroos were talking to each other, and one said, "Gee, I hope it doesn't rain today. I hate it when the children play inside."
—*Henny Youngman*

**Lions**

I take my pet lion to church every Sunday. He has to eat.
—*Marty Pollio*

**Platypus**

If you look at a platypus, you think that God might get stoned, "OK, let's take a beaver and put on a duck's bill. It's a mammal, but it lays eggs. Hey Darwin, kiss my ass!"
—*Robin Williams*

**Rabbits**

A couple of rabbits were being chased by a pack of coyotes. They stopped in a haystack, and one rabbit said to the other, "We gonna make a run for it, or stay here and out-number them?"
—*Red Skelton*

The other day when I was walking through the woods, I saw a rabbit standing in front of a candle making shadows of people on a tree.
—*Steven Wright*

**Rescue**

My wife works at an animal rescue place. So at home we now have a dog with two anuses and half a dachshund.
—*Jon Stewart*

**Rights**

My feeling is, we ran from animals for three million years. It's our time now. If a cow could eat you, it would. And it wouldn't care how comfortable your truck ride over was, either.
—*Greg Proops*

**Size**

You know why fish are so thin? They eat fish.
—*Jerry Seinfeld*

Size isn't everything. The whale is endangered, while the ant continues to do just fine.
—*Bill Vaughan*

**Snails**

What does a snail say when he rides on the back of a turtle? "Whee!"
—*Will Durst*

I hate snails. I don't trust them. Pulling their house on their back. Walking around, "Nothing can harm me, I've got my house on my back." *Crunch*. "Where did that foot come from? Bastard broke my house. I don't have insurance for that."
—*Jeremy Hotz*

Snakes

I found a snake in my yard, and got a shovel and whacked the hell out of it. Then I didn't have cable for a week.

—*Charlie Viracola*

Testing

They do a lot of animal testing in the cosmetics industry. Maybe they should brag about it in their commercials: "Aquanet hair spray, if it can blind a Spider Monkey, it can make your hair look luscious." Or "Gillette, because four thousand bald squirrels can't be wrong."

—*Vernon Chapman*

I think animal testing is a terrible idea; they get all nervous and give the wrong answers.

—*Fry and Laurie*

Wrongs

Dolphin-safe tuna, that's great if you're a dolphin. What if you're a tuna? Somewhere there's a tuna flopping around a ship going, "What about me? I'm not cute enough for you?"

—*Drew Carey*

To me, the most blatant example of cruelty to animals is the rotisserie. It's just a really morbid Ferris wheel for chickens.

—*Mitch Hedberg*

**ANSWERING MACHINES**

See: **TELEPHONES**

**APARTMENTS**

See also: **HOUSING**

Painting

I've been living in this apartment for years, and every time I paint it, it's a little bit smaller. The thickness of the paint keeps coming in closer. I don't even know where the wall outlets are anymore. I look for a lump with two slots in it. Looks like a pig is trying to push his way through from the other side. That's where I plug in.

—*Jerry Seinfeld*

**Rent**

I don't get no respect. I told my landlord I want to live in a more expensive apartment. He raised the rent.
—*Rodney Dangerfield*

My landlord comes by. Tries to be nice. He tells me, "Bernard, I like you, but the rent's way overdue, and I've got people lining up around the block for this apartment." "Lining up around the block?" I ask that sumbitch. "Who wants to live in this crack house?" And he says, "You livin' here, ain't you?"
—*Bernie Mac*

I've been sort of crabby lately. It's that time of the month again—the rent's due.
—*Margaret Smith*

**When Single**

The only good thing about a singles apartment is that you never had to clean it up. At least not until the day you moved and tried to get the security deposit back. Then you'd argue with the landlord. "No sir, the back door was missing when we moved in here. The pizzas were always on the ceiling."
—*Jeff Foxworthy*

**APOLOGIES**

Mexican people never say they're sorry. My grandmother, when I was young, hit me with her car. I was in the driveway—pang! "You know where I park, *cabron*. *Mira*, where the oil is." Did she say she was sorry? "*Ta loco*, he's seven. When he starts paying the bills, then I'll say sorry."
—*George Lopez*

**ARCHITECTURE**

See also: **HOUSING**

I think the most memorable experience I had in France was visiting the Cathedral at Chartres. It's a four-hundred-year-old cathedral, beautiful stained glass, and it's a very, very moving experience, and as I was writing my name on it with a can of spray paint . . .

—*Steve Martin*

**ARGUMENTS**      See also: **MARRIAGE**

I got into an argument with my girlfriend inside a tent. A tent is not a good place for an argument. I tried to walk out on her and had to slam the flap.

—*Mitch Hedberg*

I got into a fight one time with a really big guy, and he said, "I'm going to mop the floor with your face." I said, "You'll be sorry." He said, "Oh yeah? Why?" I said, "Well, you won't be able to get into corners very well."

—*Emo Philips*

Never pick a fight with an ugly person; they've got nothing to lose.

—*Robin Williams*

**ART**      See also: **MUSEUMS**

I'm taking an art class, and the nude model just quit. Because I like to finger paint.

—*Wendy Liebman*

There is nothing funny about dogs playing poker. There is nothing remotely cute about animals with gambling problems. If you look closely at those paintings, you can tell that most of those dogs are playing with money they can't afford to lose. And sadder still, it takes seven of their dollars to make one of ours.

—*Dennis Miller*

I've been doing a lot of abstract painting lately, extremely abstract. No brush, no paint, no canvas, I just think about it.

—*Steven Wright*

**ASSEMBLY**

I got a gas grill, but it came unassembled. It looked like a car bomb. Every guy's been where I've been. You finish building it, it looks great, but there's a weird bag of important-looking stuff left over. "Honey? Why don't you try the grill out first? I'll be in the basement with my welding hat on."

—*Tim Allen*

**ASSES**

Never comment on a woman's rear end. Never use the words "large" or "size" with "rear end." Never. Avoid the area altogether. Trust me.

—*Tim Allen*

I like nothing more in the world than sitting on my ass doing nothing. And it's not my fault I have this attitude, because I happen to have an amazingly comfortable ass. It may not look like much, but if you could sit on this baby for two minutes, you'd realize that getting off this ass would be a crime against nature. I'm fighting the will of God every time I step on a Stairmaster, and that's an uphill battle, let me tell you.

—*Lori Chapman*

I've been working out. I work out everything, except my ass. I don't work out my ass because I never think of it, I never see it. Unless something has gone horribly wrong. To me, it's a safety device to prevent me from falling in the toilet. So as long as it's doing its job, I don't have to make it look attractive, too. That's just a little too much pressure.

—*Garry Shandling*

**ASTROLOGY**

My wife's an earth sign. I'm a water sign. Together we make mud.

—*Henny Youngman*

**ASTRONOMY**

Interestingly, according to modern astronomers, space is finite. This is a very comforting thought, particularly for people who cannot remember where they left things.

—*Woody Allen*

> I've been getting into astronomy, so I installed a skylight. The people who live above me are furious.
>
> —*Steven Wright*

## ATTITUDES

Bad Temper

The worst-tempered people I have ever met were those who knew that they were wrong.
—*David Letterman*

Chip on Shoulder

The chip on my shoulder's a little heavy. I have back problems now.
—*Janeane Garofalo*

Pessimism

I got to a traffic light, and it turned red. I said, "Why me?"
—*Geoff Bolt*

I guess I just prefer to see the dark side of things. The glass is always half empty. And cracked. And I just cut my lip on it. And chipped a tooth.
—*Janeane Garofalo*

It seems like I'm always an hour late or a dollar short. I'm the kind of guy who will have nothing all my life, and then they'll discover oil while they're digging my grave.
—*George Gobel*

Some mornings, it's just not worth chewing through the leather straps.
—*Emo Philips*

Pet Peeves

I don't have pet peeves like some people. I have whole kennels of irritation.
—*Whoopie Goldberg*

Positive

I think it's really important to maintain a positive attitude. It might not solve all your problems, but keep it up long enough

and it will piss off enough people to make it worthwhile.
—*Margot Black*

If a man smiles all the time he's probably selling something that doesn't work.
—*George Carlin*

Seminars

I was forced to go to a positive-thinking seminar. I couldn't stand it. So I went outside to the parking lot and let half the air out of everybody's tires. As they came out I said, "So, are your tires half-full, or half-empty?"
—*Adam Christing*

**AUTOMOBILES**

See also: **ACCIDENTS, DRIVING, GASOLINE**

American

I have one of those real old American-built cars. The kind that just punches through accidents.
—*Jim Samuels*

Car Alarms

I was on my way to work the other day, and I guess I got too close to someone's car, because the alarm started going off. I didn't want them to come back and be confused as to why it was going off, so I threw a brick through the windshield. I figured that would explain it.
—*Jessica Delfino*

They design the car alarm so it will behave as if it was a nervous hysterical person. Anyone goes near it, disturbs it, "Aaaaaahhhhhhh!" Lights flashing on and off, acting all crazy. Wouldn't it be nice to have a car alarm that was a little more subtle? Somebody tries to break in, it goes, "Ahem. Ahem. Excuse me?"
—*Jerry Seinfeld*

Crappy

I've finally got a car that turns heads. Mostly because of the knocking, rattling, and backfiring.
—*Reno Goodale*

Knowledge of

I know a lot about cars. I can look at a car's headlights and tell you exactly which way it's coming.
—*Mitch Hedberg*

License Plates

My license plate says PMS. Nobody cuts me off.
—*Wendy Liebman*

and Men

My aunt, thirty years a feminist, says, "A car is just an extension of your penis." Oh, I wish.
—*Tim Allen*

I've never known a man who wasn't deeply attached on a very emotional level to his beloved vehicle. Whether it was a piece of junk or a masterpiece made no difference. They rode in their metal boxes and were in control of their lives. I think I know why so many men are afraid to make a commitment to women. It's because we can't be steered.
—*Rita Rudner*

When you're a dad you can't keep your cool car. Fancy stereo, power windows, sunroof; the kids are going to kill all that stuff. Take an ordinary cookie. In the hands of a kid it becomes a sugar hand grenade. You have to take the car into the shop because chocolate chips are clogging the carburetor.
—*Sinbad*

Men Versus
Women

My boyfriend, like a lot of men, takes great pride in his car. Honey, his car is detailed, waxed, and vacuumed weekly. On the other hand, my car looks like a really big purse.
—*Diane Nichols*

There is truth in what they say about the sexes. Men like cars; women like clothes. I also like cars because they take me to clothes.
—*Rita Rudner*

Minivans

In a Jeep you can at least pretend to be cool. When you're at a stoplight and an attractive woman pulls up alongside you, you

can still smile and convince yourself, "Maybe she thinks I'm
enormously rugged and the car is loaded up with equipment for that very dangerous geological expedition." But in
a minivan, you're fooling no one. You're on your way to
Gymboree, the side compartments are stuffed with diaper
wipes, and the interior is all sticky with apple juice. You
know what? You're not Indiana Jones; you're a dad.
   *—Paul Reiser*

Mirrors
Driving hasn't been the same since I installed fun-house
rearview mirrors.
   *—Steven Wright*

Pintos
My brother gave me his Pinto, but he neglected to tell me
one thing: It doesn't handle well on pavement.
   *—Christine Crosby*

Problems
I'm having car problems. My Check Engine light came on
today. But I couldn't check it; there was too much smoke.
Then the Game Over light came on. I hadn't seen that
one before.
   *—Dobie Maxwell*

Recalls
They recall a lot of cars. "We gotta get those cars back. We
don't recall putting brakes in them."
   *—Evan Davis*

Rentals
Anybody abuse rental cars? The thing that bothers me is
when you have to return one with a full tank of gas. You
know what I do now? I just top it off with a garden hose.
   *—Will Shriner*

Repairs
Every time I go to a mechanic, they look at me like I'm stu-
pid, "It's a gasket, honey." I know what a gasket is; it's $150.
But a "gasket, honey" is $200.
   *—Emily Levine*

Start-up Speed

My husband's car goes from zero to sixty in ten seconds, and that makes him happy. I just don't know why he'd ever want to do that. Maybe someday he'll find an open stretch of road and play Frisbee with himself.
—*Rita Rudner*

SUVs

See also: **ADVERTISING**

I hate those new Sport Utility Vehicles. I just got cut off by that new one, you know, the Ford Exhibitionist.
—*Daryl Hogue*

SUVs, why must they be so big? Americans need their space. Just ask the Indians.
—*Mo Rocca*

According to some commercials, driving an SUV means you support terrorists. The answer is the hybrid gas-electric car, which only supports terrorists when going uphill.
—*Jon Stewart*

Tires

The gas station attendant looks at the car and says, "You got a flat tire." I said, "No, the other three just swelled up."
—*Bill Engvall*

Towing

I had my car towed. There's nothing wrong with it. That was just cheaper than buying a tank of gas.
—*Jay Leno*

Trade-ins

I took my car down to see what I could get for it on a trade-in. The dealer took a look at it and offered me a ballpoint pen.
—*Henny Youngman*

**BABIES**      See also: **BIRTH, FATHERHOOD, MOTHERHOOD, PREGNANCY**

Avoiding

I still can't believe that people I know, my peers, are making babies. I'm too lazy to make a salad.
—*Hellura Lyle*

I'll never have a baby because I'm afraid I'll leave it on top of my car.
—*Lizz Winstead*

Babysitting

As far as babysitting tips go, I recommend a few quick questions to the parents when you want to get out early. Like, "Is it all right for the baby to have . . . bleach?"
—*Jake Johannsen*

Circumcisions

My son was circumcised by his father. Who's not a doctor, just cheap.
—*Daryl Hogue*

The hardest thing in the world is making a kid happy after he's been circumcised.
—*Damon Wayans*

Considering

I've thought about having a family. I just haven't seen any that really appeal to me.
—*Laura Kightlinger*

I want to have kids some day, but I have to consider the crying, changing clothes, the bottles, the late night feedings . . . and then there's also a baby to take care of.
—*Tracey MacDonald*

I can't decide if I want a baby. And my friends who have kids don't make very good salesmen. They're like, "Oh you learn all this great stuff, like how to survive on two hours' sleep." If I want to learn that I'll just become a political prisoner or something.
—*Cathryn Michon*

I was asking my friend who has children, "What if I have a baby and I dedicate my life to it and it grows up to hate me. And it blames everything wrong with its life on me." And she said, "What do you mean, 'if'?"

—*Rita Rudner*

## Crying

For about a month after my baby was born I bragged to everyone that I had the perfect baby because he never cried. Then I realized those baby monitors have volume control.

—*Frances Dilorinzo*

We have a baby now at my house, all day long. And all night long. I wonder why they say you have a baby? The baby has you.

—*Gallagher*

## Cute

I think God made babies cute so we don't eat them.

—*Robin Williams*

## Diapers

You have got to change those diapers every day. When it says "six to twelve pounds" on the side of the Pampers box, they're not lying. That is all those things will hold.

—*Jeff Foxworthy*

I hate changing my baby's diapers after he poops. I know exactly what he ate at daycare. Yesterday, it was carrots. Tomorrow I'm hoping for long-stem roses.

—*Shirley Lipner*

Shouldn't there be some kind of relationship between how much a baby eats and how much comes out the other end? It's like at the circus, where they've got the tiny VW bug but the clowns just keep coming out and out and out. . . . Eventually you learn how to hold your breath like a Hokkaido pearl diver.

—*Dennis Miller*

My friend has a sixteen-month-old. The baby's crawling around, and he has an accident in his diaper. And the mother comes over and says, "Isn't that adorable? Brandon made a gift for Daddy." I'm thinking this guy must be real easy to shop for on Father's Day.
—*Garry Shandling*

Baby caca is like Kryptonite to a father. Even the dog says, "You don't rub his face in it."
—*Robin Williams*

Doctors

You always get drugs when you go and see the doctor with the baby. The drugs are for me and Mama.
—*Gallagher*

Hopes for

See also: **PARENTS**

When my son was born I had this dream that one day he might grow up to be a Nobel Prize winner. But I also had another dream that he might grow up to say, "Do you want fries with that?"
—*Robin Williams*

Naming

Always end the name of your child with a vowel, so that when you yell the name will carry.
—*Bill Cosby*

We gave our kids old-fashioned names. Our little boy is Hunter, and our little girl is Gatherer.
—*Brian Kiley*

In some cultures they don't name their babies right away. They wait until they see how the child develops. Like in *Dances with Wolves*. Unfortunately, our kids' names would be less romantic and poetic. "This is my oldest boy, Falls off His Tricycle, his friend, Dribbles His Juice, and my beautiful daughter, Allergic to Nuts."
—*Paul Reiser*

It gets harder to name children when you get older. Because by the time you're in your thirties every name you think of reminds you of someone you hate. We have to hurry; we're down to Jethro and Nefertiti.

—*Rita Rudner*

Naming our kid was a real trial. I seize up when I have to name a document on my computer. I didn't name my son after me. What if he turns into a maniac? How'd you like to be Jeffrey Dahmer, Senior?

—*Jeff Stillson*

Photographs

People seldom live up to their baby pictures.

—*Rodney Dangerfield*

Potty Training

The baby is great. My wife and I have just started potty training. Which I think is important, because when we want to potty train the baby we should set an example.

—*Howie Mandel*

Spitting up

If you pull at babies too hard, they'll spew like a can of beer. I used to shake up my daughter and hand her to people I didn't like. "Hold her just a minute, would ya?"

—*Jeff Foxworthy*

Temperatures

Studies show rectal thermometers are still the best way to take a baby's temperature. Plus, it really shows them who's boss.

—*Tina Fey*

Work

There's a lot to do when you have a baby. The first thing, which is taking me a really long time: I have to figure out who the father is.

—*Heidi Joyce*

**BALDNESS**

See: **HAIR**

**BANKING**          See also: **FINANCES**

ATMs

For safety's sake, I try not to go to the ATM at night. I also try not to go with my four-year-old who screams, "We've got money! We've got money!"

—*Paul Clay*

At the ATM they ask if you'd like to conduct your business in English or Spanish. I suggest you try Spanish, because your account balance will look much better in pesos.

—*Tere Joyce*

When someone's using an ATM, you want be about six feet back. People get edgy around that ATM. They got their money out, their eyes are darting around. The other place I wanna be six feet away is urinals. ATMs and urinals—whenever someone's taking something valuable out of their pants you want to give them as much room as possible.

—*Jerry Seinfeld*

Checks

The lady at the bank asked, "What do you want on your checks: wildlife, scenery?" I said, "I want a picture of a big, thick-necked guy on my checks. What's that? A bouncer, that's what my checks are going to be."

—*Bob Kubota*

Friendly

The banks have a new image. Now you have "a friend." Your friendly banker. If the banks are so friendly, how come they chain down the pens?

—*Alan King*

Loans

I had a hard time at the bank today. I tried to take out a loan, and they pulled a real attitude with me. Apparently, they won't accept the voices in my head as references.

—*Steve Altman*

A bank is a place that will lend you money, if you can prove that you don't need it.
—*Bob Hope*

**Savings Accounts**  I don't even have a savings account because I don't know my mom's maiden name, and apparently that's the key to the whole thing.
—*Paula Poundstone*

I went to the bank and went over my savings. I found out I have all the money that I'll ever need. If I die tomorrow.
—*Henny Youngman*

**Tellers**  They usually have two tellers in my local bank. Except when it's very busy, when they have one.
—*Rita Rudner*

**BANKS**  See also: **BANKING**

**Blood**  A blood bank called the other day to see if I was interested in making a donation. For free. That just didn't seem right. Not when I'm still using my blood and I've got bills to pay. The sperm bank pays me for my generosity, even though we all know there's always plenty more where that came from. And the blood bank doesn't even let you keep their magazines. I know, because I asked.
—*Brian Beatty*

I tried to give blood the other day. The blood bank refused to take it, though. Because I wouldn't tell them where I got it from.
—*Wally Wang*

**Sperm**  I know that some lesbians are getting pregnant by going to sperm banks. I couldn't do that. I'm exactly like my grandmother, "What? Everything's frozen! Nothing's fresh?"
—*Judy Carter*

I have nothing against sperm banks, but they should really get rid of those automatic teller machines.
—*David Corrado*

For a woman the worst thing about a sperm bank is that sperm is no longer free. Just go into a bar, and a sperm container will try to pick you up.
—*Tina Georgie*

I saw this ad in the paper, "Safe Sex. Get Paid. Men 18 to 40." Sounds like the kind of scam I go for. So I call 'em up, and it's a guidebook to sperm banks. And I think: Why not get paid? After all, I've done charity work for so long.
—*Norman K.*

People make a living donating to sperm banks. Last year I let $500 slip through my fingers.
—*Robert Schimmel*

**BARS**

See also: **ALCOHOL**, **DRINKING**

I went to the bar to have a few drinks. The bartender asked me, "What'll you have?" I said, "Surprise me." He showed me a naked picture of my wife.
—*Rodney Dangerfield*

Two guys walk into a bar. You'd think one of them would have seen it.
—*Daniel Lybra*

I was at a bar nursing a beer. My nipple was getting quite soggy.
—*Emo Philips*

Never buy a drink for the road, because the road is already laid out.
—*Flip Wilson*

Pickups

I was in a bar the other night, hopping from barstool to barstool, trying to get lucky. But there wasn't any gum under any of them.
—*Emo Philips*

I went up to a girl in a bar once and asked her where she was from. I guess she wasn't interested, because she said, "Mars." So I asked, "You need a ride home?"
—*Ray Romano*

I once said to a woman in a bar, "What's your name?" She said, "Don't even bother." I said, "Is that an Indian name, because I'd like to meet Hot to Trot. Is she here?"
—*Garry Shandling*

## BASEBALL

Infield Chatter

One of the things that stays behind in childhood is baseball infield chatter. "Hey batter, hey batter, batter . . . swing!" For instance, as an adult, I've never seen courtroom proceedings start with "Hey lawyer, hey lawyer, lawyer . . . sue!"
—*Dobie Maxwell*

Little League

I was never an athletic kid. One year I played Little League baseball, and my dad was the coach. Halfway through the season he traded me to another family.
—*David Corrado*

I was in Little League. I was on first base: I stole third. I ran straight across the diamond. Earlier in the week, I learned the shortest distance between two points is a straight line. I argued with the ump that second base was out of my way.
—*Steven Wright*

Season Openers

Are you excited about the opening of the baseball season? Ah, the leather, the pine tar, the rosin—and that's just the hot dogs.
—*Conan O'Brien*

and Sex

Baseball is so associated with sex. "He's playing the field," "He scored," "He didn't get to first base." "I struck out." Why? "She wanted a diamond."

*—Jerry Seinfeld*

Spitting

Every time a baseball player grabs his crotch, it makes him spit. That's why you should never date a baseball player.

*—Marsha Warfield*

Stealing

I used to steal second base, and feel guilty and go back.

*—Woody Allen*

Umpires

Another umpire was attacked by a fan. That's not fair. With their poor eyesight you know umpires can't pick suspects out of lineups.

*—Jay Leno*

Versus Football

Baseball and football are the two most popular spectator sports in this country. And as such, it seems they ought to be able to tell us something about ourselves and our values. In baseball, during the game, in the stands, there's kind of a picnic feeling; emotions may run high or low, but there's not too much unpleasantness. In football, during the game in the stands, you can be sure that at least twenty-seven times you're capable of taking the life of a fellow human being.

*—George Carlin*

## BEAUTY

Contests

I can't believe we still have the Miss America pageant. This is America! Where we're not supposed to judge people based on how they look; we're supposed to judge people based on how much money they make.

*—Heidi Joyce*

"As Miss America, my goal is to bring peace to the entire world, and then get my own apartment."

*—Jay Leno*

The Miss America pageant is very pro-education. They give the winner a full college scholarship. Which is just what Harvard needs, more bulimics who play the ukulele.
—*Sheila Wenz*

Men

There are a lot of good-looking men out there. But keep in mind that no matter how cute and sexy a guy is, there's always some woman somewhere who is sick of him.
—*Carol Henry*

Not

I'm so ugly, as a kid, I once stuck my head out the window and got arrested for mooning.
—*Rodney Dangerfield*

Standards

Standards of beauty change. If Mona Lisa went into a modeling agency today, they'd say, "Sorry, we don't need a janitor."
—*Jim Gaffigan*

Society's idea of beautiful has much too much to do with thin. My feeling is that when you can actually see a woman digesting, she's too thin.
—*Jonathan Katz*

Women

There's no leeway for a woman's looks. You never see a man walking down the street with a woman who has a little pot belly and a bald spot.
—*Elayne Boosler*

**BEDDING**

I bought an irregular electric blanket. It's solar-powered.
—*Nick Arnette*

**BEER**

See: **ADVERTISING**, **ALCOHOL**, **BEVERAGES**

**BEVERAGES**

See also: **ALCOHOL**, **COFFEE**, **WATER**, **WINE**

Beer, Nonalcoholic

The people who invented nonalcoholic beer are working on liver without vitamins.
—*Elayne Boosler*

Nonalcoholic beer is kinda like a Nerf vibrator. It's not really going to work.
—*Robin Williams*

Diet Sodas

The odds of getting a diet soda when you order one at the drive-through are roughly better than chance.
—*Jason Love*

I'm drinking a Diet Coke, because frankly I ate a whole box of Pop Tarts yesterday and this will take it away.
—*Paula Poundstone*

Dr. Pepper

I went out to lunch today and ordered a Dr. Pepper. The waitress said, "We don't have Dr. Pepper; we have Mr. Pibb. It's the same thing." It's not the same thing at all. Dr. Pepper went to school an extra four years. He's much more qualified to be a soft drink. We don't even know if Mr. Pibb has a G.E.D.
—*Livia Squires*

Tea

Tea, tea! What is it with tea? I have passed urine samples that are stronger than this. Gimme a coffee, now!
—*Colin Mocherie*

**BIRDS**

See also: **ANIMALS, PETS**

Eagles

Eagles mate while flying at eighty miles an hour. And when they start to drop, they don't stop until the act is completed. So, it's not uncommon they both hit the ground and die. That's how committed they are. Boy, don't we feel like wimps for stopping to answer the phone? I don't know about you, but if I'm one of those two birds and we're getting close to the ground, I would seriously consider faking it.
—*Ellen DeGeneres*

Feeders

I bought a bird feeder. It was expensive, but I figured in the long run it would save me money on cat food.
—*Linda Herskovic*

Parakeets

My parakeet died. We were playing badminton.
      —*Danny Curtis*

Ever let your parakeet out of its cage? My parakeet will fly across the room, right into the mirror. . . . He will hit that mirror: *Bang!* He's so stupid. Even if he thought the mirror was another room, you'd think he'd try to avoid hitting the other parakeet.
      —*Jerry Seinfeld*

**BIRTH**

See also: **BABIES, FATHERHOOD, MOTHERHOOD, MOTHERS**

When I was born I was so surprised I couldn't talk for a year and a half.
      —*Gracie Allen*

I don't get no respect. When I was born, the doctor smacked my mother.
      —*Rodney Dangerfield*

It was probably a coincidence, but right after I was born, my mom and dad left town.
      —*Bob Hope*

I've always, always wanted to give birth. To kittens. I figure it would hurt less, and when you're done, you'd have kittens!
      —*Betsy Salkind*

When I was a baby, I kept a diary. Recently I was rereading it. It said: "Day One: Still tired from the move. Day Two: Everybody talks to me like I'm an idiot."
      —*Steven Wright*

Alternatives

People are giving birth underwater now. They say it's less traumatic for the baby because it's in water. But certainly more traumatic for the other people in the pool.
      —*Elayne Boosler*

This is exciting. A woman recently had a baby from an embryo that had been frozen for seven years. She said, "I had no idea if I was having a little boy, a little girl—or fish sticks."
—*Conan O'Brien*

**Cesarean**

We had a C-section. That's when the baby comes out like toast.
—*Bobcat Goldthwait*

I was born by Cesarean section, but you can't really tell. Except that when I leave my house, I always go out the window.
—*Steven Wright*

**Classes**

See also: **EXERCISE**

You take Lamaze classes. I went. It was a total waste of time. Ain't nobody going to breathe a baby out. There's going to be a fight.
—*Sinbad*

In the natural childbirth classes my wife and I took, the birthing process was represented by a hand puppet being pushed through a sock. So at the actual birth I was shocked to see all this blood. The thing I had prepared myself for was a lot of lint.
—*Steve Skrovan*

Lamaze expects the husband, me, to be there, so that I can witness this festivity. I did not want to be there. This was remarkably painful for my wife. There was nothing my presence could really do to relieve her pain. In other words, I didn't see why my evening should be ruined too.
—*Dennis Wolfberg*

**Cutting the Cord**

The doctor turned to me and asked, "Mr. Goldthwait, would you like to cut the cord?" And I said, "Isn't there anyone more qualified?"
—*Bobcat Goldthwait*

Drugs

We planned this beautiful, totally natural, unmedicated delivery. What kind of stupid-ass idea is that? Next time I want the epidural at the moment of conception. Numb for nine months.
                —*Heidi Joyce*

Filming

My friends want to show me films of their baby's birth. No, thank you. But I'll look at a video of the conception, if you've got one.
                —*Garry Shandling*

When my daughter was born, we videotaped the birth. Now when she makes me angry, I just hit rewind and put her back in.
                —*Grace White*

Labor

My wife, God bless her, was in labor for thirty-two hours. And I was faithful to her the entire time.
                —*Jonathan Katz*

If you don't yell during labor, you're a fool. I screamed. Oh, how I screamed. And that was just during the conception.
                —*Joan Rivers*

I want to have children, but my friends scare me. One of my friends told me she was in labor for thirty-six hours. I don't even want to do anything that feels good for thirty-six hours.
                —*Rita Rudner*

She's screaming like crazy. . . . You have this myth you're sharing the birth experience. Unless you're circumcising yourself with a chainsaw, I don't think so. Unless you're opening an umbrella up your ass, I don't think so!
                —*Robin Williams*

Natural

We had natural childbirth. We had our baby on a bed of lettuce at the Sizzler.
                —*Bob Saget*

**BIRTH CONTROL**     See: **CONTRACEPTION**

**BIRTHDAYS**     For my birthday, my old man showed me a picture of a cake. I sat there all day trying to blow out the candles.
        —*Rodney Dangerfield*

        I'm getting sick of pretending to be excited every time it's somebody's birthday. What is the big deal? How many times do we have to celebrate that someone was born? Every year, over and over. All you did was not die for twelve months. That's all you've done, as far as I can tell.
        —*Jerry Seinfeld*

Cakes     Why is it that with birthday cakes you can blow on them and spit on them and everyone rushes to get a piece?
        —*Bobby Kelton*

Candles     You know you're getting old when the candles cost more than the cake.
        —*Bob Hope*

Parties     I had the worst birthday party ever when I was a child, because my parents hired a pony to give rides. These ponies are never in good health, but this one dropped dead. It just wasn't much fun after that. One kid would sit on him and the rest of us would drag him around in a circle.
        —*Rita Rudner*

        These big birthday parties my friends make for their kids. One of my friends had a surprise party for her child. He was one year old. We all snuck in around the crib, jumped up, and yelled, "Surprise!" He's in therapy now.
        —*Rita Rudner*

Presents     On my sixteenth birthday my parents tried to surprise me with a car, but they missed.
        —*Tom Cotter*

My childhood was rough. Once for my birthday, my old man gave me a bat. The first day I played with it, it flew away.
—*Rodney Dangerfield*

I walked into a store and said, "It's my wife's birthday. I'd like to buy her a beautiful pen." The clerk winked at me and said, "A little surprise, heh?" I said, "Yes, she's expecting a Cadillac."
—*Henny Youngman*

**BOOKS**

Outside of a dog, a book is man's best friend. Inside of a dog it's too dark to read.
—*Groucho Marx*

Authors

I wrote a book under a pen name, Bic.
—*Buzz Nutley*

in Bed

I honestly believe there is absolutely nothing like going to bed with a good book. Or a friend who's read one.
—*Phyllis Diller*

Bookcases

I own 150 books, but I have no bookcase. Because nobody will lend me a bookcase.
—*Henny Youngman*

Bookstores

A bookstore is one of the only pieces of evidence we have that people are still thinking.
—*Jerry Seinfeld*

Dictionaries

If a word in the dictionary was misspelled, how would we know?
—*Steven Wright*

Encyclopedias

Encyclopedia is a Latin term. It means "to paraphrase a term paper."
—*Greg Ray*

Poetry

I recently bought a book of free verse. For $12.
      —*George Carlin*

**BOYFRIENDS**

See also: **BREAKING UP, DATING, MARRIAGE, RELATIONSHIPS**

I haven't had a boyfriend for, like, a hundred years, and I'm at that point where I could really use a guy on a Saturday for about six hours. You know what I mean? Because everything in my apartment is broken.
      —*Karen Bergreen*

Boyfriend. This is such a weird word. There's no good word about someone if you're not married. Even calling a guy you live with your boyfriend makes you sound eleven years old. Old man? If you're not living with Willie Nelson, that one doesn't work, either.
      —*Elayne Boosler*

We were incompatible in a lot of ways. Like for example, I was a night person, and he didn't like me.
      —*Wendy Liebman*

After two years I said to my boyfriend, "Either tell me your name or it's over."
      —*Rita Rudner*

**BREAKING UP**

See also: **DIVORCE, RELATIONSHIPS**

I recently broke up with my tractor provider. I was scared to do it in person, so I just sent a John Deere letter.
      —*Myq Kaplan*

I broke up with someone, and she said, "You'll never find anyone like me again." And I'm thinking, I hope not! If I don't want you, why would I want someone just like you? Does anybody end a bad relationship and say, "By the way, do you have a twin?"
      —*Larry Miller*

I've upped my standards. Now, up yours.
—*Pat Paulsen*

When somebody says to you, "The last thing I want to do is hurt you" what they really mean is, "It's on the list. I've just got some other things to do first."
—*Mark Schiff*

**Back Together** When you get back together with an old boyfriend, it's pathetic. It's like having a garage sale and buying your own stuff back.
—*Laura Kightlinger*

I asked my ex-girlfriend, "Do you think we'll get back together?" She said, "I think the chances are better of me putting Super Unleaded into a rented car."
—*David Spade*

How many people still have that relationship with their ex, where you call each other up just to yell? It's like you're married: You're not having sex, and you're fighting.
—*Rosie Tran*

**Friendship after** When men break up they want to remain friends. Why? Why can't they just get lost?
—*Rita Rudner*

**with Her** I just broke up with my girlfriend because I caught her lying. Under another man.
—*Doug Benson*

If you're going to break up with your old lady, and you live in a small town, make sure you don't break up at three in the morning. Because you're screwed; there's nothing to do. So make it about nine in the morning. Bullshit around, worry her a little, then come back at seven in the night.
—*Lenny Bruce*

There is one thing I would break up over, and that is if she caught me with another woman. I wouldn't stand for that.
—*Steve Martin*

I broke up with my girlfriend. She moved in with another guy, and I draw the line at that.
—*Garry Shandling*

with Him

I once had a man break up with me. He said I was using him because right after making love I would weigh myself.
—*Emily Levine*

I wasn't the easiest guy to live with. I had multiple personalities, but what bothered her was that none of them made any money.
—*Danny Liebert*

I was going with someone for a few years, but we broke up. It was one of those things. He wanted to get married, and I didn't want him to.
—*Rita Rudner*

Moving on

A woman broke up with me, and sent me pictures of her and her new boyfriend in bed together. Solution? I sent them to her dad.
—*Christopher Case*

After you've dated someone it should be legal to stamp them with what's wrong with them, so the next person doesn't have to start from scratch.
—*Rita Rudner*

The last girl I went out with blew me off. Now I call her with lame excuses to see her, "Hey, did I leave a penny over there?"
—*David Spade*

when Older    The thing about breaking up when you get older, you just
              don't have the steam anymore. "Oh, that's it. I can't start
              shaving my legs above the knee again."
                              —*Elayne Boosler*

What to Say   If you want to get rid of a man, I suggest saying, "I love you.
              I want to marry you. I want to have your children."
              Sometimes they leave skid marks.
                              —*Rita Rudner*

              Refusal to accept reality does not change reality. My girl-
              friend broke up with me. I said, "I can't imagine you leaving
              me." She said, "Well, let me help. You stay here. I'm going
              to turn around. Then I'm going to start walking. To you,
              it'll seem like I'm getting smaller."
                              —*Basil White*

## BREASTS

Breast-Feeding   A child is too old to breast-feed when he can unhook
                 mommy's bra with one hand.
                              —*Anthony Clark*

                 What a childhood! I was breast-fed by my father.
                              —*Rodney Dangerfield*

                 My mom breast-fed me. It was only 2 percent.
                              —*Wendy Liebman*

                 My mother breast-fed me with powdered milk. It was my
                 first real do-it-yourself project.
                              —*Buzz Nutley*

                 I can't get past the fact that food is coming out of my wife's
                 breasts. What was once essentially an entertainment center
                 has now become a juice bar.
                              —*Paul Reiser*

I'm not going to breast-feed. I've put this off so long, I'm sure my milk has expired.

—*Rita Rudner*

Women breast-feeding in public always defend themselves by saying, "It's a beautiful thing." Yeah, so is sex, but I've never done it in the middle of Denny's. Although that at least would be a Grand Slam Breakfast.

—*Traci Skene*

Implants

Fake breasts: Women always say, "You know they're not real, don't you? She bought them." Do you know I don't care if they're real? I want to buy some, too. For the house, put them in different rooms. And on the dashboard of the car, for when I'm driving.

—*Arsenio Hall*

The women who got implants sued Dow Corning because they felt betrayed by their implant company. Betrayed? "What, you mean I can't put a petroleum by-product in a baggie and insert it in my chest cavity, safely? I am shocked! And betrayed!"

—*Dani Klein*

This one girl I saw in *Playboy* was so amazing. I don't think she had silicone; I think she had helium. She was so big I couldn't keep the magazine closed.

—*Rita Rudner*

Real

My husband would look at the women in those nudie magazines and say, "How come you don't have any chest?" And I said to him, "When you married me, I didn't have a chest. But when I married you, you had a full head of hair."

—*Sue Costello*

I've never had plastic surgery. I still have my own real breasts. I know, because when I lay on my back they roll underneath my arms, and I look like a hammerhead shark.

—*LeMaire*

Size

See also: **CHILDREN**, **HEALTH CLUBS** Members, **WOMEN** in Business

A lot of guys think the larger a woman's breasts are, the less intelligent she is. I think it's the opposite. I think the larger a woman's breasts are, the less intelligent the men become.
—*Anita Wise*

**BREATH**

We should have a way of telling people they have bad breath without hurting their feelings. "Well, I'm bored. Let's go brush our teeth." Or, "I've got to make a phone call. Hold this gum in your mouth."
—*Brad Stine*

**BRIDAL SHOWERS**    See: **WEDDINGS**

**BRIDESMAIDS**    See: **WEDDINGS**

**BROTHERS**    See: **FAMILY**

**BUSINESS**    See also: **EMPLOYMENT**

CEOs

In Japan, the highest-paid executive earns only fifteen times what the average worker does. Here, CEOs earn five hundred times more, but that's supposed to motivate the American worker. To do what, kidnap his boss?
—*Norman K.*

These CEOs are scary. I walk past a gang banger; I don't even flinch. But I see a white dude with a *Wall Street Journal*, I haul ass. Cutting through the projects, you might lose what you have on you that day, but I ain't never been mugged of my future. No thug ever said, "Give me your 401K. I want your college fund, your IRA. I want it all."
—*Wanda Sykes*

Corporations

Congress voted for tougher laws on corporations. So now when a corporation buys a senator, they need a receipt.
—*Jay Leno*

We're one corporate meltdown away from having the dollar be the peso's bitch.
—*Dennis Miller*

Lemonade
Stands

I tried to make money as a kid. I had a lemonade stand for about six weeks. I made no money. I had to burn it down and collect insurance.
—*Brian Kiley*

At my lemonade stand I used to give the first glass away free and charge $5 for the second glass. The refill contained the antidote.
—*Emo Philips*

Show

There's no business like show business, but there are several businesses like accounting.
—*David Letterman*

**BUSES**        See: **TRANSPORTATION**

**CABS**          See: **AUTOMOBILES**

**CAMERAS**       See also: **PHOTOGRAPHS**

I have an underwater camera just in case I crash my car into a river, and at the last minute I see a photo opportunity.
—*Mitch Hedberg*

**CAMPING**       Camping: That's what I call getting drunk outside.
—*Dave Attell*

I went camping and borrowed a circus tent by mistake. I didn't notice until I got it set up. People complained because they couldn't see the lake.
—*Steven Wright*

**CANCER**        You show me something that doesn't cause cancer, and I'll show you something that isn't on the market yet.
—*George Carlin*

A study in Italy showed that people who eat a lot of pizza are less likely to get colon cancer. And another study says masturbation reduces risk of prostate cancer. It's what I've always said: diet and exercise.
—*Jay Leno*

**CANDY**         Everyone loves Hershey's Kisses and Hugs. I'm waiting for Hershey's Gropes.
—*Myq Kaplan*

Candy is the only reason you want to live when you're a kid. And you have your favorite candies that you love. Kids actually believe they can distinguish between twenty-one different versions of pure sugar. When I was a kid, I could taste the difference between different colored M&Ms. I thought the red was heartier, more of a main course M&M. And the light brown was a mellower, kind of after-dinner M.
—*Jerry Seinfeld*

**CANNIBALS**

A cannibal is a person who walks into a restaurant and orders a waiter.

—*Morey Amsterdam*

Cannibals love Domino's Pizza. Not for the pizza, but for the delivery guy.

—*Shang*

**CARDS**

Greeting

Chicanos never say congratulations when people do well. "I got a job over at the hospital." "'S about time." Do we say good luck? No, we say, "Don't fuck it up like last time." Or, "So now you think you're all bad, or what?" Go to the Hallmark store and look for that card. "Do you have a Now-You-Think-You're-All-Bad card?"

—*George Lopez*

If you're going to get a card for somebody you don't really care about, they should make cards that say that. "You're a friend of my wife's cousin—the hell with you." "We hardly know you. What did you expect, cash?"

—*Paul Reiser*

Playing

See also: **GAMBLING**

I was once asked to play strip poker, but I'm more comfortable with strip solitaire.

—*Rob O'Reilly*

I stayed up one night playing poker with tarot cards. I got a full house and four people died.

—*Steven Wright*

**CARS**

See: **AUTOMOBILES**

## CATS

Bathing

One thing you can say about cats. They don't have to worry about kissing each other's asses. They can do that for themselves.

*—Dwight*

I gave my cat a bath the other day; they love it. He enjoyed it, it was fun for me. The fur would stick to my tongue, but other than that . . .

*—Steve Martin*

Falling

If toast always lands butter-side down and cats always land on their feet, what happens if you strap toast on the back of a cat and drop it?

*—Steven Wright*

Fleas

I have three cats, and they have fleas. But they never go out, so if they have fleas, they got them from me. I feel like kind of an ass for making them wear the collars.

*—Paula Poundstone*

Illness

My cat was up all night throwing up. So obviously I was up all night holding her hair.

*—Sarah Silverman*

My cat was limping, and the vet said he had a bad knee. I didn't even know cats had knees. But I know nothing about the feline anatomy; if the vet told me the cat needed new batteries I couldn't argue. But I'm not at the complete mercy of the vet. There's a built-in price constraint. I can always get a new kitty for nothing. Let's face it: High vet bills make it difficult to respect the sanctity of life. Fluffy might be cute and you might love Fluffy, but Fluffy's not getting a liver transplant. No donor list for kitty cats.

*—Jeff Stilson*

Intelligence    Cats are smarter than dogs. You can't get eight cats to pull a sled through snow.
—*Jeff Valdez*

Kittens    See: **BIRTH**, **CLICHÉS** Life

Looks    The problem with cats is that they get the same exact look whether they see a moth or an ax-murderer.
—**Paula Poundstone**

Lost    I found our cat the other day. I would have found him a week ago, but we've got a grass bag on the lawn mower.
—**Emo Philips**

Love    In my more depressed moments, I believe my cats suffer from Stockholm syndrome. You know, where the hostage falls in love with the captor, as an adaptive mechanism.
—**Betsy Salkind**

Neutered    My wife's cats have been neutered and declawed, so they're like pillows that eat.
—**Larry Reeb**

Ownership    I bought a generic cat. It only had five lives.
—**Buzz Nutley**

I have cats because they have no artificially imposed, culturally prescribed sense of decorum. They live in the moment. If I had an aneurysm in the brain, and dropped dead, I love knowing that as the paramedics carry me out, my cats are going to be swatting at that little toe tag.
—**Paul Provenza**

Purpose    I don't see the purpose of cats. Dogs can protect you, can sniff out things, and can be your eyes if you're blind. Could you imagine a seeing-eye cat? The first person who walks by with an untied shoelace, and you're history.
—*Christine O'Rourke*

and Toilets

I found out why cats drink out of the toilet. My mother told me it's because it's cold in there. And I'm like, "How did my mother know that?"
—*Wendy Liebman*

Training

I've been trying to train my cat to understand the meaning of the word "no." Which seems to be roughly equivalent to teaching a dog Latin.
—*Judy Brown*

Wrestling

People do crazy things when bored. I'm sitting at home with nothing to do, looking at the cats, and think, "I'll teach the cats to wrestle." You should never teach cats to wrestle, but if you do, here's how: Get two cats. Take cat number one, and rub catnip all over him. Put him next to cat number two. The rest just sort of happens.
—*Basil White*

**CELIBACY**

See: **SEX**

**CHILDHOOD**

See also: **FATHERHOOD**, **FATHERS**, **MOTHERHOOD**, **MOTHERS**, **PARENTS**

When you're eight years old, nothing is your business.
—*Lenny Bruce*

As I have discovered by examining my past, I started out as a child.
—*Bill Cosby*

My childhood was kind of a blur, to tell you the truth. I needed better glasses.
—*Wendy Liebman*

Babysitters

See also: **BABIES**

We used to terrorize our babysitters when I was little, except for my grandfather because he used to read to us from his will.
—*Janine DiTullio*

As a child I experienced a lot of betrayal. One time I ran into my babysitter, and she was with another kid. They were holding hands, and the kid wasn't even cute. And I recently found out my babysitter was only with me for the money.
    —*Wendy Spero*

Chores

Before my mother would give you that dime allowance, she'd want you to do a little chore around the house. Like build a porch.
    —*Ray Romano*

I grew up hearing such stupid things. My mother would say, "That's the last time I'm gonna tell you to take out the garbage." Well, thank God.
    —*George Wallace*

Friendships

When I was a kid I got no respect. I had no friends. I remember the seesaw. I had to keep running from one end to the other.
    —*Rodney Dangerfield*

When I was a girl I only had two friends, and they were imaginary. And they would only play with each other.
    —*Rita Rudner*

Nerdy

I was so nerdy as a kid, the only thing that would have made beating me more attractive is if I'd been filled with candy.
    —*Larry Getlen*

Nostalgia for

I'm nostalgic. I miss childhood. I miss first grade. I miss thinking girls are gross. Do you know how much money I could save if I still thought girls were gross?
    —*Patrick Keane*

I miss being a kid. I got food, clothing, and shelter for free. Grownups only get that in jail.
    —*Leighann Lord*

**Only Child**

I'm an only child, and it wasn't always easy. There were a lot of games that were hard to play. Like catch. God, that was tiring.

—*Dominic Dierkes*

When I was a kid we had a quicksand box. I was an only child, eventually.

—*Steven Wright*

**Poverty**

When I was little boy, I wanted a dog desperately, and we had no money. My parents got me an ant. I called it "Spot." Coming home late one night, Sheldon Finklestein tried to bully me. Spot was with me; I said "Kill!" and Sheldon stepped on my dog.

—*Woody Allen*

We were poor. If I wasn't a boy, I wouldn't have had nothing to play with.

—*Redd Foxx*

We were so poor the only family pet we could afford was dust bunnies.

—*Kelly*

I was a poor kid. My mom saved money by shopping at the Army-Navy Surplus store, but I felt stupid going to kindergarten dressed as a Chinese General.

—*Blamo Risher*

**Playing**

The essence of childhood, of course, is play, which my friends and I did endlessly on streets that we reluctantly shared with traffic.

—*Bill Cosby*

I don't get no respect. When I played in the sandbox the cat kept covering me up.

—*Rodney Dangerfield*

One day when I was little, and my parents were having a party, I went around to all the adults and said, "Drink this, it'll make you taller, it's magic." And they all drank it and said, "How cute. How weird." And then I snuck off into the room where they kept all the coats and hemmed everyone's sleeves an inch shorter.

—*Steven Wright*

**Safety**

When you were a little kid, remember how hard it was to get a cookie? Way in the back, unless your mom was really mean: Then they'd be on top of the refrigerator. Nowhere, any place on a package of Oreos does it say, "Keep out of reach of small children." Where was the Liquid Drano? Under the sink, right next to the rest of the poisons.

—*Mike Bullard*

Once when I was lost I asked a policeman to help me find my parents. I asked him, "Do you think we'll ever find them?" He said, "I don't know, kid. There are so many places they can hide."

—*Rodney Dangerfield*

**Tooth Fairy**

How can any child resist the tooth fairy? That single shining example of selfless generosity in this slimy veil of greed. When I was broke, I pulled out my brother's teeth. Naturally, it was too good to last. Just one more nonrenewable resource on a diminishing planet.

—*A. Whitney Brown*

**CHILDREN**

See also: **BABIES, CHILDHOOD, FATHERS, MOTHERS, PARENTHOOD, PARENTS**

Kids are cute, but they're so rude. I was taking a shower, when my daughter came in and said, "Gosh Mom, I hope when I grow up my breasts are nice and long like yours."

—*Roseanne Barr*

Poets have said that the reason to have children is to give yourself immortality. Immortality? Now that I have five children, my only hope is that they are all out of the house before I die.

—*Bill Cosby*

Kids today have the attention span of high-speed lint.

—*Will Durst*

My wife is about to have our second child, and we're very happy because we were told we couldn't have kids. By our landlord.

—*Brian Kiley*

Kids are cute, babies are cute, puppies are cute. The little things are cute. See, nature did this on purpose so that we would want to take care of our young. Made them cute. Tricked us. Then gradually they get older and older, until one day your mother sits you down and says, "You know, I think you're ugly enough to get your own apartment."

—*Cathy Ladman*

Kids? It's like living with homeless people. They're cute but they just chase you around all day long going, "Can I have a dollar? I'm missing a shoe! I need a ride!"

—*Kathleen Madigan*

You never know what you're going to get, and children have their own personalities immediately. I was watching little kids on a carousel. Some kids were jumping on the horses; some kids were afraid of the horses; some kids were betting on the horses.

—*Rita Rudner*

**CHILD SUPPORT**    See: **PARENTHOOD**

## CHRISTMAS

Fruitcakes

Here's a money-saving tip for Christmas: Glue a jujube on a brick and mail it out as fruitcake.
—*Julie Brown*

Gifts

I have all these people to give Christmas gifts to, and you know what I've found? There are some very nice things at the 99-cents store.
—*Ellen DeGeneres*

If you want to restore your faith in humanity, think about Christmas. If you want to destroy it again, think about Christmas shopping. But the gifts aren't the important thing about the holidays. The important thing is having your family around resenting you.
—*Reno Goodale*

The day after Christmas: When we all have two more ugly sweaters.
—*Craig Kilborn*

When I was little my grandfather one Christmas gave me a box of broken glass. He gave my brother a box of Band-Aids, and said, "You two share."
—*Steven Wright*

I love Christmas. I receive a lot of wonderful presents I can't wait to exchange.
—*Henny Youngman*

while Jewish

Jesus never put up a tree and exchanged gifts, or left cookies out for Santa. He never made a harried last-minute trip to the mall, or spent Christmas Eve cursing at a toy that he couldn't put together. He celebrated Passover. So, if you want to be more like Jesus, pass the matzo.
—*Drew Carey*

Probably the worst thing about being Jewish during Christmas time is shopping, because the lines are so long. They should have a Jewish express line, "Look, I'm a Jew. It's not a gift. It's just paper towels!"
—*Sue Kolinsky*

December 25 is National Jews Go to the Movies Day.
—*Jon Stewart*

Lights

I haven't taken my Christmas lights down. They look so nice on the pumpkin.
—*Winston Spear*

Mail

Mail your packages early so the post office can lose them in time for Christmas.
—*Johnny Carson*

Nativity Scenes

The Supreme Court has ruled they cannot have a nativity scene in Washington, D.C. This wasn't for any religious reasons. They couldn't find three wise men and a virgin.
—*Jay Leno*

Office Parties

What I don't like about office Christmas parties is looking for a job the next day.
—*Phyllis Diller*

I used to work in a Fotomat booth. Talk about the world's worst office Christmas party. I sat in a mall parking lot with a punchbowl and a candy cane.
—*Dobie Maxwell*

Santa Claus

My husband is so cheap. On Christmas Eve he fires one shot and tells the kids Santa committed suicide.
—*Phyllis Diller*

I never believed in Santa Claus because I knew no white dude would come into my neighborhood after dark.
—*Dick Gregory*

Santa is very jolly because he knows where all the bad girls live.
—*Dennis Miller*

Christmas always sucked when I was a kid because I believed in Santa Claus. Unfortunately, so did my parents. So I never got anything.
—*Charlie Viracola*

**Trees**

I tell you one thing I'm upset about: the day after Christmas my tree is all dried up, all brown. I went back to where I bought it, and the whole place is gone. This is the last year I buy my Christmas tree from one of those fly-by-night businesses.
—*Jay Leno*

The Christmas tree inspires a love/hate relationship. All that time spent selecting and decorating, and a week after, you see it by the side of the road, like a mob hit. A car slows down, a door opens and a tree rolls out. People snap out of Christmas spirit like it was a drunken stupor, "There's a tree inside the house! Throw it anywhere."
—*Jerry Seinfeld*

**Stockings**

Last Christmas, I got no respect. In my stocking I got an Odor-Eater.
—*Rodney Dangerfield*

The best stocking stuffer is a human leg.
—*Norm Macdonald*

**CIRCUSES**

See also: **FUNERALS**

It's a traveling syphilitic sideshow: I don't like the circus. Diseased animals and hermaphrodite clowns throwing anthrax spores at the children. This is like entertainment from the ninth century. Geeks, trolls, mutants, all these inbred circus people. They come out from under bridges, releasing disease and pestilence into the air. I don't like the circus.

—*Jay Leno*

**Clowns**

The good thing about being a circus clown must be that you never have to worry about how your hair looks.

—*Reno Goodale*

The hardest part about being a clown, it seems to me, would be that you're constantly referred to as a clown. "Who was that clown?" "I'm not working with that clown. Did you hire that clown?" "The guy's a clown!"

—*Jerry Seinfeld*

## CLICHÉS

Is "tired old cliché" one?

—*Steven Wright*

**Apple a Day**

An apple a day keeps the doctor away. My HMO also says that's the best they can do for me.

—*Charlotte Lobb*

**Barrel of Monkeys**

Did you ever hear someone say this: "It was more fun than a barrel of monkeys." Did you ever smell a barrel of monkeys?

—*Steve Bluestein*

**Beat Them**

If you can't beat them, arrange to have them beaten.

—*George Carlin*

**Caught My Eye**

I was walking down the street. Something caught my eye, and dragged it fifteen feet.

—*Emo Philips*

**College Try**

Why do they say, "Give it the old college try?" Based on our experience, "the old college try" would consist of sleeping in for four years and not giving a damn.

—*Lee Curtis and Jon Berahya*

| | |
|---|---|
| Day without Sunshine | A day without sunshine is like, you know . . . night.<br>—*Steve Martin* |
| Do Unto Others | Do unto others, then run.<br>—*Benny Hill* |
| Early Bird and Worm | See also: **MOTHERS** Advice |

The early bird gets the worm. I'd rather sleep in and have toaster muffins.
    —*Shirley Lipner*

Remember, the early worm gets devoured by the early bird.
    —*Jason Love*

**Family**

My father would say things that make no sense, like, "If I were the last person on earth, some moron would turn left in front of me."
    —*Louie Anderson*

My mother used to say, "You can eat off my floor." You can eat off my floor, too. There are thousands of things there.
    —*Elayne Boosler*

My father wore the pants in the family—at least, after the court order.
    —*Vernon Chapman*

Blood may be thicker than water, but it is still sticky, unpleasant, and generally nauseating.
    —*Janeane Garofalo*

My mom always says, "Keep your chin up." That's how I ran into the door.
    —*Daryl Hogue*

My granddad used to say, "If everybody liked the same thing, they'd all be after your grandma."
—*Gary Muledeer*

Where's there's a will, there's a family fighting over it.
—*Buzz Nutley*

Whenever anything went wrong in my life, my mother would say, "All things happen for the best." And I'd ask, "Who's best?" And she'd say, "Gotta go."
—*Rita Rudner*

**Glass Houses**

People who live in glass houses might as well answer the door.
—*Morey Amsterdam*

**Happens for a Reason**

I agree with New Age philosophy that everything happens for a reason. But not always for a good reason. A tornado is not especially interested in your self-actualization.
—*Judy Brown*

Everything happens for a reason. My aunt Juanita lost her trailer in a tornado, but when she got her insurance settlement she got enough money to buy a new, black all-lace body suit. So she now sees the inside of lots of trailers. Dreams do come true.
—*Melissa McQueen*

**Hard Work Pays**

Hard work pays off in the end, but laziness pays off now.
—*Al Lubel*

**Have Everything**

You can't have everything. Where would you put it?
—*Steven Wright*

**Heads, Two**

Two heads are better than one, unless you're cleaning them.
—*Craig Sharf*

**Heart on Sleeve**

I wear my heart on my sleeve. I wear my liver on my pant leg.
—*Steven Wright*

**If Shoe Fits**

If the shoe fits, get another one just like it.
    —*George Carlin*

**Life**

I was high on life, but eventually I built up a tolerance.
    —*Arj Barker*

Life's a bitch. Then you marry one.
    —*Steve Carell*

If life was fair, Elvis would be alive, and all the impersonators would be dead.
    —*Johnny Carson*

If life gives you lemons, make some sort of fruity juice.
    —*Conan O'Brien*

The best things in life really are free. So, how many kittens do you want?
    —*Nancy Jo Perdue*

Life isn't like a box of chocolates. It's like a jar of jalapeños: You never know what's going to burn your ass.
    —*Paul Rodriguez*

At first I thought that my life was going around in circles. Then I got to looking closer, and it's actually a downward spiral.
    —*Tom Ryan*

The cost of living is going up, and the chance of living is going down.
    —*Flip Wilson*

**Light at End of Tunnel**

There's a light at the end of the tunnel. And it's a train.
    —*Margaret Smith*

They say when you die there's a light at the end of the tunnel. When my father dies, he'll see the light, make his way toward it, and then flip it off to save electricity.
—*Harland Williams*

Lonely at Top

Just remember: It's lonely at the top, when there's no one on the bottom.
—*Rodney Dangerfield*

Love

Love is the answer, but while you're waiting for the answer, sex raises some pretty good questions.
—*Woody Allen*

Love is blind. I guess that's why it proceeds by the sense of touch.
—*Morey Amsterdam*

They say, "If you have true love, let it go and it will come back." I don't think so. True love is like a cupcake, it should be enjoyed immediately.
—*Vinny Badabing*

You can't buy love, but you can pay heavily for it.
—*Henny Youngman*

the Meek

The meek shall inherit the earth. They won't have the nerve to refuse it.
—*Jackie Vernon*

Minds Think Alike

Blank minds think alike.
—*Tony Invergo*

Misery Loves Company

It's true that misery loves company. If you ever doubt that, look at a No-Pest Strip. It's covered with flies. You'd think that the first fly would tell any others "Go around! Go around!"
—*Margaret Smith*

**Money**

A fool and his money were lucky to get together in the first place.
—*Harry Anderson*

Money can't buy happiness, but it helps you look for it in more places.
—*Milton Berle*

Money can't buy you happiness, but it does bring you a more pleasant form of misery.
—*Spike Milligan*

If money can't buy happiness, then I guess I'll have to rent it.
—*Weird Al Yankovic*

What's the use of happiness? It can't buy you money.
—*Henny Youngman*

**Nature Abhors a Vacuum**

Nature also abhors a vacuum salesman.
—*Jason Love*

**Watched Pot**

A watched pot never boils. But it does get paranoid.
—*Lesley Wake*

**Way to a Man's Heart**

The quickest way to a man's heart is through his chest.
—*Roseanne Barr*

**What's on the Inside**

Some say it's what's on the inside that counts. If that were true about women, *Playboy* would be running centerfolds of brain tissues and gall bladders.
—*Christy Murphy*

**with the Universe**

Every once in a while I feel that I am at two with the universe.
—*Woody Allen*

**Words**

You can get more with a kind word and a gun than you can with a kind word alone.
—*Johnny Carson*

A word to the wise ain't necessary. It's the stupid ones who need the advice.
—*Bill Cosby*

**You Are What You Eat**

You are what you eat. Which makes me cheap, quick, and easy.
—*Dave Thomas*

**CLOCK, BIOLOGICAL**    See: **PREGNANCY**

**CLONING**

"Human cloning would not lead to identical souls, because only God can create a soul," a panel set up by Pope John Paul has concluded. They also took care of a couple other things that were burning issues: Apparently, Trix are indeed for kids.
—*Janeane Garofalo*

Now that we can clone humans they've removed the one pleasurable thing about having a child.
—*David Letterman*

**CLOTHING**    See also: **FASHION, LEATHER JACKETS, SHOES**

**Bathing Suits**

Men have an easier time buying bathing suits. Women have two types: depressing and more depressing. Men have two types: nerdy and not nerdy.
—*Rita Rudner*

**Bras**

Push-up bras are like breasts on the half-shell.
—*Dom Irrerra*

I stuff my bra. So if you get to second base with me, you'll find that the bases are loaded.
—*Wendy Liebman*

My favorite marketing gimmick, the WonderBra. Doesn't your date notice that your chest feels like a stuffed animal? And what happens when you get home and take it off? It's called the WonderBra because the guy is sitting there thinking, "I wonder where her boobs went?"

—*Rebecca Nell*

Compliments

When people are complimented on what they're wearing, they accept as if it was about them. "Nice tie." "Thank you very much!" That's the job of clothes: to get compliments, because it's hard to get them based on human qualities. No matter how nice you are, nobody will say, "Nice person." It's easier to be a bastard and match the colors up.

—*Jerry Seinfeld*

Dressing

Men don't feel the urge to get married as quickly as women do because their clothes all button and zip in the front. Women's dresses usually button and zip in the back. We need men emotionally and sexually, but we also need men to help us get dressed.

—*Rita Rudner*

Fit

When a woman tries on clothing from her closet that feels tight, she will assume she has gained weight. When a man tries on clothing from his closet that feels tight, he will assume the clothing has shrunk.

—*Rita Rudner*

Men

See also: Bathing Suits

For men, upon marriage you lose the ability to choose clothing for yourself. "Honey, what do you think? A striped shirt and a solid tie, or a solid shirt and a pair of mukluks? A Beatle wig and a grass skirt? Tell me, because I haven't used that part of my brain in several years. Why don't you just choose something, lay it out, and I'll be in the crib until we have to leave."

—*Paul Reiser*

They should put expiration dates on clothing so we men will know when they go out of style.
—*Garry Shandling*

**Pantyhose**

I hate pantyhose. Although I occasionally wear Control Top because I've found there's no quicker way to flatten my tummy, and shut down my whole digestive tract.
—*Mercedes Wence*

**Shoes**

See also: **PENISES**

They say you can compare a man's shoe size to his manhood. So that's why I keep my skis on everywhere I go.
—*Garry Shandling*

**Socks**

I went into this bar and sat down next to a pretty girl. She looked at me and said, "Hey, you have two different colored socks on." I said, "Yeah, I know, but to me they're the same because I go by thickness."
—*Steven Wright*

**Sweaters**

I'm reading *Hints from Heloise*, and she says that if you put an angora sweater in the freezer for an hour, it won't shed for the rest of the day. And I'm thinking, "My cat sheds an awful lot."
—*Ellen DeGeneres*

**Underwear**

You ever wear a bathing suit because you've run out of clean underwear?
—*Louis C.K.*

It is a point of pride for the American male to keep the same size Jockey shorts for his entire life. And so you have a man with a brand-new 40-inch waist who is trying to get into size 36 Jockey shorts, a man who is now wearing a combination of supporter and tourniquet. Proud men have gone to the brink of gangrene to maintain the interior fashion of their youth.
—*Bill Cosby*

If women were in charge, all men's underwear would come with an expiration date.
—*Diane Ford*

I can tell I'm getting older, because I find myself using words like "spacious," "roomy," and "comfortable" when I'm buying underwear.
—*Reno Goodale*

Why does women's underwear have lace and flowers all over it? You never see men's underwear with a big wrench in the middle of it.
—*Heidi Joyce*

I got some new underwear the other day. Well, new to me.
—*Emo Philips*

The older you get, the higher you wear your underwear. Like rings on a tree. Eighty, ninety years old, your breasts are inside them. When you die, they just pull them up over your head.
—*Margaret Smith*

Warning Labels    See: **DRY CLEANING**

**CODEPENDENCE**    See: **NEUROSES**

**COFFEE**

Causes Cancer    Coffee has carcinogens, causes cancer. And it also has caffeine. So not only are you dying, you watch yourself go.
—*Jackie Mason*

Decaffeinated    I'm on decaf now. What I miss most is the road rage.
—*David Letterman*

I can't handle most stimulants. Anybody else like me? You ever call the IHOP at about four in the morning and yell into the phone, "I said decaf!"
> —*Tom Ryan*

Houses

There is now a Starbucks in my pants.
> —*George Carlin*

They just opened a new Starbucks, in my living room.
> —*Janeane Garofalo*

as Meal

You know what's great about coffee? It's the only meal for which the name of the food is also the official name of the event: coffee. "We'll get together for coffee." We don't know what we're doing, but we know what we'll be having: coffee. No one ever talks about getting together for lamb or Fresca or grapes. You never hear it because it doesn't quite have the same draw as coffee.
> —*Paul Reiser*

Ordering

You can tell a lot about someone's personality by how he orders coffee. "Decaf please, skim milk, no sugar." That's the kind of a guy who goes through the car wash wearing a seat belt.
> —*Margot Black*

**COFFEE HOUSES**     See: **COFFEE**

**COLLEGE**

College: A fountain of knowledge where all go to drink.
> —*Henny Youngman*

Cheating

I was thrown out of college. I cheated on my metaphysics final. I looked within the soul of the boy sitting next to me.
> —*Woody Allen*

Classes

I took biology two years in a row just to eat the specimens.
> —*Pat Paulsen*

I took a course called Statistical Analysis. And there was a guy in the course who used to make up all his computations, and he never used sigma. He used his own initials. Because he was the standard deviation.

—*Mort Sahl*

I got an A in philosophy because I proved that my professor didn't exist.

—*Judy Tenuta*

College is supposed to prepare you for the real world, but if that's the case, they should have a class on standing in line. The post office line. DMV line. Grocery store line. Unless Shakespeare's clever wordplay can help me cut in front of that mom and screaming baby at the market, he's of no use to me.

—*Rosie Tran*

Faculty

Faculty: The people who get what's left after the football coach receives his salary.

—*Henny Youngman*

Graduating

I went to the University of South Florida for five and a half years. Then I sobered up, got dressed, and went home. They still have my earrings.

—*Tracy Smith*

Law School

My parents sent my brother through law school. He graduated. Now he's suing them for wasting seven years of his life.

—*Mike Binder*

Loans

The student loan director from my bank called. He said, "You've missed seventeen payments, and the university never received the $17,000. We'd like to know what happened to the money." I said, "Mr. Jones, I'll give it to you straight. I gave the money to my friend Slick, and he built a nuclear weapon with it. And I'd appreciate it if you'd never call again."

—*Steven Wright*

Majors

I went to college: majored in philosophy. My father said, "Why don't you minor in communications so you can wonder out loud?"
—*Mike Dugan*

I majored in animal husbandry in college, which is good, because I married a couple of pigs.
—*Sheila Kay*

I majored in nursing. I had to drop it. I ran out of milk.
—*Judy Tenuta*

ROTC

I was in the ROTC program. I remember once I was walking through campus and my instructor grabs me, and he's a real big guy, and yells, "It's been six weeks since I've seen you in camouflage class!" I said, "I'm getting good."
—*Emo Philips*

Sororities

Being in a sorority was like flying coach. Both had bitchy women telling me all I was allowed to eat was a small bag of pretzels and a diet Coke.
—*Stephanie Schiern*

Studying

I had the worst study habits in the history of college, until I found out what I was doing wrong: highlighting with black magic marker.
—*Jeff Altman*

College is where I realized that God didn't need seven days to create the earth. He could party for six days, and pull an all-nighter.
—*Tommy Koenig*

**COLOGNE**          See also: **PERFUME**

What are men wearing? Why do they think women like horse saddles and pine sap? If a man wanted me to follow him down

the street, he should wear something called "Butter Cookie" or, even better, "Croissant."
—*Rita Rudner*

**COMEDY**          See also: **LAUGHTER**

Comedy is when you accidentally fall off a cliff and die. Tragedy is when I have a hangnail.
—*Mel Brooks*

That is the saving grace of humor: If you fail no one is laughing at you.
—*A. Whitney Brown*

It only seems like it would be funny to enter a bank wearing a ski mask.
—*Jason Love*

Black          You all know how black humor started? It started on slave ships. Cat was rowing and dude says, "What you laughin' about?" And he says, "Yesterday I was a king."
—*Richard Pryor*

Sense of Humor          Women claim that what they look for in a man is a sense of humor, but I don't believe it. Who do you want removing your bra—Tom Cruise or the Three Stooges?
—*Bruce Smirnoff*

Men always say the most important thing in a woman is a sense of humor. You know what that means? He's looking for someone to laugh at his jokes.
—*Sheila Wenz*

Satire          People say satire is dead. It's not dead; it's alive and living in the White House.
—*Robin Williams*

**COMMERCIALS**          See: **ADVERTISING**

**COMMITTEES**     A committee is a group that keeps minutes and loses hours.
                   —*Milton Berle*

**COMMUNICATION**  See also: **LANGUAGE**

                   That movie *Fatal Attraction* really ruined things for women. I
                   mean, you can't even call a guy 150 times a day anymore with-
                   out having them get all bent out of shape.
                   —*Lisa Goich*

                   I really feel as human beings, we need more training in our
                   basic social skills. Conversational distance: Don't you hate
                   these people that talk into your mouth like you're a clown at a
                   drive-through?
                   —*Jerry Seinfeld*

Electronic         I have e-mail, a pager, a cell phone, a fax line. I've got an
                   answering machine, three phone lines at home, one in my
                   purse, and a phone in my car. The only excuse I have if I
                   don't return your call is I just don't like you.
                   —*Alicia Brandt*

Male               Only a man will think of a burp as a greeting for another man.
                   —*Tim Allen*

Misspeak           I'm always putting my foot in my mouth. I met this woman
                   recently, and I could have sworn she was pregnant. I think the
                   rule is don't guess at that ever, ever, ever.
                   —*Brian Regan*

**COMMUNISM**      Communism doesn't work because people like to own stuff.
                   —*George Carlin*

**COMPLAINING**    Complaining burns calories. That's why skinny women are
                   always such bitches.
                   —*Debbie Kasper*

**COMPUTERS**          See also: **CYBERSPACE**

Computers are like dogs. They smell fear.
—*Simone Alexander*

I got a computer. I wrote an apology note to my VCR for ever thinking it was difficult. You find someone in this country who can print out an envelope. Maybe the fifth envelope, but you have to kill four to get to the fifth one.
—*Elayne Boosler*

I shop at a computer store called, "Your Crap Is Already Obsolete."
—*Jeff Cesario*

I just bought a computer. Fifteen hundred bucks, with extra memory. Then I find out that for an extra $10, you can get one that holds a grudge.
—*Jonathan Katz*

I don't know anything about computers. I don't even know how often to change the oil.
—*Buzz Nutley*

They say that computers can't think, but I have one that does. It thinks it's broken.
—*Gene Perret*

Geeks          When I'm around hard-core computer geeks I wanna say, "Come outside, the graphics are great!"
—*Matt Weinhold*

Internet          See: **CYBERSPACE**, **SEX**

Not          I don't own a computer. I'm waiting for the kind where I can look at the screen and say, "Hey, I need a pizza," and one comes out and hits me in the eyebrows.
—*Kathleen Madigan*

Office

They've finally come up with the perfect office computer. If it makes a mistake, it blames another computer.

—*Milton Berle*

**CONGRESS**

See also: **POLITICS**

You can lead a man to Congress, but you can't make him think.

—*Milton Berle*

We have the best congressmen that money can buy.

—*JoAnn Dearing*

If con is the opposite of pro, and progress is good, what is Congress?

—*Gallagher*

the House

Fourteen members of the House of Representatives got stuck in an elevator together, and it ended badly. They got out.

—*Jay Leno*

the Senate

See also: **DRIVING** Violations

The reason there are two senators for each state is so that one can be the designated driver.

—*Jay Leno*

The Senate decided they will be smoke-free. They ordained that all public areas in the Senate are now smoke-free. However, the senators themselves will still be allowed to blow smoke up each other's asses.

—*Bill Maher*

We've got fourteen women in the Senate. Fourteen women in the Senate? We are 52 percent of the population. Apparently women do suck at math.

—*Paula Poundstone*

**CONTRACEPTION**

Contraceptives should be used on every conceivable occasion.
—*Spike Milligan*

Effectiveness

I've got three kids. I had one with the birth control pill, one with a diaphragm, and another with the IUD. I don't know what happened to my IUD, but I have my suspicions. That kid picks up HBO.
—*Roseanne Barr*

The best contraceptive is the word "no" repeated frequently.
—*Margaret Smith*

The most effective birth control I know is a toddler with the croup and diaper rash.
—*Kate Zannoni*

Condoms

See also: Oral

I don't understand why some guys get self-conscious when they buy condoms. I don't get embarrassed when I buy condoms. I get embarrassed when I throw them out after they expire.
—*Jack Archey*

Recently someone asked if I minded wearing a condom. Au contraire, I prefer them. There's no difference in the sensation, unless you count the total lack of any.
—*Richard Jeni*

According to a new survey, 56 percent of women carry condoms. The other 44 percent are carrying babies.
—*Jay Leno*

New York City hotels have free condoms in the rooms. All these years I've been using the free shower cap.
—*David Letterman*

I was insecure about sex. I've grown more secure. I used to use the amateur phylactics, and I only use the prophylactics now.
—*Steve Martin*

I wear two condoms all the time. Then when I make love, I take one off, and I feel like a wild man.
—*Dennis Miller*

Condoms aren't completely safe. A friend of mine was wearing one and got hit by a bus.
—*Bob Rubin*

Magnum condoms are a marketing gimmick, because what guy is going admit he doesn't require them? "No thanks. They're so big on me, I need to use a twist tie."
—*Robert Schimmel*

### Diaphragms

I was onstage last night talking. I said, "You know the diaphragm is a pain in the ass." Someone yelled out, "You were putting it in the wrong way."
—*Carol Montgomery*

I'm Catholic. My mother and I were unpacking and she found my diaphragm. I had to tell her it was a bathing cap for my cat.
—*Lizz Winstead*

### for Men

A birth control pill for men, that's fair. It makes more sense to take the bullets out of the gun than to wear a bulletproof vest.
—*Greg Travis*

### Oral

I was involved in an extremely good example of oral contraception two weeks ago. I asked a girl to go to bed with me, and she said "No."
—*Woody Allen*

I'm not on the pill, but I label my Tic Tacs with the days of the week. Makes me feel like I'm in a relationship.
—*Cathy Ladman*

I was dating a control freak. He insisted that he take the birth control pills.
—*Wendy Leibman*

You know what's the worst contraceptive? The pill. Because you have to keep taking it every day, regardless of what's going on in your love life. It's nice, during those two-year lulls, to have a daily reminder. "I sleep alone, but it's time for my loser pill." Can you imagine if men had to wear a condom for thirty days just in case they might need it? "It's day 28, but somebody might call."
—*Caroline Rhea*

Other women take the pill and don't get pregnant. I take the pill and get a mustache and beard.
—*Andi Rhoads*

Japanese women are refusing to take birth control pills, opting to leave contraception up to men. Do you know what they call women who leave birth control up to men? Mothers.
—*Jennifer Vally*

## COOKING

Men like to barbecue. Men will cook if danger is involved.
—*Rita Rudner*

### Bad

Every time I go near the stove, the dog howls.
—*Phyllis Diller*

My husband says I feed him like he's a god; every meal is a burnt offering.
—*Rhonda Hansome*

I can't cook. I use a smoke alarm as a timer.
—*Carol Siskind*

### Microwaves

I saw a stupid ad for a microwave that cooks in ten seconds. Are there really people who say, "I've been home for ten seconds, where the hell is dinner?"
—*Jay Leno*

I put instant coffee into the microwave. I almost went back in time.
—*Steven Wright*

**CORPORATIONS**     See: **BUSINESS**

**COSMETICS**     Makeup is such a weird concept. I'll wake up in the morning and look in the mirror: "Gee, I really don't look so good. Maybe if my eyelids were blue, I'd be more attractive."
—*Cathy Ladman*

I don't have time every day to put on makeup. I need that time to clean my rifle.
—*Henriette Mantel*

Where lipstick is concerned, the important thing is not color, but to accept God's final word on where your lips end.
—*Jerry Seinfeld*

Take it from me, wrinkle cream doesn't work. I've been using it for two years, and my balls still look like raisins.
—*Harland Williams*

**COURTS**     See also: **LAWYERS**

Juries     When you go into court you are putting your fate into the hands of twelve people who weren't smart enough to get out of jury duty.
—*Norm Crosby*

My mother is a typical Jewish mother. They sent her home from jury duty, she insisted she was guilty.
—*Cathy Ladman*

Jury: A group of twelve people selected to decide who has the better lawyer.
—*Henny Youngman*

Justice            In this country you're guilty until proven wealthy.
                   —*Bill Maher*

**CRAYONS**        See: **TOYS**

**CREATIONISM**    You ever noticed how people who believe in Creationism
                   look really un-evolved? Eyes close together, eyebrow ridges,
                   big furry hands and feet. "I believe God created me in one
                   day." Yeah, looks like He rushed it.
                   —*Bill Hicks*

**CREDIT CARDS**   I just had plastic surgery: They cut up all my credit cards.
                   Except for my Discover card, which nobody takes.
                   —*Wendy Liebman*

                   My last credit card bill was so big. Before I opened it I actu-
                   ally heard a drum roll.
                   —*Rita Rudner*

**CRIME**          See also: **GANGS, HOMICIDE, POLICE**

                   Ninety-eight percent of the adults in this country are
                   decent, hard-working, honest Americans. It's the other two
                   percent that get all the publicity. But then, we elected them.
                   —*Lily Tomlin*

Arrests            I was arrested today for scalping low numbers at the deli.
                   —*Richard Lewis*

                   The highway cop said, "Walk a straight line." I said, "Well,
                   Officer Pythagoras, the closest you could ever come to
                   achieving a straight line would be making an electroen-
                   cephalogram of your own brain waves." He said, "You're
                   under arrest. You have the right to remain silent. Do you
                   wish to retain that right?" I thought, "Oooh, a paradox!"
                   —*Emo Philips*

I was arrested for selling illegal-size paper.
            —*Steven Wright*

**Black Versus White**          See also: Suspects

Black crime tends to be stupid, not crazy. When you hear on the news that somebody chopped off his girlfriend's head, drank her blood, and used her toes to play pool, chances are it was a white guy. An old lady kicked downstairs for her welfare check? A black guy. Someone cut out the old lady's eyes and used them as knickknacks? Definitely a white guy.
            —*Chris Rock*

White criminals commit the biggest crimes. A brother might rob a bank. A white man will rob a pension fund. The brother is going to get ten to fifteen years because he had a gun. The white guy will get a congressional hearing because he had a job and a nice suit.
            —*Wanda Sykes*

**Breaking and Entering**          Some guy broke into our house last week. He didn't even take the TV. He just took the remote control. Now he drives by and changes channels on us.
            —*Brian Kiley*

We had gay burglars the other night. They broke in and rearranged the furniture.
            —*Robin Williams*

I woke up one morning and realized that someone had broken in the night before, and replaced everything in my apartment with an exact replica. I got my roommate and showed him. I said, "Look at this, everything's been replaced with an exact replica!" He said, "Do I know you?"
            —*Steven Wright*

| | |
|---|---|
| Hold-ups | A Texas bank robber wrote his hold-up note on the back of his resume, on which he lied about his earlier robberies.<br>—*Conan O'Brien* |
| of Jealousy | A woman escaped death when a bullet shot by her jealous husband lodged in her breast implant. And I almost lost a thumb.<br>—*Craig Kilborn* |
| in Laundromat | In Berlin, a laundromat was raided because it was a front for a brothel. You know what tipped police off? Men doing laundry.<br>—*Jay Leno* |
| of Passion | "Crimes of passion," that phrase drives me crazy. A man murdering his girlfriend is not a crime of passion. Premature ejaculation, that's a crime of passion.<br>—*Hellura Lyle* |
| Street Crime | I used to get beaten up by these green berets in my neighborhood. Some people call them Girl Scouts.<br>—*Tom Cotter* |

I was with my girlfriend, and we saw eight big guys pushing an old lady around. My girlfriend says, "Do something about it." So I went up to them and asked, "Is that any way to treat an elderly lady?" They said, "It's one way." So I thought, "That's reasonable."
—*Stevie Ray Fromstein*

I was walking through the park. I had a very bad asthmatic attack. These three asthmatics attacked me. I know . . . I should have heard them hiding.
—*Emo Philips*

| | |
|---|---|
| Suspects | See also: Black Versus White |

The only thing more suspicious than a black man running is a black man tippy-toeing.
—*Dave Chappelle*

All black men are born suspects. When I came out of my mother, if anything happened within a three-block radius, I was a suspect. The day I was born somebody's car got stolen from the hospital parking lot. They made me stand in a lineup. That was pretty tough considering I wasn't even a day old and couldn't crawl, much less walk. Good thing I had a couple black nurses to hold me up. I got lucky. They were in the lineup, too.
—*Chris Rock*

If you see a white man running, you think "He must be late for a meeting." When you see a black man running, you think, "I'm calling the cops. Hey, somebody stop his black ass!"
—*Wanda Sykes*

**CRUISES**     See: **VACATIONS**

**CURIOSITY**     Curiosity killed the cat. But for a while I was a suspect.
—*Steven Wright*

**CYBERSPACE**     According to a survey, 85 percent of men admit they surf the Internet wearing nothing but their underwear. Sixty-three percent said that's how they lost their last job.
—*Jay Leno*

Thanks to the Internet I had my identity stolen a few months ago, and my credit actually improved. I'm dating now, have a new car. Life is good.
—*Steve Moris*

I read an article the other day that said more and more bosses are becoming aware of their employees' need for Internet access. I don't believe that. Has anybody, anywhere, in any office actually seen somebody who is doing work on the Internet? Get real. Half the people in my office are on there looking for other jobs.
—*Livia Squires*

# DANCING

Belly
My mom took up belly dancing. In order to make it appear like she was moving, my father and I had to jiggle the furniture in back of her.
—*Rita Rudner*

Limbo
My friend would spend all of his time practicing limbo. He got pretty good. He could go under a rug.
—*Steven Wright*

Square
I have heard women say they can judge how a guy will be in bed from how he dances. I hope that's not true. Because I come from rednecks, and my people invented square dancing. Which means we're so bad at it, we have to have someone tell us what to do, as we're doing it.
—*Steve Neal*

# DATING
See also: **PERSONAL ADS**, **RELATIONSHIPS**

Whenever I want a really nice meal, I start dating again.
—*Susan Healy*

Bad Dates
I'm still going on bad dates, when by now I should be in a bad marriage.
—*Laura Kightlinger*

What is a date, really, but a job interview that lasts all night? The only difference is that in not many job interviews is there a chance you'll wind up naked.
—*Jerry Seinfeld*

I went out to dinner with a Marine. He looked across the table and he goes, "I could kill you in seven seconds." I go, "I'll just have toast then."
—*Margaret Smith*

Going out with a jerky guy is kind of like having a piece of food caught in your teeth. All your friends notice it before you do.

—*Livia Squires*

How many of you ever started dating someone because you were too lazy to commit suicide?

—*Judy Tenuta*

## Bad Luck

I don't get no respect. A girl phoned me and said, "Come on over, there's nobody home." I went over. Nobody was home.

—*Rodney Dangerfield*

I had no luck with dating. My big thrill was self-inflicted hickies.

—*Rodney Dangerfield*

I have bad luck with women. A woman I was dating told me on the phone, "I have to go, there's a telemarketer on the other line."

—*Zach Galifiankis*

I asked this one girl out, and she said, "You got a friend?" I said yes; she said, "Then go out with him."

—*Dom Irrera*

## Blind Dates

I've been on so many blind dates I should get a free dog.

—*Wendy Liebman*

## Books

I'm dating again, but it's got me confused. So I've been reading up on the differences between men and women. I read *The Rules*, the Mars and Venus books, *Dating for Dummies*. And here's the real difference: Women buy the books.

—*Daryl Hogue*

## Costs

An average guy makes a date with a girl. It costs him $100, $200. I make a date with a girl, it costs me nothing. I come up to her house. She wants to go out. I let her go! What's my business? I have to follow her around?

—*Jackie Mason*

It costs a lot of money to date. I took a girl out to dinner the other night. I said, "What'll you have?" She said, "I guess I'll have the steak and lobster." I said "Guess again."

—*Skip Stephenson*

I went out with this one guy. I was very excited about it. He took me out to dinner; he made me laugh; he made me pay. He's like, "Oh, I'm sorry. I forgot my wallet." "Really? I forgot my vagina."

—*Lisa Sunstedt*

First

Dinner is a waste on a first date, because you don't want the guy to see how much you can really eat. "He'll find out soon enough that I can put my entire head in a Häagen Dazs tub."

—*Maryellen Hooper*

My father always said, "Be the kind they marry, not the kind they date." So on our first date I'd nag the guy for a new dishwasher.

—*Kris McGaha*

Dating goes in stages. The first is the best. Conversation is new; conversation exists. You go to a restaurant, the girl goes to sit down, the guy pulls the chair out, puts the chair back in. Six, seven months go by: "What? You think I work here? Sit down and don't order the lobster, okay?"

—*John Mendoza*

I hate first dates. I made the mistake of telling my date a lie about myself, and she caught me. I didn't think she'd actually demand to see the bat cave.

—*Alex Reed*

I guess I'm looking for a woman like my mother, and on
our first date she'd put her breast in my mouth.
—*Adam Sandler*

Gifts

Men are so cheap these days. Whatever happened to guys
bringing women chocolates or flowers? I've reached the point
where the grim reaper could show up at my door and I'd be
like, "Oh my God, you brought me a scythe. That's so sweet!"
—*Jenée*

Good

I was out on a date recently and the guy took me horseback
riding. That was kind of fun, until we ran out of quarters.
—*Susie Loucks*

My sister was with two men in one night. She could hardly
walk after that. Can you imagine? Two dinners!
—*Sarah Silverman*

Is . . .

Dating is dumb. Basically you're making false judgments
based on false exteriors. Oh, sure my superficial self likes
your superficial self, but the real me likes your roommate.
—*Margot Black*

Dating is like driving on the freeway; I can never get to
where I'm supposed to be. I know I should to be at the corner of "Engaged to Be Married," but instead I'm stuck in
the "Valley of Haven't Had an Orgasm for Three Months."
—*Christine O'Rourke*

Dating is a lot like sports. You have to practice; you work
out; you study the greats. You hope to make the team, and
it hurts to be cut.
—*Sinbad*

as Kids

Dating was so much easier when we were younger because
we all spoke the same cryptic code and understood the
rules of engagement. "Shelly, ask Suzie to ask Mary to ask
Mike to ask Billy if he likes me. But tell her not to let him

know that I like him. Well OK, she can tell Billy that I like him, but not that I like him, like him."

—*Lori Gianella*

**Lying**

If a man lies to you, don't get mad; get even. I once dated a guy who waited three months into our relationship before he told me he was married. I said "Hey, don't worry about it. I used to be a man."

—*Livia Squires*

**Meetings**

I'd just like to meet a girl with a head on her shoulders. I hate necks.

—*Steve Martin*

I met a new girl at a barbecue. A very pretty blonde girl, I think. I don't know for sure. Her hair was on fire. And all she talked about was herself. "I'm on fire!" You know the type. "Jesus Christ, help me! Put me out!" Come on, can we talk about me a little bit?

—*Garry Shandling*

**Senior**

My grandmother's ninety. She's dating. He's ninety-three. They're very happy; they never argue. They can't hear each other.

—*Cathy Ladman*

**and Sex**

It's too much trouble to get laid. Because you have to go out with a guy, and go to dinner with him, and listen to him talk about his opinions, and I don't have that kind of time.

—*Kathy Griffin*

I was on a date, and this girl teased a banana in a suggestive manner, and said, "That could be you." I replied, "Well then, I should probably get that dark soft-spot looked at."

—*Deric Harrington*

A man on a date wonders if he'll get lucky. The woman knows.

—*Monica Piper*

On a date I wonder if there is going to be any sex, and if I'm going to be involved.

—*Garry Shandling*

### and Telephones

Men, if you've ever been given a fake phone number, it means you scare women. Basically, it says, "I'd reject you to your face, but I'm afraid that my head would wind up in the garbage and my body in the bay. So here's a phony phone number. Hopefully, you won't figure that out until I've made my escape."

—*Lori Chapman*

Men will say, "I'll call you. I'll call you." When they say they're going to call, they don't, and when they say they're not going to come, they do.

—*Carol Henry*

I'm standing on line at the bakery, and this really cute guy asked for my number. So I had to get another one.

—*Wendy Liebman*

When women don't want to give out their phone number, they make up a number. This one girl said to me, "My telephone number? 456-78910." "Is that by any chance in the 123 area code?"

—*Ron Richards*

### Younger Men

Younger guys have been approaching me lately. And asking me to buy them alcohol.

—*Wendy Liebman*

### DEAD END

I'm living on a one-way, dead-end street. I don't know how I got there.

—*Steven Wright*

**DEATH**          See also: **DEATH PENALTY, FUNERALS, SUICIDE**

I don't mind death. I just don't want to be there when it happens.
            —*Woody Allen*

On the plus side, death is one of the few things that can be done lying down.
            —*Woody Allen*

For three days after death, hair and fingernails continue to grow, but phone calls taper off.
            —*Johnny Carson*

One of my big fears in life is that I'm going to die and my parents are going to have to clear out my apartment and find that porno wing I've been adding on for years. There'll be more than one funeral that day.
            —*Bill Hicks*

I wanna live 'til I die. No more, no less.
            —*Eddie Izzard*

The upshot to dying is that you don't have to go to work the next day.
            —*Jason Love*

I know when I'm going to die. My birth certificate has an expiration date on it.
            —*Steven Wright*

Causes          Death is caused by swallowing small amounts of saliva over a long period of time.
            —*George Carlin*

Dying          When your life flashes before you, do you think that includes every trip you made to the bank?
            —*Carol Leifer*

How young can you die of old age?
—*Steven Wright*

When I die, I'm going to leave my body to science fiction.
—*Steven Wright*

I want to die with a smile on my face. Hopefully, it won't be mine.
—*Matt Vance*

Euthanasia

See also: **NURSING HOMES**

When you're young you say, "If I become a vegetable, pull the plug!" You get older, you hedge a little. "If I'm a turnip, kill me. If I'm a trendier vegetable, like radicchio, mist me twice a day and trim the wilted leaves."
—*Daniel Liebert*

If I'm ever stuck on a respirator or a life support system I definitely want to be unplugged. But not until I'm down to a size eight.
—*Henriette Mantel*

Immortality

If Shaw and Einstein couldn't beat death, what chance have I got? Practically none.
—*Mel Brooks*

Immortality is a long shot, I admit. But somebody has to be first.
—*Bill Cosby*

**DEATH PENALTY**

Just as the prisoner was being strapped into the electric chair, the priest said, "Son, is there anything I can do for you?" The prisoner said, "Yeah, when they pull the switch, hold my hand."
—*Dick Gregory*

If it weren't for capitol punishment, we wouldn't have Easter.
    —*Bill Hicks*

**DEBT**     See: **FINANCES**

**DENTISTS**     See also: **TEETH**

Happiness is your dentist telling you it won't hurt and then having him catch his hand in the drill.
    —*Johnny Carson*

I went to the dentist. He said, "Say 'Aaah.'" I asked, "Why?" He said, "My dog died."
    —*Tommy Cooper*

I don't get no respect. I told my dentist my teeth are going yellow. He told me to wear a brown necktie.
    —*Rodney Dangerfield*

The dentist told me I grind my teeth at night, so now before I go to sleep I fill my mouth with hot water and coffee beans and set my alarm for 7:30.
    —*Jeff Marder*

**DIETING**     See also: **WEIGHT**

Never let your caloric intake exceed your white blood cell count.
    —*Beth Donahue*

Anti-
I think everyone should go on my Fuck It Diet. Basically, if I want something that has a lot of fat or carbs, I take a moment to go within, say "Fuck it," and eat. This works really well with my Fuck That Shit exercise program.
    —*Margaret Cho*

I want to have a good body, but not as much as I want dessert.
    —*Jason Love*

Commercials

You know you're on a diet when cat food commercials make you hungry.
> —*Andy Bumatai*

Diets

I was on the grapefruit diet. For breakfast I ate fifteen grapefruit. Now when I go to the bathroom I keep squirting myself in the eye.
> —*Max Alexander*

I have a great diet. You're allowed to eat anything you want, but you must eat it with naked fat people.
> —*Ed Bluestone*

The second day of a diet is always easier than the first. By the second you're off it.
> —*Jackie Gleason*

I went on a diet, swore off drinking and heavy eating, and in fourteen days I lost two weeks.
> —*Joe E. Lewis*

I went on a diet. Had to go on two diets at the same time because one diet wasn't giving me enough food.
> —*Barry Marder*

Fasting

Do you have to brush your teeth during a fast? Why do they call it a fast if it goes so damn slow?
> —*Gallagher*

with Husband

My husband and I both gained weight after we got married, and so we went on a diet together. He lost weight, and I didn't. I had to feed him in his sleep, intravenously.
> —*Rita Rudner*

**DIFFERENTLY ABLED**

I have cerebral palsy, and I don't understand why people will go out of their way to drink so they walk like me.
> —*Geri Jewell*

I'm proud to be handicapped. If it weren't for me, you'd be spending all day looking for a place to park.
—*Gene Mitchner*

Just what is the handicapped parking situation at the Special Olympics? Is it still just the two spaces?
—*Jerry Seinfeld*

**DIVORCE**    See also: **MARRIAGE**

Our parents got divorced when we were kids, and it was kind of cool. We got to go to divorce court with them. It was like a game show. My mom won the house and car. We were all excited. My dad got some luggage.
—*Tom Arnold*

When it comes to divorce, absence may not make the heart grow fonder, but it sure cuts down on the gunplay.
—*Eileen Courtney*

I never even believed in divorce until after I got married.
—*Diane Ford*

It is a sad fact that 50 percent of marriages in this country end in divorce. But hey, the other half end in death. You could be one of the lucky ones!
—*Richard Jeni*

My wife and I had an amicable divorce. She lets me see my stuff on weekends. Last Sunday I took my sweaters to Disneyland.
—*Craig Shoemaker*

Marriage doesn't need to be protected from same-sex couples. Divorce is what ended my marriage, not Stacy and Anna getting hitched. If the Christian Conservatives really want to protect marriage they should propose a constitutional amendment to ban divorce. The murder rate would go up, but the institution of marriage would be strong and healthy.

—*Wanda Sykes*

**Definition of**    Divorce comes from the old Latin word *divorcerum*, meaning "having your genitals torn out through your wallet." And the judge said, "All the money, and we'll just shorten it to 'alimony.'"

—*Robin Williams*

**Husband's Side**    It's hard to talk to divorced men, always sensitive from the divorce. Take things the wrong way. "Nice day don't you think?" "I don't want to make a commitment." "Want half of my ice cream?" "I don't want half of anything anymore."

—*Elayne Boosler*

It wasn't actually a divorce. I was traded.

—*Tim Conway*

When I got divorced, that was group sex. My wife screwed me in front of the jury.

—*Rodney Dangerfield*

My first wife divorced me because I didn't match her shoes. I was a lazy white loafer.

—*Kelly Monteith*

It's tough. After five years of marriage, it's difficult to lose the one with the good credit rating.

—*Rich Voss*

**Separation**    The difference between divorce and legal separation is that a legal separation gives a husband time to hide his money.

—*Johnny Carson*

**Wife's Side**    I'm not upset about my divorce. I'm only upset I'm not a widow.

—*Roseanne Barr*

When I divorced I went through the various stages of grieving: anger, denial, and dancing around with my settlement check.
—*Maura Kennedy*

I got divorced recently. It was a mixed marriage. I'm human; he was Klingon.
—*Carol Leifer*

My husband and I had very messy divorce because there was a baby involved. Him. And I didn't want custody.
—*Wendy Liebman*

**DOCTORS**    See also: **MEDICINE**, **THERAPY**

I could have been a doctor, but there were too many good shows on TV.
—*Jason Love*

My father wanted me to become a doctor, but I wanted to do something that required more imagination. So we compromised, and I became a hypochondriac.
—*Wally Wang*

Appointments    I've got a doctor's appointment on Monday. I'm not sick or anything. It's just that I lost some weight, and I want someone to see me naked.
—*Tracy Smith*

Bills    Doctors are the only people that if they don't find anything wrong they still charge you. You know what you should do? Next time look into your wallet and say you can't find anything either.
—*Mark Schiff*

I've got a wonderful doctor. If you can't afford the operation, he touches up the X-rays.
—*Henny Youngman*

Diagnosis

I went to a doctor and told him, "My penis is burning." He said, "That means somebody is talking about it."
—*Garry Shandling*

A doctor said to his patient, "You're going to live until you're eighty." The patient said, "I am eighty." The doctor replied, "What did I tell you?"
—*Henny Youngman*

I said, "Doctor, it hurts when I do this." He said, "Then don't do that!"
—*Henny Youngman*

Gynecology

Recent studies show that, increasingly, women prefer female gynecologists. I, myself, am thinking about switching to a female gynecologist because I think my male gynecologist might be lying to me about being a doctor. Because last week I found out that he also works at Foot Locker. Which if he was a real doctor, I don't think he would have to do that. But his bedside manner is so soothing, and he gives me wine, and he keeps his van really clean. Anyway, I'm not gonna fire him yet. I want to see how the pictures come out.
—*Tina Fey*

I got a postcard from my gynecologist. It said, "Did you know it's time for your annual check-up?" No. But now my mailman does. Why don't you just send me a petri dish while you're at it?
—*Cathy Ladman*

It's silly for a woman to go to a male gynecologist. It's like going to an auto mechanic who never owned a car.
—*Carrie Snow*

Handwriting

My father is a doctor, with the worst handwriting. He wrote me a note once excusing me from gym class. I gave it to my teacher, and she gave me all of her money.
—*Rita Rudner*

My kid is a born doctor. He can't write anything anybody can read.
> —*Henny Youngman*

Opthamology

I went to bed with an ophthalmologist, who asked, "Is it better like this? Or like that?"
> —*Tommy Koenig*

Proctology

My father's a proctologist. My mother is an abstract artist. That's how I view the world.
> —*Sandra Bernhard*

Questionable Practices

Be suspicious of any doctor who tries to take your temperature with his finger.
> —*David Letterman*

I understand that the doctor had to spank me when I was born, but I really don't see any reason he had to call me a whore.
> —*Sarah Silverman*

Waiting Room

I hate the waiting room, so sometimes I start screwing around with stuff. Take all the tongue depressors out, lick them, put them back. Two can play at this waiting game.
> —*Jerry Seinfeld*

## DOGS

See also: **MEMORY**, **VETERINARIANS**

Dogs lead a nice life. You never see a dog with a wristwatch.
> —*George Carlin*

Barking

My neighbor has two dogs. One of them says, "Woof!" The other replies, "Moo!" The first dog is perplexed. "'Moo?' Why did you say, 'Moo?'" The other dog says, "I'm trying to learn a foreign language."
> —*Morey Amsterdam*

in Cars

Did you ever notice when you blow in a dog's face he gets mad at you? But when you take him in a car he sticks his head out the window.
—*Steve Bluestein*

Dogs hate it when you blow in their face. I'll tell you who really hates that, my grandmother. Which is odd, because when we're driving she loves to hang her head out the window.
—*Ellen DeGeneres*

I like driving around with my two dogs, especially on the freeways. I make them wear little hats so I can use the carpool lanes.
—*Monica Piper*

Chihuahuas

I just bought a Chihuahua. It's the dog for lazy people. You don't have to walk it. Just hold it out the window and squeeze.
—*Anthony Clark*

Chihuahua, there's a waste of dog food. Looks like a dog that is still far away.
—*Billiam Coronel*

and Exercise

I tell ya, my dog is lazy. He don't chase cars. He sits on the curb and takes down license plate numbers.
—*Rodney Dangerfield*

I see people rollerblading with their dogs, and I think that's cool. Unless it's a dachshund; then it's kind of a drag.
—*Dana Eagle*

as Friends

See also: **ANIMALS**

I've heard that dogs are man's best friend. That explains where men are getting their hygiene tips.
—*Kelly Maguire*

I once had a dog who really believed he was man's best friend. He kept borrowing money from me.

—*Gene Perret*

They say a dog is man's best friend, but I don't buy it. How many of your friends have had you neutered?

—*Larry Reeb*

**Ice Cream**

Some scientist spent twenty years in the lab inventing ice cream for dogs. He made it taste like vanilla, so it's hardly selling at all. If he'd made it taste like doody, dogs would be robbing stores with guns.

—*Elayne Boosler*

**IQ**

A Canadian psychologist is selling a video that teaches you how to test your dog's IQ. Here's how it works: If you spend $12.99 for the video, your dog is smarter than you.

—*Jay Leno*

**Pit Bulls**

In May this year, I bought myself a pit bull. In June, I bought myself a prosthetic arm.

—*Mark Morfey*

I have a dog that's half pit bull, half poodle. Not much of a guard dog, but a vicious gossip.

—*Craig Shoemaker*

**Pondering**

My husband and I are either going to buy a dog or have a child. We can't decide whether to ruin our carpet or ruin our lives.

—*Rita Rudner*

**Terriers**

My mother gave my grandmother a Yorkshire Terrier. It's got this affliction—it shakes and shakes. Maybe someone told him to shake once, and didn't say when to stop. He's like a shoe buffer. You can put your foot down there, and your shoe comes out shiny.

—*Garry Shandling*

I got a wire-haired terrier that wouldn't bark, so I had him rewired for sound.
—*Red Skelton*

and Toilets

Dogs are gross, they drink out of the toilet. But when you're going to the bathroom, maybe your dog is thinking, "Hey, hey, hey! I drink out of that thing! Why don't you just go in my dish, and save yourself a walk down the hallway?"
—*Garry Shandling*

Training

I sent my dog to obedience school, and she liked it. Now she wants to get tied up and whipped.
—*Ed Bluestone*

I have a dog, and I've trained him to go on the paper, but he won't wait until I've finished reading it.
—*Richard Jeni*

Walking

Oh, that dog! All he does is piddle. He's nothing but a fur-covered kidney that barks.
—*Phyllis Diller*

They have dog food for constipated dogs. If your dog is constipated, why screw up a good thing? Stay indoors and let 'em bloat.
—*David Letterman*

A lot of people walk their dogs, and I see them walking along with their little poop bags. This, to me, is the lowest activity in human life. If aliens are watching this through telescopes, they're going to think the dogs are the leaders of the planet. If you see two life forms, one of them is making a poop, the other one's carrying it for him, who would you assume is in charge?
—*Jerry Seinfeld*

My friend George walked his dog, all at once. Walked him from Boston to Ft. Lauderdale, and said, "Now you're done."
—*Steven Wright*

Washing

The Japanese have developed an automated dog-washing machine. It's bad when you unload it and find an extra paw that doesn't match.
—*Craig Kilborn*

**DOLLS**

They're going to sell a talking doll of my mother. You pull the string, and it says, "Again, with the string."
—*Fred Stoller*

Barbies

A toy company is releasing Teacher Barbie. Apparently, it's like Malibu Barbie, only she can't afford the Corvette.
—*Stephanie Miller*

If Barbie is so popular, why do you have to buy her friends?
—*Steven Wright*

**DREAMING**      See: **SLEEPING**

**DRINKING**      See also: **ALCOHOL**, **ALCOHOLISM**, **BARS**

I don't need to drink to have a good time. I need to drink to stop the voices in my head.
—*Dave Attell*

I drink too much. Last time I gave a urine sample there was an olive in it.
—*Rodney Dangerfield*

I can't hold my liquor in the winter. I'm pretty sure it's the mittens.
—*Jonathan Katz*

and Driving

Some people are against drunk driving, and I call those people the cops. But sometimes, you've just got no choice: Those kids gotta get to school.
—*Dave Attell*

Friends don't let friends drive drunk. Instead, you should shave their eyebrows and put them on a train to Chicago. It's a public service and quite entertaining at the same time.
—*Vinny Badabing*

Don't drink and drive. Instead, the next time you get too drunk to drive, walk into a local Domino's and order a pizza. Then when they go to deliver it, ask for a ride home.
—*Todd Glass*

Want to have fun when you're the designated driver? Do what I do. At the end of the evening, drop people off at strangers' houses. "Go on in Bob, kiss the wife for me."
—*Jay Leno*

There are two groups of people in the world now. Those that get pathetically drunk in public, and the rest of us poor bastards who are expected to drive these pinheads home.
—*Dennis Miller*

A bar in New York is installing a breathalyzer. If you're drunk, it advises you not to drive. If you're very, very drunk, it advises you not to call your old girlfriend.
—*Conan O'Brien*

Effects

You're drinking, you black out. You wake up in another bar. You're drinking, you black out. You wake up playing that knife game with an Indian, somewhere in South Dakota. You're drinking, you black out. You wake up, you're in White Castle, working three years, still not assistant manager.
—*Dave Attell*

I can't think of anything worse after a night of drinking than waking up next to someone and not being able to remember their name, or how you met, or why they're dead.

　　*—Laura Kightlinger*

You walk out of a bar into daylight. If you're nineteen and you stay up all night, it's a victory. But if you're over thirty, then the sun is God's flashlight. We all say the same prayer then, "I swear: I will never do this again as long as I live." And some of us have that little addition, "And this time, I mean it!"

　　*—Larry Miller*

## DRIVING

See also: **AUTOMOBILES, GASOLINE**

Hey, what do you expect from a culture that drives on parkways, and parks on driveways?

　　*—Gallagher*

### Asleep

There's a new device to wake sleepy drivers. The old device was the car crash.

　　*—Craig Kilborn*

### Bad

I am the worst driver. Let's just say I always wear clean underwear. I should drive a hearse and cut out the middle man.

　　*—Wendy Liebman*

### Cars

Driving a crappy car changes your entire mindset. If someone cuts me off on the freeway I can't flip them off, because I may need that guy to jump-start me in a few minutes.

　　*—Dobie Maxwell*

### Elderly

My dad's still driving at eighty-nine: "What red light? What open drawbridge? Why is there a baby carriage on the hood?"

　　*—Buddy Bolton*

The elderly don't drive that badly. They're just the only ones with time to do the speed limit.

　　*—Jason Love*

| | |
|---|---|
| Honking | I hate when people honk at me. Unless I'm making a left turn. Then I like it because that's how I know it's time to turn.<br>—*Rita Rudner* |
| with Husbands | When my husband and I are in the car, I usually let him drive. Because when I drive, he has a tendency to bite the dashboard.<br>—*Rita Rudner* |
| Learning | My mom taught me how to drive. I can't drive worth a damn, but I can change all my clothes at a stoplight.<br>—*Craig Shoemaker* |
| Not | I had to stop driving my car for a while. The tires got dizzy.<br>—*Steven Wright* |
| Parking | See also: **TICKETS**<br><br>Somebody actually complimented me on my driving today. They left a little note on the windscreen. It said "Parking Fine."<br>—*Tommy Cooper*<br><br>Parallel parking. What better way to do something you're already a little leery about doing, than by doing it backward?<br>—*Ellen DeGeneres* |
| Permits | I have my learner's permit, which means that I can drive with my parents in the car. Woohoo! I'm living on the edge. And driving with my parents isn't the wild ride you would think, oh no. It's awkward, especially on dates. Because, we're in the car, at a drive-in, things start getting a little hot in the back seat, and finally I just have to turn around and say, "Mom, Dad, will you cut it out! We're trying to watch the movie up here!"<br>—*Dominic Dierkes* |

**Signs**

Signs on the freeway are funny. "Orange Cones Mean Men at Work." What else could orange cones mean? Psychedelic witches embedded in asphalt?
—*Karen Babbitt*

When I'm driving I see a sign that says, "Caution: Small Children Playing." I slow down, and then it occurs to me: I'm not afraid of small children.
—*Jonathan Katz*

**Speeding**

See also: Violations

Have you noticed? Anybody going slower than you is an idiot, and anyone going faster than you is a moron.
—*George Carlin*

I got pulled over for speeding once in my Chevette. You should have seen the look on the cop's face. I didn't even think he wanted to give me a ticket. He wanted to find out how the hell I did it.
—*Jeremy Hotz*

I was stopped once for doing 53 in a 35-miles-per-hour zone, but I got off. I told them I had dyslexia.
—*Spanky*

I was pulled over for speeding today. The officer said, "Don't you know the speed limit is 55 miles an hour?" I replied, "Yes, but I wasn't going to be out that long."
—*Steven Wright*

**Steering Wheels**

One of the first things they teach you in driver's ed is where to put your hands on the steering wheel—at 10:00 and 2:00. I put mine at 9:45 and 2:17. Gives me an extra half-hour to get where I'm goin'.
—*George Carlin*

Tests

I failed my driver's test. The guy asked me, "What do you do at a red light?" I said, "I don't know. Look around, listen to the radio?"
—*Bill Braudis*

I remember learning to drive on my dad's lap. Did you guys ever do that? He'd work the brakes. I'd work the wheel. Then I went to take the driver's test and sat on the examiner's lap. I failed the exam, but he still writes me.
—*Garry Shandling*

Traffic

Fear is being stuck in traffic and you just had two cups of coffee and a bran muffin.
—*John Mendoza*

Ever been stuck behind an accident, and when you finally see the wreckage, you're actually happy? "Things should pick up now, soon as we pass this carnage."
—*Paul Reiser*

When you're driving, ugly thoughts come up. There have been times when I'm stuck on the freeway and I think to myself, "If half the city died right now, I'd be home already."
—*Paul Reiser*

I'm always in traffic with the lane expert. Constantly reevaluating their lane choice, "Is this the best lane for me? For my life? Can I get in over there?" "Yeah, come over here, pal. We're zooming here. This is the secret lane; nobody knows about it."
—*Jerry Seinfeld*

Why do they call it rush hour when nothing moves?
—*Robin Williams*

Violations     See also: Speeding

In my glove compartment, I had ten moving-violation citations, which are like savings bonds. The longer you keep them, the more they mature.
> —*Bill Cosby*

I had this dream that I was driving down the freeway and slamming into everyone, just slamming into them. From side to side to side, right to left, all the way down the freeway. Not hurting anyone, though, just knocking the phones out of their hands.
> —*Laura Kightlinger*

I've become so vain. I went through one of those traffic lights that takes a picture when you go through a red light. I hated the picture, so I went through the light again. By the third time, I was pretty confident in front of the camera.
> —*LeMaire*

I was driving down the highway, and I'm swerving all over, coz I'm trying to change the radio, and just as I get the old one taken out I hear this traffic cop behind me, "Whee-oo, whee-oo, whee-oo!" Well, I shouldn't make fun of his speech impediment.
> —*Emo Philips*

I used to have a girlfriend that would blow me when I drove. It wasn't every time I drove, but every time I drove into a tree.
> —*Adam Richmond*

One time a cop pulled me over for running a stop sign. He said, "Didn't you see the stop sign?" I said, "Yeah, but I don't believe everything I read."
> —*Steven Wright*

**DRUGS**     I used to do drugs. I still do drugs. But I used to, too.
> —*Mitch Hedberg*

I'm not pro-drug. They obviously cause a lot of damage. But I am pro-logic, and you're never going to stop the human need for release through altered consciousness. The government could take away all the drugs in the word, and people would spin around on their lawn until they fell down and saw God.

—*Dennis Miller*

The best mind-altering drug is truth.

—*Lily Tomlin*

Anti-

Drugs don't enhance your creativity. You get the same old results with heroin. Your neighbors will complain when the ambulance shows up like clockwork. The firemen are going to track footprints on the rug. Your baby's going to keep waking up because of the guy shouting, "1, 2, 3—clear!" And you always lose your job. Your boss says, "It happened on Monday and twice on Tuesday—you died. We can't have that here, there are plenty of other bike messengers."

—*Paul Alexander*

There are obvious times when you don't want people getting high. I wouldn't want my surgeon to get high before my operation. If I'm laying there on the gurney, the last thing I want to hear is, "Nurse, gimme one of those, um, pointy things. Now, refresh my memory: We're doing what here? No shit!"

—*David Cross*

If God wanted us high, He would have given us wings.

—*Arsenio Hall*

I would never advocate the use of dope. Because I'm not a professional athlete, and I can't get my hands on the good stuff.

—*Greg Proops*

Cocaine

I've asked, "What is it about cocaine that makes it so wonderful?" And they say, "It intensifies your personality." But what if you're an asshole?
—*Bill Cosby*

Stay away from cocaine. Oh, it might seem glamorous at first. But one day, one day, it will be your turn to buy.
—*Emo Philips*

Cost

You should always say no to drugs. That will drive the prices down.
—*Geechy Guy*

Crack

I would never do crack. I would never do a drug named after a part of my own ass, OK?
—*Denis Leary*

History

Drugs have been around for a long time. I read that the Incas did drugs. I guess that explains why they were building runways for UFOs.
—*Tom Rhodes*

Marijuana

See also: **EMPLOYMENT** Bosses

And on the seventh day, God stepped back and said, "There is my creation, perfect in every way. Oh damn it, I left pot all over the place. Now they'll think I want them to smoke it. Now I have to create Republicans."
—*Bill Hicks*

I used to smoke marijuana. But I'll tell you something: I would only smoke it in the late evening. Oh, occasionally the early evening, but usually the late evening, or the mid-evening. Just the early evening, mid-evening, and late evening. Occasionally, early afternoon, early mid-afternoon, or perhaps the late mid-afternoon. Oh, sometimes the early-mid-late-early morning. But never at dusk.
—*Steve Martin*

Pro-                I recently attended a pro-drug rally, in my basement.
                    —*David Cross*

                    If you don't believe drugs have done good things, then
                    burn all your records, tapes, and CDs because every one of
                    those artists who have made brilliant music and enhanced
                    your lives? *Rrrreal* fucking high on drugs. The Beatles were
                    so high they let Ringo sing a few songs.
                    —*Bill Hicks*

                    Some of our most moral leaders don't want to get rid of
                    drugs because, in their own sick way, they think drugs are
                    good for the economy. Drugs get more people in jail. Then
                    corrections officers sell inmates drugs to help them pass the
                    time. It's corrupt, but sometimes you need two jobs just to
                    make ends meet.
                    —*Chris Rock*

Quitting            I don't do drugs, because I saw what it did to my friends. I'd
                    get stoned, and they'd look really weird to me.
                    —*Wendy Liebman*

                    I've been trying to quit smoking pot. It was easier to
                    become a vegetarian, because your friends will never show
                    up at your house with a sack of beef saying, "*Star Trek*'s on:
                    Twist up a link!"
                    —*Brian Posehn*

Testing             Why is there such controversy about drug testing? I know
                    plenty of guys who'd be willing to test any drug they can
                    come up with.
                    —*George Carlin*

War on              The War on Drugs is a big waste of money. The government
                    is pissing it away just so they can put on a big show for the
                    people who are against drugs, because those people happen

to vote. I don't think marijuana smokers get to the voting booth as often as they'd like to. "What, it was yesterday?"
—*Drew Carey*

Now they're calling drugs an epidemic. That's because white folks are doing it.
—*Richard Pryor*

while Working  A recent government study reported that 8 percent of full-time employees are on drugs at work. I think this study is flawed. The figure is too low. Because that 8 percent are only the people so stoned they answered yes to the question.
—*Bill Maher*

**DRY CLEANING**  I put my clothes in the cleaner's and then don't have the money to get them out. It's like they're in jail waiting on me to spring 'em.
—*Paula Poundstone*

**DUCKS**  See: **ANIMALS**

**EARTHQUAKES**   My family and I have come up with a course of action for an earthquake. At the first tremor, we get out of bed calmly, stand in a doorway, and start screaming. Maybe you know our system under another name: panic.
—*Milton Berle*

They say animal behavior can warn you when an earthquake is coming. Like the night before that last earthquake hit, our family dog took the car keys and drove to Arizona.
—*Bob Hope*

Did you hear about the latest earthquake in Los Angeles? It destroyed everything at the Etch-a-Sketch Museum.
—*Myq Kaplan*

This is weird, and threw us off. Right before the earthquake my father went into the bathroom and closed the door, and the house jiggled a little bit.
—*Ray Romano*

One way to tell when you're having an earthquake is your Jell-O stands still.
—*Soupy Sales*

**EATING**   See also: **DIETING**, **FOOD**, **VEGETARIANS**

Bad Habits   You've got bad eating habits if you use a grocery cart in the 7-Eleven, okay?
—*Dennis Miller*

Disorders   I went to a conference for bulimics and anorexics. It was a nightmare: The bulimics ate the anorexics. But it was OK, because they were back again in ten minutes.
—*Monica Piper*

Frequency   I go through the refrigerator so many times at night my neighbors think we have a strobe light in the kitchen.
—*Max Alexander*

I'm a light eater. As soon as it gets light, I eat.
—*Henny Youngman*

**ECOLOGY**            See: **ENVIRONMENT, ENVIRONMENTALISM**

**ECONOMICS**          See also: **FINANCES**

A study of economics usually reveals that the best time to buy anything is last year.
—*Marty Allen*

**EDUCATION**          See: **COLLEGE, SCHOOLS**

**ELECTIONS**          See also: **POLITICS**

On election day I stay home. Because if you vote, you have no right to complain. You elect dishonest, incompetent people; they get in office and screw everything up. You caused the problem. I am in no way responsible, and have every right to complain as loud as I want to about the mess you people created.
—*George Carlin*

We have a presidential election coming up. And I think the big problem, of course, is someone will win.
—*Barry Crimmins*

We already know the winners of the next elections. They'll be old white men who don't care about you or your problems.
—*Craig Kilborn*

If God had wanted us to vote, he would have given us candidates.
—*Jay Leno*

Move election day to April 15. Pay your taxes and hold elections on the same day. See if any of these duplicitous

sons of bitches would try to get away with their crap if we paid their salaries on the same day we voted for them.
—*Dennis Miller*

Whatever happened to separation of Church and hate? It's amazing how, in an election year, God's name gets thrown around like a drunken dwarf at a biker rally.
—*Dennis Miller*

You have to remember one thing about the will of the people: It wasn't that long ago that we were swept away by the Macarena.
—*Jon Stewart*

It's election time, and once again isn't it amazing how many wide open spaces there are, entirely surrounded by teeth?
—*Henny Youngman*

**ELECTRICITY**    Electricity is really just organized lightning.
—*George Carlin*

If it weren't for electricity we'd all be watching television by candlelight.
—*George Gobel*

I used to live in a house that ran on static electricity. If you wanted to run the blender, you had to rub balloons on your head. If you wanted to cook, you had to pull off a sweater real quick.
—*Steven Wright*

**EMERGENCIES**    I filled out an application that said, "In case of emergency notify . . ." I wrote "Doctor." What's my mother going to do?
—*Steven Wright*

**EMOTIONS**    See also: **HAPPINESS**

I've been on an emotional roller coaster lately. The other day my mood ring exploded.
—*Janine DiTullio*

**Anger**

Whining is anger through a small opening.
—*Al Franken*

Always keep your anger bottled up. You might need a bottle of anger someday when friends come by and don't leave.
—*Laura Kightlinger*

**Guilt**

What is guilt? Guilt is the pledge drive constantly hammering in our heads that keeps us from fully enjoying the show. Guilt is the reason they put the articles in *Playboy*.
—*Dennis Miller*

**EMPLOYMENT**

See also: **OCCUPATIONS**

Most people don't know what they're doing, and a lot of them are really good at it.
—*George Carlin*

I work for a good cause: 'cause I need the money.
—*Kelly*

**Anger at**

A study came out this week that said one out of four American workers is angry at work. And the other three save it for the loved ones at home.
—*Bill Maher*

**Bad Jobs**

I work in a "you scratch my back, and I'll stab yours" kind of place.
—*Kelly*

You might want to consider a career change when you hope for natural disaster as a reason to go home for the day.
—*Jason Love*

There are many ways to know that you have a bad job. For instance, if you have to carry out the body of the guy whose place you're taking. Or, if you're employed at the post office next to a coworker who's constantly muttering under his breath, and the only word you can make out is your name.
—*Dennis Miller*

**Bosses**

Never take a job where the boss calls you "babe."
—*Brett Butler*

I hated my last boss. He asked, "Why are you two hours late?" I said, "I fell downstairs." He said, "That doesn't take two hours."
—*Johnny Carson*

Aren't bosses something? They're like gnats at a picnic. Get the fuck out of here buddy; it's just a job, doesn't mean a thing. I smoked a joint this morning; you're lucky I showed. My bed was like a womb, man.
—*Bill Hicks*

I had the meanest boss in the world, so I would call in sick a lot. I would say I had "female problems." My boss didn't know I meant her.
—*Wendy Liebman*

**Careers**

I'll tell you what a career is. It's just something you have so you can screw a better class of people.
—*Tracy Smith*

**Coffee Breaks**

I never drink coffee at work. It keeps me awake.
—*Judy Brown*

**Collaboration**

Collaborative, from the Greek *col*: with other people; *laborative*: the other people are morons.
—*Richard Jeni*

| | |
|---|---|
| Factories | I used to work in a fire hydrant factory. You couldn't park anywhere near the place.<br>—*Steven Wright* |
| First | I got my first full-time job, but it's weird. I could have sworn I was making more money in college, working for my parents as their daughter.<br>—*Melanie Reno* |
| Getting Fired | Most people work just hard enough not to get fired and get paid just enough money not to quit.<br>—*George Carlin* |

I lost my job. No, I didn't really lose my job. I know where my job is, still. It's just when I go there, there's this new guy doing it. I lost my girl. No, I didn't really lose my girl. I know where my girl is, still. It's just when I go there, there's this new guy doing it.
—*Bobcat Goldthwait*

I've been fired a few times in my life. And that's fine. In a lot of cases, it's only a little worse than getting hired.
—*Laura Kightlinger*

I used to work at the unemployment office. I hated that job because when they fired me, I had to show up at work the next day anyway.
—*Wally Wang*

My brother-in-law gave up his job because of illness. His boss got sick of him.
—*Henny Youngman*

| | |
|---|---|
| Interviews | I was applying for a job, and the person interviewing me asked me how many words per minute I typed. I said, "Well, it depends on my mood." I did not get that job.<br>—*Shashi Bhatia* |

When I was applying for a job I went from having no discernible skills to lying about having no discernible skills.
        —*Maureen Brownsey*

It's so humiliating to go on job interviews, especially when they ask, "What was the reason you left your last job?" "Well, I found that after I was fired there was a lot of tension in the office. You know, I found it difficult sitting on the new girl's lap."
        —*Caroline Rhea*

Job Fairs          I saw a sign outside of the grocery store announcing that they're having a "job fair." I love how they make it sound as though it's going to be so much fun, like a carnival. "Woohoo, come to the job fair! Take a ride on the Wheel of Minimum Wage. Stroll through the Hall of Crappy Hours."
        —*Tony Deyo*

Mornings          Nobody goes right to work. Screw the company; those first twenty minutes belong to you.
        —*George Carlin*

American workers work the first three hours every day just to pay their taxes. So that's why we can't get anything done in the morning; we're government employees!
        —*Jay Leno*

Name Tags          When you go to work if your name is on the building, you're rich. If your name is on your desk, you're middle-class. If your name is on your shirt, you're poor.
        —*Rich Hall*

Offices          In a survey, two out of three women said they'd had sex with someone in their office. I can't even get the toner cartridge to go in the copier.
        —*Jay Leno*

I used to work in an office. They're always so mean to the new girl in the office. "Oh, Caroline, you're new? You have lunch at 9:30."
    —*Caroline Rhea*

I had the most boring office job in the world. I used to clean the windows on envelopes.
    —*Rita Rudner*

Frankly, I don't believe people think of their office as a workplace any more. They think of it as a stationery store with Danish. You want to get your pastry, your envelopes, your supplies, your toilet paper, six cups of coffee, and then you go home.
    —*Jerry Seinfeld*

Office Parties    See also: **CHRISTMAS**

You moon the wrong person at an office party, and suddenly you're not "professional" any more.
    —*Jeff Foxworthy*

Pretending    To have some grins, I recommend going to a store and pretending you're an employee. When someone asks, "Do you work here?" tell them the televisions are free today.
    —*Bob Dubac*

Qualifications    This one job said they wanted a college degree or equivalent. I said, "Perfect, I have eight years of high school."
    —*Buzz Nutley*

One time I tried getting a job at a submarine sandwich shop. Only they wanted me to take a lie detector test just in order to apply for the job. What the hell am I going to lie about in a sub shop? Did they fear someone would ask for roast beef and I'd say no? "How much is the tuna?" "Thousands."
    —*Paula Poundstone*

Retirement          My father is semi-retired. He goes halfway to work, and then
                    he comes home.
                         —*Tommy Koenig*

                    When white folks retire, they go someplace warm and get
                    them a nice house and fish and play golf. But black people
                    get old, we don't go nowhere. When black folks retire, they
                    hang out at the barbershop. Some even get another job. I
                    knew this sumbitch had a job at the plant: Got old, sent
                    home. A week later he's janitor at a bus stop.
                         —*Bernie Mac*

Salaries            See also: **NORMALCY**

                    I never drew a fat salary, but I once sketched a skinny tomato.
                         —*Lou Costello*

                    The phrase Minimum Wage—What does that do for your self-
                    esteem? Can't we think of something else we can call it? "It's
                    Better Than Nothing Wage. " I'm making the "At Least I Don't
                    Live in Haiti Wage."
                         —*David Cross*

Self-Employment     I work for myself, which is fun. Except for when I call in
                    sick—I know I'm lying.
                         —*Rita Rudner*

Self-Esteem         Work, the ultimate self-esteem-sucking machine.
                         —*Kelly*

Sick Days           I wonder, will we ever find a cure for that mysterious illness
                    that turns three-day weekends into four-day weekends?
                         —*Jason Love*

Supervising         I'm tired of supervising people. Last year, right before
                    Christmas, four of my six employees didn't show up for work.
                    In my next job, I want to work with cadavers. They don't

call in sick, they don't unionize, and their health plan is pretty basic.
—*Terri Ryburn-LaMonte*

Temporary

Why do people always blame the temp when something goes wrong? My stint at Arthur Anderson didn't work out. Big deal, so I shredded a few things. Then there was that Enron assignment. So I'm not a math major, go figure.
—*Robin Bach*

I called a temp agency looking for work, and they asked if I had any phone skills. I said, "I called you, didn't I?"
—*Zach Galifianakis*

I signed up with a temp agency, and much to my dismay, they actually found me a job. It had been a couple years since I'd worked in an office, so I thought I should prepare for it. I went to the YMCA with a friend, had him tie me up in a burlap sack, and sink me to the bottom of the pool. Just as I was about to suffocate, he yanked me up and gave me a lunch break.
—*Martha Kelly*

I used to work as a temp a lot. And I think there's something about steady exposure to fluorescent lights that can dissolve every trace of a personality.
—*Laura Kightlinger*

Unemployment

See also: **ILLNESSES** Allergies

I don't have a job, which is fine with me. I don't like to waste my free time.
—*Shashi Bhatia*

I have a friend who's collecting unemployment insurance. This guy has never worked so hard in his life as he has to keep this thing going. He's down there every week, waiting in the lines and getting interviewed and making up all these

lies about looking for jobs. If they had any idea of the effort and energy that he is expending to avoid work, I'm sure they'd give him a raise.
> —*Jerry Seinfeld*

The problem with unemployment is that the minute you wake up in the morning, you're on the job.
> —*Slappy White*

and Women

Women in the workplace, we still have big strides. Girlfriend of mine just got a new job. First question the new boss asked her was if she could make a good cup of coffee. She stormed right out of that Starbucks.
> —*Carol Leifer*

When I worked in the computer industry, people often referred to me as a female executive. Is that necessary? I prefer the more politically correct "salary-impaired."
> —*Jackie Wollner*

**ENVIRONMENT**          See also: **ENVIRONMENTALISM**

It's hard for me to get used to these changing times. I can remember when the air was clean and sex was dirty.
> —*George Burns*

The environment is screwed up, but you can still have fun. I'm going brown-water rafting this summer.
> —*Barry Crimmins*

Underground nuclear testing, defoliation of the rain forests, toxic waste . . . let's put it this way, if the world were a big apartment, we wouldn't get our deposit back.
> —*John Ross*

Ozone Layer

It's absolutely stupid that we've lost the ozone layer. We've got men, rockets, Saran Wrap: Fix it!
> —*Lewis Black*

I'm glad there's a big old hole in the ozone, because you can get a tan in a split second. "Hey, I'm starting to bubble up like a bad paint job. I'm saving money on X-rays; I can see where I broke my arm as a kid."
—*Joe Keyes*

Do you ever wonder where all the farts go? They go up into the atmosphere, and they form the fart zone. It's right above the ozone layer, and that's why we have to protect the ozone layer!
—*Steve Martin*

**ENVIRON-
MENTALISM**

See also: **ENVIRONMENT**

I'm doing what I can to help the environment. I started a compost pile. It's in the back seat of my car.
—*Janine DiTullio*

Remember: A developer is someone who wants to build a house in the woods. An environmentalist is someone who already owns a house in the woods.
—*Dennis Miller*

I don't subscribe to a newspaper, but I just might so I can recycle and save a tree.
—*Paula Poundstone*

The other day I bought a wastepaper basket and carried it home in a paper bag. And when I got home I put the paper bag in the basket.
—*Lily Tomlin*

Anti-

I had a great Earth Day. I drove around with my muffler off, flicking butts out the window; then I hit a deer.
—*Drew Carey*

A new law has been enacted which will allow the timber industry to cut down excess trees. If you're in the timber industry, excess trees are the ones that haven't been cut down yet.

—*Jay Leno*

**ESCALATORS**

An escalator can never break; it can only become stairs. You would never see an "Escalator Temporarily Out of Order" sign, just "Escalator Temporarily Stairs. Sorry for the Convenience."

—*Mitch Hedberg*

**ETHICS**

What's right is what's left if you do everything wrong.

—*Robin Williams*

**ETHNICITY**

See also: **RACISM**

People always want to judge you based on your ethnic background. It's stupid. For instance, if a white guy likes rap, he's trying to be black. If a black guy gets a job, he's trying to be white.

—*Aisha Tyler*

African American

I love black women, but I like white women too. That's why I can't hate white men: We need them for breeding.

—*Alonzo Bodden*

Some people say all black people look alike. We call those people "police."

—*Dave Chappelle*

There's a stereotype that black people are lazy. I don't know if that's true, but I know white people went all the way to Africa to get out of doing work.

—*Lance Crouther*

I'm extra ghetto, if I do say so myself. I got two six-year-olds, and they ain't twins.

—*Corey Holcomb*

It's been twenty years since *Roots* came out, and black people still be givin' their kids crazy names. Zaqueeda, Jambalaya. Paradise. What happen to just plain John?

—*Bernie Mac*

I was a negro for twenty-three years. I gave that shit up: no room for advancement.

—*Richard Pryor*

Brothers are now conquering sports normally dominated by rich white people. We could take over polo, too, if they would let a brother put a horse on layaway.

—*Chris Rock*

Black names sound more like products you'd find in the drugstore. "My name is Advil, this is my wife, Cloret. Tylenol, you wanna turn the TV down, it's givin' me a headache! And the twins, Murine and Visine . . . ."

—*Daryl Sivad*

I still say black, because African American doesn't make your life easier. You don't see any of us going into Bank of America, "Excuse me, I'm here to pick up my loan." "You were rejected last week." "But I was black then; I'm African American now. I'll just go into the vault and take what I need."

—*Wanda Sykes*

Black women, we have attitude. We are the only people on earth born knowing how to roll our eyes with them closed.

—*Marsha Warfield*

Arab American      See also: **WORLD** Middle East

The people I really feel sorry for are Arab Americans who sincerely want to get into crop dusting.

—*Brian Regan*

Italian

I'm 100 percent Sicilian. But not all Sicilians are in the mob. Some are in the witness protection program.
    —*Tammy Pescatelli*

Jewish

I'm into Jewish bondage . . . that's having your money tied up in an IRA account.
    —*Noodles Levenstein*

My father is a German Jew, and my mother is a French Jew. So that makes me just really lucky to be here.
    —*Jackie Wollner*

Latino

Does it matter if someone calls you a Latino or Hispanic? I don't mind Chicano, which is a Mexican-American, but Hispanic I don't like. The U.S. Census Bureau came up with it, and who wants to be associated with a word that has "panic" in it? In a way, it's progress; we used to be "Other."
    —*George Lopez*

If you ever drive by Latino neighborhoods and they're all in the front yard at about 11:00 at night, it's because it's too loud in the house. My grandmother would yell at me, "Turn the television down!" My response was always the same, "I don't know where the pliers are. What did you do with them? You used the oven last! What did you do with them?"
    —*George Lopez*

WASP

I'm a WASP, a White Anglo-Saxon Protestant, and actually, a lot of my people are doing really well.
    —*Penelope Lombard*

**EUTHANASIA**     See: **DEATH, FAMILY**

**EVOLUTION**     See also: **CREATIONISM**

I don't understand evolution. If we came from monkeys, why are there still monkeys? What, they couldn't make it over the hump? George W. Bush made it, what's up with their raggedy asses?

—*Kathleen Madigan*

**EXERCISE**   See also: **HEALTH CLUBS**, **SPORTS**

If it weren't for the fact that the TV set and the refrigerator are so far apart, some of us wouldn't get any exercise at all.

—*Joey Adams*

Oh yeah, I'll continue to work out, until I get married.

—*Tom Arnold*

I recently started exercising, and I've got to say, Lamaze classes rock! Controlled breathing is my kind of workout. And best of all, I don't have to be embarrassed about my gut. There are some enormous women in that room. It's like they've been eating for two.

—*Brian Beatty*

Whenever I read anything, it says, "Consult your doctor before doing any exercise." Does anybody do that? I kind of think my doctor has people coming in with serious problems. I don't think I should call him and say, "Hi, this is Rita. I'm thinking of bending at the waist."

—*Rita Rudner*

They say the best exercise takes place in the bedroom. I believe it, because that's where I get the most resistance.

—*Jeff Shaw*

I get plenty of exercise carrying the coffins of my friends who exercise.

—*Red Skelton*

Avoiding   They say that exercise and proper diet are the keys to a longer life. Oh, well.

—*Drew Carey*

It takes too long to work out. It's just faster not to walk by a mirror when you're naked.
    —*Richard Jeni*

I'm so tired of exercising. I think five thousand sit-ups should be pretty much permanent. You should be at home, you're on your last and final jumping jack, and you get that phone call, "Congratulations! You have completed the exercise portion of your life. Welcome to the incessant eating section."
    —*Jann Karam*

I know I should work out, but I don't so much. I don't mind sweating, though. As long as I don't have to move. Like in a sauna. Or a good audit.
    —*Wendy Liebman*

In my view, aging is natural, exercise is not. Exercise is a lot like cleaning toilets. It's something that needs to be done regularly, but I'd like someone else to do it for me.
    —*Charlotte Lobb*

The only exercise program that has ever worked for me is occasionally getting up in the morning and jogging my memory to remind myself exactly how much I hate to exercise.
    —*Dennis Miller*

I don't exercise. What's in it for me? You've got to offer me more than my life to get me on a Stairmaster grunting for two hours. I view my body as a way of getting my head from one place to the other.
    —*Dave Thomas*

Jogging
The trouble with jogging is that the ice falls out of your glass.
    —*Martin Mull*

The first time I see a jogger smiling, I'll consider it.
    —*Joan Rivers*

I jogged for three miles once. It was the worst three hours of my life.

—*Rita Rudner*

A friend of mine jogs ten miles a day. If you ever catch me running ten miles in a row, tell the bus driver my arm is caught in the door.

—*Jeff Shaw*

Marathons

Last year I entered the Los Angeles Marathon. I finished last. It was embarrassing. And the guy who was in front of me, second to last, was making fun of me. He said, "How does it feel to come in last?" I said, "You want to know?" So I dropped out.

—*Gerry Bednob*

This is a stupid sport, marathon running: wandering through town looking for refreshments.

—*Trina Hess*

I pulled a hamstring during the New York City Marathon. An hour into the race I jumped up off the couch.

—*David Letterman*

A friend of mine runs marathons. He always talks about this "runner's high," but he has to go twenty-six miles for it. That's why I smoke and drink. I get the same feeling from a flight of stairs.

—*Larry Miller*

Nautilus

If you want to lose weight you have to exercise. I tried, went to the spa. They had this new machine there called Nautilus. I couldn't figure out how it worked, so I just strapped it on and dragged it around. I'm up to five machines now.

—*Frank D'Amico*

Nordic Tracks   I got one of those Nordic Tracks, and those are great.
Although I hit a tree the other day.
            —*Garry Shandling*

Push-ups   With me nothing comes easy. This morning I did my push-ups
in the nude. I didn't see the mousetrap.
            —*Rodney Dangerfield*

Running   See also: **OLYMPICS** Track

Running is an unnatural act, except from enemies or to
the bathroom.
            —*George Carlin*

I go running when I have to. When the ice cream truck is
doing 60.
            —*Wendy Liebman*

I ran three miles today. Finally I said, "Lady, take your purse!"
            —*Emo Philips*

Stairmasters   See also: Avoiding, **HELL**

I worked out at this really fancy health club. They had a spiral
Stairmaster.
            —*Wendy Liebman*

I'm all sore, because I got on the Stairmaster today and fell off
it for about forty-five minutes.
            —*Christopher Titus*

Step Classes   Homo sapiens did not labor to walk upright only to damage
their spines in step class.
            —*Janeane Garofalo*

| | |
|---|---|
| Trainers | I started working out with a personal trainer. The first day we trained, she bounces in, "Okay, let's get started. First we need to measure your fat content. Can I pinch your fat?" Sure, can I punch you out?<br>—*Grace White* |
| Treadmills | A new study says that one of the advantages of the treadmill is that it's the highest calorie burner of the exercises. And the other advantage is that hamsters can now laugh at us.<br>—*Johnny Robish* |
| Walking | My favorite exercise is walking a block and a half to the corner store to buy fudge. Then I call a cab to get back home. There's never a need to overdo anything.<br>—*Ellen DeGeneres* |
| | My grandmother began walking five miles a day when she was eighty-two. Now we don't know where the hell she is.<br>—*Ellen DeGeneres* |
| Yoga | I started doing yoga. Yoga is a Sanskrit word that means "heal your back without health insurance."<br>—*Norman K.* |
| | They say that yoga is a great way to use your body to reach a higher consciousness. I find it's a lot easier to just to drink to get your legs behind your neck like that.<br>—*Wendy Liebman* |
| | I enjoy yoga. I enjoy any exercise where you get to lie down on the floor and go to sleep.<br>—*Rita Rudner* |
| **EXTERMINATORS** | See: **INSECTS** |
| **EYEGLASSES** | See: **GLASSES** |

**EYESIGHT**          See also: **GLASSES**

I had a lazy eye as a kid, and it gradually spread to my whole body.

—*Tom Cotter*

FAMILY          See also: **BABIES**, **CHILDHOOD**, **CHILDREN**, **CLICHÉS**,
                **FATHERS**, **GRANDPARENTS**, **HUSBANDS**, **MOTHERS**,
                **PARENTHOOD**, **PARENTS**, **WIVES**

Brothers        Older brothers invented terrorism. "Louie, see that swamp?
                There's a monster in it." So for years I walked way around it.
                Until I got a little older, a little wiser, and a little brother.
                          —*Louie Anderson*

                My mother did not put all her eggs in one basket, so to speak:
                She gave me a younger brother named Russell, who taught
                me what was meant by "survival of the fittest."
                          —*Bill Cosby*

                I had older brothers. Growing up the only girl in the family is
                like growing up to be a tropical fruit drink, somewhere
                between spoiled rotten and beaten to a pulp.
                          —*Diane Ford*

                My brother Kevin gave me a check with 12-1 on it, so I thought
                I could cash it after December 1st. He said, "No, that was 12
                to 1. Those were the odds that the check would bounce."
                          —*Robert Murray*

                I should understand men better than I do, because I grew up
                with brothers. I wanted sisters; they're better for a girl. They
                teach you how to put on makeup, how to do your hair, give
                you dating tips. You know what brothers teach you? How to
                unhook a bra with your teeth.
                          —*Carol Siskind*

Communication   We never talked, my family. We communicated by putting Ann
                Landers articles on the refrigerator.
                          —*Judy Gold*

Daughters       I have an 18-year-old; her name is Alexis. I chose that name
                because if I hadn't had her, I'd be driving one.
                          —*Robin Fairbanks*

I have three daughters, and people ask, "Were you upset that the third child was a girl?" I say, "No, not at all. I'm whittling a boy out of wood right now."
—*Bob Saget*

Euthanasia
After watching the Kevorkian trial I asked my father, "Do you think a family should have the right to withdraw life support on a loved one?" He said, "It depends on which kid."
—*Hugh Fink*

Fun
There's no such thing as fun for the whole family; there are no massage parlors with ice cream and free jewelry.
—*Jerry Seinfeld*

Grandchildren
My grandchildren take me to the beach and try to make words out of the veins in my legs.
—*Phyllis Diller*

My mother wants grandchildren. I said, "Mom, go for it!"
—*Sue Murphy*

I asked my grandson, "What are you doing for a living now?" He said, "I'm a momback." I asked, "What's a momback?" He said, "I stand behind a truck and say, 'Momback.'"
—*Henny Youngman*

Happiness
Happiness is having a large, loving, caring, close-knit family in another city.
—*George Burns*

In-Laws
My brother-in-law is always there for me when he needs a favor.
—*David Corrado*

I told my mother-in-law that my house was her house, and she said, "Get the hell off my property."
—*Joan Rivers*

My mother-in-law finally died. For the twenty-one years of my marriage she always referred to me as "Edgar's first wife."
—*Joan Rivers*

I couldn't ask for a better mother-in-law, as much as I'd like to.
—*Mary Lou Terry*

I want to send my brother-in-law a gift. How do you wrap up a saloon?
—*Henny Youngman*

Love

I love my husband, I love my children, but I want something more. Like a life.
—*Roseanne Barr*

Your family is a pack of idiots whom you have to love. We exist on earth to love each other, and our family is the test.
—*Jeff Foxworthy*

Meals

As a child my family's menu consisted of two choices: Take it, or leave it.
—*Buddy Hackett*

Nephews

I go visit my nephews. I get out of the car. They see me and drop what they're doing and hug my legs. I feel like the most important person on God's earth. Seven minutes later I would trade their pelts for whiskey. I look down at them. "How could you be so obnoxious?" Then I look at my brother.
—*Brent Cushman*

When I babysit my nephew, we play Twister. I lock him in the storm cellar and pretend a tornado is coming.
—*Craig Sharf*

Poverty

When I was a kid we were so poor that when my dad was in a car accident, we couldn't afford a steel plate for his head, so we had to use a paper plate.
—*Shang*

Returning to    Thomas Wolfe wrote, "You can't go home again." You can,
but you'll get treated like an eight-year-old.
                —*Daryl Hogue*

I'm going home next week. It's kind of a family emergency.
My family is coming here.
                —*Rita Rudner*

Sons    I was the youngest of five boys. After they had me, Mom
and Daddy never spoke to each other again.
                —*Bob Hope*

Trees    I looked up my family tree and found out I was the sap.
                —*Rodney Dangerfield*

I come from a typical American family. Me, my mother, her
third husband, his daughter from a second marriage, my
stepsister, her illegitimate son.
                —*Carol Henry*

I love my family, but I hate family reunions. Family reunions
are that time when you come face to face with your family
tree and realize some branches need to be cut.
                —*René Hicks*

It's fun to study your family tree and learn old customs. For
example, a stranger is too close to you, fling your poo.
Respect our monkey heritage.
                —*Basil White*

Vacations    Every year my family would pile into the car for our vacation and drive eighty trillion miles just to prove we couldn't
get along in any setting.
                —*Janeane Garofalo*

Family vacation. Some vacation sitting in the back seat of a
'72 Ford Country Squire station wagon, with a flatulent old
English sheep dog and my annoying brother chanting, "I

know you are, but what am I?" I know if you don't leave me alone you're going to be bludgeoned to death in your sleeping bag. Which, by the way, is flammable.
—*Joel Warshaw*

**FANTASIES**          See: **SEX**

**FARMING**          See also: **GARDENING**

A guy bought a farm. He didn't know anything about farms, but he bought one anyway. He decides he's going to plant something. Anything. "What are you going to plant?" his friend asks. "Razor blades and cabbages." His friend looks at him. "Razor blades and cabbages? What could you possibly get out of that?" "Coleslaw."
—*Buddy Hackett*

**FASHION**          See also: **CLOTHING**

Advice          Never let a panty line show around your ankle.
—*Joan Rivers*

Colors          I'm glad earth tones are popular again. It means I don't have to do laundry as often.
—*Reno Goodale*

Future          I hate clothes. I can't stand every day trying to come up with little outfits for myself. I think fashion won't even exist eventually, because anytime I see a movie or a TV show where there's people from the future of another planet, they're all wearing the same thing. Somehow they decided, "This is going to be our outfit: one-piece silver jumpsuit, V-stripe, and boots."
—*Jerry Seinfeld*

and Women          There are weird rules for girls; we get all the uncomfortable crap. We get all the S&M clothes, like the high heels that make us easier to hunt.
—*Sue Murphy*

Why do women dress to emphasize body parts men are already looking at? The short skirts, the pushup bras—do we really need the coaching? I'm sure men are total failures at every aspect of conducting a relationship, but you're going to tell me we need help with the leering and the gawking?
—*Jerry Seinfeld*

**FATHERHOOD**

See also: **BABIES**, **BIRTH**, **CHILDHOOD**, **CHILDREN**, **FATHERS**, **PARENTHOOD**, **PARENTS**

If the children's name for me is "Dad-Can-I" then my name for them is "Yes-You-May."
—*Bill Cosby*

If the new American father feels bewildered and even defeated, let him take comfort from the fact that whatever he does in any fathering situation has a 50 percent chance of being right.
—*Bill Cosby*

Fashion

In schools, you can always identify the children who were dressed by their fathers. Such children should have signs pinned to their strange attire that say, "Please do not scorn or mock me. I was dressed by my father, who sees colors the way Beethoven heard notes."
—*Bill Cosby*

Games

The worst thing that can happen to a man is to have his wife come home and he has lost the child. "How did everything go?" "Great, we're playing hide and seek and she's winning."
—*Sinbad*

Gifts

Fatherhood is pretending the present you love most is soap-on-a-rope.
—*Bill Cosby*

Homework

Let's face it, by the second grade you can no longer do the math. We didn't have that stuff in college. It is truly a shame

when your seven-year-old son says, "Daddy, will you check my math?" and you have to lie and say, "I trust you, son."
          —*Sinbad*

**Impending**          My wife just let me know I'm about to become a father for the first time. The bad news is that we already have two kids.
          —*Brian Kiley*

All during the pregnancy when I was supposed to be reading baby books and taking baby classes and learning baby CPR didn't go totally to waste because I did use the time to shop for the perfect video camera.
          —*Paul Reiser*

**Wrinkles**          Now that I'm a dad, I'm sure my father is laughing in his grave. I used to ask my father, "Dad, where did all those wrinkles come from on your face?" "From you, your little brother, and your goddamn sister."
          —*Jack Coen*

**FATHERS**          See also: **BABIES**, **BIRTH**, **CHILDHOOD**, **CHILDREN**, **CLICHÉS** Family, **FATHERHOOD**, **PARENTHOOD**, **PARENTS**

**Affection**          My father carries around the picture of the kid who came with his wallet.
          —*Rodney Dangerfield*

My father hugged me only once, on my twenty-first birthday. It was very awkward. I now know what it was that made me feel so uncomfortable: the nudity.
          —*Ray Romano*

**and Automobiles**          My dad didn't like people as much as he liked his car. He even introduced it to people, "It's my Bonneville," he said. "My family's over there." Then he went on, "It's an American-made car. You can drive it head-on into a train and live." That was my cue to mutter. "You ought to try that, dad. The 7:15's coming around the bend."

—*Louie Anderson*

When his child requests a car, a father will wish that he were a member of some sect that hasn't gone beyond the horse. "Dad, all my friends say that I should have my own car," the boy says earnestly one day. "Wonderful. When are they going to buy it?"

—*Bill Cosby*

Wherever we had to be we were usually late because Dad was always implementing some plan or theory to avoid traffic.

—*Ray Romano*

Cheap

My father was so cheap that one year he told us Santa didn't come because he wears red and we lived in a Crips zone.

—*A. J. Jamal*

My father was so cheap. We'd eat Hamburger Helper with no hamburger.

—*A. J. Jamal*

My father was cheap. Every year he'd say "I'm glad Christmas comes but once every other year."

—*John Roy*

My father refused to spend money on me as a kid. One time I broke my arm playing football, and my father tried to get a free X-ray by taking me down to the airport and making me lie down with the luggage.

—*Glenn Super*

Childhood

According to my dad, he had a really tough childhood. He had to walk twenty miles to school in five feet of snow, and he was only four feet tall.

—*Dana Eagle*

**College**

My dad went back to college, and we're all so proud of him. Except when he comes home from a keg party and pees out the window.
        —*Brian Kiley*

**and Daughters**

My father's not a warm and fuzzy guy. He can't bring himself to ask about my feelings or emotions. All he ever asks is, "How's the car doing?" Finally, I said, "The car is experiencing low self-esteem and financial distress. The car could use a new computer, and probably a new car."
        —*Dana Eagle*

I'm a grown woman, but my father still thinks I know nothing about my car. He always asks me, "You changing the oil every 3,000?" "Yes, Dad. I'm also putting sugar in the gas tank. That way my exhaust smells like cotton candy."
        —*Mimi Gonzalez*

**and Discipline**

My father would give us a preview of coming attractions. "Do I have to get the belt?" "Oh no dad, we'd prefer that shovel with the nails in it."
        —*Jack Gallagher*

Whenever my dad got mad at me or my brother, he would never actually hit us. But he did have one of the great belt movements. He'd say, "Do I have to go for the belt?" Then he'd wiggle his waistband around a little, kind of a fatherly Morse code.
        —*Jay Leno*

My father used to ground me—and then run electricity through me.
        —*Taylor Negron*

**and Fashion**

You can tell what was the best year of your father's life, because they seem to freeze that clothing style and ride it out. And it's not like they don't continue shopping; they just some- how manage to find new, old clothes. Every father is this fashion time capsule. They should be on a pedestal, with someone next to them going: "This was 1965."

—*Jerry Seinfeld*

Gifts to

See also: **FATHERHOOD**, **HOLIDAYS** Father's Day

I never know what to get my father for his birthday. I gave him $100 and said, "Buy yourself something that will make your life easier." So he bought a present for my mother.

—*Rita Rudner*

Good

My dad asked me, "Stuey, have I been a good father?" I said, "Dad, you're the best; why do you ask?" He said, "I wanted to make sure the way you turned out is your fault."

—*Stu Trivax*

Hairy

My father was very hairy. When my brother and I were little, to amuse us he would light his chest hairs on fire and then blow them out. Still not conclusive proof that I come from carnie people.

—*Grace White*

Idolizing

When you're young, you think your dad is Superman. Then you grow up, and you realize he's just a regular guy who wears a cape.

—*Dave Attell*

Intelligence

"Don't get smart with me," my father would growl. That was my favorite expression of his. Don't get smart with me. Just once I wanted to make a weird face and go, "Duh! Is this dumb enough for you, dad?"

—*Louie Anderson*

Fathers are the geniuses of the house because only a person as intelligent as we could fake such stupidity. Think about your father: He doesn't know where anything is. You ask him to do something; he messes it up, and your mother sends you, "Go down and see what your father's doing before he blows up the house." He's a genius at work because he doesn't want to do it, and knows someone will be coming soon to stop him.

—*Bill Cosby*

My dad is not real bright. But I love the guy. We go into this trophy shop because my basketball team won second place. We were in this shop, and there are trophies everywhere. My dad looks around and goes, "This guy is really good."

—*Fred Wolf*

Intimidation

All fathers are intimidating, because they're fathers. Once a man has children, his attitude is, "To hell with the world, I can make my own people. I'll eat whenever I want, I'll wear whatever I want, and I'll create whoever I want."

—*Jerry Seinfeld*

Leaving Home

My father didn't ask me to leave home. He took me down to the highway and pointed.

—*Henny Youngman*

and Maps

If you ever want to torture my dad, tie him up and right in front of him, refold a road map incorrectly.

—*Cathy Ladman*

and Money

My dad always maintained he didn't care about money. That's because he never had any.

—*Louie Anderson*

Hey, kids! It's mostly bullshit and garbage, and none of the stuff they tell you is true. And when your dumb-ass father says he wants you to amount to something, he means make a lot of money. How do you think the word amount got in there?

—*George Carlin*

My dad said I'd never amount to anything. Lucky guess.

—*David Cousins*

My father makes money the American way. He trips over stuff and sues people.
—*Dominic Dierkes*

**Senior Dads**

My dad's pants kept creeping up on him. By sixty-five he was just a pair of pants and a head.
—*Jeff Altman*

My dad, eighty-six years old and he's still working, God bless him. He's a pimp, and he's out there every night.
—*Jonathan Katz*

My dad's hearing is gone, and he won't admit it. When he reads, he goes, "What?" The mind is slowly following. He called me up the other night, very excited. He says, "Jonathan, when I get up to go to the bathroom in the middle of the night I don't have to turn on the light; the light goes on automatically. When I'm done, the light goes off automatically." I said, "Dad, you're peeing in the fridge, and it's got to stop."
—*Jonathan Katz*

I love my dad because, even though he has Alzheimer's, he still remembers the important things. He can't remember my name, but last week he told me exactly how much money I owe him.
—*Thyra Lees-Smith*

**Smoking**

I phoned my dad to tell him I had stopped smoking. He called me a quitter.
—*Steven Pearl*

**and Sons**

When I was born my father spent three weeks trying to find a loophole in my birth certificate.
—*Jackie Vernon*

**FAX MACHINES**    For Christmas I bought my brother a combination fax
machine and paper shredder. Either we hooked it up wrong
or a lot of people are faxing him confetti.
—*Anthony Clark*

**FEET**    I bought Odor Eaters. They ate for half an hour, and then
threw up.
—*Howie Mandel*

**FEMININITY**    See: **WOMEN**

**FEMINISM**    When I say I'm a feminist, I make it clear I'm not anti-male,
just anti-asshole. Having been an asshole myself, I realize that
it's a gender-free concept.
—*Mimi Gonzalez*

I'm a male feminist. I'd never call a nasty sales clerk a bitch. I
use gender-neutral terms like asshole.
—*Danny Liebert*

Anti-    I don't call myself a feminist. I call myself a killer bitch.
—*Roseanne Barr*

I wanted to be a feminist in high school, but my boyfriend
wouldn't let me.
—*Denise Munro Robb*

I don't agree with feminists. I saw a feminist on TV saying
"If women ruled the world, there'd be no crime, no pollution,
and no war." I'm thinking "Great. What happens if there's
a spider?"
—*Livia Squires*

**FIGHTING**    See: **ARGUMENTS**, **SPORTS** Boxing

**FINANCES**          See also: **BANKING**

Bankruptcy

If a parsley farmer goes bankrupt, can they garnish his wages?
——*Bruce Baum*

I used to worry about paying my bills until I read about Chapter 11. You don't have to pay anyone off, and you don't go to jail. What's Chapter 12? "Run Like Hell."
——*Rita Rudner*

Bouncing Checks          See also: **BANKING**

You ever know anybody that bounced a check to pay a bounced check? Yeah, that was me. But what about those fools that let you pay a bounced check with a check? They deserve not to get paid.
——*Herb Clark*

Cost of Living

Americans are getting stronger. Twenty years ago it took two people to carry ten dollars' worth of groceries. Today, a five-year-old can do it.
——*Henny Youngman*

in Debt

I am heavily in debt. Right now my goal in life is to be just broke. I wanna get back to zero. Someday, I'm gonna have nothing. I'll leave it to my kids. "See this? None of this is all yours."
——*Tom Ryan*

Strange things happen when you're in debt. Two weeks ago, my car broke down, and my phone got disconnected. I was one electric bill away from being Amish.
——*Tom Ryan*

Expenses

No matter how much money you make, you always need an extra $40 a week. I'm sure it was Einstein who first stated: "Expense equals salary, plus forty bucks."
     —*Jeff Jena*

Investing

I had one stock that dropped to the point where I owed them money.
     —*Wanda Sykes*

Loans

It's the people who ask for loans that you don't want to lend money to.
     —*Jason Love*

You ever have somebody owe you money, and have the nerve to wear new clothes around you? Brand new clothes, and they point them out like. "Hey, look what I just picked up?" Well, did you see my money while you were down there?
     —*Chris Rock*

Misers

Misers aren't fun to live with, but they make wonderful ancestors.
     —*David Brenner*

Money

Money is better than poverty, if only for financial reasons.
     —*Woody Allen*

If you had a penny and threw it off the Empire State Building and it hit somebody in the head, it would kill him. Talk about getting your money's worth.
     —*Heywood Banks*

Our money looks like baseball cards with slave owners on it.
     —*Dave Chappelle*

The average American has less money these days, and the pictures on our dollar bills are getting bigger. That's so we'll remember what it looks like from far away.
     —*Erica Doering*

I don't like money, but it quiets my nerves.
—*Joe E. Lewis*

My grandfather always said, "Don't watch your money; watch your health." So one day while I was watching my health, someone stole my money. It was my grandfather.
—*Jackie Mason*

Money won't buy friends, but you get a better class of enemy.
—*Spike Milligan*

I've got all the money I'll ever need, if I die by four o'clock this afternoon.
—*Henny Youngman*

**Penniless**

People always say, "He died penniless," as if it's a terrible thing. Sounds like good timing to me.
—*Al Cleathen*

I never had a penny to my name. So I changed my name.
—*Henny Youngman*

**Poor**

Conservatives say if you don't give the rich more money, they will lose their incentive to invest. As for the poor, they tell us they've lost all incentive because we've given them too much money.
—*George Carlin*

Poor people have more fun than rich people, they say. And I notice it's the rich people who keep saying it.
—*Jack Paar*

I'm always amazed how the poor can take so much of our money and still remain poor. What are they doing with it?
—*Greg Proops*

Savings

I had a nest egg, but I lost it gambling. I was betting I'd be dead by now.
—*Drew Carey*

Wealth

No matter how bad it gets, I'm rich at the dollar store.
—*Jason Love*

I worked myself up from nothing to a state of extreme poverty.
—*Groucho Marx*

We got no wealthy black people; we got rich people. Shaq is rich. The white man that signs his check is wealthy. "Here you go, Shaq. Buy yourself a bouncing car." Maybe if we didn't spend all our money on rims, we might have some to invest.
—*Chris Rock*

Someday I want to be rich. Some people get so rich they lose all respect for humanity. That's how rich I want to be.
—*Rita Rudner*

**FIREPLACES**

I have a microwave fireplace in my house. The other night I laid down in front of the fire for the evening in two minutes.
—*Steven Wright*

**FISH**

See: **FOOD**, **PETS**

**FISHING**

See also: **HUNTING**

There's a fine line between fishing and standing on the shore looking like an idiot.
—*Steven Wright*

Ice Fishing

Whoever came up with ice fishing must have had the worst marriage on the planet.
—*Jeff Cesario*

Intelligence

Fish aren't that smart. For example, I once caught a fish by dangling a worm in the ocean. Shouldn't he have been

suspicious when he saw it? I'm not saying I'm a genius, but if I dive into a swimming pool and there's a sausage in the drain, I don't care how hungry I am. I'm going to ask a question or two before I chow down.
                    —*Richard Jeni*

Killing

We're fishing, and my wife had a problem with killing the fish. I wasn't crazy with that part either, but I figured, if we just wait for them to die naturally, it could take forever. Certainly until after supper.
                    —*Paul Reiser*

Patience

I like fishing, but I don't have any patience. So I use an aquarium.
                    —*Craig Sharf*

Quitting

I used to go fishing until one day it struck me: You can buy fish. What the hell am I doing in a boat at 4:30 in the morning? If I want a hamburger, I don't track cattle down.
                    —*Kenny Rogerson*

**FITNESS**            See also: **HEALTH CLUBS**, **PHYSIQUE**

I get winded when I use a rotary phone.
                    —*Jonathan Katz*

**FLOWERS**            Flowers are one of the few things we buy, bring home, watch die, and we don't ask for our money back.
                    —*George Carlin*

**FLYING**             If God wanted us to fly, he would have given us tickets.
                    —*Mel Brooks*

Airplanes

I hate flying in small planes. When you go in the airport you see, Flight 109: Departures—Arrivals—Odds.
                    —*Billy Crystal*

I flew in one of these little-bitty-ass planes—it was playing Buddy Holly music. I'm like, "Can we change the station or something, man?" They didn't have any departure schedule or arrival schedule or nothin'. They didn't even have an intercom. They were just outside, "We're leaving! Bring your ass; we're leaving!"

—*Jamie Foxx*

We don't know how old the airplanes are, and there's really no way for us to tell, because we're laymen. But I figure if the plane smells like your grandmother's house, get out. That's where I draw the line.

—*Garry Shandling*

Airports

When people ask me how I'm getting to the airport I say, "Well, I'm flying to one of them."

—*Steven Wright*

and Babies

My wife began to breast-feed our baby to relieve his ear pressure during takeoff. Which, I understand, hands-down beats the hell out of chewing gum.

—*Paul Reiser*

When we got on the plane, I finally understood why they let people with small children get on board first. It's not because you need more time to put things away; it's because they want to spare you all those dirty looks.

—*Paul Reiser*

There ought to be an FAA requirement that crying babies have to go into the overhead compartment.

—*Bobby Slayton*

Coach

If you have a DVD player, it's rude to watch porn in coach.

—*Adam Ferrara*

I think I was flying in Assistant Coach.

—*Jeffrey Ross*

Fear of

I don't have a fear of flying. I have a fear of not flying.
—*Andrew Dice Clay*

I'm terrified of dying in a plane crash. I'd hate the thought
that peanuts would be my last meal.
—*Tanya Luckerath*

I'm afraid of planes. I don't trust the oxygen mask. The little orange cup—attached to that bag that's full of nothing.
Maybe I'm cynical. I don't even think that it's an oxygen
mask. I think it's more to just muffle the screams.
—*Rita Rudner*

Fear of flying is quite rational because human beings cannot fly. Humans have fear of flying the same way fish have
fear of driving. Put a fish behind the wheel, and they go, "I
shouldn't be doing this. I don't belong here."
—*Jerry Seinfeld*

First Time

I'd never been on a plane before. I told them I wanted seats
over the wing, because I figured we'd be safer with a wing
under us. I was like a big kid grinning from takeoff to landing. White people wouldn't understand that feeling. White
people get on planes all the time. They were born on planes.
—*Bernie Mac*

Luggage

Limited carry-on—the stewardess said your carry-on bag
had to fit in the ass of the passenger in front of you.
—*Dennis Miller*

They have luggage stores in airports. Who forgets their suitcase? Have you ever seen a guy with an armload of shirts
going, "Hurrah, a suitcase!"
—*Jay Mohr*

I went to the airport. I had three pieces of luggage. I said, "I
want this piece to go to Cleveland, this piece to go to

Toronto, and this piece to Florida." The airline agent said, "We can't do that." I replied, "Well, you did it last week."
                —*Henny Youngman*

Metal Detectors    Some people have the audacity to put a little bolt through their penis. Which makes me think it must be fun at the airport metal detector. "Will you take out your keys? Do you have any other metal on you? Yes? Will you take that out, too?"
                —*Robin Williams*

Passengers    I was flying, and this guy was sitting next to me, and I could tell he really wanted me—to shut up. Because he kept saying, "Shut up!" I'm chatting and chatting, and he's busy, flying the plane. And he's, like, very focused, on that bottle of vodka.
                —*Wendy Liebman*

Pilots    See also: Passengers

There's debate now on whether pilots should carry guns. On the one hand, the skies would be safer. On the other hand, guns and alcohol don't mix.
                —*Conan O'Brien*

Are there keys to a plane? Maybe that's what those delays are. They tell you it's mechanical because they don't want to come on the P.A. system, "Ladies and gentlemen, we're going to be on the ground for awhile. I, uh, I left the keys to the plane in my apartment. They're in this big ashtray by the front door. I'm sorry; I'll run back and get them."
                —*Jerry Seinfeld*

The flight attendant will always tell you the name of your pilot. Like anyone goes, "Oh, he's good. I like his work."
                —*David Spade*

Safety    If airline travel is so safe, how come the flight attendants sit right next to the emergency exits?
                —*Johnny Carson*

I'd better not get too comfortable in my three-quarter-of-an-inch recline because toward the end of the flight, the flight attendant is going to say, "You're going to have to put your seat in the upright position for landing." They're so adamant about that every single time, like that's gonna make a difference. Because if we crash, the investigators are going to say, "Oh, that's a shame, her seat was reclined. When will they learn? What was that, thirty thousand feet? She could have made that. Sheesh. If only she'd been upright."
　　—*Ellen DeGeneres*

At JFK airport, security guards made a woman drink a container of her own breast milk to prove that it was not a dangerous substance. What was even worse was that during the flight they asked to her to walk down the aisle when they served coffee.
　　—*Conan O'Brien*

If airline seat cushions are such great flotation devices, why don't you ever see anyone take one to the beach?
　　—*Jerry Seinfeld*

At the airport they asked me if anybody I didn't know gave me anything. Even the people I know don't give me anything.
　　—*George Wallace*

and Sex　　See also: Coach

Did you hear about those two strangers who were arrested for having sex in first class on American Airlines? You know who I feel sorry for? The guy in the middle seat.
　　—*Jay Leno*

Stewardesses　　When did stewardesses in this country get so cranky? They treat you with that highly contrived air of mock civility, that tight, pursed-lip grin where they nod agreement with everything you say. I'd rather they just come out in the open and say, "Listen, asshole: When I was eighteen years old, I made

a horrible vocational error. I turned in my entire adult life for cheap airfare to Barbados. Now I'm a waitress in a bad restaurant at thirty thousand feet."
—*Dennis Miller*

**FOOD**     See also: **CANDY, DIETING, EATING, VEGETARIANS**

Allergies     Too much food in America, man. We got so much food in America; we're allergic to food. Hungry people ain't allergic to shit. Do you think anybody in Rwanda is lactose intolerant?
—*Chris Rock*

Animal     I bought a box of animal crackers, and it said on it, "Do
Crackers     not eat if seal is broken." So I opened up the box, and sure enough . . .
—*Brian Kiley*

I opened a box of animal crackers, but there was nothing inside. They'd eaten each other.
—*Lily Tomlin*

Cereal     Fuck whole-grain cereal. When I want fiber, I eat some wicker furniture.
—*George Carlin*

Little kids in a supermarket buy cereal the way men buy lingerie. They get stuff they have no interest in just to get the prize inside.
—*Jeff Foxworthy*

I like any cereal. I like the idea of just eating and drinking with one hand, without looking.
—*Jerry Seinfeld*

Chocolate     See also: Fruit

I'm addicted to chocolate; I used to snort cocoa.
—*Marilyn*

Scientists say that chocolate affects your brain the same way sex does. Which means that after they eat a Snickers, guys roll over and go to sleep. And women ask the wrapper, "What are you thinking?"

—*Jim Wyatt*

Cinnamon Rolls

I like cinnamon rolls, but I don't always have time to make a pan. That's why I wish they would sell cinnamon roll incense. After all, I'd rather light a stick and have my roommate wake up with false hopes.

—***Mitch Hedberg***

Cookies

See also: **CHILDHOOD** Safety

I'm enjoying adulthood for a lot of reasons. Reason number one: As an adult, if I want a cookie, I have a cookie. I can have three cookies or four cookies, or eleven cookies. And then I call my mother to tell her. "Hello, Mom? I just ruined my appetite."

—***Jerry Seinfeld***

Deprivation

I just gave up dairy, caffeine, and sugar because I was feeling sluggish, tired, and anxious. Now I have a lot more energy to feel angry and deprived.

—***Jennifer Siegal***

Eggs

A government report says raw eggs may have salmonella and may be unsafe. In fact, the latest government theory says it wasn't the fall that killed Humpty Dumpty; he was dead before he hit the ground.

—***Jay Leno***

Fast

McDonald's "Breakfast for Under a Dollar" actually costs much more than that. You have to factor in the cost of coronary bypass surgery.

—***George Carlin***

Fish            See also: Sushi

                I will not eat oysters. I want my food dead. Not sick, not
                wounded, dead.
                        —*Woody Allen*

                Have you ever seen these places that feature fish sandwiches? I
                always think, "Well, that's kind of general." I wouldn't order
                something called a meat sandwich. At least not without a cou-
                ple of follow-up questions: "Does anyone know where this meat
                came from? Are any of the waitresses missing?"
                        —*George Carlin*

Foreign         In Europe they use all the parts of the animal we throw away.
                Look in their Dumpsters; there's the prime rib. They're saving
                the lungs and the pancreas for some kind of colon tartar.
                        —*Jay Leno*

Fruit           Fruit only angers my need for chocolate.
                        —*Jason Love*

Health          I just started eating health food. I had an avocado-and-wood
                sandwich and some pigeon milk. It was great. I went outside
                and went to the bathroom on the windshield of my car.
                        —*Garry Shandling*

                Tofu! Why do people eat tofu? I throw out my old sponges.
                        —*Karen Williams*

Hot Dogs        There's only one food I won't eat, which is hot dogs at the
                movie theater, because I feel like there's no USDA preparation
                guidelines for this meat. They used to be impaled on spears
                rotating inside a Timex case. Suddenly that's gone and
                replaced by the foot massage–log roll jamboree. And they never
                look like they're cooking; they just look like they're sweating.
                        —*Wayne Federman*

Liver

When I was a kid my mother would make chopped liver for company, and I thought, "Who wants to eat liver?" That's the organ that filters out all the crap you eat. I'd look at the liver on my plate and worry, "That could have been an alcoholic cow."

—*Joel Warshaw*

Meat

See also: Fish, Foreign

PETA, the People for the Ethical Treatment of Animals, are against eating meat. They say, "Don't eat anything that has a face." My standards are a little more relaxed. I won't eat anything that has a job.

—*Nosmo King*

Scientists are now saying eating meat is as bad for you as smoking. And if you eat smoked meat . . . But what you really have to watch out for is secondhand meat.

—*Jay Leno*

Red meat is not bad for you. Now blue-green meat, that's bad for you.

—*Tommy Smothers*

Pizza

I love pizza better than sex. Of course that's only because I can get pizza.

—*Doug Graham*

Poisoning

I got food poisoning today. I don't know when I'll use it.

—*Steven Wright*

Poverty

Know how to tell if a person's poor? You look in the fridge. If there's nothing there but bologna, you're talking serious poor. Lots of beans in our house too. And cereal. Only you be eating it with a fork, leave the milk at the bottom for the next guy. If you think I'm lying, you don't know what poor is.

—*Bernie Mac*

**Preparation**     Food tastes better when other people make it.
                    —*Jason Love*

**Salads**          If a man prepares dinner for you and the salad contains three
                    or more types of lettuce, he is serious.
                    —*Rita Rudner*

**Sandwiches**      Someone said to me, "Make yourself a sandwich." Well, if I
                    could make myself a sandwich, I wouldn't make myself a sand-
                    wich. I'd make myself a horny, eighteen-year-old billionaire.
                    —*George Carlin*

**Soup**            You ever wonder if illiterate people get the full effect of
                    alphabet soup?
                    —*John Mendoza*

**Sushi**           I never eat sushi. I have trouble eating things that are merely
                    unconscious.
                    —*George Carlin*

**Trail Mix**       You want my recipe for trail mix? Plain M&Ms, Kraft
                    Caramels, Peanut M&Ms. It gets me over the mountain.
                    —*Roseanne Barr*

**Unhealthy**       See also: Fast

                    I saw a product in the market, Mr. Salty Pretzels. Isn't that
                    nerve? Everything nowadays is low-salt or salt-free. Here's a
                    guy, "The hell with you: Mr. Salty Pretzels." Like Mr. Tar and
                    Nicotine Cigarettes, Mr. Gristle and Hard Artery Beefsteak.
                    —*Bill Maher*

**Vegetables**      Nobody says, "Can I have your beets?"
                    —*Bill Cosby*

                    If carrots are so good for my eyes, how come I see so many
                    dead rabbits on the highway?
                    —*Richard Jeni*

# FOOTBALL

**Cheerleaders**

The NFL cheerleaders are gorgeous and sexy, but are their cheers helping anybody? Ever see a player interviewed after the game say, "We were down pretty big in the fourth quarter, but then the cheerleaders started chanting 'Defense!' That's when it dawned on the coach, 'Them gals are right!'"
—*Gary Gulman*

**College**

It's reassuring to see that colleges are putting the emphasis on education again. One school has gotten so strict they won't give a football player his letter, unless he can tell which one it is.
—*Henny Youngman*

**Halftime**

Halftime shows really stink. The announcers don't even want to watch. "Now, the Phillips High School band pays a tribute . . . to mayonnaise!" They form a gigantic mayonnaise jar on the field. One kid missed practice, doesn't know where to go. He's running around. From the stands it looks like a fly in the mayonnaise jar. And they announce it: "There's a fly in the mayonnaise jar! Very clever."
—*Robert Klein*

**Playing**

The first time the coach called me from the bench I jumped up. I said I was ready to go! I'm gonna score out there! And he said, "Gimme your jersey." I said, "What?" He said "Gimme your jersey, Johnson just ripped his." It was twenty degrees below zero out there, and my skin stuck to the metal bench, and then I started to root for my jersey! I said "Go ahead jersey, get a touchdown!" And my jersey scored! Then I started to root for Johnson's pants. I was afraid that was next.
—*Bill Cosby*

In high school football, the coach kept me on the bench all year. On the last game of the season, the crowd was yelling,

"We want Youngman! We want Youngman!" The coach said, "Youngman, go see what they want."
—*Henny Youngman*

Professional

The hardest part of being a professional football player is, on the one hand you're a millionare, on the other, they blow a whistle and you have to run around after a football. To me, the whole idea of being a millionare is: Somebody throws a football at me—maybe I catch it, maybe I don't. I'd think you could get someone to hand you the ball at that point.
—*Jerry Seinfeld*

and Sex

A poll shows women think men are sexiest playing football. And they're at their least sexy watching football.
—*Jay Leno*

Super Bowl

Super Bowl Sunday is the one day of the year where everyone in the country, regardless of their religious beliefs, completely stops what they're normally doing. Especially the team I'm rooting for.
—*Dennis Miller*

I was watching the Super Bowl with my ninety-two-year-old grandfather. The team scored a touchdown. They showed the instant replay. He thought they scored another one. I was gonna tell him, but I figured the game he was watching was better.
—*Steven Wright*

Understanding Men

I've been trying to understand men by watching football, and I noticed that they treat the football like a woman. They hold on to it; they take it places and never let it out of their sight. Until the moment they score, when they toss it aside.
—*Maureen Murphy*

Versus Baseball

In football the object is for the quarterback to be on target with his aerial assault. With short bullet passes and long

bombs, he marches his troops into enemy territory with a
sustained ground attack that punches holes in the forward
wall of the enemy's defensive line. In baseball, the object is
to go home. And to be safe! "I hope I'll be safe at home."
        —*George Carlin*

and Women    The reason women don't play football is because eleven of
them would never wear the same outfit in public.
        —*Phyllis Diller*

My husband is from England, and has never seen a football
game before. So I could tell him anything I wanted. I told
him it was over at half time.
        —*Rita Rudner*

**FRIENDSHIPS**    You got friends, then you've got your best friend. Big difference. To me, a friend is a guy who will help you move. A
best friend is a guy who will help you move a body.
        —*Dave Attell*

He's the kind of friend who will always be there when he
needs you.
        —*Adam Christing*

Men, I'm telling you: If you have a woman and she has a best
friend, they have drawn your penis on a napkin at Denny's.
        —*Monique Marvez*

When you're in your thirties it's hard to make a new friend.
Whatever the group you've got, that's who you're going
with. You're not taking applications. If I meet a guy at the
gym or the club, it's like, "I'm sure you're a nice person;
you seem to have a lot of potential. We're just not hiring
right now."
        —*Jerry Seinfeld*

Your friend gets involved with someone, it affects the friend-ship. Whenever a friend of mine has a new girlfriend, we should say, "I look like the person you used to know, but I've been modified to survive in this relationship. If we have an argument and she's there, I may disagree with you. I'd rather continue to see her naked."
    —*Jerry Seinfeld*

Friends are very important. I have lots of friends in very high places. I hope the police can talk them down.
    —*Craig Sharf*

My best friend ran away with my wife. I really miss him.
    —*Henny Youngman*

**FUNERALS**    When black people die, they want a good send off. That's why they always have life insurance, so they can get themselves a nice casket and have a fancy catered affair and impress their friends from beyond the grave.
    —*Bernie Mac*

Death is the last big move of your life. The hearse is like the van; the pallbearers are your close friends, the only ones you could really ask to help you with a big move like that. And the casket is that great, perfect box.
    —*Jerry Seinfeld*

My uncle was a clown for the Ringling Brothers Circus, and when he died all of his friends went to the funeral in one car.
    —*Steven Wright*

Cemeteries    I tell ya I get no respect from anyone. I bought a cemetery plot. The guy said, "There goes the neighborhood!"
    —*Rodney Dangerfield*

Coffins    The proof that we don't understand death is that we give the dead people a suit and a pillow. If you can't stretch out and get some solid rest at that point, I don't think there are any bedding accessories that can make any difference. What situation are you going into with a suit and a pillow? There's no business nap meetings.

—*Jerry Seinfeld*

Cremation

An undertaker calls a son-in-law, "About your mother-in-law, should we embalm her, cremate her, or bury her?" He says, "Do all three. Don't take chances."

—**Myron Cohen**

Before he died, my father asked to be cremated and have his ashes spread on a golf course. I put him in a sand trap. He could never get out of the bunkers when he was alive; now he's spending eternity there.

—*Jeff Jena*

I got a coupon in the mail: Ash Burial at Sea, $478. What an affordable way to die. The only thing is, I don't want my ashes scattered at sea. I want them thrown on all the people who have ever blown smoke in my face. Let's see if their dry cleaners can get that out.

—**Cathy Ladman**

Eulogies

I'm always relieved when someone is delivering a eulogy and I realize I'm listening to it.

—**George Carlin**

**FURNITURE**

My mother wrapped the living room furniture in plastic. We practiced safe sitting in our household.

—**Adam Ferrara**

My favorite furniture brand is the La-Z-Boy. This is very flattering to the prospective customer, isn't it? Why don't we just call it the "Half-conscious-deadbeat-with-no-job-home-all-day-eating-Cheetos-and-watching-TV" recliner?

—*Jerry Seinfeld*

Last week, I went to a furniture store to look for a decaffeinated coffee table.

   —*Steven Wright*

My grandfather had a special rocking chair built that would
lean forward rather than backward, so that he could fake
interest in any conversation.

   —*Steven Wright*

**GAMBLING**          See also: **CARDS** Playing

I used to be a heavy gambler. Now I just make mental bets. That's how I lost my mind.
> —*Steve Allen*

Americans spend $300 billion every year on games of chance, and that doesn't include weddings and elections.
> —*Argus Hamilton*

Blackjack

I love blackjack, but I'm not addicted to gambling. I'm addicted to sitting in a semi-circle.
> —*Mitch Hedberg*

Gambler's Anonymous

I don't get no respect. I joined Gambler's Anonymous. They gave me two to one I don't make it.
> —*Rodney Dangerfield*

Las Vegas

You know what I like best about going to Vegas? When I tell people I'm going, they say, "Here's ten dollars, put it on red for me." I've always considered this to be, like, gas money.
> —*Dave Pavone*

A man went to Las Vegas with a $30,000 Cadillac and came home on a $100,000 bus.
> —*Henny Youngman*

I'll tell you how to beat the gambling in Las Vegas. When you get off the airplane, walk right into the propeller.
> —*Henny Youngman*

Lotteries

A man wins the lottery. He says to his wife, "I've got it made! Start packing." She says, "Am I packing for cold weather or warm?" He says, "How the hell should I know? Just be out by the time I get back."
> —*Red Buttons*

According to statistics, it's a lot easier to get hit by lightning than to win a Lotto jackpot. The good side: You don't hear from your relatives.
—*Johnny Carson*

**Roulette**

In Vegas, I got into a long argument with the man at the roulette wheel over what I considered to be an odd number.
—*Steven Wright*

## GAMES

See: **TOYS**

## GANGS

My homeboy, Tito, was always trying to get me to join a gang. Tito, with two black eyes, arm in a sling and crutches, saying, "Hey Willie, why don't you join the gang? You get protection!"
—*Willie Barcena*

I do not understand gang violence; it's totally crazy. Blacks killing blacks; Latinos killing Latinos. If gang members have to kill, kill constructively. Kill some Ku Klux Klan.
—*René Hicks*

I have no respect for gangs today. None. They just drive by and shoot people. At least in the old days, like in *West Side Story*, the gangs used to dance with each other first.
—*Robert G. Lee*

You know the good thing about gangs is, they carpool.
—*John Mendoza*

## GARAGE SALES

There's nothing more pathetic on earth than a garage sale. You sit in your driveway with all your crap, and it's not even your good crap.
—*Sue Murphy*

## GARDENING

If you water it and it dies, it's a plant. If you pull it out and it grows back, it's a weed.
—*Gallagher*

When my wife asked me to start a garden, the first thing I dug up was an excuse.
>          —*Henny Youngman*

Black Thumbs

I do not have a green thumb. I can't even get mold to grow on last month's takeout.
>          —*Johnnye Jones Gibson*

I've killed so many plants. I walked into a nursery once, and my face was on a wanted poster.
>          —*Rita Rudner*

I have no plants in my house. They won't live for me. Some of them don't even wait to die; they commit suicide. I once came home and found one hanging from a macramé noose; the pot kicked out from underneath. The note said, "I hate you, and your albums."
>          —*Jerry Seinfeld*

All the plants in my house are dead; I shot them last night. I was teasing them by watering them with ice cubes.
>          —*Steven Wright*

## GASOLINE

Cost

Gasoline may go to $3 a gallon to cover the ever-increasing cost of screwing us.
>          —*Craig Kilborn*

I bought a gallon of gas, as an investment.
>          —*Jay Leno*

Gas Stations

Why do they lock gas station bathrooms? Are they afraid someone will clean them?
>          —*George Carlin*

My car has this feature that I guess is standard, because it was on my last car, too. It has a rotating gas tank. Whatever side of the pump I pull up to, it's on the other side.
—*Rita Rudner*

I drove past a gas station the other day. There were two signs in the window: "Help Wanted," "Self Service." So I went in and hired myself. Made myself the boss. I took all the money and I left.
—*Steven Wright*

**Running out**

I'm the only person I know who ran out of gas at a car wash. I've also run out of gas at a drive-thru window at 1:00 A.M. I had to push the car five feet, wait for someone to make an order, push it another five feet, wait for someone else to make an order, push it another five feet to give my order and buy something for the tow truck driver, too.
—*Dobie Maxwell*

**GAY**

See: **HOMOSEXUALITY**, **LESBIANS**

**GENDER DIFFERENCES**

See also: **MEN**, **WOMEN**

Men look at women the way men look at cars. Everyone looks at Ferraris. Now and then we like a pickup truck. And we all end up with a station wagon.
—*Tim Allen*

Men and women are a lot alike in certain situations. Like when they're both on fire, they're exactly alike.
—*Dave Attell*

Men are stupid, and women are crazy. And the reason women are so crazy is because men are so stupid.
—*George Carlin*

Share your feelings with your woman. And she'll leave you for a guy who never cries and who spanks her.
    —*Jim Carrey*

Men and women belong to different species, and communications between them is still in its infancy.
    —*Bill Cosby*

Do we know much about women? Do we? We don't. We know when they're happy; we know when they're crying; we know when they're pissed off. We just don't know what order those are going to come at us.
    —*Evan Davis*

Men are superior to women. For one thing, men can urinate from a speeding car.
    —*Will Durst*

Men and women both care about smell, but women go to the trouble to smell good. Men are like, "Does this stink too bad to wear one more time? Maybe I should iron it."
    —*Jeff Foxworthy*

Women interrogate you. You can't lie, because women are like lawyers when they ask you where you been. "So you left at 2:20, and it takes fifteen minutes to get from here to the club. It's now 5:15 in the morning—let the court show I'm about to bust your ass!"
    —*Jamie Foxx*

Women look in a mirror, and no matter what they look like in real life, they always think they look worse. Guys look in a mirror and think they look substantially better than they are. No matter how much of a three-toed, knuckle-dragger a guy is, he figures he's four or five sit-ups away from being in the hot tub with Elle McPherson.
    —*Richard Jeni*

Women are the most powerful magnet in the universe. All men are cheap metal. And we know where north is.
—*Larry Miller*

Women get their heart broke, they cry. Men don't do that. Men hold it in like it don't hurt. They walk around and get hit by trucks. "Didn't he see that truck?" "Man, he wouldn't have seen a 747. His heart was broke."
—*Richard Pryor*

Women need to like the job of the guy they're with. Men, if they are physically attracted to a woman, are not that concerned with her job. "Slaughterhouse? You're just lopping their heads off? Great! Why don't you shower, and we'll get some burgers."
—*Jerry Seinfeld*

If there were no women in the world, men would be naked, driving trucks, living in dirt. Women came along and gave us a reason to comb our hair.
—*Sinbad*

Men only have two feelings: We're either hungry or horny. I tell my wife, if I don't have an erection, make me a sandwich.
—*Bobby Slayton*

Men and women have always had problems relating. As children, men were told: "Be a man. Don't cry!" and women were told, "Let it out. Cry, you'll feel better!" And that's why as adults, women become very emotional, and men become snipers.
—*Pam Stone*

Men are hunters; women are gatherers. Men risk death to bring back meat. Women bring back useful things like fruit, water, and hunters.
—*Basil White*

**GIFTS**

What do you give a kid with seven fingers on one hand? Firecrackers.

—*Emo Philips*

Flowers

Why do people give each other flowers? To celebrate various important occasions, they're killing living creatures. Why restrict it to plants? "Sweetheart, let's make up. Have this deceased squirrel."

—*Jerry Seinfeld*

What do you send to a sick florist?

—*Henny Youngman*

**GIRLFRIENDS**

See also: **BREAKING UP, DATING, MARRIAGE, RELATIONSHIPS**

I don't have a girlfriend. But I do know a woman who'd be mad at me for saying that.

—*Mitch Hedberg*

My girlfriend is not a ball and chain; she's more of a spring-loaded trap.

—*Kevin Hench*

You can't please everybody. Like, I have a girlfriend. My girl-friend to me is the most wonderful, most remarkable person in the world. That's to me. But to my wife . . .

—*Jackie Mason*

**GIRL SCOUTS**

See: **SCOUTING**

**GLASSES**

People always want to try on my glasses. That's rude. I don't go to people with hairpieces, "Hey, let me try on your wig." "Let me sit in your wheelchair. Oh my God, you are so crippled."

—*Jim Gaffigan*

My wife made me get glasses. I wasn't seeing things her way.
—*Mark Klein*

Yesterday I was walking down the street wearing my eyeglasses, and all of a sudden my prescription ran out.
—*Steven Wright*

My mother was eighty-eight years old. She never used glasses. Drank right out of the bottle.
—*Henny Youngman*

**GLOBES**

I have the world's oldest globe. It's flat.
—*Buzz Nutley*

**GOD**

See also: **RELIGION**

In the beginning there was nothing. God said, "Let there be light!" And there was light. There was still nothing, but you could see it a whole lot better.
—*Ellen DeGeneres*

Belief in

I believe there is something out there watching us. Unfortunately, it's the government.
—*Woody Allen*

Religion has actually convinced people that there is an invisible man living in the sky, who sees everything you do and wants you to follow a special list of ten things or he'll send you to a place of fire, smoke and death, and crying forever and ever. But he loves you.
—*George Carlin*

Guilt

See also: **RELIGION** Judaism

Guilt is simply God's way of letting you know that you're having too good a time.
—*Dennis Miller*

Is a Woman

What if God's a woman? Not only am I going to hell, I'll never know why.
—*Adam Ferrara*

Judgments

I think God's going to come down and pull civilization over for speeding.
—*Steven Wright*

No Belief in

Not only is God dead, but just try to find a plumber on weekends.
—*Woody Allen*

I strongly believe there is no God; I hope He doesn't hold it against me.
—*Rick Reynolds*

Pleading

A Jewish grandmother is watching her grandchild playing on the beach when a huge wave comes and takes him out to sea. She pleads, "Please God, save my only grandson. I beg of you, bring him back." And a big wave comes and washes the boy back onto the beach, good as new. She looks up to heaven and says, "He had a hat!"
—*Myron Cohen*

Power

If I had the power of God, I would use it to open my CDs.
—*Jim Carrey*

Proof

I've had people say to me, "Look at the sky, the fields, the ocean, the beautiful sunset. Isn't that proof positive of God?" Following that line of thought, look at the magnificent rainbows after a big rainstorm. Isn't that proof positive that God is gay?
—*Ray Romano*

War, disease, death, destruction, hunger, filth, poverty, torture, crime, corruption, and the Ice Capades. If this is the best God can do, I'm not impressed. Results like these do not belong on the resume of a Supreme Being. This is the kind of stuff you'd expect from an office temp with a bad attitude.
—*George Carlin*

| | |
|---|---|
| Satan | And God said, "Let there be Satan, so people don't blame everything on Me. And let there be lawyers, so people don't blame everything on Satan."<br>*—John Wing* |
| Signs | If only God would give me a clear sign! Like making a large deposit in my name at a Swiss bank.<br>*—Woody Allen* |
| Sneezes | I fear that one day I'll meet God, he'll sneeze, and I won't know what to say.<br>*—Ronnie Shakes* |
| Worship | Let's face it. God has a big ego problem. Why do we always have to worship Him? "Oh, you're the greatest. You're perfect. We're fuckups. You know everything. We're in the dark." Secure people don't need to hear that all the time.<br>*—Bill Maher* |

**GOING OUT**   See: **DATING**, **SOCIALIZING**

**GOLF**   Give me my golf clubs, fresh air, and a beautiful partner, and you can keep my golf clubs and the fresh air.
*—Jack Benny*

If you watch a game, it's fun. If you play it, it's recreation. If you work at it, it's golf.
*—Bob Hope*

| | |
|---|---|
| Carts | I don't rent a golf cart. I don't need one. Where I hit the ball, I can use public transportation.<br>*—Gene Perret* |
| Clothing | Golf is not a sport. It's men in ugly pants, walking.<br>*—Rosie O'Donnell* |

Golf is one of the few sports where a white man can dress like a black pimp.
—*Robin Williams*

## Golfers

It takes Latinos nine hours to play golf. Four hours for eighteen holes, and five hours to do the lawn.
—*George Lopez*

The world's coming to an end. The world's best golfer is black, and the world's best rapper is white.
—*Chris Rock*

My dad's a golfer. Well not really, he watches it on TV. But it takes the same amount of energy to get a sweat going on that vinyl seat after nine hours.
—*Mike Rowe*

## Old Pros

I play golf even though I hate it. I'm not done with that game yet. I hate those windmills.
—*Mark Guido*

I'm getting faster at ninety-five. After I hit my tee shot, it doesn't take nearly as long to walk to the ball.
—*Bob Hope*

## Playing

Whenever I come home from playing golf, my son always asks me excitedly, "Did you win, Dad?" I have explained to him time and time again that you're really just playing against yourself. This time the family was on vacation, and I had gone out to play a round. When I returned, the kids were swimming in the hotel pool, which was full of young kids and surrounded by dozens of parents. From across the pool, at the top of his lungs, my son yelled, "Hey, Dad! Were you just playing with yourself?" We checked out that night.
—*Ray Romano*

Scores

I played golf. I did not get a hole in one, but I did hit a guy.
That's way more satisfying.
——*Mitch Hedberg*

I went to play golf and tried to shoot my age, but I shot my
weight instead.
——*Bob Hope*

Playing golf the other day I broke seventy. That's a lot
of clubs.
——*Henny Youngman*

While playing golf today I hit two good balls. I stepped on
a rake.
——*Henny Youngman*

Swings

I'm into golf now. I'm getting pretty good. I can almost hit
the ball as far as I can throw the clubs.
——*Bob Ettinger*

I can safely say that before me, no one in the history of my
family ever swung a golf club that wasn't swung in anger.
——*George Lopez*

on Television

Anyone can be a golf announcer. All you have to do is use
that voice you use when you call in sick at work. "I won't be
coming in today, I have a golf game to announce."
——*Mike Rowe*

**GOVERNMENT**

See also: **POLITICS, PRESIDENTS**

ATF

Do you know that there's a Bureau of Alcohol, Tobacco,
and Firearms? Only in America would we combine these
three hobbies into a government agency. I called them up.
Some guy answered, "Alcohol, Tobacco, and Firearms." I
asked, "What bourbon goes with an M-16?"
——*Wayne Cotter*

Census
Census workers have been attacked by people they're trying to interview. No one knows how many.
—*Jon Stewart*

Debt
We're a trillion dollars in debt. Who do we owe this money to? Someone named Vinnie?
—*Robin Williams*

Foreign Policy
There's nothing wrong with our foreign policy that faith, hope, and clarity couldn't cure.
—*Henny Youngman*

the Pentagon
The Pentagon's so greedy it has an extra side on its building.
—*Barry Crimmins*

Social Security
Social Security. You don't get the money till you're sixty-five; meanwhile, the average black man dies at fifty-four. We don't live that long. Hypertension, high blood pressure, NYPD—something will get you.
—*Chris Rock*

Spending
If you want to put an end to government spending, don't pay our president, senators, and representatives a salary. Give them 10 percent of our tax refunds every year. In three months, the entire federal bureaucracy would be run out of a windowless basement in Georgetown, by a ninety-year-old guy named Frankie with an unlisted rotary-dial phone.
—*Dennis Miller*

State Legislators
State legislators are merely politicians whose darkest secret prohibits them from running for higher office.
—*Dennis Miller*

Washington, D.C.
Washington, D.C., is no longer an honored and revered institution commanding the respect of its republic, but a soap opera circus, a tabloid dart board, a Hollywood with better acting,

and a bemusement park where the rides are four years long, and the popcorn is a billion dollars a bucket.
—*Dennis Miller*

Waste

To call our government a cesspool of waste is to do a disservice to all the plucky amoeba out there who thrive on human excrement.
—*Dennis Miller*

**GRANDPARENTS**    See also: **FAMILY**, **HELL**

Grandfathers      See also: **CHILDHOOD** Babysitters, **NURSING HOMES**

I only have one grandpa. We call him Grandpa Alive. He still beats me at checkers, but I kick his ass at full-contact karate.
—*Dave Attell*

I played with my grandfather a lot when I was a kid. He was dead, but my parents had him cremated and put his ashes in my Etch-a-Sketch.
—*Alan Havey*

My grandfather lived to be 103 years old. The truth is, nobody knows what's good for you. Every morning he would eat an entire raw onion and smoke a cigar. You know what his dying words were? Nobody knows; they couldn't get near the guy.
—*Jonathan Katz*

My grandparents gave me Scratch and Cough books when I was growing up, Scene of the Accident coloring books.
—*Richard Lewis*

I'll always remember the last words of my grandfather, who said, "A truck!"
—*Emo Philips*

My grandfather is a little forgetful, and he likes to give me advice. One day he took me aside, and left me there.
　　　—*Ron Richards*

My friends have a baby. All you hear is, "You've got to come over and see the baby!" Nobody ever wants you to come over to see their grandfather. "He's so cute, 164 pounds and four ounces; he's a thousand months. He went to the bathroom by himself today."
　　　—*Jerry Seinfeld*

Grandmothers　　See also: **HUSBANDS**, **TELEPHONES** Call Waiting

My Nana, ninety years old and still driving. Not with me, that would be stupid.
　　　—*Tim Allen*

My grandmother is eighty-five years old and she's starting to lose her memory. Everybody's upset about it except me, because I got eight checks for my birthday from her. Hey, that's forty bucks.
　　　—*Tom Arnold*

I just saw my grandmother, probably for the last time. She's not sick or anything, she just bores the hell out of me.
　　　—*A. Whitney Brown*

I was going to be a nice guy and mow my grandmother's grass, but then I thought, "Hey, the cemetery takes care of that."
　　　—*Ken Ferguson*

My husband's granny is eighty-seven, and she just got two new hearing aids, and cataracts removed from both eyes. I tell her we're going to fix her up just a little more and then sell her.
　　　—*Tina Fey*

My grandmother lives in Florida now. She just moved, which is great because we thought that coma was permanent.
> —*Myq Kaplan*

Getting your grandma a cell phone that sends emails and takes pictures is a great way to confuse her three times with one gift.
> —*Craig Kilborn*

I never will forget my granny. . . . One day she's sitting out on the porch and I said, "Granny, how old does a woman get before she don't want no more boyfriends?" She was around 106 then. She said, "I don't know, honey, you'll have to ask somebody older than me."
> —*Moms Mabley*

My grandmother was a very tough woman. She buried three husbands. Two of them were just napping.
> —*Rita Rudner*

## GUNS

See also: **HUNTING**

**Assault Weapons**

What's with the NRA? They don't want to outlaw automatic weapons. I guess you have to understand where they're coming from. They feel it's okay to shoot a human, as long as you eat the meat after.
> —*Elayne Boosler*

They keep saying assault weapons can be used as legitimate hunting rifles. Okay, I can buy that. You can also use a chainsaw to cut butter. It's just going to get a little messy around muffin time.
> —*Will Durst*

**Bullets**

Guns don't kill people; it's those bullets ripping through the body.
> —*Eddie Izzard*

We don't need no gun control; we need bullet control. All bullets should cost $5,000; then people would think before they killed somebody. "Man, I would blow your head off—if I could afford it. I'm going to get me another job, save my money. You better hope I can't get no bullets on layaway."

—*Chris Rock*

Control

You can buy a gun at Wal-Mart, but your 4th of July sparklers you have to smuggle across the state line.

—*Jeff Cesario*

I'm a proponent of gun control. For those of you in the National Rifle Association, proponent means I'm in favor of gun control.

—*Barry Crimmins*

I'm all for gun control. Sometimes I shake a little; I've got to use two hands.

—*Tom Kearney*

The NRA has their cute little bumper sticker, "You'll get my gun when you pry it from my cold dead hands." Whatever. In a perfect world.

—*Dennis Miller*

You want gun control? Get rid of metal detectors around the Capitol building. Take away Secret Service protection for politicians. By next week the worst thing you'll have to worry about is drive-by shoutings. Which, I might add, are protected by the First Amendment.

—*Dennis Miller*

Want gun control? Get Crips and Bloods, Nation of Islam, the JDL, Mexicans, Arab Americans, any minority group, to join the NRA. All us card-carrying members legally owning hand-guns would scare the shit out of those boys. The next meeting

they'd say, "Mohammed, Jose, Chang, Dante, and the Queer
Eye guys have guns. We need some goddamn gun control."
        —*Wanda Sykes*

Deaths          I've never owned a gun. I won't allow one in the house.
                Guns kept in the home for protection are forty-three times
                more likely to kill a family member than an assailant. Maybe
                if the number was only thirty-three, I'd take my chances.
                        —*Al Franken*

                They say "Guns don't kill people, people kill people." But I
                think the guns help. Just standing there saying "bang" doesn't
                really hurt anybody.
                        —*Eddie Izzard*

                Last year in this country there were more people killed as a
                result of firearms than as a result of automobile accidents. A
                trend that will continue until we can develop a more
                accurate automobile.
                        —*Jonathan Katz*

                The Centers for Disease Control reports that guns are now
                the second leading cause of premature death in America,
                just behind AIDS. So, if you must have unprotected sex,
                don't use a gun.
                        —*Johnny Robish*

for Hunting     Why does man kill? He kills for food. And not only food,
                frequently there must be a beverage.
                        —*Woody Allen*

                I'm all for hunters having guns. Or anything else that increases
                the odds of two rednecks blowing each other's heads off.
                        —*Bobcat Goldthwait*

Outlawed        If guns are outlawed, only outlaws will have guns. Fine, part
                of their job.
                        —*Barry Crimmins*

Pro-            Of course we need firearms. You never know when some nut
                is going to come up to you and say something like, "You're
                fired." You gotta be ready.
                            —*Dave Attell*

                This country loves guns; we even have salad shooters. This
                country thinks that salad is too peaceable; you have to find
                some way to shoot it.
                            —*Bill Maher*

                Please people, if you don't have a gun, for God's sake go out
                and get one. Because you never know when you're gonna be
                downtown someday; it's cold and dark, and all of a sudden
                you're gonna need some money.
                            —*Harland Williams*

and Republicans    There was another school shooting, and the Republicans are
                commenting on it: "The problem isn't guns, it's a problem of
                the heart." Which I guess is true, when you take six rounds to
                the chest, that is a problem of the heart.
                            —*Bill Maher*

Waiting Periods    You have to wait ten days to buy a gun in LA. I can't stay mad
                that long.
                            —*Emo Philips*

**GYMS**            See: **HEALTH CLUBS**

# HAIR

Balding

All your friends are like, "Hey Dave, is that a bald spot, or what?" "No, friend, it's a blowhole. I'm a dolphin."
—*Dave Attell*

This kind of thing would bum out any young guy. I just found out my father lost his hair—in a slap fight.
—*Vernon Chapman*

I prefer balding men. Why would you want to run your hands through a man's hair, when you could shove your fist right into his skull?
—*Stephanie Hodge*

My son has a new nickname for me, "Baldy." Son, I've got a new word for you, "Heredity."
—*Dan Savage*

I don't consider myself bald. I'm simply taller than my hair.
—*Tom Sharp*

When I hit my thirties I found there's less hair on my head and more in my ears.
—*Robert Wuhl*

Blondes

Blondes have more fun, don't they? They must. How many brunettes do you see walking down the street with blonde roots?
—*Rita Rudner*

Cut

I just had my hair cut. They cut my hair too short, and now I can't get it to do what I want it to. I want it to type.
—*Paula Poundstone*

I got a bad haircut recently. It was a haircut that actually redefined head trauma.
—*Cindee Weiss*

Dye

See also: **HAIR** Blondes

I got my hair highlighted, because I felt that some strands were more important than others.
—*Mitch Hedberg*

I dye my hair so much, my driver's license has a color wheel.
—*Nancy Mura*

Eyebrows

I refuse to think of them as chin hairs. I like to think of them as stray eyebrows.
—*Janette Barber*

If I don't tweeze every day, my eyebrows need barrettes.
—*Nancy Mur*

Gray

Gray hair is God's graffiti.
—*Bill Cosby*

It's great to have gray hair. Ask anyone who's bald.
—*Rodney Dangerfield*

I found my first gray hair today. On my chest.
—*Wendy Liebman*

Mustaches

I love a man with a mustache. And fortunately for me, I've found a man who loves a woman with one.
—*Aurora Cotsbeck*

Guys are lucky because they get to grow mustaches. I wish I could. It's like having a little pet for your face.
—*Anita Wise*

Removal

Women definitely go to maintenance extremes. One of the great mysteries to me is the fact that a woman could pour hot wax on her legs, rip the hair out by the roots, and still be afraid of a spider.
—*Jerry Seinfeld*

Toupees                Hair replacement techniques mean your wife's running her
                       fingers through your hair while you're not at home.
                       —*Richard Jeni*

Unhappy with           Nobody is really happy with what's on their head. People with
                       straight hair want curly, people with curly want straight, and
                       bald people want everyone to be blind.
                       —*Rita Rudner*

Wigs                   I don't like women who wear wigs because they make your
                       head smell like a foot.
                       —*David Allen Grier*

Women's                You see those fucked-up hairdos our women be wearing? Look
                       like chandeliers. And that hair gotta last. If they get it done
                       Thursday, you ain't getting any all weekend. Not till it starts
                       itching. When you see them takin' a pencil to that hard, high
                       hair, see them poking and scratching in there, you're going to
                       be getting' some pokin' of your own.
                       —*Bernie Mac*

**HANDICAPPED**        See: **DIFFERENTLY ABLED**

**HANDSOMENESS**       See: **BEAUTY** Men

**HAPPINESS**          Happiness is finding a book that's three weeks overdue, and
                       you're not.
                       —*Totie Fields*

                       Happiness is the quiet lull between problems.
                       —*Paul Reiser*

**HARASSMENT**

Sexual                 I quit a job once because of sexual harassment. There was
                       nowhere near enough of it going on to keep me around.
                       I got needs.
                       —*Mel Fine*

on the Street    I really hate it when strange men on the street say, "Smile! You'd look so much prettier if you'd smile." I always feel like saying, "Get hard! You'd look so much more useful if you had an erection."
                 —*Cathyrn Michon*

                 Honking the horn at a woman amazes me. What's she supposed to do? Kick off the heels, start running after, hang on to the bumper? "It's a good thing you honked, or I wouldn't have known how you felt."
                 —*Jerry Seinfeld*

                 I'm walking down the street, and a bunch of construction workers working on a building are whistling down at women. I pretend they're whistling at me, and I wave back, shake a little hip. They throw their Thermos bottles at me; I sell them on eBay. I think that makes me the winner.
                 —*Basil White*

**HEALTH**         See also: **MEDICINE**

                 I know a man who gave up smoking, drinking, sex, and rich food. He was healthy right up to the day he killed himself.
                 —*Johnny Carson*

                 When it comes to my health, I think of my body as a temple. Or at least a moderately well-managed Presbyterian Youth Center.
                 —*Emo Philips*

Nuts             Health nuts are going to feel stupid someday, lying in hospitals dying of nothing.
                 —*Redd Foxx*

Supplements      I take geranium, dandelion, passionflower, hibiscus. I feel great, and when I pee, I experience the fresh scent of potpourri.
                 —*Sheila Wenz*

Vitamins

How do vitamins know where to go? A is supposed to help the eyes, E the heart; do they have a map? I take them, but I don't feel better. But I guess when you take your vitamins with vodka, they get tipsy and confused, lose the map, and go straight to my breasts. Like most guys after a couple drinks.
—*Jayne Warren*

Warnings

I think tobacco and alcohol warnings are too general. They should be more to the point: "People who smoke will eventually cough up brown pieces of lung." And, "Warning! Alcohol will turn you into the same asshole your father was."
—*George Carlin*

**HEALTH CLUBS**          See also: **EXERCISE**

It's difficult to find the right gym to suit your fitness concerns. I'm looking for one that has ashtrays attached to the Stairmaster.
—*Michele Balan*

Joined a health club last year; spent four hundred bucks. Haven't lost a pound. Apparently, you have to show up.
—*Rich Ceisler*

Family

Why would anyone want to go to a place called a family fitness center? Why should your family burn off their pent-up energies at a gym when you can all accomplish the same thing for free at home with a series of ugly, confrontational shouting matches?
—*Dennis Miller*

Machines

My favorite machine at the gym is the vending machine.
—*Caroline Rhea*

Members

Health club patrons: men with breasts the size of lobby furniture.
—*Richard Jeni*

I joined a Nautilus club to meet men, but these guys are all bulk and no brains, like human sequoia trees. This one guy was so stupid he couldn't walk while I was chewing gum. I blew a bubble, and he stubbed his toe.
—*Cathy Ladman*

Have you been to the gym lately? Boy, some of those guys overdevelop. If your neck is as wide as your head, take a day off.
—*Margaret Smith*

Renewals

I never work out. I only go to the gym once a year—to renew. When I get the urge to exercise, I just lie down till it passes.
—*LeMaire*

## HEARING

Aids

A man brags about his new hearing aid. "It's the most expensive one I've ever had: It cost $2,500. His friend asks, "What kind is it?" He says, "Half-past four."
—*Henny Youngman*

Impaired

For years I was getting a ringing in my ears. It's getting worse. Now I'm getting busy signals.
—*Rodney Dangerfield*

My grandfather is hard of hearing. He needs to read lips. I don't mind him reading lips, but he uses one of those yellow highlighters.
—*Brian Kiley*

## HEIGHT

When I was a kid, I was so short I had to blow my nose through my fly.
—*Rodney Dangerfield*

Being a tall woman, I always dated guys for their height rather than their wealth, because I wasn't thinking.
—*Frances Dilorinzo*

**HEIGHTS**

A lot of people are afraid of heights. Not me, I'm afraid of widths.
—*Steven Wright*

**HELL**

Most major religions use hell as a deterrent to bad activity. But I find the concept of hell quite comforting because, hey, at least I'll know people there.
—*Margot Black*

Maybe there is no actual place called hell. Maybe hell is just having to listen to our grandparents breathe through their noses when they're eating sandwiches.
—*Jim Carrey*

I think hell will be whatever your mind's eye idea of hell is. Unfortunately, I've come face-to-face with mine: to be sentenced to the Stairmaster ring of Dante's Inferno. And Stairmaster time is the slowest increment of time known to man. And the only music I'll get is Michael Bolton, karaoke-style from a drunken secretary on Margarita Night.
—*Janeane Garofalo*

People in hell: where do they tell someone to go?
—*Red Skelton*

**HEROS**

See also: **SUPERHEROS**

Our heros used to be Teddy Roosevelt and Babe Ruth. Today it's different; we worship political blowhards and overpaid sports figures.
—*Vinny Badabing*

**HETERO-SEXUALITY**

See: **SEXUALITY**

**HISTORY**

If you think you have it tough, read history books.
—*Bill Maher*

A new study reveals U.S. students have very little knowledge of American history. In fact, test scores are the lowest since the Lincoln-Nixon debates.
—*Conan O'Brien*

Civil War

I joined a Civil War reenactment club. Next weekend, we're burning down Atlanta.
—*Craig Sharf*

Columbus

See also: **HOLIDAYS** Columbus Day

Columbus is the guy who, except for the Indians, the Vikings, the Egyptians, and possibly the space aliens, discovered America.
—*Craig Kilborn*

Do you know how Columbus discovered America? He was drawn by the lights from the Indian casinos.
—*Jay Leno*

Colonists

On the American colonists: They said, "We discovered new lands and territories." Hey, if you believe that, I can go to court and say, "Your honor, I was exploring some fire escapes and discovered this man's apartment. I planted my flag in his living room, and now all his stuff is mine. Him and his wife came home; I had to shoot them—they were savages!"
—*Warren Hutcherson*

Declaration of Independence

A copy of the Declaration of Independence is being auctioned over the Internet. The copy has never been handled, and, judging by events, seldom been read.
—*Jon Stewart*

Abraham Lincoln

You don't know who to believe. Like Abraham Lincoln. Abe Lincoln said all men are created equal. He never went to a nude beach.
—*Rodney Dangerfield*

Do you know the real reason Abraham Lincoln was shot in the theater? His cell phone kept going off.

—*Jay Leno*

Based on what you know about him in history books, what do you think Abraham Lincoln would be doing if he were alive today? 1. Writing his memoirs of the Civil War. 2. Advising the president. 3. Desperately clawing at the inside of his coffin.

—*David Letterman*

President Lincoln wore a stovepipe hat. The guy that sat behind him at Ford's Theatre only saw the second half of the show.

—*David Letterman*

Native Americans

The people with brown skins were here first. The rest of you are lucky that the Indians didn't ask Columbus for his Green Card.

—*Charlie Hill*

George Washington

Do you think when they asked George Washington for his ID he just took out a quarter?

—*Steven Wright*

**HOBBIES**

I've been working out lately, it's my new hobby. I thought I already had a hobby, but apparently going out, getting stinking drunk, and giving creepy guys phony phone numbers is not actually considered a hobby, but a "lifestyle."

—*Andi Rhoads*

I have a large seashell collection, which I keep scattered on beaches all over the world.

—*Steven Wright*

**HOLIDAYS**        See also: **CHRISTMAS**

April Fools' Day

April first is the day disc jockeys announce the deaths of people who are still alive.

—*Mo Rocca*

Columbus Day    On Columbus Day Native Americans put out ice cream and
                cake, and then watch the white people take it from them.
                        —*Conan O'Brien*

Easter          See also: **DEATH PENALTY**

                My father was so cheap. For Easter, we'd wear the same
                clothes, but he'd take us to a different church.
                        —*A. J. Jamal*

                A guy comes down to earth, takes your sins, dies, and comes
                back three days later. You believe in him and go to heaven
                forever. How do you get from that to Hide-the-Eggs? Did
                Jesus have a problem with eggs? Did he go, "When I come
                back if I see any eggs, the whole salvation thing is off."
                        —*Jon Stewart*

Father's Day    I have mixed emotions when I receive my Father's Day gifts.
                I'm glad my children remember me; I'm disappointed that
                they actually think I dress like that.
                        —*Mike Dugan*

                Father's Day is coming, but I figure, why get a tie for a guy
                who only goes out to the liquor store?
                        —*David Letterman*

                Father's Day, when you get that lethal combination of
                alcohol and new power tools.
                        —*David Letterman*

                I got my dad one of those typical Father's Day cards. You
                know, with a picture of a hunting coat hanging on a peg, a
                duck decoy and some golf clubs leaning in the corner.
                Perfect card for him, because there's nothing dad loves
                more than going out in the woods on a frosty morning and
                beating ducks to death with a four iron.
                        —*Daniel Liebert*

Father's Day: I hate this occasion. I can never find the right card, because they are all too nice.
—*Margaret Smith*

Going Home

My mom wanted to know why I never get home for the holidays. I said, "Because I can't get Delta to wait in the yard while I run in."
—*Margaret Smith*

Halloween

When I was twelve I went as my mother for Halloween. I put on a pair of heels, went door to door, and criticized what everyone else was wearing.
—*Robin Bach*

I learned something the other day. I learned that Jehovah's Witnesses do not celebrate Halloween. I guess they don't like strangers going up to their door and annoying them.
—*Bruce Clark*

When I was in college, I came up with the perfect Halloween costume. I wore cat ears and angel wings and carried a pitchfork, and went as every girl on campus.
—*Steve Hofstetter*

On Halloween I ran out of candy and had to give the kids nicotine gum.
—*David Letterman*

When I was a kid my parents always sent me out as a tramp: high heel shoes, fishnet stockings . . .
—*David Letterman*

Last Halloween was bad for me. I got real beat up. I went to a party dressed as a piñata.
—*Jim Samuels*

Independence Day

Why is there so much pressure to spend Independence Day with other people?
—*Betsy Salkind*

Jewish

For the holidays I bought my mother a self-complaining oven.
—*Richard Lewis*

Jews have a lot of holidays; sometimes I stay home for no reason. "Jon, is it a holiday?" "Yeah, it's Achm Blacm day."
—*Jon Stewart*

Labor Day

As you know, Labor Day is the day when we honor hard-working people in America. So let's take a moment to thank all those people by saying, "Gracias, amigos!"
—*Jay Leno*

I like Labor Day. Do you have the campout and picnic thing with all the relatives? It's fun, for about eighteen minutes. We had problems with my Uncle Earl. He's eighty years old, and he ate about half a bag of those mesquite wood chips.
—*David Letterman*

Mother's Day

Mothers stress the lovely meaning of Mother's Day by gathering their children and tenderly saying, "I carried every one of you in my body for nine months and then my hips started spreading because of you. I wasn't built like this until you were born, and I didn't have this big blue vein in the back of my leg. You did this to me."
—*Bill Cosby*

The worst Mother's Day gift is sending your mother a song over the telephone. Basically, you're putting Mom on hold.
—*Craig Kilborn*

Mother's Day is the biggest day of the year for long-distance telephone calls. Makes you wonder why so many people move long distances from Mom, doesn't it? I'm off the hook this year, though. Mom thinks I'm still in the hospital.
—*David Letterman*

Mother's Day is the day we honor the woman we blame for all our personal problems.

—*David Letterman*

When I was little I asked my mother, "Do you love me?" She said "I love you when you're sleeping." When I was fourteen, I asked, "Mom, am I ugly?" She said, "It's OK; when you're sixteen you can get a nose job." When I was leaving for school, she said, "I don't know why we're spending any money to send you to college—you don't deserve it." When I came home for Mother's Day, she asked, "Where is my present?" I said, "Your present is, I still only have one personality, and it's not planning to kill you!"

—*Robin Roberts*

Not romantic, my husband. Do you know what he gave me for Mother's Day? A George Foreman grill. I gave it back to him for Father's Day, in a sort of forceful upward motion.

—*Sandi Selvi*

New Year's Eve

Women get a little more excited about New Year's Eve than men do. It's like an excuse: You get drunk; you make a lot of promises you're not going to keep; the next morning as soon as you wake up you start breaking them. For men, we just call that a date.

—*Jay Leno*

I'm still keeping my New Year's resolutions. I actually only make one because it's the only one easy to keep: I resolve to spend less time with my family.

—*Maria Menozzi*

I have the same New Year's resolution every year: I decide to drink heavily. Because I know I can do it, which will build my self-esteem.

—*Betsy Salkind*

Religious

All religions are the same: basically guilt, with different holidays. "I feel so guilty. Let's eat."
—*Cathy Ladman*

Traditions

Holiday traditions mean a lot to people, particularly people in retail.
—*Michael Feldman*

St. Patrick's Day

The legend of St. Patrick is that he drove all the snakes out of Ireland, and into law school.
—*David Letterman*

St. Valentine's Day

Hallmark is coming out with a new card for guys who forget Valentine's Day. The card is small and gold and maxes out at ten grand.
—*Craig Kilborn*

Valentine's Day. Or, as men like to call it: Extortion Day.
—*Jay Leno*

I don't understand why Cupid was chosen to represent Valentine's Day. When I think about romance, the last thing on my mind is a short, chubby toddler coming at me with a weapon.
—*Paul McGinty*

I wanted to make it really special on Valentine's Day, so I tied my boyfriend up. And for three solid hours I watched whatever I wanted to on TV.
—*Tracy Smith*

Thanksgiving

At Thanksgiving, my mom always makes too much food, especially one item, like seven or eight hundred pounds of sweet potatoes. She's got to push it during the meal. "Did you get some sweet potatoes? There's sweet potatoes. They're hot. There's more in the oven, some more in the garage. The rest are at the Johnson's."
—*Louie Anderson*

You know that just before that first Thanksgiving dinner there was one wise, old Native American woman saying, "Don't feed them. If you feed them, they'll never leave."
     —*Dylan Brody*

We're having something a little different this year for Thanksgiving. Instead of a turkey, we're having a swan. You get more stuffing.
     —*George Carlin*

Thanksgiving is an emotional time. People travel thousands of miles to be with people they only see once a year. And then discover once a year is way too often.
     —*Johnny Carson*

Thanksgiving: When the Indians said, "Well, this has been fun, but we know you have a long voyage back to England."
     —*Jay Leno*

You can tell you ate too much for Thanksgiving when you have to let your bathrobe out.
     —*Jay Leno*

Thanksgiving is the day when you turn to another family member and say, "How long has Mom been drinking like this?" My mom, after six Bloody Marys looks at the turkey and goes, "Here, kitty, kitty."
     —*David Letterman*

There's a lot of New York City Thanksgiving traditions. For example, a lot of New Yorkers don't buy the frozen Thanksgiving turkey. They prefer to buy the bird live and then push it in front of a subway train.
     —*David Letterman*

When I was a kid in Indiana, we thought it would be fun to get a turkey a year ahead of time and feed it and so on for the following Thanksgiving. But by the time Thanksgiving came

around, we sort of thought of the turkey as a pet, so we ate the dog. Only kidding. It was the cat.
—*David Letterman*

Last Thanksgiving I shot my own turkey. It was fun. That shot gun going, "Blam! Blam!" Everybody at the supermarket just staring. Why track them when I know where they are?
—*Kenny Rogerson*

This Thanksgiving is gonna be a special one. My mom says I don't have to sit at the card table.
—*Jim Samuels*

I celebrated Thanksgiving in the traditional way. I invited everyone in my neighborhood to my house; we had an enormous feast. And then I killed them and took their land.
—*Jon Stewart*

**HOMELESSNESS**    My family was homeless for a long time. I grew up in Canada, so I thought we had just gone camping. And my parents kept me in the dark, because they were embarrassed. I'd ask, "Dad, are we living below the poverty line?" And he'd say, "No son, we're rich as long as we have each other. Now get in the Dumpster."
—*Jim Carrey*

I always give homeless people money, and my friends yell at me, "He's only going to buy more alcohol and cigarettes." And I'm thinking, "Oh, like and I wasn't?"
—*Kathleen Madigan*

**HOMICIDE**    They caught the first female serial killer in Florida. Eight men. But she didn't kill them. She gained access to their homes, hid the remote controls, so they killed themselves.
—*Elayne Boosler*

Serial killers always say, "I heard voices." Why don't those voices ever say, "Go dancing"? Or "Bake a cake?"
—*Dexter Madison*

You're not gonna believe this. I saw a murder. I got there five minutes after it happened. Apparently, from what I saw, the body fell onto a chalk line exactly the same shape.
—*Howie Mandel*

Probably the toughest time in anyone's life is when you have to murder a loved one because they're the devil. Other than that, it's been a good day.
—*Emo Philips*

**HOMO-SEXUALITY**

See also: **LESBIANS**, **RELIGION**, **SCOUTING**, **SEXUALITY**

Cause of

The next time someone asks you, "Hey, how did you get to be a homosexual anyway?" tell them, "Homosexuals are chosen first on talent, then interview. The swimsuit and evening gown competition pretty much gets rid of the rest of them."
—*Karen Williams*

Coming out

Here is a little tip for all of you: Don't come out to your father in a moving vehicle.
—*Kate Clinton*

as Disease

If homosexuality is a disease, let's all call in queer to work. "Hello, can't work today. Still queer."
—*Robin Tyler*

in High School

My high school had a Head Start program for homosexuals; it was called Drama Club.
—*Bob Smith*

Homophobia

Homophobia: The irrational fear that three fags will break into your house and redecorate it against your will.
—*Tom Ammiano*

**Laws**

The sodomy laws have been overturned, so now we can overturn each other.
—*Craig Kilborn*

**Male**

I thank God for creating gay men. Because if it wasn't for them, us fat women would have no one to dance with.
—*Roseanne Barr*

My brother is gay, and my parents don't care, as long as he marries a doctor.
—*Elayne Boosler*

I love the word "faggot," because it describes my kind of guy. I am a fag hag. Fag hags are the backbone of the gay community. Without us, you're nothing. We have been there all through history guiding your sorry ass through the underground railroad. We went to the prom with you.
—*Margaret Cho*

**Marriage**

I'm against gay marriage. I think marriage is a sacred union between a man and a pregnant woman.
—*Craig Kilborn*

I'm in favor of gay marriage. Then at least both people are excited about planning the wedding.
—*Jay Leno*

I was once involved in a same-sex marriage. There was the same sex over and over and over.
—*David Letterman*

My parents were worried about me getting married, so I got married. But they have a problem with it: She's black. But she's also doctor, so it's OK.
—*Marla Lukofsky*

Canada said, "We'll see your legalization of sodomy and raise you gay marriage." But here in the U.S. marriage is a sacred act between two people chosen by the studio audience.
    —*Jon Stewart*

**Organs**

The Kinsey Institute says gay men have bigger sex organs. Hence the origin of gay pride.
    —*Jay Leno*

**Parents of**

My parents were in denial about my being gay. I wasn't afraid of the dark; I was afraid of unflattering light.
    —*Bob Smith*

**and Religion**

See also: **RELIGION** Bible

If all gay people are going to hell, I'd like to see everyone in heaven get their hair done.
    —*Judy Carter*

**Republicans**

Gay Republicans, how exactly does that work? "We disapprove of our own lifestyle. We beat ourselves up in parking lots."
    —*Paula Poundstone*

**Rights**

As women, as lesbians and gay men, we are denied certain very basic human rights. The last time most people in this society cared about my rights, I was a fetus. And the next time they'll care about my rights is when I die and come back as a whale.
    —*Sara Cytron*

**Signs of**

They say you can't tell guys are gay just by looking. But if two guys are kissing, you can figure at least one of them is gay.
    —*Bill Braudis*

**and Straight**

Straight people are fine. I have one of them fix my car. They do great work.
    —*Michael Rasky*

In college I experimented with heterosexuality: I slept with a straight guy. I was really drunk.
—*Bob Smith*

Terminology

Using the word "gay" as a euphemism for homosexual is fine, I guess. But I've always thought a word like "fabulous" might have been better. Sure would be a lot easier to tell your parents, "Mom, Dad: I'm fabulous! And my friends are fabulous, too!"
—*Michael Greer*

Wrongs

The heterosexuals who hate us should just stop having us.
—*Lynda Montgomery*

## HONESTY

Best Policy

Honesty may be the best policy, but it's important to remember that apparently, by elimination, dishonesty is the second-best policy.
—*George Carlin*

Honesty is the best policy, but insanity is a better defense.
—*Steve Landesberg*

Lessons

I was walking down Fifth Avenue today and I found a wallet. I was gonna keep it, rather than return it, but I thought: Well, if I lost $150, how would I feel? And I realized I would want to be taught a lesson.
—*Emo Philips*

## HOTELS

I saw a billboard for a small hotel that said, "We Treat You Like Family." And sure enough, nine o'clock the next morning, someone was banging on my door yelling, "When the hell are you gonna get a place of your own?"
—*Brian McKim*

Furniture

In hotel rooms I worry. I think I can't be the only guy who sits on the furniture naked.
—*Jonathan Katz*

What a hotel! The towels were so fluffy I could hardly close my suitcase.
—*Henny Youngman*

Nonsmoking Rooms

Hotels and I appear to differ on the precise definition of what constitutes a nonsmoking room. Hotels' definition appears to be "Nobody's smoking in there right now." Two months ago in New York, I stayed in a nonsmoking room that smelled like the guy before had been curing a ham.
—*Dennis Miller*

Wake-up Calls

Here's a little tip from me to you as an experienced traveler. Wake-up calls: worst way to wake up. The phone rings; it's loud; you can't turn it down. I leave the number of the room next to me, and it just rings kind of quiet, and you hear a guy yell, "What are calling me for?" Then you get up and take a shower. It's great.
—*Garry Shandling*

## HOUSEWIVES

See: **WIVES**

## HOUSEWORK

I do clean up a little. If company is coming, I'll wipe the lipstick off the milk container.
—*Elayne Boosler*

So I live in this apartment that's disgusting; it's really dirty. And the kitchen floor is, like, sticky. I had to do something about it, so finally I went out and bought some slippers.
—*Sarah Silverman*

Anti-

It is better to light just one candle than to clean the whole apartment.
—*Eileen Courtney*

Cleaning the house before your kids are done growing is like shoveling the walk before it stops snowing.
—*Phyllis Diller*

Housework can't kill you, but why take a chance?
—*Phyllis Diller*

Don't cook. Don't clean. No man will ever make love to a woman because she waxed the linoleum. "My God, the floor's immaculate. Lie down, you hot bitch."
—*Joan Rivers*

**Cleaning Ladies**

Never hire a cleaning lady named Dusty.
—*David Corrado*

**Dusting**

Dusting is a good example of the futility of trying to put things right. As soon as you dust, the fact of your next dusting has already been established.
—*George Carlin*

**Laundry**

See also: **CLOTHING**, **CRIME** in Laundromat

You know it's time to do the laundry when you dry off with a sneaker.
—*Zach Galifiankis*

I hate doing laundry. I don't separate the colors from the whites. I put them together and let them learn from their cultural differences.
—*Rita Rudner*

**Men Versus Women**

Men leave their socks lying around because we can use them for oven mitts.
—*Mike Dugan*

Even though women work all day long, they still come home and clean up about 99 percent of the things cleaned up around the house. There is still a problem here. Women aren't as proud of their 99 percent as men are of their 1 percent. We clean up something; we're going to talk about it all week long. It might be on the news.

*—Jeff Foxworthy*

When I get mad it makes me want to clean. So my wife spends most of the day following me around trying to piss me off.

*—Reno Goodale*

My wife comes home, and I've spread crap all over the house. I come home, and she's organized the refrigerator magnets into perfect rows and columns. Tell me again which one of us is crazy.

*—Basil White*

and Single Men    We're single guys; nobody washes dishes. I had to go to the closet and get the Yahtzee game to find a clean cup to drink out of.

*—Dobie Maxwell*

Vacuuming    The day I worry about cleaning my house is the day Sears comes out with a riding vacuum cleaner.

*—Roseanne Barr*

My mother is a clean freak. She vacuumed so much, the guy downstairs went bald.

*—Steve Bridges*

Vacuuming sucks.

*—Jason Love*

**HOUSING**    See also: **APARTMENTS**

Architecture    My house is made out of balsa wood. When no one is home across the street except the little kids, I lift my house up over my head. I tell them to stay out of my yard, or I'll throw it at them.

*—Steven Wright*

Carpeting

I wanted to buy some carpeting, you know how much they want for carpeting? $15 a square yard! And I'm sorry, I'm not going to pay that for carpeting. So what I did, I bought two square yards, and when I go home I strap them to my feet.
—*Steve Martin*

Doors

I have French doors in the bedroom. They don't open unless I lick them.
—*Judy Gold*

House Buying

I just bought a new house. It has no plumbing. It's uncanny.
—*Morey Amsterdam*

I just bought a new house. I don't want to brag, but it's in a golf-course community. A famous golf course, you may have heard of: the Putt-Putt. It's a beautiful place—my deck overlooks the third, fourth, seventh, twelfth, fifteenth fairways, the windmill, and the clown's mouth. I'm living the dream.
—*Tony Deyo*

We just bought a house. My husband calls it a "fixer-upper." I call it a piece of crap.
—*Maryellen Hooper*

I can't believe I actually own my own house. I'm looking at a house; it's five hundred grand. The realtor says, "It's got a great view." For five hundred grand I better open up the curtains and see breasts against the window.
—*Garry Shandling*

I saw a commercial that said you can get a house with no money down. How in the hell can you do that? Kill the people who live in it?
—*Shang*

Mobile

I grew up in a mobile home. When I was a kid, I ran away from home, and it followed me.
—*Jimmy Brogan*

Hey, there are advantages to living in a mobile home. One time, it caught on fire. We met the fire department halfway there.
—*Ronnie Shakes*

**Mother's**

My mother's house: exposed bricks and nerves. She lives in a predominantly anxious part of town.
—*Richard Lewis*

**Remodeling**

We did some remodeling, and the workmen could have an attitude. The painter came, and I asked, "Could you fill in some of these holes before you start, please?" He said, "Lady, I don't spackle, I don't sand, I just paint." Then the exterminator came in. I said, "Kill the painter."
—*Rita Rudner*

**Selling**

I sold my house this week. I got a pretty good price for it, but it made my landlord mad as hell.
—*Garry Shandling*

**HUMANITY**

More than any other time in history, mankind faces a crossroads. One path leads to despair and utter hopelessness. The other, to total extinction. Let us pray we have the wisdom to choose correctly.
—*Woody Allen*

I think I'm a pretty good judge of people, which is why I hate most of them.
—*Roseanne Barr*

I believe there's a commonality to all humanity: We all suck.
—*Bill Hicks*

I had a linguistics professor who said that it's man's ability to use language that makes him the dominant species on the planet. I think there's one other thing that separates us from animals: We aren't afraid of vacuum cleaners.
—*Jeff Stilson*

**HUMIDIFIERS**

I got a humidifier, and a dehumidifier. I put them in the same room and watch them fight it out.

—*Steven Wright*

**HUMOR**

See: **COMEDY**

**HUNTING**

See also: **GUNS**

Do you know how the Amish hunt? They sneak up on a deer and build a barn around it.

—*Tim Bedore*

If God didn't want man to hunt, he wouldn't have given us plaid shirts.

—*Johnny Carson*

You ask people why they have deer heads on the wall. They say, "Because it's such a beautiful animal." I think my mother's attractive, but I have photographs of her.

—*Ellen DeGeneres*

They call hunting and fishing "game." It's the only game where the other team never volunteered to play.

—*Matt North*

**HUSBANDS**

See also: **MARRIAGE**, **WIVES**

I want my husband to take me in his arms and whisper those three little words that all women long to hear: "You were right."

—*Kelly Smith*

at Birth

I asked my husband if he wanted to be in the room with me when I gave birth. He said, "It would have to be a big room, and there would have to be a bar at one end."

—*Rita Rudner*

Cheap

I've been asked to say a couple of words about my husband, Fang. How about, short and cheap?
          —*Phyllis Diller*

Cheating

He was cheating on me with his secretary. I found lipstick on his collar, covered with Wite-Out.
          —*Wendy Liebman*

Dead

My husband is dead. At least I know where he is. He's on the mantelpiece.
          —*Dame Edna Everage*

Dressing

Men are married about six months, and they can't even dress themselves anymore, "Honey, does this tie go with my underwear?"
          —*John Mendoza*

For men, upon marriage you lose the ability to choose clothing for yourself. "Honey, what do you think? A striped shirt and a solid tie, or a solid shirt and a pair of mukluks? A Beatle wig and a grass skirt? Tell me, because I haven't used that part of my brain in several years. Why don't you just choose something, lay it out, and I'll be in the crib until we have to leave."
          —*Paul Reiser*

Ex-

Regarding her ex-husband: In lovemaking, what he lacked in size, he made up for in speed.
          —*Roseanne Barr*

Never bad-mouth your ex-husband to your kids. Because if you do, then you ruin the moment when they figure it out all by themselves.
          —*Cory Kahaney*

My ex-husband cheated on me, even though I was a good wife and mother. I cleaned; I cooked. The way to a man's heart

may be through his stomach, but that's only if you twist the blade and lift up.
                                        —*Sheila Kay*

Mr. Right

I married Mr. Right. Mr. Always Right.
                                        —*Lotus Weinstock*

Multiple

My grandmother had four husbands, but she had all her orgasms in the fruit section of the supermarket.
                                        —*Tami Yellin*

Need Space

My husband said he needed more space. So I locked him outside.
                                        —*Roseanne Barr*

My husband and I used to fight about that night out with the guys, but it's not like I was doing it every night.
                                        —*Jenny Jones*

Roles

They think it's your destiny to clean, and I guess it's their destiny to have a couch surgically implanted on their behind. You may marry the man of your dreams, ladies, but years later you're married to a couch that burps.
                                        —*Roseanne Barr*

Role Playing

My husband and I were role playing the other night, and I started to cry when I realized that he'd cleaned the apartment.
                                        —*Alex House*

Self-Image

I don't see myself as a married guy. I still see myself as a pirate.
                                        —*Adam Ferrara*

Things in Common

The only thing my husband and I have in common is that we were married on the same day.
                                        —*Phyllis Diller*

Trust

Trust your husband, adore your husband, and get as much as you can in your own name.

—*Joan Rivers*

**HYENAS**          See: **ANIMALS**

**IDEAS**

I got a lot of ideas. Trouble is, most of them suck.
   —*George Carlin*

**ILLNESSES**

See also: **CANCER, DOCTORS, MEDICINE**

Allergies

My brother-in-law has an allergy. He's allergic to work.
   —*Henny Youngman*

Comas

A woman woke up from four and a half years in a coma. Her husband spent the whole time by her bedside, and when she came to, he said, "Honey, can you get me a beer?"
   —*Jay Leno*

Diseases

First the doctor told me the good news: I was going to have a disease named after me.
   —*Steve Martin*

Headaches

Ever get one of those ice cream headaches? You know, when you tell your girlfriend she's gaining weight, and she hits you with the scoop? "Ow! I said that too fast!"
   —*Jeff Shaw*

**IMMIGRATION**

Immigration is the sincerest form of flattery.
   —*Jack Paar*

All the problems we face in the United States today can be traced to an unenlightened immigration policy on the part of the American Indian.
   —*Pat Paulsen*

**INCENSE**

What's the deal with incense? It smells like somebody set fire to a clothes hamper. Gym socks and jasmine. Do we need that smell? You what incense smells like? If flowers could fart.
   —*Billiam Coronel*

## INSECTS

Ants

Ants can carry twenty times their own body weight, which is useful information if you're moving and you need help carrying a potato chip across town.

—*Ron Darian*

Ever watch ants just crawling around? They walk in that single straight line, a long, long mile of ants. Sometimes they will walk over and pick up their dead friends and carry those around. I'm pretty sure it's because they can get in the carpool lane and pass up that line.

—*Ellen DeGeneres*

I bought an ant farm. I don't know where I'm gonna find a tractor that small.

—*Steven Wright*

Bees

As yet there have been no deaths attributed to the killer bees. However, two bees were caught this week planning a murder.

—*Dennis Miller*

Extermination

Some women think that any aerosol can kill a bug. My wife says, "Deodorant! Use that! I've killed bugs with deodorant!" Try killing a monster with deodorant. It's not easy, and all I could find was the roll-on.

—*Ray Romano*

Exterminators

I called a discount exterminator. A guy came by with a rolled-up magazine.

—*Wil Shriner*

Flies

I don't kill flies, but I like to mess with their minds. I hold them above globes. They freak out and yell, "Whoa, I'm way too high!"

—*Bruce Baum*

Spiders

See also: **HAIR** Removal

I was reading how a female spider will eat the male spider after mating. I guess female spiders know that life insurance is easier to collect than child support.
—*Janine DiTullio*

**INSOMNIA**

See: **SLEEPING**

**INSTRUCTIONS**

I once went to Sears to buy a workbench. It came in a big, big box, and there was some assembly required. There were instructions, but I didn't need those. Hey, I'm a guy; my balls will tell me how it all fits together.
—*Tim Allen*

**INSURANCE**

Dental

I finally have a dental plan. I chew on the other side.
—*Janine DiTullio*

Health

See also: **PARENTS** Dreams

I have really bad health insurance. The only hospital on my plan is the Imitation Mayo Clinic.
—*Craig Sharf*

HMOs

See also: **CLICHÉS** Apple a Day, **INVENTIONS**, **LAUGHTER**, **MEDICINE** HMOs, **MEDICINE** X-rays

Life

See also: **INSECTS** Spiders, **MONSTERS** Godzilla

The insurance man told me that the accident policy covered falling off the roof, but not hitting the ground.
—*Tommy Cooper*

My wife and I took out life insurance policies on one another, so now it's just a waiting game.
—*Bil Dwyer*

I used to sell life insurance. But life insurance is a really weird concept. You really don't get anything for it. It works like this: You pay me money. And when you die, I'll pay you money.

—*Bill Kirchenbauer*

**IRS**          See: **TAXATION**

**INTERNET**     See: **CYBERSPACE**

**INTIMACY**     I have a tremendous fear of intimacy. I feel lucky just to get aroused, because my penis is usually in the shape of a question mark. If I am lucky enough to get an erection, fortunately for me, my hard-on points to the nearest counseling center.

—*Richard Lewis*

My friends tell me I have an intimacy problem. But they don't really know me.

—*Garry Shandling*

**INVENTIONS**   Who invented the brush they put next to the toilet? That thing hurts!

—*Andy Andrews*

My uncle invented the solar-powered funeral home. It's got basic solar technology: Big solar panels on the roof, the sun beats down, it heats up the panels. Trouble is, it can't cremate; it can only poach.

—*Heywood Banks*

My father invented the burglar alarm, which unfortunately was stolen from him.

—*Victor Borge*

There's now a glove that lets doctors see a patient's vital signs just by touching him. Unless you're in an HMO. Then your doctor gets an oven mitt and a meat thermometer.

—*Jay Leno*

I don't know if I want a fuzzy cover on my toilet seat, but I want to meet whoever invented them. Who lifted a toilet seat and thought, "That needs a hat."
>—*Rita Rudner*

I invented the cordless extension cord.
>—*Steven Wright*

**JAIL**            See: **PRISONS**

**JEWELRY**         A recent marketing poll shows that 32 percent of all diamonds are purchased right before Christmas. And 50 percent are purchased right after the test strip turns pink.
>—*Conan O'Brien*

When I was a boy my mother wore a mood ring. When she was in a good mood it turned blue. In a bad mood, it left a big red mark on my forehead.
>—*Jeff Shaw*

**JOBS**            See: **EMPLOYMENT**

**JUGGLING**        Some people think a juggler is talented. Could be a schizophrenic playing catch.
>—*Bob Dubac*

**JURIES**          See: **COURTS**

**JUSTICE**         See: **COURTS**

**KANGAROOS**       See: **ANIMALS**, **PREGNANCY** Pondering

**KIDS**            See: **BABIES**, **CHILDREN**, **FATHERHOOD**, **MOTHERHOOD**, **PARENTHOOD**

**KISSING**         People who throw kisses are hopelessly lazy.
>—*Bob Hope*

**KU KLUX KLAN**      See: **GANGS, RACISM**

**LAND**      See: **REAL ESTATE**

**LANGUAGE**      See also: **COMMUNICATION**

I personally think we developed language because of our
deep inner need to complain.
      —*Lily Tomlin*

Alphabet      Why is the alphabet in that order? Is it because of the song?
      —*Steven Wright*

English      I've heard people say, "If you don't speak the American
language, you should get out of here." Really? You don't
sound like you're from here, Navaho.
      —*Bobcat Goldthwait*

I've always tried to be a good American citizen. So I've made
it a point to not learn any other language but English.
      —*Becky Pedigo*

Foreign      Certain tribes in Borneo do not have a word for "no" and
consequently turn down requests by nodding their heads
and saying, "I'll get back to you."
      —*Woody Allen*

French      I think my French is peccable.
      —*Steve Martin*

Spanish      I'm learning to speak Spanish by calling my bank and press-
ing the number two button.
      —*Paul Alexander*

I bought one of those tapes to teach you Spanish in your
sleep. During the night, the tape skipped. Now I can only
stutter in Spanish.
      —*Steven Wright*

**LATENESS**

Mexicans are always late. You want to piss somebody off, be early. "Hey, wassup? You mad at me? I just got here. How come I'm late? I thought you were going to be late; that's why I'm late."

—*George Lopez*

**LAUGHTER**

See also: **COMEDY**

Laughter is the shortest distance between two people.

—*Victor Borge*

He who laughs last didn't get it in the first place.

—*Rodney Dangerfield*

Laughter is the best medicine, but only because it's cheaper than an HMO.

—*Buzz Nutely*

If you can laugh at yourself loud and hard every time you fall, people will think you're drunk.

—*Conan O'Brien*

**LAWS**

See also: **LAWYERS**

I'm against any law that I wouldn't break if I could get away with it.

—*A. Whitney Brown*

**LAWYERS**

A lawyer shows up at the pearly gates. St. Peter says, "Normally we don't let you people in here, but you're in luck; we have a special this week. You go to hell for the length of time you were alive, then you get to come back up here for eternity." The lawyer says, "I'll take the deal." St. Peter says, "Good, I'll put you down for 212 years in hell." The lawyer says, "What are you talking about? I'm sixty-five years old!" St. Peter says, "Up here we go by billing hours."

—*Orson Bean*

Most attorneys practice law because it gives them a grand and glorious feeling. You give them a grand, and they feel glorious.
—*Milton Berle*

Criminal lawyer. Or is that redundant?
—*Will Durst*

I call my lawyer and ask, "Can I ask you two questions?" My lawyer says, "What's the second question?"
—*Henny Youngman*

Lawyer is swimming in the water. A shark comes toward him and veers away. Professional courtesy.
—*Henny Youngman*

**LEATHER JACKETS**

I had a leather jacket that got ruined. Now, why does moisture ruin leather? Aren't cows outside most of the time? When it's raining do cows go up to the farmhouse, "Let us in, we're all wearing leather!"
—*Jerry Seinfeld*

Leather jackets scare me. Think about it, people are wearing dried meat for clothing. They're spending $500 to wear beef jerky.
—*Brad Stine*

**LESBIANS**

See also: **HOMOSEXUALITY**, **SEXUALITY**

Introductions

Introductions are tricky in a lesbian relationship. It's a word game. To my friends she's my lover; to strangers and family members in denial she's my roommate; to Jehovah's Witnesses at the door she's my lesbian sex slave; and to my mother she's Jewish, and that's all that matters.
—*Denise McCanles*

and Men            They say that lesbians hate men. Why would a lesbian hate a
                   man? They don't have to fuck them.
                                        —*Roseanne Barr*

                   I was performing at a comedy club, and when I said I'm a les-
                   bian, a guy in the audience yelled out, "Can I watch?" I said,
                   "Watch me what? Fix my car?"
                                        —*Sabrina Matthews*

                   Some men think that they can convert gay women, make
                   them straight. I couldn't do that. I could make a straight
                   woman gay, though.
                                        —*Jeff Stilson*

                   One man asked, "Hey, did you get that way because you had
                   some kind of bad sexual experience with a guy?" I'm like, "If
                   that's all it took, the entire female population would be gay, sir."
                                        —*Suzanne Westenhoefer*

Parents of         Most parents of gay children are unprepared to give them
                   guidance. It's not advisable for a lesbian daughter to try to use
                   her father's method of keeping a woman happy: Agree to
                   whatever she says, and then do what you want anyway.
                                        —*Bob Smith*

and Penises        It's not that I don't like penises. I just don't like them on men.
                                        —*Lea DeLaria*

Sexual Practices   Heterosexuals are rude sometimes, get right in your face and
                   ask you rude questions, "What do you lesbians do in bed?"
                   Well, it's a lot like heterosexual sex. Only, one of us doesn't
                   have to fake an orgasm.
                                        —*Suzanne Westenhoefer*

Signs              A study claims that the relative lengths of the index and ring
                   fingers indicates whether a woman is a lesbian. If between her

thumb and index finger is another woman's nipple, that's an even better indication.
—*Bill Maher*

Terminology

Some women can't say the word lesbian, even when their mouth is full of one.
—*Kate Clinton*

Labels can be misleading. I saw a news report about a lesbian protest march, and the reporter said, "Coming up next, a lesbian demonstration." My first thought was, "Cool. I always wondered how those things work."
—*Michael Dane*

That word lesbian sounds like a disease. And straight men know, because they're sure that they're the cure.
—*Denise McCanles*

**LIBERALS**    See: **POLITICS**

**LIFE**    Life is a sexually transmitted disease.
—*Guy Bellamy*

Life is a near-death experience.
—*George Carlin*

Life is tough. What do you get at the end? Death. What's that, a bonus? The life cycle is backward. You should die first, get it out of the way, then live in an old age home. Get kicked out when you're too young, get a gold watch, go to work forty years until you're young enough to enjoy your retirement. Do drugs, alcohol, party, and get ready for high school. Go to grade school, become a kid, play, have no responsibilities, become a baby, go back to the womb, spend your last nine months floating, finish off as an orgasm.
—*George Carlin*

If I've learned one thing in life it's that I can always count on pinkeye at the most inappropriate moment.

—*Janeane Garofalo*

The world is like a ride in an amusement park. You think it's real because that's how powerful our minds are. The ride goes up and down, round and round; it has thrills and chills; it's brightly colored, loud and fun, for a while. Some people have been on the ride for a long time, and they begin to question, "Is this real, or is this just a ride?" And other people remember. They come back to us and say, "Hey, don't worry, don't be afraid, ever, because this is just a ride." We kill those people.

—**Bill Hicks**

Most people think life sucks, and then you die. Not me. I beg to differ. I think life sucks, then you get cancer, your dog dies, your wife leaves you, the cancer goes into remission, you get a new dog, get remarried, owe ten million dollars in medical bills, but you work hard for thirty-five years and pay it back, and then one day you have a massive stroke, your right side is paralyzed, you have to limp along the streets and speak out of the left side of your mouth and drool, but you go into rehabilitation and regain the power to walk and the power to talk, and then one day you step off a curb, and, bang, you get hit by a city bus and then you die. Maybe.

—**Denis Leary**

Life is what happens when you're not watching television.

—*Jason Love*

God knows life sucks. It's right there in the Bible. The book of Job is all about Job asking God to take away pain and misery. And God says, "I can't take away pain and misery because then no one would talk to me."

—**Bill Maher**

Life is a ride. We're strapped in, and no one can stop it.
When the doctor slaps your behind, he's ripping your ticket.
As you make each passage from youth to adulthood to
maturity, sometimes you put your arms up and scream;
sometimes just hang on to that bar in front of you. But the
ride is the thing. I think the most you can hope for at the
end is that your hair is messed, you're out of breath, and
you didn't throw up.
　　　*—Jerry Seinfeld*

I like life. It's something to do.
　　　*—Ronnie Shakes*

**LIPSTICK**　　See: **COSMETICS**

**LITTERING**　　Doesn't it bother you when people litter? Their most cre-
ative rationale for throwing an apple core out the window
is, "It will plant seeds for other trees to grow." And of course
our highways are lined with apple trees, right next to the
cigarette bush.
　　　*—Nick Arnette*

**LOOKS**　　See: **BEAUTY**

**LOVE**　　The difference between love and sex is that sex relieves
tension and love causes it.
　　　*—Woody Allen*

I urge you all to love yourselves without reservation, and to
love each other without restraints. Unless you're into
leather. Then, by all means, use restraints.
　　　*—Margaret Cho*

I am certainly not an authority on love because there are no authorities on love, just those who've had luck with it and those who haven't.
        *—Bill Cosby*

If you open your heart up and let all the love you have flow out of you, I promise that some highly dysfunctional, emotionally unavailable man will glom himself onto you and never let go.
        *—Wendy Kamenoff*

When you're in love, it's the most glorious two-and-a-half days of your life.
        *—Richard Lewis*

Love is like playing checkers. You have to know which man to move.
        *—Moms Mabley*

What is my favorite romantic spot? You mean in the whole world or on somebody's body?
        *—Jackie Mason*

Don't you hate it when you date someone and they say this, "I love you, but I'm not in love with you." You just want to go, "I want you, but not inside me."
        *—Felicia Michaels*

My mother always said that a rose is the perfect symbol of romance. It dies after a few days; its pretty petals fall off; and all you're left with is the ugly prickly thing.
        *—Maureen Murphy*

There's a fine line between true love and a stalking conviction.
        *—Buzz Nutley*

A lot of people wonder how you know if you're really in love. Just ask yourself this one question: "Would I mind being financially destroyed by this person?"

—*Ronnie Shakes*

I've been in love with the same woman for forty-one years. If my wife finds out, she'll kill me.

—*Henny Youngman*

Falling in

Before I met my husband I'd never fallen in love, though I've stepped in it a few times.

—*Rita Rudner*

I fall in love really quickly, and this scares guys away. I'm like, "I'm in love with you; I want to marry you; I want to move in with you.' And they're like, "Ma'am, could you give me the ten bucks for the pizza, and I'll be outta here."

—*Penny Wiggins*

Is . . .

What is love? An extension of like. What is lust? An extension.

—*Rodney Dangerfield*

Love is staying awake all night with a sick child. Or a very healthy adult.

—*David Frost*

Love is a feeling you feel when you're about to feel a feeling you never felt before.

—*Flip Wilson*

and Men

A guy knows he's in love when he loses interest in his car for a couple of days.

—*Tim Allen*

Fifty percent of the American population spends less than ten dollars a month on romance. You know what we call these people? Men.

—*Jay Leno*

Ah, those three magic words. You want to start a fight, ask a man this question: "Do you love me?" "Ah fuck, here we go. I told you a long time ago. When you got that income tax check. Not the state, the federal. Memmer?" "But do you love me?" "I'm here, ain't I? All my tools are at your mom's house. You cosigned on the truck. Where am I going?"

—*George Lopez*

## MAGAZINES

Health

I know I need some kind of athletic activity in my life, so I subscribed to a couple of health magazines. There's nothing better than kicking back with a cigarette, a Budweiser, and *Prevention* magazine, and reading about what nicotine, alcohol, and sloth will do to me. The anxiety alone raises my heart rate.
—*Cindee Weiss*

Nudie

We should pass a new law: Nobody can get famous just by sleeping with a celebrity and getting naked in a magazine. You have to make a contribution to society, first. You can still be in *Playboy*; you just have to do something worthwhile beforehand. "I developed a vaccine, and I'd like to show you my breasts." Go ahead, you've earned it.
—*Elayne Boosler*

My old boyfriend used to say, "I read *Playboy* for the articles." Right, and I go to shopping malls for the music.
—*Rita Rudner*

There's very little advice in men's magazines, because men don't think there's a lot they don't know. Women want to learn. Men think, "I know what I'm doing; just show me somebody naked."
—*Jerry Seinfeld*

Soap Opera Digest

Why would anyone want to read *Soap Opera Digest?* You're reading gossip about people who don't exist!
—*Margot Black*

Sports Illustrated

I don't understand the *Sports Illustrated* swimsuit issue. Bikini models in a magazine about sports? That'll make sense the day I see Dick Butkus in the Victoria's Secret catalog.
—*Sheila Wenz*

## MAGIC

I don't like magic, because I try to figure out how it's done, and I get frustrated. Just like porn videos.
—*Garry Shandling*

**MAINSTREAM**     The reason the mainstream is thought of as a stream is
                   because of its shallowness.
                          *—George Carlin*

**MAPS**           At home I have a map of the United States, actual size. I
                   spent all summer folding it.
                          *—Steven Wright*

**MARRIAGE**       See also: **DIVORCE, HUSBANDS, MEN, SINGLE, WED-
                   DINGS, WIVES**

                   I love being married. It's so great to find that one special
                   person you want to annoy for the rest of your life.
                          *—Rita Rudner*

Adultery           Never tell. Not if you love your wife . . . in fact, if your lady
                   walks in on you, deny it. Yeah. Just flat out: "I'm telling ya.
                   This chick came downstairs with a sign around her neck,
                   'Lay on Top of Me, or I'll Die.'"
                          *—Lenny Bruce*

                   I will not cheat on my wife. Because I love my house.
                          *—Chas Elstner*

                   It's a good marriage, but I think my wife has been fooling
                   around. Because our parrot keeps saying, "Give it to me
                   hard and fast before my husband Jonathan Katz comes
                   home. And yes, I'd love a cracker."
                          *—Jonathan Katz*

                   I went home and saw a trail of clothes leading to my bed-
                   room. A bra here, another bra there, two pairs of panties,
                   jeans over by the chair. I hear moanin' and groanin'. My
                   heart pounding, I opened the door, and my wife was in bed
                   with a beautiful young woman. I said with disgust, "You
                   nasty, no-good, double-crossing, unfaithful—move over!"
                          *—Bernie Mac*

I discovered my wife in bed with another man, and I was crushed. So I said, "Get off of me, you two!"
    —*Emo Philips*

You can't just have an adultery; you "commit" adultery. And you can't commit adultery unless you already have a commitment. Once you commit, then you can commit the adultery—and then you get caught, get divorced, lose your mind, and they have you committed.
    —*Jerry Seinfeld*

Anniversaries

I celebrated twenty years of marriage and I did it the hard way: four men.
    —*Joanne Astrow*

My husband and I celebrated our thirty-eighth wedding anniversary. You know what I finally realized? If I had killed the man the first time I thought about it, I'd have been out of jail by now.
    —*Anita Milner*

For my parents' fiftieth wedding anniversary I sent them on a trip to Florida. I paid for everything—they were thrilled. First time they'd been on a bus.
    —*Stu Trivax*

Arguments

Never go to bed mad. Stay up and fight.
    —*Phyllis Diller*

My parents only had one argument in forty-five years. It lasted forty-three years.
    —*Cathy Ladman*

Avoiding

I have a Y chromosome that makes me ask, "Why get married?" But I wouldn't want to put down marriage as a whole—which it is.
    —*Kevin Hench*

My take on marriage is this: Why buy the butcher when you can get the sausage for free?
—*Jen Kerwin*

Why get married and make one man miserable, when I can stay single and make thousands miserable?
—*Carrie Snow*

Before

You know what I did before I married? Anything I wanted to.
—*Henny Youngman*

Better or Worse

They say marriage is a contract. No, it's not. Contracts come with warrantees. When something goes wrong, you can take it back to the manufacturer. If your husband starts acting up, you can't take him back to his mama's house. "I don't know; he just stopped working. He's just laying around making a funny noise."
—*Wanda Sykes*

We were married for better or worse. I couldn't have done better, and she couldn't have done worse.
—*Henny Youngman*

Completion

A man is incomplete until he's married. Then he's really finished.
—*Henny Youngman*

Confidence

You get more confident when you're married. When you're single and you don't hear from your boyfriend, you wonder, "Should I call him?" When you're married and you don't hear from your husband, you wonder what you should call him.
—*Rita Rudner*

Control

Let us now set forth one of the fundamental truths about marriage: The wife is in charge.
—*Bill Cosby*

As soon as you say "I do," you'll discover that marriage is like a car. Both of you might be sitting in the front seat, but only one of you is driving. And most marriages are more like a motorcycle than a car. Somebody has to sit in the back, and you have to yell just to be heard.
—*Wanda Sykes*

I know a man who thinks marriage is a fifty-fifty proposition, which convinces us that he doesn't understand women or percentages.
—*Henny Youngman*

**Difficulty**

Marriage is very difficult. Marriage is like a five-thousand-piece jigsaw puzzle, all sky.
—*Cathy Ladman*

It's not easy to keep a marriage together in Hollywood because, well, we sleep with so many people.
—*Steve Martin*

Marriage is real tough because you have to deal with feelings, and lawyers.
—*Richard Pryor*

**End of**

What happened to my marriage? It was broken up by my mother-in-law. My wife came home from work early, and she found us in bed together.
—*Lenny Bruce*

My wife left me. I should have seen it coming; for the past year she called me her insignificant other. By the end of the marriage her favorite position was man on top, woman visiting her mother.
—*Daniel Liebert*

**and Exercise**

Married people don't have to exercise, because our attitude is "They've seen us naked already, and they like it."
—*Carol Montgomery*

Gay      See: **HOMOSEXUALITY**

Gifts

For our anniversary, I got my wife one of those fur coat kits. A Velcro coat with a hundred gerbils.
    *—Tom Arnold*

After a fight I'd bring my wife one red rose. Of all the presents you can get a woman there really is nothing like that one rose to say, "Honey, sweetheart, this is just to let you know I'm so cheap."
    *—Danny Liebert*

Happy

Your marriage is in trouble if your wife says, "You're only interested in one thing," and you can't remember what it is.
    *—Milton Berle*

Being happily married is like having a shit job with people you dig.
    *—Jack Coen*

I think the bottom-line difference between being single and being married is this: When you're single you're as happy as you are. When you're married, you can only be happy as the least happy person in the apartment.
    *—Tom Hertz*

You know your marriage is in trouble when your wife starts wearing the wedding ring on her middle finger.
    *—Dennis Miller*

There's a study in Maine that found if you marry someone who doesn't appreciate you, tries to control you, and always has to be right, you may be unhappy. They also discovered that going without water for long periods of time makes you thirsty.
    *—Caroline Rhea*

A man doesn't know what real happiness is until he's married. Then it's too late.
—*Henny Youngman*

The secret of a happy marriage remains a secret.
—*Henny Youngman*

**Licenses**

Never, ever, discount the idea of marriage. Sure, someone might tell you that marriage is just a piece of paper. Well, so is money, and what's more life-affirming than cold, hard cash?
—*Dennis Miller*

**Living Together**

That married couples can live together day after day is a miracle that the Vatican has overlooked.
—*Bill Cosby*

My wife wouldn't live with me before we were married. Now that we've been married for fifteen years I'm trying to talk her into getting her own place again.
—*Jeff Jena*

**Longevity**

My parents stayed together for forty years, but that was out of spite.
—*Woody Allen*

My parents have been married for fifty-five years. The secret to their longevity? "Outlasting your opponent."
—*Cathy Ladman*

I was married for a short time. Just long enough to realize all those comedians weren't joking.
—*Daniel Lybra*

After seven years of marriage, I'm sure of two things: First, never wallpaper together; and second, you'll need two bathrooms, both for her.
—*Dennis Miller*

Getting married is a lot like getting into a tub of hot water. After you get used to it, it ain't so hot.
> —*Minnie Pearl*

My mom had good advice for me about how to stay married for a long time. She said, "Always remember, honesty is very important. It must be avoided. And the most important thing is, you have to let your husband be himself, and you have to pretend he's someone else."
> —*Rita Rudner*

I was married for two years. Which is a long time if you break it down into half-hour segments.
> —*Charisse Savarin*

They say married men live longer. It just seems longer.
> —*Bobby Slayton*

Maybe

I've never been married. I'd like to find that special someone I can grow old with. Someone I can nurture. Someone who can straighten out my finances.
> —*Mike Dugan*

I'd marry the right girl. Someone beautiful, successful, and independent who only wants to talk about me.
> —*Richard Jeni*

Every single one of my friends from high school has long since tied the knot. And I'm getting older. I guess I should think about hanging myself, too.
> —*Laura Kightlinger*

I'm in my thirties, and my parents really want me to get married. My father wants me to stop using his name . . . Kenny.
> —*Wendy Liebman*

Men Versus
Women

A woman marries hoping that he will change, and he doesn't.
A man marries hoping she won't change, and she does.
   —*Joey Bishop*

Now, of course, I realize that a mixed marriage means one
between a man and a woman.
   —**Michael Feldman**

The problem with marriage is that it involves men and
women. And that's a pretty bad match.
   —**Cathy Ladman**

Marriage is not a man's idea. A woman must have thought of
it. Years ago some guy said, "Let me get this straight, honey. I
can't sleep with anyone else for the rest of my life, and if
things don't work out, you get to keep half my stuff? What a
great idea."
   —**Bobby Slayton**

Money

My mother always said, "Don't marry for money. Divorce
for money."
   —*Wendy Liebman*

Monogamy

If variety is the spice of life, marriage is the big can of
leftover Spam.
   —*Johnny Carson*

Being married is like getting to have your favorite soft drink
any time you want. But only your favorite soft drink. It's
monogamous. You feel like a hot drink, you better heat
up some Mr. Pibb.
   —*Jeff Cesario*

A study shows that monogamous couples live longer. And
cheaters who don't get caught live longer than cheaters who
do get caught.
   —*Jay Leno*

It can take a man several marriages to understand the importance of monogamy.
—*Jason Love*

Newly Wed

My wife and I have been married almost a year. The first year's the hardest, and then the second's even harder.
—*Tom Arnold*

We've been married three months. I'm just not used to being wrong so often.
—*Dennis Regan*

All men make mistakes, but married men find out about them sooner.
—*Red Skelton*

The first part of our marriage was very happy. But then, on the way back from the ceremony . . .
—*Henny Youngman*

to Older Men

I married an older man. Foreplay took a little longer, but at least his hand shook.
—*Jenny Jones*

The old saying was, "Marry an older man because they're mature." The saying now is, "Marry a young man because men don't mature."
—*Rita Rudner*

Prenuptial Agreements

My husband and I didn't sign a prenuptial agreement. We signed a mutual suicide pact.
—*Roseanne Barr*

Remarriage

Remarrying a husband you've divorced is like having your appendix put back in.
—*Phyllis Diller*

I don't understand couples who break up and get back together, especially couples who divorce and remarry. That's like pouring milk on a bowl of cereal, tasting it, and saying, "This milk is sour. Well, I'll put it back in the refrigerator; maybe it will be okay tomorrow."

      *—Larry Miller*

My wife and I got remarried. Our divorce didn't work out.

      *—Henny Youngman*

**Second**

I just got married. It's my husband's second marriage. If you think it's hard to get a guy who's never been married to commit, try to get a guy to go back and do it all over again. It's like talking a vet back into Vietnam.

      *—Cory Kahaney*

I'm going to marry again because I'm more mature now, and I need some kitchen stuff.

      *—Wendy Liebman*

**Separation**

We sleep in separate rooms; we have dinner apart; we take separate vacations. We're doing everything we can to keep our marriage together.

      *—Rodney Dangerfield*

**Sex**

Before I got married, my wife told me, "Don't talk about sex until we get married." We got married and she said, "Now you can talk about it all you want."

      *—Rodney Dangerfield*

When we got married, I told my wife I like sex twice a day. She said, "Me, too." Now we never see each other.

      *—Rodney Dangerfield*

Sex when you're married is like going to the 7-Eleven: There's not much variety, but at three in the morning, it's always there.

      *—Carol Leifer*

A survey asked married women when they most want to have sex. Eighty-four percent of them said right after their husband is finished.

*—Jay Leno*

Making love while you're married is like being a bad Little League player. Even if you suck, they still have to put you in for two innings.

*—Buzz Nutley*

**Shared Beliefs**

My father says, "Marry a girl who has the same beliefs as the family." I said, "Dad, why would I want a girl who thinks I'm a schmuck?"

*—Adam Sandler*

**Standards**

The older you get the lower your standards get. I used to be so picky. Oh when I get married he's going to be tall, handsome, rich . . . and I'm down to: registered voter. I'd marry a midget just for the handicapped parking.

*—Kathleen Madigan*

**Tricked into**

He tricked me into marrying him. He told me he was pregnant.

*—Carol Leifer*

**Versus Single**

Married or single? I have to compare the disadvantages of each. You've got to say to yourself, "Hey, do I want to stay a single guy, and run around in bars with a bunch of different morons? Or, do I want to be married with a family, and stay home with the exact same group of morons?"

*—Richard Jeni*

I love being married. I was single for a long time, and I just got so sick of finishing my own sentences.

*—Brian Kiley*

When you're single, you're the dictator of your own life: "I give the order to fall asleep on the sofa in the middle of the day!" When married, you're part of a vast decision-making body, and this is if the marriage works. That's what's so painful about divorce: You get impeached, and you're not even the president.

*—Jerry Seinfeld*

**MASSAGES**

I'm trying to get stress out of my life. I had a massage about a month ago. Have you had one? Did they put the whipped cream on you, too? It's a weird thing the first time getting a massage because you're lying on a table naked, being touched by a stranger. Which is very, very nice. They try and relax you. He played music, which was a little aggravating. The trombone kept hitting me in the head . . . at least I think it was a trombone.

*—Ellen DeGeneres*

My husband likes massages. I booked a masseuse to come to the house. Wasn't that a good idea? I thought so, until the doorbell rang, and there was an eighteen-year-old blonde girl standing there, saying, "I'm here to give your husband a massage." I said, "He's dead."

*—Rita Rudner*

**MASTURBATION**     See: **SEX**

**MATURITY**

The older I get, the simpler the definition of maturity seems: It's the length of time between when I realize someone is a jackass and when I tell them that they're one.

*—Brett Butler*

**MEDICINE**     See also: **DOCTORS**

Alternative

The only difference between alternative medicine and an HMO is that more doctors believe HMOs don't work.

*—Wally Wang*

Ambulances

I don't get no respect. The time I got hurt, on the way to the hospital the ambulance stopped for gas.
— *Rodney Dangerfield*

I was in front of an ambulance the other day, and I noticed that the word "ambulance" was spelled in reverse print on the hood. I thought, "Well, isn't that clever?" In the rearview mirror, I can read the word "ambulance" behind me. Of course, while you're reading, you don't see where you're going; you crash; you need an ambulance. I think they're just trying to drum up some business, on the way back from lunch.
— *Jerry Seinfeld*

Anesthesia

Can you imagine what a nightmare it must have been before they invented painkillers? What did they do, have a guy bite a bullet? They could have done better than that. Bring in a big-breasted woman. That would distract any man. Stick a knife through their arm: They see those big breasts, they don't feel a thing.
— *Joy Behar*

I had general anesthesia. That's so weird. You go to sleep in one room, and then you wake up four hours later in a totally different room. Just like college.
— *Ross Shafer*

Cholesterol

I had my cholesterol checked, and it's higher than my SATs. I can now get into any college based on my cholesterol check.
— *Garry Shandling*

I had a cholesterol test: They found bacon.
— *Bob Zany*

HMOs

See also: X-rays

Some people have physicians who are in an HMO or a PPO. Mine are in a UFO: You want to believe they exist, but there's really no evidence.

—*Reno Goodale*

Hospitalization

My dad's in the hospital, and he's critical. He's okay. He just complains about the room; he can't stand the nurses; he hates the food. . . .

—*Reno Goodale*

Mammograms

Mammogram. You ever get one of those things? They put your breast in a vise, and take it hostage. Start cranking it shut, like you have the secret rocket formula. You don't think it's ever going to get back into its natural shape; you'll be rolling it up to get it back in the bra. Put a little ham key on the end of it.

—*Margaret Smith*

Medication

Anything wrong, black people take aspirin. "He got a fever." "Give him some aspirin." "He got chills." "Give him some aspirin." "He stepped on a nail." "Crush up some aspirin, and rub it all over." "He got shot." "Take the whole jar of aspirin, and put it right in that hole, with some duct tape or newspaper or something."

—*Bernie Mac*

What's great about aspirin is that no matter how long you suck on it, it never loses its flavor.

—*Gregg Rogell*

The pain-relieving ingredient, there's always got to be a lot of that. Nobody wants anything less than Extra-Strength. "Give me the maximum allowable human dosage. Figure out what will kill me, and then back it off a little bit."

—*Jerry Seinfeld*

None

We could be coughing blood, but Latino people never go to the doctor. Your family encourages you not to go: "If I were you, I wouldn't go, because they're gonna find something wrong. Have you drank 7-UP? Drink it, and burp it up, *mira*. Because two years ago I had leukemia, *muchingo un* Sprite, with a lemon. And *si*, look at me now!"
          *—George Lopez*

I just got a vasectomy. I didn't mean to; my pocketknife opened by mistake.
          *—Reno Goodale*

I had my appendix removed. There was nothing wrong with it. I just did it as a warning to the other organs in my body to shape up or they're out of there.
          *—Charlie Viracola*

Patches

My male roommate and I mixed up our nicotine and testosterone patches. He got cranky and hungry. I got a raise and a corner office.
          *—Karen Ripley*

Placebos

I'm addicted to placebos. I'd give them up, but it wouldn't make any difference.
          *—Jay Leno*

X-rays

I had a chest X-ray last month, and they found a spot on my lung. Fortunately, it was barbecue sauce.
          *—George Carlin*

Do you know how to avoid overexposure to X-rays? Join an HMO.
          *—Jay Leno*

**MEDITATION**

My son has taken up meditation. At least it's better than sitting doing nothing.
          *—Max Kauffman*

I took up meditation. I like to have an espresso first just to make it more challenging.
—*Betsy Salkind*

## MEMORY

Did you ever walk into a room and forget why you walked in? I think that's how dogs spend their lives.
—*Sue Murphy*

### Men

Men forget everything; women remember everything. That's why men need instant replays in sports. They've already forgotten what happened.
—*Rita Rudner*

### Women

Women don't get mad at you about something you just did. They have precision memory, for everything you've ever done: time, date, place, what you said, and your hand position when you said it. This memory will never crash; it probably keeps ticking after she does. You bury her, and from six feet under you'll hear a muffled shout, "AT THE CHURCH PICNIC, 1985, WHAT KIND OF LOOK WAS THAT YOU GAVE KENE-SHA, MISTER BIG EYES?"
—*Sinbad*

## MEN

See also: **GENDER DIFFERENCES, WOMEN**

### Are . . .

Men are liars. We'll lie about lying if we have to. I'm an algebra liar. I figure two good lies make a positive.
—*Tim Allen*

Men are pigs. Too bad we own everything.
—*Tim Allen*

Men are like flowers. If you don't know how to handle a rose, you get stuck by a couple of pricks.
—*Margot Black*

Men are like pay phones. Some of them take your money. Most of them don't work, and when you find one that does, someone else is on it.

—*Catherine Franco*

Men are simple things. They can survive a whole weekend with only three things: beer, boxer shorts, and batteries for the remote control.

—*Diana Jordan*

Men are delusional. Hugh Hefner lounges around in a bathrobe with three live-in girlfriends. You know guys are sitting at home watching the *Playboy* channel and thinking, "That could be me. I've got a bathrobe."

—*Denise Munro Robb*

Get two women together, one will say, "Men are dogs." Men are not dogs, because you can trust dogs. I never found panties in my dog's car. My dog never ran up my phone bill calling 900-numbers to talk dirty to some nasty ho. My dog doesn't have another family across town he's hiding. Dogs are loyal, they protect you, and they can lick their own balls.

—*Wanda Sykes*

I was talking to a businessman, and I said, "Don't you think most men are little boys?" And he said, "I'm no little boy! I make $75,000 a year." And I said, "Well, the way I look at it, you just have bigger toys."

—*Jonathan Winters*

**and Bathrooms**    All I have to say about men and bathrooms is: They're not too specific.

—*Rita Rudner*

**Bragging Rights**    When men get together there's a lot of ego at stake. Ever see two guys meet each other for the first time? Within five minutes, there's a top-it contest of life achievements. The first guy will say something innocuous like, "When I was a kid, I went to the last game when the Mets won the World Series." The other guy goes, "I went to Woodstock. Sat on a speaker." "I'm on a first-name basis with the Unknown Soldier." "I was the busboy at the Last Supper." "I remember you. How did you like the tip?"

—*Joe Bolster*

Men brag about the bad shit that happens. "Tell 'em about the time you got electrocuted." "My feet were wet, man, and I plugged the thing in. I felt the 'lectric going through me, but somehow my mind told my hands, because I was holding a beer, and I didn't drop one drop!"

—*George Lopez*

Crying

Men do cry, but only when assembling furniture.

—*Rita Rudner*

Faithfulness

A man is only as faithful as his options.

—*Chris Rock*

Feminine Side

I wish men would get more in touch with their feminine side, and become self-destructive.

—*Betsy Salkind*

and Marriage

Men don't settle down. Men surrender.

—*Chris Rock*

Nipples

Here's something I've never understood: How come men have nipples? What's the point? They're like plastic fruit.

—*Carol Leifer*

Perfect

The only perfect man is Mr. Ed. He's hung like a horse and can hold a conversation.

—*Traci Skene*

Plans

All plans between men are tentative, if one man should have an opportunity to pursue a woman. It doesn't matter how important the arrangements are: When they scrub a space shuttle, it's because an astronaut met someone on his way to the launch pad. They hold the countdown; he's leaning against the rocket talking to her, "What do you say we get together for some Tang?"

—*Jerry Seinfeld*

Reason for Living

My mom said the only reason men are alive is for lawn care and vehicle maintenance.

—*Tim Allen*

Sensitivity

Men are sensitive in strange ways. If a man has built a fire and the last log does not burn, he will take it personally.

—*Rita Rudner*

and Sex

My mom always said, "Men are like linoleum floors. You lay them right, and you can walk on them for thirty years."

—*Brett Butler*

Researchers say Stonehenge was built in the form of the female sex organ. No wonder it's baffled men for five thousand years.

—*Jay Leno*

Women say they have sexual thoughts too. They have no idea. It's the difference between shooting a bullet and throwing it. If they knew what we were really thinking, they'd never stop slapping us.

—*Larry Miller*

Men and women behave like our basic sexual elements. Single men on a weekend act like sperm: disorganized, bumping into each other, swimming in the wrong direction. "Let me through!" "You're on my tail!" They're the Three Billion Stooges. But the egg is cool: "Well, who's it going to be? I can divide. I can wait a month. I'm not swimming anywhere."

—*Jerry Seinfeld*

They say men get sexier as they get older. No, sexy men get sexier as they get older; the rest of us get red sports cars.
   —*Jeff Shaw*

**Thinking**

Men always scratch their ass when they're thinking. Because that's where their brain is.
   —*Tim Allen*

Guys, have you ever been quiet for a minute around your girl? What's the first thing women ask? "What are you thinking?" And guys always reply, "Nothing." Ladies, believe them! They can actually do that. Leave the man alone. If you keep bugging him, he's gonna be thinking, "Will you shut the fuck up? That's what I was thinking."
   —*Wanda Sykes*

**Versus Women**

Guys are like dogs. They keep comin' back. Ladies are like cats. Yell at a cat one time, they're gone.
   —*Lenny Bruce*

**Want**

I know what men want. Men want to be really, really close to someone who will leave them alone.
   —*Elayne Boosler*

What do men want? Men want a mattress that cooks.
   —*Judy Tenuta*

**MENOPAUSE**

I exercise; I diet; I meditate. I still want to rip someone's head off. The only good thing about menopause is that it helps me get in touch with my inner bitch. Do you know why the menopausal woman crossed the road? To kill the chicken.
   —*Jane Condon*

A new study found that menopausal women who smoke are more likely to have hot flashes, and women who smoke while having a hot flash are more likely to burst into flames.
   —*Caroline Rhea*

**MENSTRUATION**     See also: **PREMENSTRUAL SYNDROME**

I needed a pint of Ben and Jerry's Super Fudge Chunk and box of tampons. Pretty much if you're shopping for one, you're shopping for the other. The cashier checked me out and asked, "Paper or plastic?" I said, "Oh, I don't want a bag. I just want to walk down the street with these things out in front of me, and watch people get out of my way."
    —*Sabrina Matthews*

and Men

I would like it if men had to partake in the same hormonal cycles to which we're subjected monthly. Maybe that's why men declare war, because they have a need to bleed on a regular basis.
    —*Brett Butler*

**MENTAL DISORDERS**     See also: **NEUROSES, THERAPY**

Depression

Studies show that 80 percent of the population suffers from depression, and the other 20 percent of you cause it.
    —*Dana Eagle*

Mood Swings

When I was little I had a mood swing set.
    —*Steven Wright*

Obsessive Compulsive

I'm an obsessive compulsive. I joined the Obsessive Compulsive Society because they said I could join as many times as I want.
    —*Chuck Johnson*

**MICROWAVES**     See: **COOKING**

**MILITARY**     See also: **WEAPONS**

The whole idea of the military strikes me as completely absurd. What sense does it make to go off somewhere thousands of miles away to a scorching desert, to kill a lot of people who have never done anything to me, when I can sit

in air-conditioned comfort of my own home and take out a few
people who really matter?
—*E. L. Greggory*

I was serving my country. It was either that, or six months.
—*Richard Pryor*

Air Force

Why does the Air Force need expensive new bombers?
Have the people we've been bombing over the years been
complaining?
—*George Wallace*

Army

Being in the Army is like being in the Boy Scouts, except that
the Boy Scouts have adult supervision.
—*Blake Clark*

I joined the Army because I was eighteen and bored with the
tenth grade.
—*Robert Hawkins*

Gays

I'd like to see gays in the military. If my wife will give me a
night off now and then.
—*Dylan Brody*

I spent five years in the Air Force, and if it wasn't for sexual
harassment no one would have talked to me at all. An officer
accused me of being a lesbian. I would have denied it, but I
was lying naked on top of her at the time.
—*Lynda Montgomery*

Why can't they have gay people in the Army? Personally, I
think they are just afraid of a thousand guys with M16s going,
"Who'd you call a faggot?"
—*Jon Stewart*

Money for

We spend so much money on the military, yet we're slashing education budgets throughout the country. No wonder we've got smart bombs and stupid fucking children.
—*Jon Stewart*

Planes

There's the stealth plane, the invisible plane. What good is an invisible airplane going to do? The enemy looks down on their radar and says, "We'll, there's no aircraft here. But there's two little guys in a sitting position at 40,000 feet."
—*Will Durst*

The stealth bomber replaced the B-1 bomber, which was supposed to avoid enemy radar by flying at treetop level. Unfortunately, trees are at treetop level.
—*Jack Mayberry*

Senior Service

Why have we always insisted on asking our young men, and now young women, in the flower of their lives, to risk themselves in combat? Why not use a human wave of our elderly to scare the enemy? What do these people really have to lose? The worst four years of their lives?
—*Al Franken*

Women in

Remember the whole controversy about whether or not women in the service should be in combat? Can women fight? Can women kill? Yeah, I think so. Just have the general come over and say, "Hey, see the enemy over there? I just heard them talking. They say you look fat in your uniform."
—*Elayne Boosler*

If we wanted to be part of an institution that is hostile to gays and women, we could just stay home with our families.
—*Georgia Ragsdale*

Veterans

Vietnam vets, I have a lot of empathy for them. They had to go to a horrible place and perform a hideous job for people

who didn't even appreciate it. I know what that's like; I used
to be a waitress at Denny's.

    *—Roseanne Barr*

**MILITIAS**      Militias are a bunch of crazy white dudes who are mad at the
government. But the government of this country was con-
structed for white men, by white men. Wasn't nobody else covered in the Constitution. No black people, no Indians, no
Jews, no women. We might have been there when they was
writing the Constitution, but y'all had us serving the tea.
Didn't ask us what it should say.

    *—D. L. Hughley*

**MIMES**      Some things aren't funny. Beatings aren't funny. Stabbings
aren't funny. Mimes aren't funny. But beating and stabbing a
mime—why is that hilarious?

    *—Dave Attell*

I'm walking to work this morning, and I see one of those mime
performers. So the mime is doing that famous mime routine
where he's pretending to be trapped in a box. And, he finishes
up, and thank God he wasn't really trapped in a box. And I see
on the sidewalk there he's got a little hat for money. So I went
over and I pretended to put a dollar bill in his hat.

    *—David Letterman*

My uncle was thrown out of a mime show for having a seizure.
They thought he was heckling.

    *—Jeff Shaw*

If you shoot a mime, should you use a silencer?

    *—Steven Wright*

**MODELS**      The world would be a safer place if supermodels used their
powers to fight more than just fashion crime.

    *—Brian Beatty*

I'm not a model, and that's OK with me. Because I don't want to look like a whippet or any other shaky dog.
—*Karen Kilgariff*

I found this site where models are selling their eggs over the Internet. Oh great, that's what this world needs, more vanity. Not more Einsteins or Picassos: more anorexic, cat-walking hat racks.
—*Kris McGaha*

## MONKEYS

See: **PETS**

## MONSTERS

### Frankenstein

If I was Dr. Frankenstein, I would take out the appendix before bringing the creature to life.
—*Vinny Badabing*

Frankenstein was a strange monster. He never caught any black people. No Mexicans, either. He only went after very scared white people. He never went into the ghetto. A black guy with Nikes would have run circles around his ass. "Yeah, come on, Frankie, bring your green ass over here." If Frankenstein went into the barrio, the Mexicans would've taken those bolts right out of his head. "Well, thanks, man. We need that shit for our tires. I'm glad you showed up. My wheel was loose."
—*Paul Rodriguez*

### Godzilla

A lot of the movies that were made in Japan had monsters in them. Can you imagine a widow trying to collect on her husband's insurance policy? "Tell me once again, Mrs. Ochichoba. How did Hideo die?" "He was bitten in half by Godzilla." "That is most unfortunate, because I see he's only covered for Rodan."
—*Franklin Ajaye*

Loch Ness

Here's a news item: The Loch Ness Monster surfaced today and asked if she had any messages.
—*George Carlin*

Vampires

In scary movies, people always get bitten in the neck. To me, that means they don't even try to run. If a vampire gets close to me, I'm off and running away! When they find my body, the police will say, "Call the *X-Files*. This man has two holes in his butt, and no blood in his body."
—*Sinbad*

Werewolves

During a lunar eclipse, werewolves get stuck with just sideburns and a goatee.
—*Craig Kilborn*

**MOONING**

See also: **EMPLOYMENT** Office Parties

Never moon a werewolf.
—*Mike Binder*

Here's a health warning: Don't moon a pit bull after sitting in A-1 sauce.
—*Johnny Carson*

**MOTHERHOOD**

See: **BABIES, BIRTH, MOTHERS, PARENTHOOD, PARENTS, PREGNANCY**

I've been married fourteen years, and I have three kids. Obviously, I breed well in captivity.
—*Roseanne Barr*

Difficulty

You get a lot of tension, you get a lot of headaches. I do what it says on the aspirin bottle: Take two and keep away from children.
—*Roseanne Barr*

Being a mother is harder than being a surgeon. At least you get schooling and training first before they let you start cutting people open. Also you can quit being a surgeon when

you're ready. Patients aren't going to keep following you
around with a snotty nose: "Doc, Doc, Doc!"
—*Wanda Sykes*

Intuition

I don't think I'll ever have a mother's intuition. My sister
left me alone in a restaurant with my ten-month-old nephew.
I said, "What do I do if he cries?" She said, "Give him some
vegetables." It turns out jalapeño is not his favorite.
—*Janine DiTullio*

as Job

The way I feel, if the kids are still alive when my husband
comes home from work, I've done my job.
—*Roseanne Barr*

I have one of those 24/7 jobs: I'm a divorced mom with
no alimony.
—*Sully Diaz*

and Love

I tell you there is no love sweeter than the love between a
mother and a child. Now I know my wife loves me, but I am
reasonably sure that she doesn't look at me the same way
she looks at them. You know it's kind of humbling because
you realize at some point you're just a date that worked out.
—*Dennis Miller*

Maybe

I think I'd be a good mother, maybe a little overprotective.
Like I'd never let the kid out—of my body.
—*Wendy Liebman*

I'd like to have kids. I get those maternal feelings. Like when
I'm laying on the couch and I can't reach the remote control.
—*Kathleen Madigan*

Surrogates

The Vatican came down with a new ruling: no surrogate
mothers. Good thing they didn't make this rule before Jesus
was born.
—*Elayne Boosler*

In this day and age women can have kids for other women through surrogate motherhood. Is this the ultimate favor or what? I think I'm a good friend. I'll help you move. But whatever comes out of me after nine months, I'm keeping. I don't care if it's a shoe.

*—Sue Kolinsky*

Surrogate mothers make me wonder: When is the right time to ask someone if you can borrow their uterus? Probably not right after you realize you didn't return their lawn mower.

*—Cyndi Stiles*

**MOTHERS**          See also: **BABIES**, **BIRTH**, **MOTHERHOOD**, **PARENTHOOD**, **PARENTS**, **PREGNANCY**

I know how to do anything: I'm a mom.

*—Roseanne Barr*

My mother has gossip dyslexia. She has to talk in front of people's backs.

*—Richard Lewis*

My mother loved children. She would have given anything if I had been one.

*—Groucho Marx*

The relationship between mothers and children never changes, and that's because no matter how rich or powerful you are your mother still remembers when you were three and put Spaghetti-Os up your nose.

*—Dennis Miller*

Adoption          I asked my mother if I was adopted. She said, "Not yet, but we placed an ad."

*—Dana Snow*

Advice

My mother thinks everything can be fixed with crafting and prayer: "Let God and glue into your life."
—*Monique Marvez*

My mom taught me everything I needed to know. Don't talk to strangers; don't pay retail; and the size of your hair should always match the size of your ass.
—*Stephanie Schiern*

My mom, she wakes me at six in the morning and says, "The early bird catches the worm." If I want a worm, Mom, I'll drink a bottle of tequila.
—*Pam Stone*

Angry

If you're looking for a way to piss your mother off, here's what I suggest: Next time you're driving with your mother, stop in front of the local strip joint. Put the car in park and say, "I'll be right back. I just have to run in and pick up my check."
—*Judy Gold*

My mom is one of those really angry moms who gets mad at absolutely everything. Once when I was a little kid, I accidentally knocked a Flintstones glass off the kitchen table. She said, "Well, dammit, we can't have nice things."
—*Paula Poundstone*

Cleaning

Moms will clean up everything. Scientists have proven that a mom's spit is the exact chemical composition of Formula 409. Mom's spit on a Kleenex—you get rust off a bumper with that.
—*Jeff Foxworthy*

My mother from time to time puts on her wedding dress. Not because she's sentimental. She just gets really far behind in her laundry.
—*Brian Kiley*

My mom is a neat freak. If she adopted a highway, she'd mop it once a week. She'd reroute traffic: "Don't drive on my clean freeway!"

—*Daniel Liebert*

Compliments

My mom is so sweet. She said to me, "You look so young for your age. It must be your pimples."

—*Jayne Warren*

Coupons

My mom thinks coupons are money, and gives them for gifts.

—*Jayne Warren*

Criticism

My mother just wrote her autobiography. Pick it up. It's in the stores right now. It's entitled, *I Came, I Saw, I Criticized*.

—*Judy Gold*

Discipline

In my day, adults were in control. Every time my mamma set down the law, she'd say, "I know you don't like it, Bean, and I know you're mad at me. But life isn't a popularity contest." Good thing, too. Lots of days she would have finished last for damn sure.

—*Bernie Mac*

and Food

The cheapest thing my mother ever bought was the peanut butter with the jelly inside. Peanut butter with jelly in the same jar—how low can you go? That's like buying a shoe with a sock sewn inside.

—*Chris Rock*

My mother complained about her order in a restaurant and tried to send it back. I had to stop her, "Ma, you can't send back food after you've finished eating it!"

—*Roberta Rockwell*

When it comes to food, my mother is neurotic. I tell my friends when they come over, "When you're done with the meal, my mother's going to try to give you more. If you want a little bit more, tell her, 'I'm full.' Boom, a little bit more. If you want a lot more, you tell her 'just a tiny bit.' Boom, another meal, just like that. But if you don't want any more, you have to shoot her."

—*Ray Romano*

**Haircuts by**

Why did Mom insist on cutting my hair herself until I was fourteen? She had a home haircut kit that looked like Mengele's briefcase and the barber skills of Dr. Leatherface brandishing a Flow-Bee.

—*Dennis Miller*

**Humor**

I got my sense of humor from my mother. When I was growing up, she refused to bake. She said, "Well, you just eat it."

—*Betsy Salkind*

**Love**

A mother's claim to your psyche is wholly substantiated because you love her. And you love her because she was your arrival terminal. She created you, so you always owe her and can never repay the debt. Being born is like asking Don Corleone a favor.

—*Dennis Miller*

I have trouble telling women my feelings. I think it goes back to the first time I told my mom I loved her. I said, "I love you, Mommy." And she said, "Slow down, I'm not ready for that kind of commitment. You're going way too fast."

—*Mike Rubin*

**Loyalty to**

I'm very loyal in a relationship, all relationships. When I'm with my mother, I don't look at other moms, "Wow. I wonder what her macaroni and cheese tastes like."

—*Garry Shandling*

**Name Calling**

My mother never saw the irony in calling me a son-of-a-bitch.

—*Richard Jeni*

When we were growing up my mother told my brother he was a pain in the neck. He became a chiropractor. I'm glad she didn't call him a pain in the ass.

—*Joel Warshaw*

Neurotic

My mom was a little weird. When I was little Mom would make chocolate frosting, and she'd let me lick the beaters. And then she'd turn them off.

—*Marty Cohen*

My mom is very possessive. She calls me up and says, "You weren't home last night. Is something going on?" I said, "Yeah, Mom. I'm cheating on you with another mother."

—*Heidi Joyce*

My mother is so neurotic. She puts down toilet paper on the seat even at our relative's house, at the dinner table.

—*Wendy Liebman*

I hope all my blood tests come back as negative as my mother is.

—*Kate Mason*

When my mother makes out her income tax return every year, under "occupation," she writes in, "Eroding my daughter's self-esteem."

—*Robin Roberts*

There's an old saying, "Neurotics build castles in the air, and psychotics live in them." My mother cleans them.

—*Rita Rudner*

My mother is so passive-aggressive. She says things to me like, "You just can't seem to do anything right, and that's what I really love about you."

—*Laura Silverman*

and Puberty      Once I was riding my bike, and my mom was waving to me
                 from her window. She said, "Judy, soon your body will
                 change." I said, "I know, like in puberty." She said, "No, that
                 Good Humor truck."
                           —*Judy Gold*

Seeing           You know you can put up a front in the real world, but your
                 mom sees through that faster than Superman sees through
                 Lois Lane's pantsuits.
                           —*Dennis Miller*

                 Saw my Mom today. It was all right; she didn't see me.
                           —*Margaret Smith*

Senior Moms      I'm so mad at my mother. She's 102 years old and she called
                 me up last week, said she wanted to borrow $10 for some
                 food. I told her, "Hey, I work for a living." So I lent her the
                 money, had my secretary bring it down, and yesterday she
                 calls me up and says she can't pay me back for a while.
                 What is this bullshit? So I worked it out with her. I'm gonna
                 have her carry my barbells up to the attic.
                           —*Steve Martin*

                 My mother says, "If I get senile, just put me in a home. I
                 don't want to be a burden to you." And I say, "Mom, I'd
                 shoot you dead before I would do that."
                           —*Laura Silverman*

and Sex          My mother and I had different attitudes toward sex. She
                 said, "Whatever you do, never sleep with a man until he
                 buys you a house." Well, it worked for her, and I got a swing
                 set out of the deal.
                           —*Judy Brown*

                 My mother is sixty, and her whole life she only slept with
                 one guy. She won't tell me who.
                           —*Wendy Liebman*

Single

I was raised by just my mom. See, my father died when I was eight years old. At least, that's what he told us in the letter.
—*Drew Carey*

Special
Occasions

Everything in my mother's house is for a special occasion that hasn't happened yet. My mother's waiting for the Pope to show up for dinner to break out the good stuff. Or Tony Danza.
—*Ray Romano*

Telephone
Calls

Instead of saying hello, my mother gets on the phone and says, "Guess who died?"
—*Dom Irrera*

I got on the phone, my mom said, "Hi! Is everything wrong?"
—*Richard Lewis*

I like to talk to my mother every single day, because hearing how delusional I may become one day makes me appreciate every day that I have left with my sanity.
—*Tami Vernekoff*

**MOTIVATION**

My dad's been listening to these subliminal self-help tapes. He said, "I've never felt better in my life. These are the best tapes in the world. You must buy the whole set. You must buy the whole set." I picked 'em up. I've been listening to them as I go to sleep. And I've got to tell you, I've never felt better in my life. These are the best tapes in the world. You must buy the whole set. You must buy the whole set.
—*Dylan Brody*

If you ask me, this country could do with a little less motivation. The people who are causing all the trouble seem highly motivated to me. Serial killers, stock swindlers, drug dealers, Christian Republicans. I'm not sure that motivation is always a good thing. You show me a lazy prick lying in bed all day watching TV, and I'll show you a guy who's not causing any trouble.
—*George Carlin*

**MOTOR VEHICLE AGENCY**   See also: **RELIGION** Afterlife

I've decided what the DMV needs is an arts and crafts section. If I'm going to throw away my whole day there, I might as well come out with a new potholder. And if they had a game of musical chairs set up, I think people would pay extra tax dollars for that.
— *Jeremy Beth Michaels*

**MOVIES**

Chick Flicks

I really detest movies like *Indecent Proposal* and *Pretty Woman* because they send the message to women that sleeping with a rich man is the ultimate goal, and, really, that's such a small part of it.
— *Laura Kightlinger*

My boyfriend won't see anything he terms a "chick film." That's any film where the woman talks.
— *Maura Lake*

Snack Bar

So I go to the snack bar. I don't think it should be legal to call anything that costs $18.50 a snack. "Those Twizzlers look good. Do you have financial aid?"
— *David Spade*

Talking at

I'll never understand why people go to movie theaters to have conversations. Going to the movies to talk is like going to a restaurant to cook. The idea is that you have paid your money to have someone do something better than you can do it yourself.
— *Rita Rudner*

**MOVING**

When I was about ten we moved because my father sold our house. Somehow the landlord found out about it, and we had to go.
— *A. Whitney Brown*

Last week I helped my friend stay put. It's a lot easier than helping someone move. I just went over to his house and made sure that he did not start to load shit into a truck.
—*Mitch Hedberg*

They say that moving is one of the most stressful things in life. Death in the family is the second most stressful, and moving your dead spouse is the third.
—*Kevin Nealon*

I'm moving to Mars next week. So, if you have any boxes . . .
—*Steven Wright*

**MUSEUMS**

You know it's not a good wax museum when there are wicks coming out of people's heads.
—*Rick Reynolds*

I went to a museum where they had all the heads and arms from the statues that are in all the other museums.
—*Steven Wright*

**MUSIC**

I hate music, especially when it's played.
—*Jimmy Durante*

and Age

Nothing separates the generations more than music. By the time a child is eight or nine, he has developed a passion for his own music that is even stronger than his passions for procrastination and weird clothes.
—*Bill Cosby*

When you are about thirty-five years old, something terrible always happens to music.
—*Steve Race*

Bands

I used to be in a band. You may have heard of us, the marching band. I chose the tuba based on this theory: If you're not

cool enough to be a cheerleader, make sure you're carrying something big enough to knock one on her ass.
—*Amy Barnes*

And then our band became a cappella, as we left the pawnshop.
—*Mitch Hedberg*

Concerts   Concerts are where they ruin all the songs you enjoyed on the radio.
—*Jason Love*

Country   I used to want to be a country western singer, but I took a test and I had too much self-esteem.
—*Brett Butler*

You might be a country music fan if you want to write country music but you can't think of any clean words that rhyme with truck.
—*Brian Koffman*

I don't like country music, but I don't mean to denigrate those who do. And for the people who like country music, denigrate means "put down."
—*Bob Newhart*

Discussing   Talking about music is like dancing about architecture.
—*Steve Martin*

Elvis   I got a job at Graceland. I got fired because I put up a plaque that said, "Ripping off black music for over half a century."
—*Dana Snow*

Instrumental   A friend of mine gave me a Philip Glass CD. I listened to it for five hours before I realized it had a scratch on it.
—*Emo Philips*

Instruments

I've been learning to play the banjo for almost seven years. If you do the crime, you have to do the time.
—*Brian Beatty*

I play the harmonica. The only way I can play is if I get my car going really fast, and stick it out the window.
—*Steven Wright*

Muzak

I worry that the person who thought up Muzak may be thinking up something else.
—*Lily Tomlin*

Opera

I bet opera would be popular if it was more like football, with cheerleaders and a halftime show during intermission.
—*Brian Beatty*

I love the opera. You can't sleep at home like that.
—*Larry Miller*

Rap

I was listening to rap music this afternoon. Not that I had a choice—it was coming out of a Jeep four miles away.
—*Nick DiPaulo*

Record Clubs

I joined the Columbia House Compact Disc Club. So far they've sent me over three hundred CDs for just a penny, plus court costs.
—*Jeff Shaw*

**MUSTACHES**        See: **HAIR**

**NAMES**

My son's name is Miles. Unless we're in Canada, then he's Kilometers.

    —*Jeff Jena*

I don't remember names; I remember faces. You should be introduced by the face, or whatever you remember about the person. Forget names. "Big Nose and Short Pants, come here a second. I want you to meet my buddy Hawaiian Shirt and a Bad Haircut."

    —*Paul Reiser*

**NATURE**

See: **OUTDOORS**

**NEIGHBOR-HOODS**

I tell ya, I come from a tough neighborhood. Why, just last week some guy pulled a knife on me. I could see it wasn't a real professional job. There was butter on it.

    —*Rodney Dangerfield*

I grew up in the suburbs in a neighborhood that was not very tough at all. Even our school bully was only passively aggressive. He wouldn't take your lunch. He'd just say, "You're going to eat all that?"

    —*Brian Kiley*

I grew up in such a tough neighborhood. I remember laying in bed at night and looking up at the stars and thinking, like—"Where the hell's the roof?"

    —*Rocky La Porte*

**NEIGHBORS**

I was going to do something nice for my neighbors, but I didn't want to set a precedent.

    —*Grace White*

The guy who lives across the street from me has a circular driveway, and he can't get out.

    —*Steven Wright*

## NEUROSES

See also: **MENTAL DISORDERS**

What's the difference between neurotic and eccentric? How much money you make.

—*Jason Love*

A neurotic is a person who worries about things that didn't happen in the past, instead of worrying about things that won't happen in the future, like normal people.

—*Henny Youngman*

### Codependence

I'm not codependent, myself, but aren't they great to have around?

—*Betsy Salkind*

### Hypochondria

I admit it, I'm a hypochondriac. But I manage to control it with a placebo.

—*Dennis Miller*

My friend Jerry has a severe case of hypochondria. He thinks he's dead.

—*Craig Sharf*

### Paranoia

I'm paranoid. On my stationary bike I have a rear-view mirror.

—*Richard Lewis*

Paranoids are people too; they have their own problems. It's easy to criticize, but if everybody hated you, wouldn't you be paranoid?

—*Steven Wright*

## NEWS

I'm very much against the news: "Here are ten more things to upset you. Film at 11."

—*Eric Idle*

Here's my thing with the news: I don't know what I'm supposed to do. By the time I read about something, it's obviously too late to help. If you told me that tomorrow a bus

was going to go sailing off the Himalayas, I'd pick up the
phone and warn them. "Don't get on the bus. Didn't you see
the paper?"

—*Paul Reiser*

I have a problem with the strip that runs along the bottom of
the news programs. I'm trying to read, trying to listen, "What
did he say? What did that say?" Do you want me to watch the
show, or do you want me to read the strip? Don't these idiots
who run the networks know we don't want to read? That's why
we're watching TV.

—*Jerry Seinfeld*

I don't get the newspaper anymore, because my neighbor
just moved. When I do buy the paper, I buy them out of the
coin racks; they're cheaper. They're four for a quarter out of
those things.

—*Garry Shandling*

## NORMALCY

The only normal people are the ones you don't know
too well.

—*Rodney Dangerfield*

Normal is getting dressed in clothes that you buy for work and
driving through traffic in a car that you are still paying for, in
order to get to the job you need to pay for the clothes and the
car, and the house you leave vacant all day so you can afford
to live in it.

—*Ellen DeGeneres*

Normal is just a cycle on the washing machine.

—*Whoopi Goldberg*

## NOSTALGIA

I find it difficult to reminisce with people I don't know.

—*Steven Wright*

## NURSERY RHYMES

Humpty Dumpty

I come from an Irish family in Brooklyn, a few stockbrokers, a smattering of intellectuals, and 40 percent of the New York police force. My uncle the cop used to read me bedtime stories: "Humpty Dumpty sat on the wall. Humpty Dumpty fell, or was pushed, from the wall. The perpetrator has not be apprehended. Three male Hispanics were seen leaving the area."
—*Colin Quinn*

Little Red
Riding Hood

One day Little Red Riding Hood, who although she wore red was not affiliated with any gang, was walking through the woods with a basket of goodies for her grandmother. When she met a homeless wolf who had been abused as a cub.
—*John Wing*

## NURSING HOMES

Assisted Dying is the new term for mercy killing. And nursing homes are now called Assisted Living. "If you can't pay your Assisted Living bills, we have another assisted program more in your price range, Mr. Shaprio."
—*Daniel Liebert*

I'm kinda depressed right now because we had to put Grandpa in a rest home. Well, not actually: We didn't have the money. So we drove down the turnpike and put him in a rest area.
—*Rich Vos*

## OBSCENITIES

Some guy hit my fender, and I told him, "Be fruitful and multiply." But not in those words.
—*Woody Allen*

We shouldn't curse with sexual words. It gives sex a bad name, and it doesn't make sense. You're driving, someone cuts you off on the road, almost kills you, you roll down the window, wish them the nicest possible thing in the world.

We need new curses that really mean something, like, "Oh, yeah? Audit you, buddy!"
—*Elayne Boosler*

**OBSESSIONS**

Irrational crushes, infatuations, or obsessions. Whatever you want to label it, it's important to reach out to others.
—*Janeane Garofalo*

**OCCUPATIONS**

See also: **DOCTORS, EMPLOYMENT, LAWYERS**

Accountants

I was an accountant. I wasn't a very good accountant. I always felt that if you got within two or three bucks of it, that was close enough.
—*Bob Newhart*

Assistants

I got this office job as someone's assistant. Which basically means I'm their bitch.
—*Melanie Reno*

Ballerinas

I was a ballerina. I had to quit after I injured a groin muscle. It wasn't mine.
—*Rita Rudner*

Bankers

No matter how much the boss likes you, if you work in a bank you can't take home samples.
—*Eddie Cantor*

My old man was so dumb. He worked in a bank; they caught him stealing the pens.
—*Rodney Dangerfield*

Coroners

The easiest job in the world has to be coroner. You perform surgery on dead people. What's the worst that could happen? If everything went wrong, maybe you'd get a pulse.
—*Dennis Miller*

Executioners

The leading executioner in Saudi Arabia says he likes his job and has no trouble sleeping at night. That's good. Listen, when the job stops being fun . . .
—*Jay Leno*

Firemen

According to fire department officials in Wisconsin, many of the state's communities can't find enough people to be volunteer firefighters. As a possible explanation, officials cite the extreme danger of the job, combined with the complete absence of pay.
—*Norm MacDonald*

I thought I wanted to become a fireman. But as it turns out, I just like breaking windows with axes.
—*Buzz Nutley*

Pilots

I used to be an airline pilot. I got fired because I kept locking the keys in the plane. They caught me on an eighty-foot stepladder with a coat hanger.
—*Steven Wright*

Roofers

I used to be a hot-tar roofer. Yeah, I remember that day.
—*Mitch Hedberg*

Sales

I used to sell furniture for a living. The trouble was, it was my own.
—*Les Dawson*

I once got a job at a ladies' shoe store. My plan was that chicks would be there. High heels, short skirts. But if you ever have a choice between selling shoes to young ladies or giving birth to a porcupine on fire, take my advice and look into that second, less painful opportunity.
—*Richard Jeni*

Secretaries

I'm a secretary. On a good day I type ninety-five words per minute; on a bad day I show up drunk in my pajamas.
—*Mary Beth Cowan*

Secret Service

Secret Service guys are very brave. In what other job are you asked to take a bullet for your boss? Well, other than working at 7-Eleven.
—*Jay Leno*

Stewardesses

I was a stewardess for a while on a helicopter. For about five or six people, tops. I'd ask, "Would you like something to drink? You would? Then we're going to have to land."
—*Rita Rudner*

Waitresses

See also: **RESTAURANTS** Waiters

I used to work at the International House of Pancakes. I know what you are thinking. Why? How's that possible? But you set your goals and go for them. I made it happen. It was the worst job I ever had in my entire life. When people were rude to me, I touched their eggs. It's true. I flipped them over in the back with my hand. Four times. They didn't know, but I felt better.
—*Paula Poundstone*

## OLYMPICS

Bowling

If they're making bowling an Olympic sport, why not drinking and driving, or waking up next to a fat girl?
—*Dave Attell*

Curling

If curling is an Olympic sport, then oral sex is adultery. For that matter, oral sex should be an Olympic sport. I mean, it's harder to do than curling. And, frankly, if you're good at it, you should get a medal.
—*Lewis Black*

Women like curling. They get to see men pushing brooms.
—*Jay Leno*

Gymnastics

The women gymnasts, it's like child abuse. These girls are freaks. And the announcers don't even seem to notice it's weird

anymore. "This next gymnast is eighteen years old, she weighs thirty-four pounds. Very heavy, I don't see a medal happening."
—*Kathleen Madigan*

Luge

Luge strategy? Lie flat and try not to die.
—*Tim Steeves*

Medals

That silver medal at the Olympics, that's something, isn't it? You get gold, you've won. You get bronze, "Well, at least I got something." But silver is basically saying, "Of everyone that lost, you were the best. No one lost ahead of you. You are the very best loser."
—*Jerry Seinfeld*

Skating

Whenever I watch figure skating I don't how these people have the patience to be with a partner. If I practiced with some guy for ten years and we got to the Olympics and he fell, I'd skate over to chop off a finger before he got up. I'd go up to the judges' table and say, "I don't know who that man is. He's stalking me, and I'd like him removed from the building. I don't know why his outfit matches mine."
—*Kathleen Madigan*

Swimming

I went to the Olympics, but I could only get tickets for synchronized swimming. I hate to say this, but I prayed for one of them to get a cramp because, if I understand the rules correctly, if one of them drowns, they all have to.
—*Anthony Clark*

Track

Black folks are good at the Olympic sports you can learn to do free in the park. The white guy in track knows he's coming in last. He's just running for the jacket.
—*D. L. Hughley*

Trampoline

They now include trampoline in the Olympics, but trampoline isn't a sport; it's a backyard activity. If they're going to include that, they also should have hide-and-seek. "We're

now going live to the hide-and-seek arena, where the
Canadians have been missing for eight and half hours."
                —*Kathleen Madigan*

Triathlons        The triathlons: They bike and then they swim. Why? Either
these people don't have jobs, or they have jobs that are
incredibly difficult to get to.
                —*Rita Rudner*

**OPINIONS**        I think everyone is entitled to my opinion.
                —*Victor Borge*

People always tell me stupid stuff. You know, like their
opinions.
                —*Steve Neal*

**OPPORTUNITIES**        Don't be afraid of missing opportunities. Behind every failure
is an opportunity somebody wishes they had missed.
                —*Lily Tomlin*

**OPTIMISM**        See: **ATTITUDES**

**ORGAN
DONATIONS**        Larry Flynt is now spokesman for organ donation. How novel
of him to be hocking his own body parts for a change.
                —*Betsy Salkind*

**ORGASMS**        See also: **SEX**

I have come to think of orgasms as the things that I have really
quickly while the guy gets up to look in the refrigerator for
something to drink.
                —*Merrill Markoe*

In a lifetime the average person spends four hours out of
569,500 hours experiencing orgasm. And 62 percent of that is
self-inflicted.
                —*Lily Tomlin*

Fake

Forty-six percent of women surveyed answered "Yes," when asked if they ever faked an orgasm. Actually they said, "Yes, yes! Oh God, yes!"

*—Wayne Cotter*

I found out my wife is faking orgasms. Four of my friends told me.

*—Rodney Dangerfield*

My girlfriend is taking acting lessons, so she can fake it better. And I'm nervous, because next week is the final project and the entire class is coming over to watch.

*—Craig Sharf*

Women might be able to fake orgasms. But men can fake whole relationships.

*—Jimmy Shubert*

Guys wonder why we fake it. It's called "time management." I don't need to be up all night working on something that's not going to happen; you're just cutting into my sleep time. He's working hard; you know it ain't gonna happen; and you glance at the clock, "Shoot, it's 1:30 in the morning and I got to get up at six." "Oh yes! Oh yes, baby!"

*—Wanda Sykes*

Multiple

My ex-wife was multi-orgasmic. Married nine years, two orgasms. And I wasn't there for either of them. Some guys at work told me about it.

*—Ken Ferguson*

Men can have multiple orgasms. It just takes us a week.

*—Tommy Koenig*

Simultaneous

The only time my wife and I had a simultaneous orgasm was when the judge signed the divorce papers.

*—Woody Allen*

Women                See also: Fake

I overheard these two young guys talking about women and sex. One guy says, "It's so much easier for women to have an orgasm on top." And the other guy argued, "No, it's easier for women to have an orgasm when she's on the bottom." Finally, I turned to them and said, "Guys, actually it's much easier when we're alone."

—*Cory Kahaney*

## OUTDOORS

I don't like nature. It's big plants eating little plants, small fish being eaten by big fish, big animals eating each other. It's like an enormous restaurant.

—*Woody Allen*

I don't like the outdoors. There's too much nature in it.

—*Judy Brown*

I hate the outdoors. To me the outdoors is where the car is.

—*Will Durst*

I was walking in a forest, and a tree fell right in front of me, and Keebler elves went everywhere.

—*Buzz Nutley*

**PARADES**        If you don't like a parade, walk in the opposite direction.
                   You'll fast-forward the parade.
                           —*Mitch Hedberg*

**PARENTHOOD**     See also: **BABIES, BIRTH, CHILDHOOD, FATHERHOOD,
                   FATHERS, MOTHERHOOD, MOTHERS, PARENTS**

                   Boy, parents: There's a tough job. Damn easy job to get,
                   though. I think most people love the interview. You don't have
                   to dress for it.
                           —*Steve Bruner*

                   It would seem that something which means poverty, disorder,
                   and violence every single day should be avoided entirely, but
                   the desire to beget children is a natural urge.
                           —*Phyllis Diller*

                   The way we know the kids are growing up: The bite marks
                   are higher.
                           —*Phyllis Diller*

                   What's harder to raise, boys or girls? Girls. Boys are easy. Give
                   'em a book of matches, and they're happy.
                           —*Etta May*

                   Having children is like having a bowling alley in your brain.
                           —*Martin Mull*

                   You have a baby, you have to clean up your act. You can't
                   come in drunk and go, "Hey, here's a little switch: Daddy's
                   going to throw up on you."
                           —*Robin Williams*

Affordability      The only way my wife and I could afford to have kids is if she
                   breast fed them for eighteeen years.
                           —*Paul Alexander*

Avoiding

The only real joy I'm having in not having any children is that it's driving my parents crazy, and I really like that a lot. I feel like I'm getting even for all those years in high school when they made me come home early and I couldn't have sex.

—*Elayne Boosler*

I practice birth control, which is being around my sister's children. You want to run right out and ovulate after you play with them for five minutes.

—*Brett Butler*

I'm not a breeder. I have no maternal instincts whatsoever. I ovulate sand.

—*Margaret Cho*

I thought I wanted to have kids until I spent two weeks with my nephews. Now I'll only have children if I want to go into the wrecking business.

—*Rick Duccomun*

My wife and I don't have any kids. We don't want any kids; we're happy the way we are. If we have a sudden urge to spank someone, we'll spank each other.

—*Danny Liebert*

I feel bad that I don't have children. I'm afraid if I don't have kids, my grandchildren will have no parents.

—*Paula Poundstone*

We've begun to long for the pitter-patter of little feet, so we bought a dog. Well, it's cheaper, and you get more feet.

—*Rita Rudner*

Babysitters

They say you should videotape your babysitter, but I don't think you should involve your kid in a sting operation.

—*Dave Chappelle*

I don't have a baby, but I still book a babysitter. I tell her to check on the kid after a half hour or so. Then when I return I go, "Escaped?! Well, give me fifty bucks, and we'll call it even."
        —*Harry Hill*

When you're a parent, you're a prisoner of war. You can't go anywhere without paying someone to come and look after your kids. In the old days, babysitters were fifty cents an hour; they'd steam clean the carpet and detail your car. Now they've got their own union. I couldn't afford it, so I had my mother come over. The sitters called her a scab and beat her up on the front lawn.
        —*Robert G. Lee*

**Be Nice**

Always be nice to your children, because they are the ones who will choose your rest home.
        —*Phyllis Diller*

In a nutshell, just be good and kind to your children because not only are they the future of the world, they are the ones who can eventually sign you into the home.
        —*Dennis Miller*

**Child Support**

Somewhere over the rainbow, the child support check is in the mail.
        —*Julie Kidd*

**Dating**

I have adapted the philosophy of Genghis Khan, "Give a man a fish, and he eats for a day; teach a man to fish, and he eats for a lifetime," for my slogan: "Show a teenage boy a gun, and he'll have your daughter home before 11:30."
        —*Sinbad*

**Discipline**

Never raise your hands to your kids. It leaves your groin unprotected.
        —*Red Buttons*

Parents are not quite interested in injustice; they are interested in quiet.
—*Bill Cosby*

Every minute of parenting is like hostage negotiations: "Put the kitty down. Come out with your hands up, kicking the candy bar in front of you."
—*Reno Goodale*

The thing I have the most trouble with is trying to discipline my little guy, because everything he does makes me laugh, and you don't want to send the wrong message. Like last week he'd somehow gotten hold of a carving knife, and he was stabbing my in-laws repeatedly. It was funny, but I had to be like, "No, that's bad."
—*Brian Kiley*

I've got good kids . . . love my kids. I'm trying to bring them up the right way, not spanking them. I find waving the gun around gets the same job done.
—*Denis Leary*

Latinos, when we raise kids, our first instinct is "No." "Mom?" "NO!" "You don't even know what it is." "I know what it's not."
—*George Lopez*

Everyone should have kids. They are the greatest joy in the world. But they are also terrorists. You'll realize this as soon as they are born, and they start using sleep deprivation to break you.
—*Ray Romano*

Fights

No matter how calmly you try to referee, parenting will eventually produce bizarre behavior, and I'm not talking about the kids.
—*Bill Cosby*

Freedom

When you're a parent you give up your freedom. You sleep according to someone else's schedule; you eat according to someone else's schedule. It's like being in jail, but you really love the warden.
    —*Lew Schneider*

Homework

It's a myth that you will be able to help your children with their homework. I'm taking remedial math so I can help my son make it to the third grade.
    —*Sinbad*

Intelligence

All parents think their kids are the smartest kids ever born. My mom thought my daughter was a genius because she would lie on the floor and talk to the ceiling fan. I said, "Mom, Uncle Harold does that, and y'all call him an alcoholic."
    —*Jeff Foxworthy*

Children are smarter than any of us. Know how I know that? I don't know one child with a full-time job and children.
    —*Bill Hicks*

Learning

My childhood should have taught me lessons for my own parenthood, but it didn't because parenting can be learned only by people who have no children.
    —*Bill Cosby*

People have always told me that I'd learn more from my kids than they'd learn from me. I believe that. I've learned that as a parent, when you have sex your body emits a hormone that drifts down the hall into your child's room and makes them want a drink of water.
    —*Jeff Foxworthy*

Love

You don't know what love is until you become a parent. You don't know what love is until you fish a turd out of the bathtub for someone.
    —*Margaret Smith*

New

How much being a parent would change my life didn't occur to me until I was heaving up my dinner the day my daughter was born.
—*Tim Allen*

Next time you're at the park, do yourself a favor and look at the new parents. At first they appear to be basking in their newfound parental bliss. But look close. See that facial twitch? That's no twitch, my friend. That man is a hostage, and he's trying to blink you a message.
—*Ray Romano*

Pondering

Why do I want a child? Does giving birth make me a real woman? No, earning less than a man makes me a real woman.
—*Suzy Berger*

I think about having children, because time is running out. I want to have children while my parents are still young enough to take care of them.
—*Rita Rudner*

We've been married six years, so people are trying to force us to have kids. They all say the same thing, "Kids, they a lot of work, but they worth it." But I noticed something: They never look you in the eye when they say that.
—*Wanda Sykes*

Preparation

Since childhood is a time when kids prepare to be grown-ups, I think it makes a lot of sense to completely traumatize your children. Gets 'em ready for the real world.
—*George Carlin*

Pre-teens

My eleven-year-old daughter mopes around the house all day waiting for her breasts to grow.
—*Bill Cosby*

These kids are nuts today. I got a kid myself, ten years old. He's going to be eleven, if I let him.

*—Henny Youngman*

**Purpose**

Having children gives your life purpose. Right now my purpose is to get some sleep.

*—Reno Goodale*

**Ready**

I'm getting ready to be a parent. I just turned thirty, and I'm tired of mowing the grass.

*—Jeff Foxworthy*

You wake up one day and say, "You know what, I don't think I ever need to sleep or have sex again." Congratulations, you're ready to have children.

*—Ray Romano*

Once you survive growing up, the next step is to have your own kid. When everyone you know has caught on to you, you need to create a new person, someone who doesn't know you. You have a kid; the relationship is off to a great start. You give the kid food and toys, and immediately they are impressed with you.

*—Jerry Seinfeld*

**Relaxed**

I have two kids, and over the years I've developed a really relaxed attitude about the whole child-rearing thing. I don't cry over spilt milk. Spilt vodka, that's another story.

*—Daryl Hogue*

**Returning Home**

Human beings are the only creatures that allow their children to come back home.

*—Bill Cosby*

**Running Away**

Most children threaten at times to run away from home. This is the only thing that keeps some parents going.

*—Phyllis Diller*

My teenage daughter has threatened to run away from home. Oh, pinch me, I'm dreaming; let me help you pack. But even if she did run away, I know she'd come back. Just like a bad check, "Insufficient Funds."

—*Sheila Kay*

## Teenagers

Teenagers. They say they don't need you to be their friend. Yeah, no kidding. I know who my friends are, and they don't steal money out of my purse in the middle of the night.

—*Cory Kahaney*

I have a teenage daughter who wants to go to college. But I wonder why I should pay for her education, when she already knows everything.

—*Sheila Kay*

Having a teenage daughter is like being stuck in a hurricane. All you can do is board up your windows and look out in four years to see what the damage is.

—*Buzz Nutley*

My friends complain that their teenagers sleep all day. Not me. Can you imagine if they were awake all day? Teenagers, like espresso, are meant to be taken in small doses.

—*Buzz Nutley*

Is your teenage son or daughter out for the evening? If so, take advantage of the opportunity. Pack your furniture, call a moving van, and don't leave a forwarding address.

—*Henny Youngman*

## Toddlers

I called a friend, and his three-year-old answered the phone. "My Daddy is the best daddy in the world. My Daddy took me to the animal zoo. I love my Daddy." He got on the phone. I said, "Carl, enjoy her while she's stupid."

—*Bob Alper*

We spend the first twelve months of our children's lives teaching them to walk and talk, and the next twelve telling them to sit down and shut up.
——*Phyllis Diller*

What's the best way to keep two-year-old children from biting their fingernails? Make them change their own diapers.
——*Paul Lynde*

A child of one can be taught not to do certain things, such as touch a hot stove, pull lamps off of tables, and wake Mommy before noon.
——*Joan Rivers*

A two-year-old is like having a blender, but you don't have a top for it.
——*Jerry Seinfeld*

**Twins**

I have two-year-old twins in my house; it's nuts. I make excuses to get out, "You need anything from anywhere? Anything from the Motor Vehicle Bureau? C'mon let me register something. I was going out anyway, to apply for jury duty. Please!"
——*Ray Romano*

When I gave birth, I had twins, my daughter and my husband. They were both immature and bald.
——*Grace White*

If I ever had twins, I'd use one for parts.
——*Steven Wright*

**PARENTS**

See also: **BABIES, BIRTH, CHILDHOOD, CHILDREN, MOTHERHOOD, MOTHERS, FATHERHOOD, FATHERS, PARENTHOOD**

I don't think my parents liked me. They put a live teddy bear in my crib.
——*Woody Allen*

I'll tell you when I first got the feeling my parents never wanted me. It was right after my fourth bris.
—*Ed Bluestone*

My parents never felt I was good-looking. When they made home movies, they'd hire an actor to play me.
—*Ed Bluestone*

If your parents never had children, chances are you won't either.
—*Dick Cavett*

My parents used to take me to the pet department and tell me it was a zoo.
—*Billy Connolly*

You finally get old enough to stay home alone when your parents go away on vacation, but they call back and ask stupid questions like, "How's the house?" I used to answer things like, "Oh, the house is sick. Yesterday it threw up all over the place."
—*George Wallace*

Advice

Your parents are always giving you advice: "Never take money from strangers." So I used to take it out of her purse instead.
—*George Wallace*

Cheap

When I went to college, my parents threw a going away party for me, according to the letter.
—*Emo Philips*

My parents were both cheap. I'm sure that's why they got married in the first place. They weren't in love. They just realized, "We could save a lot of money if we was together."
—*Chris Rock*

Dreams　　　　See also: **FATHERS**

My parents' dream was for me to have everything they didn't.
And thanks to ozone holes, fear of AIDS, and no health
insurance, their dream has come true.
　　　—*Brad Slaight*

Living with　　I've moved back in with my mom and dad. It was my wife's idea.
She suggested—in fact, demanded—that while we're apart we
have sex with other people. I hear it's going great for her.
　　　—*Chris Elliot*

I lived at home until my mid-twenties, with my mother. If
you're twenty-five and you're sleeping on *Star Wars* sheets, the
force is not with you.
　　　—*Gary Gulman*

I lived at home until I was twenty-four. I was trying to find
myself. Then one day, boom, I found myself, out in the front
yard with all my shit.
　　　—*Jeff Jena*

Mexican dudes, we never move out. White kids, first chance
they get they're out the door to college or some exotic
backpacking trip. We live at home forever. That's why you see
very few Latino homeless. Because you gotta leave home to
be homeless.
　　　—*George Lopez*

People think living in your parents' basement until you're
twenty-nine is lame. But what they don't realize is that while
you're there, you save money on rent, food, and dates.
　　　—*Ray Romano*

Not Perfect　　I could tell that my parents hated me. My bath toys were a
toaster and a radio.
　　　—*Rodney Dangerfield*

In high school my parents told me I ran with the wrong crowd. I was a loner.

—*Jeff Shaw*

There are no perfect parents. Even Jesus had a distant father and a domineering mother. I'd have trust issues if my father allowed me to be crucified.

—*Bob Smith*

Fortunately, my parents were intelligent, enlightened people. They accepted me for what I was: a punishment from God.

—*David Steinberg*

Peer Pressure

There's a new book, *Parents Don't Matter,* which says that growing up, your peer group affects you more than your parents. I'm not sure I believe that. It's much easier to blame your parents. I still have their phone number.

—*Norman K.*

Retired

Every Sunday I talk to my parents in Arizona. They live in a retirement community, which is basically a minimum-security prison with a golf course.

—*Joel Warshaw*

Seniors

Parents can scare you once they reach a certain age. Every year mom starts earlier and earlier. About 9:00 A.M. yesterday Mom started drinking margaritas. Before long it got dark out, and no one could find her. Well, turns out she passed out on the lawn. The next day she was woken up by a deer licking the salt off her lips.

—*David Letterman*

and Sex

My parents are in their late sixties, and they still have sex. Because they want grandchildren.

—*Wendy Liebman*

You don't ever really want to visualize your parents having sex. It's very uncomfortable. Sex is a great thing and all. But you don't want to think that your whole life began because somebody had a little too much wine with dinner.
—*Jerry Seinfeld*

**Single**

According to an article in *USA Today*, children from single parent homes have much better verbal skills than children from two parent homes. However, children from two parent homes are far superior at bitterly sarcastic repartee.
—*Dennis Miller*

**and Teenagers**

The only thing I ever said to my parents when I was a teenager was, "Hang up, I got it!"
—*Carol Leifer*

**Visits**

I got even with my parents. My parents came to stay with me for the weekend in my apartment. I made them sleep in separate bedrooms. My mother said, "What? Are you crazy? I've been sleeping with this man for years." I said, "Look, I don't care what you do on the outside. But when you're in my house . . ."
—*Elayne Boosler*

I took my parents back to the airport today. They leave tomorrow.
—*Margaret Smith*

**PARTIES**

Single people throw the best parties. They don't have to worry about their furniture getting messed up. Their friends can destroy everything they own; they're out fifteen bucks.
—*Jeff Foxworthy*

I used to walk into a party and scan the room for attractive women. Now I look for women to hold my baby so I can eat potato salad sitting down.
—*Paul Reiser*

**PATRIOTISM**

If every man was as true to his country as he was to his wife, we'd be in a lot of trouble.

—*Rodney Dangerfield*

I fucking hate patriotism. It's a round world last time I checked.

—*Bill Hicks*

**PENISES**

I'm just a huge fan of the penis. Can I just say I love penises? They're just the greatest. And they're all different, like snowflakes.

—*Margaret Cho*

Women think men are led around by our penises. It points us in a direction, I'll give you that. But we're adult enough to make a decision whether to follow it. Granted, I put my back out trying to reel it back in

—*Garry Shandling*

The problem is that God gives men a brain and a penis, and only enough blood to run one at a time.

—*Robin Williams*

Enhancement

There's a product called Mr. Big Cream. Just rub it on your dick, and it gets bigger. Well, if it worked, then wouldn't your hands get bigger, too?

—*Robert Schimmel*

Envy

My theory is that women don't suffer from penis envy. Every man just thinks his penis is enviable. Maybe Freud suffered from penis doubt.

—*Bob Smith*

Freud accused women of having penis envy. I have no reason to be jealous of a penis. At least when I get out of the ocean, all my bodily parts are still the same size.

—*Sheila Wenz*

Naming

Why do men name them? You hear them saying things like, "Well, Bobby's awake." You never hear women saying things like, "I'm sitting on Margaret."
    —*Marsha Warfield*

Sizes

My penis is about ten inches long, if you include part of my large intestine.
    —*David Corrado*

Women say it's not how much men have, but what we do with it. How many things can we do with it? What is it, a Cuisinart? It goes two speeds: Forward and Reverse.
    —*Richard Jeni*

I've done a little survey, guys, and size does matter. But not as much as smell.
    —*Danny Liebert*

I love sex, and I'm blessed. If I take this thing out, whole room goes dark.
    —*Bernie Mac*

See also: **COLOGNE**

**PERFUME**

Why are women wearing perfume that smells like flowers when men don't like flowers? I've been wearing a great scent; it's called New Car Interior.
    —*Rita Rudner*

I love watching women put on their perfume. They always hit the inside of the wrist. Women are convinced that this is the most action-packed area. Why? In case you slap the guy, he still finds you intriguing? *Crack!* "Ouch . . . Chanel!"
    —*Jerry Seinfeld*

**PERSONAL ADS**     See also: **DATING**

A truly honest personal ad would say, "I want to date myself, only with more money."
— *Maureen Brownsey*

I saw a personal ad that looked interesting. It said she loved long walks, running on the beach, going to parks. As it turns out, she was a German shepherd.
— *David Corrado*

It's hard to trust when dating through personal ads. To make the personals more truthful, I think there should be a Pinocchio effect. Whenever a guy lies, his nose would grow. No, better yet, his member would shrink. This would cut down on both the betrayal and the birth rate.
— *Caryl Fuller*

Everyone is putting up personal ads now; it's not sleazy like it used to be. Listen to this one, "Professor emeritus instructor of anthropology looking for female kindred spirit to travel, seek, and explore. Must have enormous hooters."
— *Monica Piper*

Saw this personal ad in the paper, "Democratic man would like to meet young woman Republican. Object: Third party."
— *Henny Youngman*

**PESSIMISM**     See: **ATTITUDES**

**PETS**     See also: **ANIMALS, BIRDS, CATS, DOGS**

I've always had pets. I know I should have a child someday, but I wonder, could I love something that doesn't crap in a box?
— *Sheila Wenz*

Fish     An aquarium is like a lava lamp with feces.
— *David Corrado*

I have fish for pets. That's what I have. Goldfish. It was originally for the stress thing. They say if you watch fish, it helps you relax, to fall asleep. Which explains why I always doze off when I'm snorkeling.
—*Ellen DeGeneres*

My goldfish got a bladder infection. I didn't know it was urinating thirty-seven times a day until its bowl tipped over, full.
—*Howie Mandel*

My parents never wanted me to be upset about anything. They couldn't tell me when a pet had died. Once I woke up, and my goldfish was gone. I asked, "Mom? Where's Fluffy?" She said, "He ran away."
—*Rita Rudner*

Goats

My pet goat, and that precious moment when I was all of thirteen and my little buddy got eliminated. We were playing "*Vamonos,* c'mon *Chivo.* Jump, jump!" when my grandmother starts yelling from the porch. "What should I call him?" I asked her. "How about Temporary. I told you not to play with the food!"
—*George Lopez*

Hamsters

My brother had a hamster. He took it to see the vet; that's like bringing a disposable lighter for repair.
—*Wayne Cotter*

Turtles

Has any turtle ever outlived a shaker of turtle food?
—*Jerry Seinfeld*

**PHILOSOPHY**

What if everything is an illusion and nothing exists? In that case, I definitely overpaid for my carpet.
—*Woody Allen*

Some people see things that are and ask, "Why?" Some people dream of things that never were and ask, "Why not?" Some people have to go to work and don't have time for all that shit.
—*George Carlin*

I didn't invent the hypothetical situation, but let's just suppose for a second that I did.
—*Auggie Cook*

Imagine if there were no hypothetical situations.
—*John Mendosa*

I'm not a fatalist. But even if I were, what could I do about it?
—*Emo Philips*

**PHOBIAS**

My wife was afraid of the dark. Then she saw me naked. Now she's afraid of the light.
—*Rodney Dangerfield*

I suffer from peroxide-aphobia. Every time I've gotten near a blonde woman, something of mine has disappeared. Jobs, boyfriends . . . once, an angora sweater just leapt right off my body.
—*Rita Rudner*

**PHOTOGRAPHS**  See also: **CAMERAS**

Someone handed me a picture and said, "This is a picture of me when I was younger." Every picture of you is when you were younger. "Here's a picture of me when I'm older." Where'd you get that camera, man?
—*Mitch Hedberg*

Family

I came across this picture in our family photo album, and I don't know what to make of it. My mom, pregnant, cigarette dangling, mowing the lawn, and my little sister in an overturned playpen with a rock on top of it. And then there's me, tied to a tree with a jump rope.
—*Janeane Garofalo*

Rare

I have some very rare photographs. One is of Houdini locking his keys in his car.
—*Steven Wright*

Vacation

Don't you love looking at your friends' vacation pictures?
Especially when they owe you money.
—*J. Chris Newberg*

**PHYSIQUE**

Feeling shitty about your physique is an important state of
mind, for it leads one into a series of diverse, unfulfilling relationships. As opposed to just one monogamous journey into
the banal.
—*Janeane Garofalo*

I have the body of an eighteen-year-old. I keep it in the fridge.
—*Spike Milligan*

Abs

I'm so sick of athletic types bragging about their six packs. I
have a four pack: a roll here, a roll there.
—*Kathie Dice*

I don't have six-pack abs; I have the whole case.
—*Reno Goodale*

Some people have six-pack abs; I have a keg.
—*Craig Sharf*

out of Shape

I'm chunky. In a bathing suit I look like a Bartlett pear with a
rubber band around it.
—*Drew Carey*

I'm in very bad shape. I hurt myself playing Scrabble.
—*Rodney Dangerfield*

Men try forever to preserve their old football image. My husband is shaped like one.
—*Phyllis Diller*

My doctor told me to exercise. He said walking would get me
into shape. I said, "Doc, I've already chosen a shape, and it's
round."
—*Irv Gilman*

I sacrificed my body to the goddess of motherhood. I used to have a waist. I'm still keeping the pants because they fit around my head now.
—*Stephanie Hodge*

I don't have an hourglass figure. I have an hour and a half.
—*Wendy Liebman*

**Shapely**

I'm from the South, and I like a big woman. Cute in the face and thick in the waist. And with a big woman you ain't even got to buy them drinks; they get high from food. "Oooh, these chicken wings got me fucked up."
—*Jamie Foxx*

**Thighs**

I have flabby thighs, but fortunately my stomach covers them.
—*Joan Rivers*

**Thin**

I hate skinny women, because no matter how thin, they're still always on a diet. My friend Cynthia is 5'9" and 102 pounds, has been on Fen Phen, Metabolife, and lives on Slim Fast. Used to be she'd ask, "Do I look fat in this?" Now she says, "Can you still see me? Am I still visible to the naked eye?"
—*Kelly Maguire*

**PICKETING**    See: **ACTIVISM**

**PIERCINGS**

When considering whether or not to have a metal stud put through your tongue or your belly button or your genitalia, take lightning into account.
—*Dennis Miller*

I don't understand the body piercing movement. I see some guy's got eight rings through his eyebrows. I ran up and hung a shower curtain on his face.
—*Harland Williams*

There are a lot of people into body piercing. They get to where they look like they've been mugged by a staple gun. Fifteen earrings here, a little towel rack there.
—*Robin Williams*

Clitoral

A friend of mine got her clitoral hood pierced. I think that's disgusting. I would never do that. I'd get a clip-on.
—*Sarah Silverman*

Ears

I saw a sign in a jewelry store window, "Ears Pierced While You Wait." The alternative just staggers the imagination.
—*Emily Levine*

I think men who have a pierced ear are better prepared for marriage. They've experienced pain and bought jewelry.
—*Rita Rudner*

Nose

I used to have an apartment in LA with roommates that had nose rings, and I couldn't concentrate on a word they were saying without staring at their nostrils. They could've told me the apartment just burned down and I'd say, "Uh, did that hurt going in? Can you pick your nose?"
—*Judy Gold*

The people with the rings in their noses: Wouldn't it be great if you could walk up to those freaks, rip the rings out, and ten seconds later they'd blow up?
—*Harland Williams*

## PLASTIC SURGERY

See also: **BREASTS** Implants

Facelifts

I've had so much plastic surgery if I have one more facelift it will be Cesarian.
—*Phyllis Diller*

I don't have anything against facelifts, but I think it's time to stop when you look permanently frightened.

—*Susan Norfleet*

I don't plan to grow old gracefully. I plan to have facelifts until my ears meet.

—*Rita Rudner*

Rhinoplasty

The technical term for a nose job is rhinoplasty. They have a big nose, that's why they're coming in. Do they need the abuse of being compared to a rhinoceros? When someone goes in for a hair transplant, they don't say, "We're going to perform a cue-ballectomy on you, Mr. Johnson; remove the skinheadia of your chrome-domus, which is the technical term."

—*Jerry Seinfeld*

**PMS**

See: **PREMENSTRUAL SYNDROME**

**POETS**

Are poets imaginative people? Yes, they imagine people like listening to their poems. Is there a lot of money in poetry? Yes. But first you must be completely dead.

—*Paul Alexander*

**POISON**

My cousin accidentally swallowed some poison. So to induce vomiting, we gave him a beer and rushed him right to the nearest college fraternity.

—*Wally Wang*

**POLICE**

See also: **ETHNICITY** African American

If you ever see me getting beaten up by the police, please put your video camera down and help me.

—*Bobcat Goldthwait*

We live in an age when pizza gets to your home before the police.

—*Jeff Marder*

A recent police study found that you're much more likely to get shot by a fat cop if you run.
—*Dennis Miller*

A cop pulled me over the other day and scared me so bad I thought I stole my own car.
—*Chris Rock*

Sometimes the police get carried away with those uniforms. I got a ticket for jaywalking, and I was petrified. This policeman comes up to me. He has this great big helmet, big black boots, sunglasses, and the belt with all the stuff hanging off it. And he says, "Excuse me, little lady. Did you know you crossed against the light?" I had this terrible desire to say, "No, and do you know that you look like one of the Village People?"
—*Rita Rudner*

**POLITICIANS**      See: **AFFIRMATIVE ACTION, GUNS**

**POLITICS**         See also: **GOVERNMENT, PRESIDENTS**

Too bad the only people who know how to run the country are busy driving cabs and cutting hair.
—*George Burns*

I looked up the word "politics" in the dictionary, and it's actually a combination of two words: "poli," which means "many," and "tics," which means "bloodsuckers."
—*Jay Leno*

Bipartisan       The word "bipartisan" usually means some larger-than-usual deception is being carried out.
—*George Carlin*

Conservatives    These conservatives are all in favor of the unborn; they'll do anything for the unborn. But once you're born, you're on your own. They're not interested in you until you reach military age. Conservatives want live babies, so they can raise them to be dead soldiers.

—*George Carlin*

"My kid is a conservative, why is that?" you ask. Remember in the sixties, when we told you if you kept using drugs your kids would be mutants?

—*Mort Sahl*

Conservatives Versus Liberals

Liberals feel unworthy of their possessions. Conservatives feel they deserve everything they've stolen.

—*Mort Sahl*

I'm liberal on some issues and conservative on others. For example, I would not burn a flag, but neither would I put one out.

—*Garry Shandling*

Corruption

Politics is so corrupt, even the dishonest people get screwed.

—*George Carlin*

Democrats Versus Republicans

What's the difference between a Democrat and a Republican? A Democrat blows; a Republican sucks.

—*Lewis Black*

May you be as rich as a Republican and have the sex life of a Democrat.

—*Johnny Carson*

A Democrat sees the glass of water as half-full, a Republican looks at the same glass, and wonders who the hell drank half his glass of water.

—*Jeff Cesario*

There's a nickel's worth of difference between Democrats and Republicans. If you put a nickel on the table, a Democrat will steal it from you and a Republican will kill you for it.

—*Barry Crimmins*

Democrats are gas, Republicans are brakes, and everyone else is just a bump in the road.
—*Jason Love*

**Jokes**

Personally, I'm against political jokes. Too often they get elected to office.
—*Henny Youngman*

**Liberals**

It's easy to be politically correct and a liberal when you live in a gated community.
—*Bobcat Goldthwait*

**Political Parties**

See also: **HOMOSEXUALITY** Republicans

We have a two-party system. One party wins the election, and the other tells us about the mistake we made for the next four years.
—*Tommy Koenig*

Assuming that either the left wing or the right wing gained control of the country, it would probably fly around in circles.
—*Pat Paulsen*

**Republicans**

They say there's a struggle to find the soul of the Republican Party. What are they using? Tweezers and an electron microscope?
—*Barry Crimmins*

The Republicans keep talking about returning power to the states. Oh great, let's have more things run by the people who brought you the Department of Motor Vehicles.
—*Andy Kindler*

The Republicans, whose health care plan consists of "Just Say No to Sickness."
—*Kevin Pollack*

I'm not a Republican because I just don't make enough money to be that big an asshole.

—*Paula Poundstone*

Conservative Republicans don't believe anything should be done for the first time, and moderate Republicans say, "It should be, but not now."

—*Mort Sahl*

The Republication Party should change their national emblem from an elephant to a prophylactic, because it stands for inflation, halts production, protects a bunch of pricks, and gives a false sense of security when one is being screwed.

—*Robin Tyler*

**PORNOGRAPHY**     See also: **BREASTS**

Definition of

The Supreme Court says pornography is anything without artistic merit that causes sexual thoughts; that's their definition, essentially. No artistic merit, causes sexual thoughts. Hmm . . . sounds like every commercial on television, doesn't it?

—*Bill Hicks*

and Men

Men love to watch two women make love. I wonder, does this turn them on, or are they just trying to figure out how to do it right?

—*Joy Behar*

To men, pornos are beautiful love stories with all the boring stuff taken out.

—*Richard Jeni*

I had to learn sex from porno movies. That doesn't work. Learning sex from porno, that's like learning how to drive by watching the Indianapolis 500.

—*Norman K.*

You know what I like more than women? Pornography.
Because I can get pornography.
— *Patton Oswalt*

Music

I saw a blind man rent a porno video. He must really like
bad music.
— *Mark Gross*

Titles

Every porno movie should be called *Stuff That Never Happens to You.*
— *Richard Jeni*

and Women

My husband says I don't understand pornography because I'm
always fast-forwarding to the story.
— *Alicia Brandt*

**POSTAL SERVICE**

The other day I went to the post office, and I saw they had
bulletproof glass. I realized that it wasn't to keep the bullets
from coming in, but the other way around.
— *Louie Anderson*

Today a post office was shut down, but a vibrating box turned
out to contain a vibrator. Police suspect a single woman
acting alone.
— *Craig Kilborn*

The postal service has gone from slow to inert. It's ironic that
the only people in America unwilling to push the envelope
are postal employees.
— *Dennis Miller*

Why do they put wanted posters in the post office? Do they
expect us to write to them? "It's about time you straightened
up, a guy with your potential."
— *Jerry Seinfeld*

**PREGNANCY**     See also: **BIRTH**

Pregnancy is amazing. To think that you can create a human being just with the things you have around the house.
—*Shang*

and Alcohol

They caution pregnant women not to drink alcohol. It may harm the baby. I think that's ironic. If it wasn't for alcohol most women wouldn't be that way.
—*Rita Rudner*

Artificial Insemination

I prefer the old-fashioned way of having children. By accident.
—*Phyllis Diller*

Artificial insemination. That's a scary concept. You know why? I don't want to have coffee with a stranger, never mind have their child.
—*Rosie O'Donnell*

and Beauty

They say, "A woman is at her most beautiful when she's pregnant." Then how come you go into the Bears' locker room and never see a poster of some nude babe in her third trimester?
—*Judy Tenuta*

Biological Clock

My girlfriend is at that stage where her biological clock is telling her it's time for her to be making me feel guilty and immature.
—*Kevin Hench*

The hands on my biological clock are giving me the finger.
—*Wendy Liebman*

I'm getting older, and I'm thinking about having my eggs frozen. Well, just the egg whites. I'm trying to cut back on my cholesterol.
—*Brenda Pontiff*

Causes

On the reproductive front, researchers say the number one cause of pregnancy is sex. The number two cause is sex ten minutes later.
—*Kevin Nealon*

Fertility

My husband and I tried really hard to have a baby, including having sex. But nothing happened. So we went to one of those fertility clinics where they charge you twelve million dollars every time your husband jerks off into a jar, but he was too uncomfortable there. Finally, to get a sample I had to fly him back home to his old room in his mother's house.
—*Karen Haber*

When I was growing up, the fertility drug was alcohol.
—*Kelly Monteith*

Men

Doctor says to a man, "You're pregnant." The man asks, "How does a man get pregnant?" The doctor says, "The usual way: a little wine, a little dinner . . ."
—*Henny Youngman*

Natural Childbirth

See also: **BIRTH** Natural

Natural childbirth class. A great place to find chicks, if you're into the full-figured gals. And you can be reasonably sure these girls put out.
—*Jonathan Katz*

Older Women

An eighty-year-old woman in Pakistan is pregnant. You know what she said? "Damn prom."
—*Craig Kilborn*

Women forty-nine years old are having their first child. Forty-nine! I couldn't think of a better way to spend my golden years. What's the advantage of having a kid at forty-nine? So you can both be in diapers at the same time?
—*Sue Kolinsky*

**Pondering**  I don't need a baby growing inside me for nine months. For one thing, there's morning sickness. If I'm going to feel nauseous and achy when I wake up, I want to achieve that state the old-fashioned way: getting good and drunk the night before.
*—Ellen DeGeneres*

I envy the kangaroo. That pouch setup is extraordinary; the baby crawls out of the womb when it is about two inches long, gets into the pouch, and proceeds to mature. I'd have a baby if it would develop in my handbag.
*—Rita Rudner*

I know lots of women who have had children. But I'm not sure it's for me. "Feel the baby kicking, feel the baby kicking," says my friend who is deliriously happy about it. To me, life is tough enough without having someone kick you from the inside.
*—Rita Rudner*

**Pregnancy Tests**  I took a pregnancy test, but I failed. I didn't expect to pass it, though. I didn't even study. And I got hammered the night before.
*—Jessica Delfino*

**Sonograms**  The sonogram. We had fun looking for early traces of family resemblance. "Gee, honey, it looks just like your mother, if she were bald, had no eyelids, and was floating in amniotic fluid." "Yeah, but from this side, it looks like your father. Presuming, of course, he was a Hawaiian prawn."
*—Paul Reiser*

**Twins**  I'm pregnant with twins. They throw a lot of elbows, but I really can't blame them. My brother and I couldn't share a back seat without fighting. Can you imagine having to share a womb? "Your umbilical cord is on my side!"
*—Eileen Kelly*

Worry

My period was late, and I had nothing to worry about, but I worried anyway: "Maybe I am going to have the Lord's child."
—*Penelope Lombard*

**PREMENSTRUAL SYNDROME**

See also: **AUTOMOBILES** License Plates, **MENSTRUATION**

Women complain about premenstrual syndrome, but I think of it as the only time of the month I can be myself.
—*Roseanne Barr*

I thought I had PMS, but my doctor said, "I've got good news and bad news. The good news is, you don't have PMS. The bad news is, you're a bitch."
—*Rhonda Bates*

PMS is this very difficult hormonal syndrome that causes women, for four or five days out of every month, to behave exactly the way men do all the time.
—*Dylan Brody*

Science has found that men may suffer from PMS. Men suffer, too. The saddest part? I have my mother's thighs.
—*Craig Kilborn*

**PRESIDENTS**

See also: **ELECTIONS**

In the United States, anybody can be president. That's the problem.
—*George Carlin*

I'd never run for president. I've thought about it, and the only reason I'm not is that I'm scared no woman would come forward and say she had sex with me.
—*Garry Shandling*

George W. Bush

George W. Bush taught me a valuable lesson: Vote!
—*Jason Love*

George Bush is anti-abortion yet pro–death penalty. I guess it's all in the timing, huh George?
—*Dennis Miller*

George W. Bush. A black C-student can't even manage Burger King. A white C-student just happened to be the president of the United States of America.
—*Chris Rock*

Choosing

We need a president who's fluent in at least one language.
—*Buck Henry*

So how do I pick a president? Much the same way I choose a driver to the airport. Which one will cost me the least, and not get me killed.
—*Dennis Miller*

Every politician we have, liberal or conservative, who gets caught drinking or chasing women is thrown out of office. It's backward. It's more dangerous to have a clean-living president with his finger on the button. He thinks he's going right to heaven. You want to feel safe with a leader? Give me a guy who fights in bars and cheats on his wife. This is a man who wants to put off Judgment Day as long as possible.
—*Larry Miller*

Bill Clinton

I think President Clinton misunderstood the role of the president, which is to screw the country as a whole, not individually.
—*Betsy Salkind*

Women

They say we will never have a woman president of the United States because our hormones change once a month and it makes us crazy. Yeah, right. If a woman was president, she'd be like this: "Are you nuts? You take hostages on a day when I'm retaining water? I can't believe I have to sit here

and waste my time with a morally bankrupt terrorist like you
when there's a sale on and the stores close at six!"
    —*Elayne Boosler*

It doesn't surprise me that Washington, D.C., is such a sexist
place; it's a town that lives in the shadow of the Washington
Monument, the world's largest dick. And there's never going
to be a woman president until somebody digs a seven-hundred-
foot tunnel honoring Eleanor Roosevelt.
    —*Cathryn Michon*

All the old sexist arguments against a woman president have
been shot down by, ironically, men. Women are ruled by their
biology? For chrissakes, a red-assed monkey masturbating at
the zoo is in more control of his impulses than three-quarters
of Congress. Women are too shallow, too concerned with frilly
fashions and feminine makeup? Yes, I suppose those are traits
best left out of the Oval Office, because they're much more
suited to the head of the FBI.
    —*Dennis Miller*

**PRISONS**

A prisoner escaped using a fake gun made of paper. He was
captured while frantically trying to fold a getaway car.
    —*Craig Kilborn*

My friend Larry's in jail now. He got twenty-five years for
something he didn't do. He didn't run fast enough.
    —*Damon Wayans*

**PRO-CHOICE**

I'm getting an abortion. I don't need one, but I feel that as an
American I should exercise that right before it gets taken away.
    —*Betsy Salkind*

**PROCRASTINATION**

Procrastinate now; don't put it off.
    —*Ellen DeGeneres*

My mother said, "You won't amount to anything because you procrastinate." I said, "Just wait."
—*Judy Tenuta*

**PRO-LIFE**          See also: **HOMICIDE**

These guys say they're against abortion because birth is a miracle. Popcorn is a miracle, too, if you don't know how it's done.
—*Elayne Boosler*

I'd like the names of the anti-abortion people so that when all those kids start having babies, we can take them to their house.
—*Whoopi Goldberg*

I say to this dude with a "Stop Abortion" picket sign, "I have the answer to abortion: Shoot your dick. Take that tired piece of meat down to the ASPCA and let them put it to sleep."
—*Whoopi Goldberg*

If you're so pro-life, don't lock arms and block medical clinics; lock arms and block cemeteries. Let's see how committed you are to this premise.
—*Bill Hicks*

The right-to-life movement killed a doctor. Let me use their own terminology against them: They aborted a child in the 200th trimester. People in the right-to-life movement should get a life before they tell other people what to do theirs.
—*Dennis Miller*

Pro-life people shoot up a clinic and then say, "Jesus told me to do it." It's always somebody you can't get on the phone and verify.
—*Shang*

## PROSTITUTION

for Men
You wanna hear my personal opinion on prostitution? If men knew how to do it, they wouldn't have to pay for it.
—*Roseanne Barr*

I don't get no respect. I went to a massage parlor. It was self-service.
—*Rodney Dangerfield*

I don't respect prostitutes. I think they've sold out.
—*Craig Sharf*

for Women
I'd like to open a whorehouse for women so we can get it the way we really want it. Like, we pay our money, and guys pretend they like talking to us, and they care about our lives. Then they have to hold us real tight and say, "Oooo, you're so thin!" Even if they've never seen us before, they have to say, "Have you lost weight?" And then we have sex, and right before that fabulous moment, they have to shout, "I can't believe how great your shoes match your dress!"
—*Karen Haber*

## PROTESTS
See: **ACTIVISM**

## PSYCHICS
I called the Psychic Friends hotline. We spoke for six hours, and she didn't realize that I wasn't going to pay my bill.
—*Michael Aronin*

Psychics should be licensed. We could give them the regular DMV test, only with silver dollars and pizza dough over the eyes. If you can parallel park like that, you're a psychic.
—*Jerry Seinfeld*

**RABBITS**          See: **ANIMALS**

**RACISM**          See also: **ETHNICITY**

I think racism is a terrible thing. I think we should all learn to hate each other on an individual basis.
          —*Cathy Ladman*

On being black: I was born a suspect. I can walk down any street in America, and women will clutch their purses tighter, hold onto their Mace, lock their car doors. If I look up into the windows of the apartments I pass, I can see old ladies on the phone. They've already dialed "91 . . . " and are just waiting for me to do something wrong.
          —*Chris Rock*

Ku Klux Klan

This man was a bigot and a bed wetter. He used to go to Ku Klux Klan meetings wearing a rubber sheet.
          —*Woody Allen*

Last time I was down South, I was in a restaurant and ordered some chicken, and these three cousins, you know the ones I mean, Ku, Kluck, and Klan, come up and say, "Boy, we're givin' you fair warnin'. Anything you do to that chicken, we're gonna do to you." So I put down my knife and fork, and I picked up that chicken. And I kissed it.
          —*Dick Gregory*

North Versus South

For a black man, there's no difference between the North and the South. In the South they don't mind how close I get so long as I don't get too big. In the North they don't mind how big I get so long as I don't get too close.
          —*Dick Gregory*

Racial Slurs

I was walking down the street, and this man actually calls me a Chink! I was so mad: Chinks are Chinese; I'm Korean—I'm a

Gook. If you're going to be racist, at least get the terminology correct. Okay, Bubba?

—*Margaret Cho*

Those country guys all over Texas, big hat, boots, weather-beaten face, belt buckle holding up a stomach well into its last trimester, and calls Latinos "Nachos." "Well, there they go, "*habla, habla, habla.* Why can't yawl learn how to talk rightly?"

—*George Lopez*

The funniest racists are those who don't even realize when they're being racist. This old man came up to me on the street, and demanded, "Pick up my cane, Poncho." "Sir, I'm Vietnamese," I said. "I don't care what part of Mexico you're from," he replied.

—*Dat Phan*

**Reverse**

Just what is reverse racism? Is there something white people are not getting? Reverse racism is like Mike Tyson saying, "It's not fair, me always having to fight the heavy guys. From now on, I only want to fight lightweights."

—*Chris Rock*

**RADIO**

I am amazed at radio DJs today. I am firmly convinced that AM on my radio stands for Absolute Moron. I will not begin to tell you what FM stands for.

—*Jasper Carrott*

The hardest thing about getting out of a relationship is listening to the radio. Because every song is about being in love, or being heartbroken. And I found that the only song I was comfortable with is that Peter, Paul, and Mary song, "If I Had a Hammer."

—*Ellen DeGeneres*

If you break up you can't listen to the radio. "You're listening to the All Love Songs station, nothing but stick-your-head-in-the-oven-and-turn-up-the-gas love songs. And now for everybody who just broke up, here's a song you'll enjoy, "You'll be Alone for the Rest of Your Life" from the CD, *You'll Die in a Puddle of Your Own Urine in a Welfare Hospital*."
      *—Richard Jeni*

How about a radio station that keeps its giveaway money and plays some bloody music?
      *—Jason Love*

**READING**      See also: **BOOKS**

I took a course in speed-reading and was able to read *War and Peace* in twenty minutes. It's about Russia.
      *—Woody Allen*

I went to a Waffle House, I'm eating and I'm reading a book. Waitress walks over to me, "Tch, tch. Hey, what you readin' for?" Is that the weirdest question you've ever heard? Not what am I reading, but what am I reading for. I read for a lot of reasons, and the main one is so I don't end up being a fucking waffle waitress.
      *—Bill Hicks*

I just got out of the hospital. I was in a speed-reading accident. I hit a bookmark.
      *—Steven Wright*

**REAL ESTATE**      See also: **HOUSING**

I have property in LA; a hotel is holding two of my suitcases.
      *—Soupy Sales*

I brought some land. It was kind of cheap. It was on some-body else's property.
—*Steven Wright*

**REALITY**

Reality is the leading cause of stress amongst those in touch with it.
—*Lily Tomlin*

Reality, what a concept.
—*Robin Williams*

**REDNECKS**

Check your neck. You might be a redneck if . . .
There is a stuffed possum anywhere in your house.
Any of your kids were conceived in a car wash.
You've ever financed a tattoo.
You've worn a tube top to a wedding.
You've ever used lard in bed.
You have to go outside to get something out of the 'fridge.
In tough situations you ask yourself, "What would Curly do?"
You've ever hitchhiked naked.
—*Jeff Foxworthy*

**RELATIONSHIPS**

See also: **BOYFRIENDS**, **BREAKING UP**, **DATING**, **GIRLFRIENDS**, **MARRIAGE**

I deserve someone who likes me for who I am pretending to be.
—*Arj Barker*

the Beginning

At the beginning of a relationship wouldn't it save so much time if you could just ask the guy, "Hey, are you an asshole?" And the guy, could say, "Yeah." Which would be OK with me, because I go out with assholes. Exclusively.
—*Karen Haber*

Cheating

My girlfriend found out I was messing around with this other chick. So she called my wife.
—*Corey Holcomb*

Communication

If you are married or living with someone, then there is one thing that gets said day and night that drives both of you absolutely crazy. But one or both of you always say it. It is "What?" The word, the phrase, the implication, the irritation. "What?" "You're deaf?" you mumble. "What?" "I don't mumble, stupid." "I heard that." "That you heard."
    —*Elayne Boosler*

Once a relationship is underway, then I would say deafness would come in handy. Then once you're married and have kids, paralysis. "I'd love to drive you kids to that game, but I've got to sit in that chair and watch football on television."
    —*Jerry Seinfeld*

Dependency

Relationships are a lot like drugs. You develop a dependency, and if you're not really careful you could wind up losing your house.
    —*Mike Dugan*

End of

You always know when the relationship is over. Little things start grating on your nerves, "Would you please stop that! That breathing in and out, it's so repetitious!"
    —*Ellen DeGeneres*

Relationships are hard. It's like a full-time job, and we should treat it like one. If your boyfriend or girlfriend wants to leave you, they should give you two weeks' notice. There should be severance pay, and before they leave you, they have to find you a temp.
    —*Bob Ettinger*

Honesty

Honesty is the key to a relationship. If you can fake that, you're in.
    —*Richard Jeni*

Men Versus Women

Men and women just look at life completely different. Women are playing chess; we plan relationships ten moves ahead.

Meanwhile, the guy is playing checkers, thinking just one move ahead: "Jump me!"

—*Margot Black*

Not

When I'm not in a relationship, I shave one leg. So when I sleep, it feels like I'm with a woman.

—*Garry Shandling*

I'm not in a relationship now, but I have a stalker. Which is kind of nice, because at least he calls. And I never have to make plans with him, because he's always there for me.

—*Pamela Yager*

Perfect Person

You're never going to meet the perfect person. The timing's off. You're married; she's single. You're a Jew; he's Palestinian. One's a Mexican; one's a raccoon. One's a black man; one's a black woman. It's always something.

—*Chris Rock*

Short

Relationships don't last anymore. When I meet a guy, the first question I ask myself is, "Is this the man I want my children to spend their weekends with?"

—*Rita Rudner*

I can't get a relationship to last longer than it takes to burn their CDs.

—*Margaret Smith*

Versus Prison

The difference between being in a relationship and being in prison is that in prison they let you play softball on the weekends.

—*Bobby Kelton*

**RELIGION**

See also: **CREATIONISM**, **GOD**, **HELL**

I was walking across a bridge one day, and I saw a man standing on the edge, about to jump off. So I ran over and said "Stop! Don't do it! There's so much to live for!" He

said, "Like what?" I said, "Well, are you religious or atheist?"
"Religious." I said, "Me too! Are you Christian or Buddhist?"
"Christian." I said, "Me too! Are you Catholic or Protestant?"
"Protestant." I said, "Me too! Are you Episcopalian or Baptist?"
"Baptist." I said, "Wow! Me too! Are you Baptist Church of
God or Baptist Church of the Lord?" "Baptist Church of God."
I said, "Me too! Are you original Baptist Church of God, or
are you Reformed Baptist Church of God?" "Reformed Baptist
Church of God." I said, "Me too! Are you Reformed Baptist
Church of God, Reformation of 1879, or Reformed Baptist
Church of God, Reformation of 1915?" He said, "Reformed
Baptist Church of God, Reformation of 1915." I said, "Die,
heretic scum," and pushed him off.
——*Emo Philips*

Afterlife

Eternal nothingness is fine if you happen to be dressed for it.
——*Woody Allen*

I do not believe in an afterlife. Although I am bringing a
change of underwear.
——*Woody Allen*

Saw a guy with a sign that said, "Where will you spend eternity?"
Which freaked me out, because I was on my way to the Motor
Vehicle Agency.
——*Arj Barker*

The Baptists believe in life after death, but it's a privilege you
have to earn by spending the interim in guilt-ridden misery. At
an early age I decided that living a life of pious misery with the
hope of going to heaven is like keeping your eyes shut during
a movie, in the hope of getting your money back at the end.
——*A. Whitney Brown*

Atheism

To you I'm an atheist; to God, I'm the Loyal Opposition.
——*Woody Allen*

I was raised an atheist. Every Sunday, we went nowhere. We prayed for nothing. And all our prayers were answered.
—*Heidi Joyce*

Do you know what you get when you cross a Jehovah's Witness with an atheist? Someone who knocks on your door for no apparent reason.
—*Guy Owen*

Most people past college age are not atheists. Because you don't get any days off. And if you're an agnostic you don't know whether you get them off or not.
—*Mort Sahl*

And God said, "The only people I like are the atheists, because they play hard-to-get."
—*Lotus Weinstock*

Baptists

The Baptists' basic theology is that if you hold someone underwater long enough, he'll come around to your way of thinking. It's a ritual known as "Bobbing for Baptists."
—*A. Whitney Brown*

Old ladies in the Baptist church always competing about how blessed they are. "I'm blind in one eye; the arthritis is killing me; I take heart pills; my blood pressure is sky-high, but I'm blessed." "Oh yes, sister. My diabetes is acting up fierce. I got so much pain in my legs I can't walk. I ain't had a decent movement in years, but I'm blessed."
—*Bernie Mac*

The story of Adam and Eve made no sense to me. Eve is responsible for the entire decline of humanity because she was tempted by an apple. Don't you think God overreacted just a tad? It's not like Eve ate God's last Oreo.
—*Margot Black*

**Bible**

If it was the exact word of God—you ready?—it would be real clear and easy to understand. God's got a way with words, being the creator of language and all.

—*Bill Hicks*

The Bible contains six admonishments to homosexuals and 362 to heterosexuals. This doesn't mean God doesn't love heterosexuals; it's just that they need more supervision.

—*Lynn Lavner*

They have a politically correct Bible now. They didn't want Jesus to be killed by Jews, an ethnic group, so he dies of secondhand smoke.

—*Bill Maher*

The Bible looks like it started out as a game of Mad Libs.

—*Bill Maher*

"The wages of sin are death." I would imagine so, but by the time they take the taxes out, it's just kind of a tired feeling, really.

—*Paula Poundstone*

Thou shall not kill. Thou shall not commit adultery. Don't eat pork. I'm sorry, what was the last one? Don't eat pork? Is that the word of God, or is that pigs trying to outsmart everybody?

—*Jon Stewart*

Even if you don't believe a word of the Bible, you've got to respect the person who typed all that.

—*Lotus Weinstock*

**Born Again**

Born again? No, I'm not. Excuse me for getting it right the first time.

—*Dennis Miller*

I was recently born again. I must admit it's a glorious and wonderful experience. I can't say my mother enjoyed it a whole lot.

—*John Wing*

**Buddhism**

How come people always flip and think they're Jesus? Why not Buddha? Particularly in America, where more people resemble Buddha than Jesus. "Ah'm Buddha!" "You're Bubba!" "Ah'm Buddha now. All I gotta do is change three letters on ma belt."

—*Bill Hicks*

I spent a week at a Buddhist monastic retreat, where I sat silently for hours at a time in an uncomfortable position trying to shatter my ego. Why bother? Two minutes with my wife and kids does the same thing.

—*Brian Koffman*

Was the Buddha married? His wife would say, "Are you just going to sit around like that all day?"

—*Garry Shandling*

I've been studying Zen Buddhism. Zen teaches the value of doing and thinking nothing. I thought, " Cool, I was fired for being a Zen Master."

—*Dana Snow*

**Catholicism**

The Pope is a hard guy to please, isn't he? No weird sex. Well, what's this kiss my ring stuff?

—*Elayne Boosler*

The Dodge-Plymouth dealers have just had their annual raffle, and they've given away a Catholic church.

—*Lenny Bruce*

I have as much authority as the Pope. I just don't have as many people who believe it.

—*George Carlin*

When I was growing up my mother wanted me to be a priest, but I think it's a tough occupation. Can you imagine giving up your sex life, and once a week people come in and tell you all the highlights of theirs?
    —*Tom Dreesen*

I thought about being a nun for awhile, and believed I'd make a gol-darned good nun. Then I had sex and thought, "Well, fuck that."
    —*Diane Ford*

I stepped into the confessional today and said, "You first."
    —*Dennis Miller*

People ask me what I think about that woman priest thing. Women priests. Great, great. There would be priests of both sexes I don't listen to.
    —*Bill Hicks*

I'm Catholic and we don't read the Bible; we pay a priest to do that for us. Man's got the week off, and no wife; he can give us a forty-five-minute book report once a week. "Just weed through the crap and get to the plot, Padre."
    —*Kathleen Madigan*

I was raised Roman Catholic, and according to the Catholic church it's OK to be homosexual, as long as you don't practice homosexuality. Which is interesting, because I think it's OK to be Catholic as long as you don't practice Catholicism.
    —*Bob Smith*

We were skeptical Catholics. We believed Jesus walked on water. We just figured it was probably winter.
    —*John Wing*

Christianity

Every day people are straying away from the church, and going back to God.
    —*Lenny Bruce*

When I taught Sunday school I was really strict. I used to tell the kids, "If one more of you talks, you're all going to hell!"
—*Margaret Cho*

I think what went wrong with Christianity is exactly like what happens when you try to get your dog to look at something on TV. Jesus pointed at God, and everybody just stared at his finger.
—*Frank Miles*

Episcopalian

When I was a kid my mother switched religions from Catholic to Episcopalian. Which is what, Catholic Lite? One-third less guilt than regular religion.
—*Rick Corso*

Fundamentalism

Fundamentalists are to Christianity what paint-by-numbers is to art.
—*Robin Tyler*

Holy Men

If you want to be a holy man, you have to be committed. When you make a decision you cannot waver in any way. You'd never see Gandhi during a hunger strike sneaking into the kitchen in the middle of the night. "Gandhi, what are you doing down there?" "I, um, I thought I heard a prowler and was going to hit him over the head with this giant bowl of potato salad."
—*Jim Carrey*

Jesus

Hey, doncha think the real reason Jesus Christ hasn't returned is those crosses you wear? "They're still wearing crosses: I'm not going, Dad. They totally missed the point. When they start wearing fishes, I might show up again."
—*Bill Hicks*

If Jesus is my friend, why won't he lend me money?
—*Warren Hutcherson*

In pictures of Jesus he's always a blond, blue-eyed, surfer dude. I don't know why. Jesus was Semitic, so he would have had dark eyes and hair, and a five-o'clock shadow. Basically, Jesus would look like a guy who'd make you nervous if he sat next to you on an airplane.

—*Jennifer Post*

Jesus had twelve disciples who followed him wherever he went. How annoying is that? Do you think he ever turned to them and said, "What?"

—*Jon Stewart*

**Judaism**

There's only one difference between Catholics and Jews. Jews are born with guilt, and Catholics have to go to school to learn it.

—*Elayne Boosler*

My mother is Jewish, my father Catholic. When I went to confession, I'd pray, "Bless me father for I have sinned, and I think you know my lawyer, Mr. Cohen."

—*Bill Maher*

I'm Jewish, but I only go to temple twice a year: Christmas and Easter.

—*Jeffrey Ross*

**Mormonism**

Mormons can have multiple wives. The funny thing is, most guys I know don't even want one.

—*Joel Warshaw*

**Pentecostal**

We were Pentecostal. That's just a light bulb and a car away from being Amish.

—*René Hicks*

**Prayer**

What's with some of these prayers they make little kids recite? "Now I lay me down to sleep, I pray to the Lord my soul to keep. If I should die before I wake . . ." If I should die before I wake? Yeah, someone's going to have an extra donut at

breakfast tomorrow morning. Seriously, I'm not going to sleep, Mom. Get cable, because I'm staying up.
> —*Dennis Miller*

When I was a kid, I used to pray every night for a new bicycle. Then I realized that the Lord, in his wisdom, didn't work that way. So I stole one, and asked Him to forgive me.
> —*Emo Philips*

Why is it when we talk to God we're said to be praying, but when God talks to us we're schizophrenic?
> —*Lily Tomlin*

Dial-a-Prayer hung up on me.
> —*Jackie Vernon*

Reincarnation

I used to believe in reincarnation, but that was in a previous lifetime.
> —*Paul Krassner*

I spend money with reckless abandon. Last month I blew $5,000 at a reincarnation seminar. I got to thinking, "What the heck, you only live once."
> —*Ronnie Shakes*

I believe in reincarnation. I've had other lives. I know. I have clues. First of all, I'm exhausted.
> —*Carol Siskind*

Religious Right

The religious right is really getting out of control. Today they were at the grocery store blocking the home pregnancy test aisle.
> —*Melissa Maroff*

TV Evangelists

Every time I see a TV evangelist I can't help but think that if God wanted to talk to me through the TV, I think he could get a spot on a major network.
> —*Margot Black*

Wouldn't it be great if we found you could only get AIDS from giving money to TV preachers?
— *Elayne Boosler*

TV evangelists are the pro wrestlers of religion.
— *Rick Overton*

Unitarianism

If you were a bigot and wanted to drive a Unitarian out of your town, you'd burn a question mark on his lawn.
— *Mort Sahl*

and War

On going to war over religion: You're basically killing each other to see who's got the better imaginary friend.
— *Richard Jeni*

**REMOTE CONTROLS**

See also: **CRIME** Breaking and Entering, **TELEVISION** Men Versus Women

A new survey reveals that women would rather give up sex than give up the remote for the TV. Men, on the other hand, would be willing to have sex with the remote for the TV.
— *Conan O'Brien*

I want one more remote control unit in my life. I want twelve of those suckers lined up on the coffee table, bring the friends over and go "See those? I don't know how to work any of them. Zero for twelve."
— *Paul Reiser*

I couldn't find the remote control to the remote control.
— *Steven Wright*

**REPAIRS**

If it can't be fixed by duct tape or WD-40, it's a female problem.
— *Jason Love*

## RESTAURANTS

Buffets

Buffet is a French term. It means "Get up and get it yourself."
—*Greg Ray*

I went to this restaurant last night that was set up like a big buffet in the shape of a Ouija board. You'd think about what kind of food you want and the table would move across the floor to it.
—*Steven Wright*

Checks

My husband has never picked up a check in his life. People think he has an impediment in his reach.
—*Phyllis Diller*

Costs

Eating out is very expensive. I was in one restaurant; they didn't even have prices on the menu. Just pictures of faces with different expressions of horror.
—*Rita Rudner*

Doggie Bags

If you're a guy and you ask for the doggie bag on a date, you might as well have them wrap up your genitals, too. You're not going to be needing those for a while, either.
—*Jerry Seinfeld*

I can't leave a restaurant without leftovers. Some restaurants actually get uncomfortable wrapping something up in tin foil, so they disguise it as a swan figurine. I'm like, "You might want to make that swan some babies, because I'm taking these Sweet 'n' Low, too."
—*Margaret Smith*

Family

The other night I ate at a real nice family restaurant. Every table had an argument going.
—*George Carlin*

McDonald's     I went into a McDonald's yesterday and said, "I'd like some
               fries." The girl at the counter asked, "Would you like some
               fries with that?"
                    —*Jay Leno*

               I started a grease fire at McDonald's. Threw a match in the
               cook's hair.
                    —*Steve Martin*

Names          You know how Mexican restaurants always have "border" in
               the name: Border Grill, Border Café. You wouldn't do that to
               black people: Kunta's Kitchen or Shackles. They don't do it to
               white people. You don't see the Honkey Grill, the Cracker
               Barrel . . . oh, never mind.
                    —*George Lopez*

               I stopped for breakfast at the International House of
               Pancakes. As soon as you walk in the establishment, you catch
               the distinct, worldwide feel of the place. I was completely baf-
               fled by the complex menu. So I just had the flapjack du jour,
               and my syrup steward helped me select a very dry maple that
               was busy but never precocious.
                    —*Dennis Miller*

Ordering       Last night I ordered an entire meal in French, and even the
               waiter was surprised. It was a Chinese restaurant.
                    —*Henny Youngman*

Party of One   If I ever got money, I would open a restaurant for single peo-
               ple. And I'd make 'em feel comfortable, too. Name it "Just
               One." You walk in, nice long row of sinks. No tables and chairs.
               Everyone eats standing over the sink. All the food comes in the
               package, so you can read the back while you're eating.
                    —*Elayne Boosler*

               When going to a restaurant, "party of one" is rarely cause for
               celebration.
                    —*Ellen DeGeneres*

Pizza | There's a pizza place near where I live that sells only slices. In the back you can see a guy tossing a triangle in the air.
        *—Steven Wright*

Seafood | Don't sit in a restaurant by the tank where they keep the lobsters—it's very depressing. Lobsters always have that look of, "Any word from the governor?"
        *—Richard Jeni*

Why does Sea World have a seafood restaurant? I'm halfway through my fishburger and I realize, "Oh my God, I could be eating a slow learner."
        *—Lynda Montgomery*

Waiters | I once dated a waitress. In the middle of sex she'd say, "How is everything? Is everything okay over here?"
        *—David Corrado*

I was at a fancy restaurant. They had a waiter for everything. The butter waiter came over and gave us butter; the water waiter came over and gave us water; the head waiter came over . . . oh, it was so fancy.
        *—George Miller*

Waiters and waitresses are becoming much nicer and more caring. I used to pay my check, they'd say "Thank you." That graduated into "have a nice day." That's now escalated into, "You take care of yourself, now." The other day I paid my check—the waiter said, "Don't put off that mammogram."
        *—Rita Rudner*

When I go to a restaurant I always ask the manager, "Give me a table near a waiter."
        *—Henny Youngman*

**REVERIES** | I was trying to daydream, but my mind kept wandering.
        *—Steven Wright*

**RIGHTS**            Everybody says they have rights. But you also have responsibilities. You have the right to choose any religion, but you also have the responsibility to pick one that doesn't wake me up on Sunday morning by knocking on my door.
                      —*Bill Maher*

**RIGHT-TO-LIFE**     See: **PRO-CHOICE, PRO-LIFE**

**ROMANCE**           See: **LOVE**

**ROOMMATES**         Roommates are tough. Even if you shared an apartment with the Pope, I guarantee that three weeks into it you'd be going, "Hey, you mind picking up the cape, man? And quit leaving the papal miter on the kitchen counter."
                      —*Jeff Foxworthy*

**RUNNING**           See: **EXERCISE**

**RUTS**              I feel like I'm in a rut. Every time I go to bed at night, I find myself getting up again in the morning.
                      —*Brad Stine*

**SAFETY**        See also: **SECURITY**

Men and women perceive crime differently. Once I was walking in New York with a boyfriend. He said, "Gee, it's a beautiful night. Let's go down by the river." "What? Are you nuts?" I asked. "It's midnight! I'm wearing jewelry! I'm carrying money! I have a vagina with me! Tomorrow," I added, "I'll leave it in my other pants. Then we'll go down."
        —*Elayne Boosler*

Safety was not a big thing when I was growing up. A seat belt was something that got in the way, "Ma, the seat belt is digging into my back." "Stuff it down into the seat. And roll those windows up, you're letting my cigarette smoke out."
        —*Margaret Smith*

**SATELLITES**        Every so often, I like to go to the window, look up, and smile for a satellite picture.
        —*Steven Wright*

**SCHOOLS**        See also: **COLLEGE**

A lot of stuff in school you don't appreciate 'til you get to be older. Little things, like being spanked every day by a middle-aged woman. Stuff you'd pay good money for later in life.
        —*Emo Philips*

Education        I had a terrible education. I attended a school for emotionally disturbed teachers.
        —*Woody Allen*

You know there is a problem with the education system when you realize that out of the three Rs, only one begins with an R.
        —*Dennis Miller*

**Elementary**

When I was a kid in elementary school, the teacher asked me to discuss *Moby Dick*. So I said, "It strikes me as a plug for the whaling industry."
—*John Astin*

My first-grade teacher said, "Okay Mark, tell us everything you know about the letter H." I said, "That's Jesus' middle name."
—*Mark Lundholm*

Nothing I learned in school prepared me for life on any level. My first book should have read, "See Dick balance his checkbook. See Jane leave an unhealthy relationship. Run, Jane, run!"
—*Kate Mason*

**Fire Drills**

In elementary school, in case of fire you have to line up quietly in a single-file line from smallest to tallest. What is the logic? Do tall people burn slower?
—*Warren Hutcherson*

**First Day**

I will never forget my first day of school. My mom woke me up, got me dressed, made my bed, and fed me. Man, did the guys in the dorm tease me.
—*Michael Aronin*

School has always been scary for me. The very first day of school, my parents dropped me off at the wrong nursery. I didn't know anyone, and there were lots of trees.
—*Brian Kiley*

**Gym**

The gym teacher, Mr. Caruso, did not speak English; he spoke "Gym." One day I was playing basketball, and Mr. Caruso told me to get an athletic supporter. He didn't say it that way, though. He said, "One day you're gonna go up for a rebound, and the family jewels aren't gonna go with ya." I had no idea what he was talking about. Next day I showed up for practice without my watch and mezuzah. He said,

"Did ya take care of the family jewels?" I said, "I left 'em in my locker." Took us a half hour to revive Mr. Caruso.
    —*Gabe Kaplan*

Any day that you had gym was a weird school day. It started off normal—English, geometry, social studies—and then suddenly you're in *Lord of the Flies* for forty minutes. You're hanging from a rope; you have hardly any clothes on. Kids are throwing dodgeballs at you, snapping towels; you're trying to survive. And then it's history, science, language. There's something off in the whole flow of that day.
    —*Jerry Seinfeld*

High School

High school classes should include one in personal finance. These kids don't know a thing about money. I had one student who thought she had money in her checking account as long as she had checks in her checkbook.
    —*Rob Bitter*

Graduation time in high schools is the moment to extend sincere congratulations to that elite 49 percent of American students who made it through the system. You all worked very hard for your diplomas, and it's just too bad that most of you won't be able to read them.
    —*A. Whitney Brown*

Children are stupid; that's why they're in school. I'd lecture for an hour about percentages and interest rates, and at the end I'd ask one simple question, "You put ten grand in a bank for one year at five and a half percent and what do you get?" Some kid would always yell out, "A toaster."
    —*Jeff Jena*

In high school my sister went out with the captain of the chess team. My parents loved him. They figured that any guy that took hours to make a move was OK with them.
    —*Brian Kiley*

My school colors were clear. We used to say, "I'm not naked, I'm in the band."
—*Steven Wright*

Homeschooling   I was homeschooled. The cat never stood a chance against me in dodgeball.
—*Eric Roth*

Kindergarten   A lot of things go on when you're a kid that you don't figure out until you're an adult. Like, I think my kindergarten teacher had a drinking problem, because naptime was every day from 9:00 to 2:30.
—*Janine DiTullio*

My kindergarten teacher hated me. She used to find any excuse to pick on me, especially during nap time. Like I'm the only guy who sleeps naked.
—*Brian Kiley*

Math   See also: **PARENTHOOD** Homework

As long as there is algebra, there will be prayer in school.
—*Larry Miller*

In high school, I could not pass a math test. I couldn't pass a drug test either. There may be a correlation.
—*Lynda Montgomery*

I'm not good at math; I've never been good at math. I accepted it from a very early age. My teacher would hand me a math test. I'd just write on it, "I'm going to marry someone who can do this."
—*Rita Rudner*

Prayer in   I'm willing to see prayer in our schools, if you're willing to find a place for algebra in our churches.
—*Dylan Brody*

Private

My kid drives me nuts. For three years now he goes to a private school; he won't tell me where it is.
—*Rodney Dangerfield*

Proms

I remember my prom—the limo, the dancing until dawn. It would have been even better if I'd had a date.
—*David Letterman*

Reunions

Don't go to a school reunion. There'll be a lot of old people there claiming to be your classmates.
—*Tom Dreesen*

Don't go to your high school reunion. You know who goes to your high school reunion? Idiots. Everybody you hated in high school shows up. The really cool people overdosed years ago, or they're living elsewhere under the witness protection program.
—*Billy Garan*

I went to the thirtieth reunion of my preschool. I didn't want to go because I've put on, like, one hundred pounds.
—*Wendy Liebman*

Sex Education

People want to take sex education out of the schools. They believe sex education causes promiscuity. Hey, I took algebra. I never do math.
—*Elayne Boosler*

Shootings

What the hell is wrong with these white kids shooting up a school? "No one would play with us. We had no friends." Hey, I saw the yearbook picture. It was six of them! I didn't have six friends in high school. I don't have six friends now. That's three-on-three with a half-court.
—*Chris Rock*

Teachers

I was a substitute teacher for a couple of years, and it's a tough job. And apparently not cool to say, "You guys work on your math problems. If you have any questions, wake me up."
—*Adam Gropman*

There's always one teacher you had a crush on. For me it's my wife's aerobics instructor.
—*Brian Kiley*

You know how to tell if the teacher is hung over? Movie Day.
—*Jay Mohr*

I like a teacher who gives you something to take home to think about besides homework.
—*Lily Tomlin*

Testing

Intelligence tests are biased toward the literate.
—*George Carlin*

Schools: I got an F one time on a question that asked my opinion.
—*Gallagher*

Tough

I won't say ours was a tough school, but we had our own coroner. We used to write essays like, "What I'm Going to Be If I Grow Up."
—*Lenny Bruce*

Uniforms

In California, some high schools are requiring students to wear uniforms. They say uniforms create a safe, stable environment. You know, like the post office.
—*Jay Leno*

## SCIENCE

Cryogenics

In cryogenics they freeze you until science discovers a cure for what killed you, and then they revive you. But what if you froze to death?
—*George Miller*

Genes

Scientists have located the gene for impulsive behavior. Not surprisingly, it was getting its nipples pierced.
—*Conan O'Brien*

| | |
|---|---|
| Human Composition | Human beings are 70 percent water, and, with some, the rest is collagen.<br>    —*Martin Mull* |
| Microwaves | The microwave oven is the consolation prize in our struggle to understand physics.<br>    —*Jason Love* |
| Robots | There are now robots that simulate dance movements. I think we call them white people.<br>    —*Jay Leno* |
| Space | If they can put a man on the moon why can't they put one in me?<br>    —*Flash Rosenberg*<br><br>Black holes are where God divided by zero.<br>    —*Steven Wright* |
| Speed of Light | It is impossible to travel faster than the speed of light, and certainly not desirable, as one's hat keeps blowing off.<br>    —*Woody Allen*<br><br>If light travels so fast, how come it takes six days to get my electricity turned back on?<br>    —*Buzz Nutley*<br><br>OK, so what's the speed of dark?<br>    —*Steven Wright* |

## SCOUTING

| | |
|---|---|
| Boy Scouts | I would be happy to have a gay child. He would be a Boy Scout, and he would teach all the other Boy Scouts how to build a fire with two sticks and a back-handed compliment.<br>    —*Margaret Cho* |

The only memory I have of being a Cub Scout was trying to get my hat back. That was all I did. Run back and forth at my bus stop going, "Quit it!"
—*Jerry Seinfeld*

They don't want gay kids in the Boy Scouts. But their motto is "Be Prepared," and nobody's more prepared than a gay scout. My survival kit had a spice rack. My Swiss Army knife had a melon-baller and garlic press. I was ready for anything.
—*Bob Smith*

When I was in Boy Scouts, I slipped on the ice and hurt my ankle. A little old lady had to help me across the street.
—*Steven Wright*

Girl Scouts

I was expelled from the Girl Scouts for creativity. They had another name for it: pyromania.
—*Aurora Cotsbeck*

I learned an awful lot as a Brownie. I learned how to start a campfire with two sticks, and a match. And how to survive in the woods on only $5 a day.
—*Donna Jean Young*

## SEASONS

Fall

Fall is my favorite season in Los Angeles, watching the birds change color and fall from the trees.
—*David Letterman*

Spring

Spring is Nature's way of saying "Let's party!"
—*Robin Williams*

Summer

Those seriously hot days this year brought back memories of my childhood summers. I remember that sizzling sound, and the delicious smell of meat cooking, when my wet thighs hit the car seat.
—*Daniel Liebert*

Winter
I've got the winter blues, but I'm not gonna raise a fuss or gonna raise a holler. That would be the summertime blues.
—*Vinny Badabing*

**SECURITY**
See also: **SAFETY**

I have six locks on my door, all in a row, and when I go out I only lock every other lock. Because I figure no matter how long somebody stands there, picks the locks, they're always locking three.
—*Elayne Boosler*

For safety's sake, I try not to go to the ATM at night. I also try not to go with my four-year-old who screams, "We've got money! We've got money!"
—*Paul Clay*

People are going to steal from you. You can't stop them. But everybody has their own little personal security thing that they think will foil the crooks. You go to the beach, go in the water, put your wallet in the sneaker. What criminal mind could penetrate this fortress of security? "I tied a bow. They can't get through that."
—*Jerry Seinfeld*

**SELF-ACCEPTANCE**
Don't compare yourself with someone else's version of happy, or thin. Accepting yourself burns the most calories.
—*Caroline Rhea*

**SELF-CONSCIOUS**
I was so self-conscious that when I was at a football game and the players went into a huddle, I thought they were talking about me.
—*Jackie Mason*

**SELF-ESTEEM**
I find low self-esteem incomprehensible. Why hate yourself, when you can hate others?
—*Amy Ashton*

Most people with low self-esteem have earned it.
　　—*George Carlin*

I'm currently dating a girl with no self-esteem. Which is good, because if she had any, she'd leave me.
　　—*Devin Dugan*

I have low self-esteem. When we were in bed together, I would fantasize that I was someone else.
　　—*Richard Lewis*

**SELF-IMAGE**

I'm getting very comfortable with my body. I'm sleeping on a full-length mirror.
　　—*Sandra Bernhard*

**SENIOR CITIZENS**

See also: **AGING**

If you live to be one hundred, you've got it made. Very few people die past that age.
　　—*George Burns*

When I was a boy, the Dead Sea was only sick.
　　—*George Burns*

Some sad news: The world's oldest man has died in Japan at the age of 114. What's the deal with this world's oldest title? It's like some kind of curse, have you noticed? As soon as you get it, like, a year later, you're dead.
　　—*Jay Leno*

It's no longer a question of staying healthy. It's a question of finding a sickness you like.
　　—*Jackie Mason*

There's one advantage to being 102. No peer pressure.
　　—*Dennis Wolfberg*

**SEX**     See also: **CONTRACEPTION, HOMOSEXUALITY, LESBIANS, MEN, ORGASMS, PENISES, PORNOGRAPHY, PROSTITUTION, SEXUALITY, STRIPPING, TELEPHONES, WIVES**

**After Children**     Sex after children slows down. Every three months now we have sex. Every time I have sex, the next day I pay my quarterly taxes. Unless it's oral sex—then I renew my driver's license.
        —*Ray Romano*

**After Fight**     Sex after a fight is often the best there is, which is why you're never allowed in the locker room right after a prizefight.
        —*Jay Leno*

**Anal**     I asked my wife to try anal sex. She said, "Sure. You first."
        —*Robert Schimmel*

**Bad**     I'm not good in bed. Hell, I'm not even good on the couch.
        —*Drew Carey*

**Beautiful**     I think sex is beautiful between the right man and the right woman, but it's difficult to get between the right man and woman.
        —*Woody Allen*

**Casual**     Casual sex is the best, because you don't have to wear a tie.
        —*John Mendoza*

        I never believed in casual sex. I have always tried as hard as I could.
        —*Garry Shandling*

**Celibacy**     I'm in kind of a sexual dry spell. For the past few years, I've only had sex in the months that end in "arch."
        —*Doug Benson*

        I'm celibate, and it ain't easy. I now know why Catholic nuns are so darn mean. I also want to hit people with a ruler for no apparent reason.
        —*René Hicks*

| | |
|---|---|
| Choice | No matter what she says or does, remember one thing—all women want it. But maybe not with you.<br>—*Bill Kalmenson* |
| Clowns | I once made love to a female clown, and she twisted my penis into a poodle.<br>—*Dan Whitney* |
| Compliments | I've had a lot of nice compliments after making love. Stuff like "I wanted to moan, but I didn't have time."<br>—*Ed Bluestone* |
| Cuddling | In Germany, police are searching for a woman who holds men at gun point and forces them to have sex with her. Actually the gun isn't for the sex; it's to keep the guy around later to make him cuddle.<br>—*Jay Leno* |
| Cybersex | I have so much cybersex, my baby's first words will be, "You've got mail."<br>—*Paula R. Hawkins* |
| and Death | The difference between sex and death is that with death you can do it alone and no one is going to make fun of you.<br>—*Woody Allen* |
| | I tell ya, I got no sex life. My dog watched me in the bedroom, to learn how to beg. He also taught my wife how to roll over and play dead.<br>—*Rodney Dangerfield* |
| Dirty | Is sex dirty? Only if it's done right.<br>—*Woody Allen* |
| | If you believe that there is a God, a God that made your body, and yet you think that you can do anything with that body that's dirty, then the fault lies with the manufacturer.<br>—*Lenny Bruce* |

How did sex come to be thought of as dirty in the first place? God must have been a Republican.
> —*Will Durst*

**Education**

I actually learned about sex watching neighborhood dogs. And it was good. Go ahead and laugh. I think the most important thing I learned was: Never let go of the girl's leg no matter how hard she tries to shake you off.
> —*Steve Martin*

When my teenage daughter told us that her sex-ed teacher had demonstrated how to put on a condom, my wife asked, "On what? A cucumber? Boy, are they letting you in for a big disappointment."
> —*Robert Schimmel*

There exists a widespread folk myth that humans should learn about sex from their parents. My relationship with my father nearly ended when he tried to teach me how to drive. I can't imagine our relationship having survived his instructing me how to operate my penis.
> —*Bob Smith*

**Ejaculation**

I went to a meeting for premature ejaculators. I left early.
> —*Red Buttons*

Premature ejaculation, I don't believe in that. If I come, it was right on time; that's the way I see it. As far as I'm concerned I can't come fast enough. They're mad at me because we have different goals in sex: I'm a speedfucker.
> —*Dave Chappelle*

My psychologist told me that a lot of men suffer from premature ejaculation. That's not true: Women suffer.
> —*Robert Schimmel*

Fantasies       My husband wanted to spice up our love life with role play. He said, "I'll fulfill your fantasy if you fulfill mine." I said, "Great. Me first: Clean the bathtub."
> —*Stephanie Blum*

Last time I tried to make love to my wife, nothing was happening, so I said to her, "What's the matter, you can't think of anybody either?"
> —*Rodney Dangerfield*

My biggest sex fantasy is we're making love and I realize I'm out of debt.
> —*Beth Lapides*

I asked my girlfriend who she fantasized about while we were having sex, and she said, "I don't really have time."
> —*Owen O'Neill*

Frequency      Engaged women have sex 2.9 times a week. And the .9 is really frustrating.
> —*Jay Leno*

In a new sex survey they found 8 percent of people had sex four or more times a week. Now here's the interesting part. That number drops to 2 percent when you add the phrase, "With partner."
> —*David Letterman*

Good       After making love I said to my girl, "Was it good for you, too?" And she said, "I don't think that was good for anybody."
> —*Garry Shandling*

Group       I tried group sex. Now I have a new problem. I don't know who to thank.
> —*Rodney Dangerfield*

I could never be comfortable at an orgy. I'd always think there would be someone making rabbit ears behind my back.
—*Diane Nichols*

My orgies are like the Special Olympics. Lots of drooling, but everybody's a winner.
—*Matt Weinhold*

High School

Back in high school, my buddies tried to put the make on anything that moved. I told them, "Why limit yourselves?"
—*Emo Philips*

Importance of

There are more important things than sex. I always thought that music was more important than sex. Then I noticed that if I don't hear a concert for a year and a half, it don't bother me.
—*Jackie Mason*

Instructions

I'm afraid to give instructions in bed because I'm afraid I'll get carried away. "Okay, pull my hair, and touch me right there. No, to the left. Now go outside and move my car so I won't get a ticket. Yeah, that's it."
—*Laura Kightlinger*

The other night I was making love to my wife, and she said, "Deeper, deeper." So I started quoting Nietzsche to her.
—*Dennis Miller*

Dr. Ruth says women should tell our lovers how to make love to us. My boyfriend goes nuts if I tell him how to drive.
—*Pam Stone*

Kinky

My last girlfriend was pretty wild in bed. She used to cover me from head to toe with oil, and then set me on fire.
—*David Corrado*

You know what I say about edible panties? I say if you're drunk enough, and your teeth are sharp enough, every panty is edible.
—*Brian McKim*

I read in *Cosmopolitan* that women like to have whipped
cream sprayed on their breasts. Unfortunately, my girlfriend
has silicone implants. So I use non-dairy topping.
—*Jeff Shaw*

and Laughter

My girlfriend always laughs during sex, no matter what
she's reading.
—*Emo Philips*

Lights off

My wife insists on turning off the lights when we make love.
That doesn't bother me. It's the hiding that seems so cruel.
—*Jonathan Katz*

without Love

Sex without love is an empty experience, but as empty
experiences go it's one of the best.
—*Woody Allen*

If you put a guy on a desert island, he'd do it to mud. A girl
doesn't understand this: "You'd do it to mud, you don't love
me!" Sex is a different emotion.
—*Lenny Bruce*

How can you have sex without emotional attachment? Use
an attachment.
—*Carrie Snow*

Lying

Everybody lies about sex. People lie during sex. If it weren't
for lies, there'd be no sex.
—*Jerry Seinfeld*

Manuals

Have you heard of this new book titled *1,001 Sex Secrets Men
Should Know*? It contains comments from 1,001 different
women on how men can be better in bed. I think that
women would actually settle for three: Slow down; turn off
the TV; call out the right name.
—*Jay Leno*

If I ever wrote a sex manual, it would be called *Ouch, You're on My Hair*.
—*Richard Lewis*

**when Married**  Sex when you're married is like going to the 7-Eleven—there's not much variety, but at three in the morning, it's always there.
—*Carol Leifer*

**Masturbation**  Having sex is like playing bridge. If you don't have a good partner, you better have a good hand.
—*Woody Allen*

If God had intended us not to masturbate he would've made our arms shorter.
—*George Carlin*

You know you have a masturbation problem when certain things won't get in your way, like the hiccups.
—*Zach Galifianakis*

**with Men**  When I was seventeen years old, I was going out with a fifty-nine-year-old man. Sexually we got along great because the things he couldn't do anymore were the things I didn't know about.
—*Carol Henry*

There is a video out now on how to please men. Here's tip number one: Just show up!
—*Jay Leno*

There ain't nothing an old man can do for me but bring me a message from a young one.
—*Moms Mabley*

**Ménage à Trois**  I'm not an advocate of three-way sex. They're like that Lucy episode where Lucy and Ethel are trying to stuff all the chocolate into their mouths. I tried a five-way once, but I'm

too needy. Afterward I was like, "So are we all in a relationship now?"
—*Margaret Cho*

*Ménage à trois* is a French term. It means Kodak moment.
—*Greg Ray*

What's the number-one fantasy for most guys? Two women. Fellows, I think that's a bit lofty. Come on, if you can't satisfy that one woman, why you want to piss off another one? Why have two angry women in bed with you at the same time?
—*Wanda Sykes*

Men Versus Women

The human race has been set up. Someone, someone is playing a practical joke on us. Apparently, women need to feel loved to have sex. Men need to have sex to feel loved. How do we ever get started?
—*Billy Connolly*

Women need a reason to have sex. Men just need a place.
—*Billy Crystal*

Men reach their sexual peak at eighteen. Women reach their sexual peak at thirty-five. Do you get the feeling God is into practical jokes? We're reaching our sexual peak right around the same time they're discovering they have a favorite chair.
—*Rita Rudner*

The basic conflict between men and women sexually is that men are like firemen. To us, sex is an emergency, and no matter what we're doing we can be ready in two minutes. Women are like fire. They're very exciting, but the conditions have to be exactly right for it to occur.
—*Jerry Seinfeld*

Making love to a woman is like baking a turkey: You have to preheat the oven, stuff, baste, make some gravy, put it in for two hours, take it out, not done yet. Another hour, another hour: Finally it's ready. Men, it's microwave cooking. Rip off the package, three minutes: Ding! Gotta nap for an hour.
—*Craig Shoemaker*

Men keep rushing through lovemaking. Which is the part I like, the beginning part. Most women are like that. We need time to warm up. Why is this hard for you guys to understand? You are the first people to tell us not to gun a cold engine. You want us to go from zero to sixty in a minute. We're not built like that. We stall.
—*Anita Wise*

Mile-High Club

Did you hear about those two strangers who were arrested for having sex in first class on American Airlines? You know who I feel sorry for? The guy in the middle seat.
—*Jay Leno*

Mirrors

I heard that having a mirror over your bed was supposed to be romantic. A week later I caught somebody shoplifting in my apartment.
—*Elayne Boosler*

I have tried a little kinky stuff. A woman called me and said "I have mirrors all over my bedroom. Bring a bottle." I brought Windex.
—*Rodney Dangerfield*

Morning

How many women like to have sex in the morning? How many like to be awake when it happens?
—*Marsha Warfield*

while Old

I once saw my grandparents have sex, and that's why I don't eat raisins.
—*Zach Galifiniakis*

In a survey for *Modern Maturity* magazine, men over seventy-five said they had sex once a week. Which proves that old guys lie about sex, too.
        —*Irv Gilman*

I'm old. I can't fuck like I used to. I'm not in shape. Sex is nothing but hard god-damn work: physical labor. Pumping away like that? My chest hurt, my back hurt, my lips are turning white. I can't breathe and she's going, "Oh yeah, baby, right there. Ooh!" What the fuck is right there? Bust a nut so we can sleep already.
        —*Bernie Mac*

One-Night Stands

I'm not into that one-night thing. I think a person should get to know someone, and even be in love with them, before you use them and degrade them.
        —*Steve Martin*

Oral

Men perform oral sex like they drive. When they get lost they refuse to ask for directions.
        —*Catherine Franco*

Men love oral sex because it combines the two activities that the average guy never gets tired of: 1. Sex. 2. Not moving at all. If the Superbowl was on I could die right now.
        —*Richard Jeni*

Nipples

See also: **MEN**

Your wife's nipples are pretty much like having a cat: They're either up and playful, or napping peacefully, at completely random intervals throughout the day. And if you're lucky, they'll be on your head when you wake up in the morning.
        —*Dave Pavone*

Partners

If you have sex and you know you've made the other person happy, it's so much better than doing it for yourself. Although if you're using your left hand, it's really like you're doing it with someone else.
—*Jim Carrey*

I've had more women than most people have noses.
—*Steve Martin*

Ladies, sexually, if your man won't do it, his best friend will.
—*Lewis Ramey*

It's stupid to be jealous of your partner's past. That's none of your business. I know Lisa had sex before we met. I can handle that. Of course, she didn't enjoy it.
—*Rick Reynolds*

Promiscuity

My sister was so promiscuous she broke her ankle in the glove compartment of a car.
—*Phyllis Diller*

There's a double standard, even today. A man can sleep around and sleep around, and nobody asks any questions. A woman, you make nineteen or twenty mistakes, right away you're a tramp.
—*Joan Rivers*

Rating

I asked my wife, "On a scale of one to ten, how do you rate me as a lover?" She said, "You know I'm no good at fractions."
—*Rodney Dangerfield*

Reason for

When my wife has sex with me there's always a reason. One night she used me to time an egg.
—*Rodney Dangerfield*

and Religion

What do atheists scream when they come?
—*Bill Hicks*

I knew this girl; her mamma told her, "If Jesus comes while you're having sex, you're going to hell." I said, "He ain't coming, woman. I put a little sign on the door: DO NOT DISTURB. Nailed it there with a cross." Man, I got some serious lovin' that night. Busted my nut three times. And the last time I thought I saw Jesus!
—*Bernie Mac*

**Responses**

It's OK to laugh in the bedroom so long as you don't point.
—*Will Durst*

If her lips are on fire and she trembles in your arms, forget her. She's got malaria.
—*Jackie Kannon*

I was with this girl the other night, and from the way she was responding to my skillful caresses, you would have sworn that she was conscious, from the top of her head to the tag on her toes.
—*Emo Philips*

**Role-Playing**

I wanted my last girlfriend to get into role-playing in bed. But she would always say, "Just put the dice away."
—*Myq Kaplan*

**Sadomasochism**

Into bondage? I am. What I do when I'm in the mood is tie her up, and gag her, and go into the living room and watch football.
—*Tom Arnold*

Those S&M people, they are bossy.
—*Margaret Cho*

I bet the Marquis de Sade would have liked the Three Stooges.
—*David Corrado*

I've been thinking about S&M lately. Because if the guy ties you up, at least you know he wants you there for a while. It's a commitment.

—*Janet Rosen*

I wonder, is pain always sexual for S&M people? If they're walking down the street, and they stub their toe, do they go, "Ow! I'm so horny."

—*Suzanne Westenhoefer*

## Safe Sex

Safe sex is very important. That's why I'm never doing it on plywood scaffolding again.

—*Jenny Jones*

The only way to really have safe sex is to abstain. From drinking.

—*Wendy Liebman*

I practice safe sex. I use an airbag. It's a little startling at first when it flies out. Then the woman realizes it's safer than being thrown clear.

—*Garry Shandling*

## Scandals

Men in power always seem to get involved in sex scandals, but women don't even have a word for "male bimbo." Except maybe "Senator."

—*Elayne Boosler*

## Talking

During sex my wife always wants to talk to me. Just the other night she called me from a hotel.

—*Rodney Dangerfield*

A study shows college girls talk about sex at least as much as college guys. They just tell the truth.

—*Jay Leno*

Don't have sex, man. It leads to kissing, and pretty soon you have to start talking to them.

—*Steve Martin*

I told my girlfriend that unless she expressed her feelings and told me what she liked, I wouldn't be able to please her. So she said, "Get off me."

*—Garry Shandling*

Terminology

In an article in *Newsweek* I noticed the phrase "sexually illiterate." I didn't understand. Does anybody's penis read? Mine doesn't. It will look at pictures. But I have never seen it yawn and put a bookmark in.

*—Garry Shandling*

Anyone who calls it "sexual intercourse" can't possibly be interested in actually doing it. You might as well announce you're ready for lunch by proclaiming, "I'd like to do some masticating and enzyme secreting."

*—Allan Sherman*

Time

I had sex for five hours once, but four and a half was apologizing.

*—Conan O'Brien*

I once made love for an hour and five minutes. It was on the day they push the clock ahead.

*—Garry Shandling*

Toys

On edible underwear: I don't know what the big deal is about these. You wear them for a couple of days, they taste just like the other ones.

*—Tom Arnold*

To me, sexual freedom meant freedom from having to have sex. And then along came Good Vibrations. As a love object, it surpasses my husband Harold by a country mile. But this is not a threat to the family unit. I think of it as a kind of Hamburger Helper for the boudoir.

*—Lily Tomlin*

Undressing

The first time I ever got undressed in front of a woman, it was horrible. She started screaming, and then they kicked me off the bus.
—*James Leemer*

According to a new survey, women say they feel more comfortable undressing in front of men than they do undressing in front of other women. They say that women are too judgmental, where, of course, men are just grateful.
—*Jay Leno*

Viagra

Viagra is the work of the devil. Now we girls can look forward to having sex with really old guys, for a really long time.
—*LeMaire*

I don't need Viagra. I need a pill to help me talk afterward.
—*Garry Shandling*

with Women

A study in a magazine asked men, "Would you rather the woman initiate sex?" Overwhelmingly, men said "Yes!" Women countered with the argument saying, "But every time we do we get rejected and criticized." Welcome to the club.
—*Jack Coen*

Making love to a woman is like buying real estate: location, location, location.
—*Carol Leifer*

You know "that look" women get when they want sex? Me neither.
—*Steve Martin*

Women are really not that exacting. They only desire one thing in bed. Take off your socks. And by the way—they're not going to invite their best girlfriend over for a threesome, so you can stop asking.
—*Dennis Miller*

**SEXUALITY**          See also: **HOMOSEXUALITY**, **LESBIANS**, **SEX**

Some men are heterosexual and some men are bisexual
and some men don't think about sex at all . . . you know,
they become lawyers.
          —*Woody Allen*

I'm a quadrasexual. That means I'll do anything with anyone for a quarter.
          —*Ed Bluestone*

Bisexuality          Lots of people think that bisexual means cowardly lesbian.
          —*Sandra Bernhard*

Am I gay? Am I straight? And I realized: I'm just slutty!
Where's my parade?
          —*Margaret Cho*

I don't even consider myself bisexual. I just think of myself
as a "people person."
          —*Michael Dane*

Bisexuals are incredibly greedy MFs. Get off the fence and
pick a hole.
          —*Dennis Miller*

Heterosexuality          See also: **HOMOSEXUALITY**

You're born a heterosexual. It's not a choice. Who would
choose this? The guilt, the shame. . . and do you think I'm
happy having to hire a decorator?
          —*Garry Shandling*

Preferences          Don't get me wrong. I support whatever your sexual
preference as long as you're committed. I myself can't
believe eventually I will have to marry someone the same
sex as my mother.
          —*Garry Shandling*

**Transsexuals**

I met this transsexual at my gym, and he was telling me about how he had a sex change to become a woman, and now he's started to date other women. I said, "Look, fellow/ma'am, I think you are making this a little bit harder than it has to be."
    —*Shashi Bhatia*

I know my sexuality, but I get so confused by other people's. I don't even know the difference between transvestites and transsexuals. As I understand it, transvestites are the ones that grow down from the ceiling and transsexuals are the ones that grow up.
    —*Pamela Yager*

**Transvestites**

Gay men in drag think it's glamorous being a woman, that it's all about the dress and makeup. Hey buddy, if you really want to impersonate a woman shove a tampon up your wazoo every month, give birth, and take a cut in pay.
    —*Michele Balan*

**SHADOWS**

I got a new shadow. I had to get rid of the other one; it wasn't doing what I was doing.
    —*Steven Wright*

**SHALLOW**

There's nothing wrong with being shallow as long as you're insightful about it.
    —*Dennis Miller*

**SHAVING**

I cut my Adam's apple shaving. What a mess . . . apple juice everywhere.
    —*Drake Sather*

**SHOES**

High heels should be outlawed. At the very least there should be a five-day waiting period before you can buy them. They destroy your feet. It should be mandatory that the Surgeon General print a warning label on high heels like they do on cigarettes. "Warning: These shoes can lead to lower back pain, aching toes, and the illusion that you are taller than you actually are."
    —*Ellen DeGeneres*

I think high heels are ridiculous. It's like putting a building on the head of a pin.

—*Cathy Ladman*

**SHOPPING**       See also: **STORES**

Batteries

I bought some batteries, but they weren't included, so I had to buy them again.

—*Steven Wright*

Compulsive

I'm a compulsive shopper. It's terrible, I buy things I don't need. Today I bought a jock strap. I use it in my kitchen to hang garlic.

—*Cathy Ladman*

Feminine Needs

I was shopping for groceries when I saw the sign for Feminine Needs and I thought to myself, "Finally, a store that sells nice, cute, well-hung guys with money, who call when they say they're gonna. Where, oh where, are my double coupons?"

—*Leah Krinsky*

I went shopping last week looking for feminine protection. I looked at all the products and decided on a .38 revolver.

—*Karen Ripley*

Home Shopping Network

I know a guy who called up the Home Shopping Network. They said, "Can I help you?" And he said, "No, I'm just looking."

—*George Miller*

Men

My husband takes me to Home Depot; I want to go home. "It's an entire aisle of nails! Get a sharp one, let's go!"

—*Maryellen Hooper*

Most men hate to shop. That's why the men's department is usually on the first floor of a department store, two inches from the door.
—*Rita Rudner*

Here's how a guy shops. He's standing outside. He goes, "I'm cold." He goes in the store, buys the coat, walks out. "I'm not cold anymore. Shopping is over."
—*Ritch Shydner*

**Sales**

My wife will buy anything marked down. Last year she bought an escalator.
—*Henny Youngman*

**Shoes**

I'm a shopaholic. I especially like to shop for shoes, because I don't have to take off the rest of my clothes. But if I do, I get a much bigger discount.
—*Bea Carroll*

I've seen a hundred women show up with one who needs shoes. It's not even shopping; it's like hunting. It's a whole primitive ritual: One of them needs shoes; they get on the edge of a cliff and call a hundred friends with a conch shell.
—*Richard Jeni*

My husband won't try anything on, not even shoes. He'll just hold the box up to the light and say, "Yeah, these fit."
—*Rita Rudner*

**SHOWERS**

I took a baby shower.
—*Steven Wright*

**SINCERITY**

Sincerity is everything. If you fake that, you've got it made.
—*George Burns*

**SINGLE**                See also: **DATING**

the Beginning      When you're first single, you're so optimistic. At the begin-
                   ning, you're like, "I want to meet a guy who's really smart,
                   really sweet, really good-looking, has a really great career." Six
                   months later, you're like, "Lord, any mammal with a day job."
                   —*Carol Leifer*

by Choice          I'm single by choice. Not my choice.
                   —*Orny Adams*

over Forty         I'm forty and single. Don't you think it's a generalization
                   that you should be married at forty? That's like looking at
                   somebody who's seventy and saying, "Hey, when are you
                   gonna break your hip? All your friends are breaking their
                   hips—what are you waiting for?"
                   —*Sue Kolinsky*

Living Alone       I'm not good at being alone. Especially at the end of the day
                   when my finances are a mess, my car is falling apart, I can't
                   find my shoe. That's when I need a big strong guy to hold
                   me close so I can look deep into his eyes, and blame him.
                   —*Simone Alexander*

                   It's pretty lonely and sad to be single. Every night was the
                   same for me: I'd go home and curl up in bed with my
                   favorite book. Well, actually it was a magazine.
                   —*Tom Arnold*

                   The thing I hate about living alone is living alone. I have
                   way too many frivolous conversations with the 411 operator.
                   —*Sue Bova*

                   Men don't live well by themselves. They don't even live like
                   people. They live like bears with furniture. I used to go over
                   to my husband's cave. Nothing on the walls, except for
                   some food. The frost was so thick in the freezer you couldn't
                   close the apartment door. The roaches in his kitchen had

stopped eating: They were full. They were on the counter doing aerobic exercise.
—*Rita Rudner*

I figure the only time I really need a man is about once a month, when it's time to flip my mattress.
—*Pamela Yager*

Men    I got married to complicate my thought process. When you're single, your brain is single-minded. Single guys think three things: "I'd like to go out with her," "I'd like to buy one of those," and "I hope those guys win."
—*Jerry Seinfeld*

Singles Groups    I joined a singles group in my neighborhood. The president called me up and asked, "I want to find out what kind of activities you like to plan." I said, "Well, weddings."
—*Lynn Harris*

Tests    It's still fun being single. You just have to be more careful. You can test people before you date them. Say, "Hi, ready in a second. I'm just sewing this button on my jacket." Then you have a little slip. "Oops, I just pricked your finger—I'll get a slide."
—*Elayne Boosler*

Terminology    I love New Age jargon. You don't have to admit to being single. You can just say, "I'm learning to be there for myself on a daily basis."
—*Vanessa Hollingshead*

**SLEEPING**    I love to sleep. It's the best of both worlds. You get to be alive, and unconscious.
—*Rita Rudner*

Alone    I was sleeping the other night; alone, thanks to the exterminator.
—*Emo Philips*

Bedtime    If I'm not in bed by eleven at night, I go home.
—*Henny Youngman*

Dreaming

I had a nightmare last night. I dreamt my parents came to visit. That's it.
— *Cathy Ladman*

It's a nightmare when people can't stop telling you about their dreams.
— *Jason Love*

Ever spend the night with someone and have a really bad dream about them? You wake up all furious and they have no idea why. "Why didn't you save me from Godzilla? He chased me all over that mall!"
— *Monica Piper*

Good

When I woke up this morning my girlfriend asked me, "Did you sleep good?" I said, "No, I made a few mistakes."
— *Steven Wright*

Insomnia

I toss and turn for hours until I realize that making salad isn't going to relax me.
— *Garry Shandling*

I'm kinda tired. I was up all night trying to round off infinity. Then I got bored and went out and painted passing lines on curved roads.
— *Steven Wright*

Naps

No day is so bad it can't be fixed with a nap.
— *Carrie Snow*

Not Enough

God help me. I'm so tired. I need my sleep. I make no bones about it. I need eight hours a day, and at least ten at night.
— *Bill Hicks*

I never get enough sleep. I stay up late because I'm a Night Guy. "What about getting up after five hours' sleep?" "That's Morning Guy's problem." So you get up in the morning, you're exhausted. Night Guy screws Morning Guy. The only

thing Morning Guy can do is oversleep enough so Day Guy loses his job and Night Guy has no money to go out.
> —*Jerry Seinfeld*

## SMOKING

See also: **HEALTH** Warnings

I tell you I don't get no respect. Why, the Surgeon General, he offered me a cigarette.
> —*Rodney Dangerfield*

### Cigars

My lady friend wants me to give up cigars. I don't want to. So we compromised. I will only smoke on nights that I'm with other women.
> —*Craig Kilborn*

### Cutting Back

I'm not really a heavy smoker any more. I only go through two lighters a day now.
> —*Bill Hicks*

### Effects

If you're saying you didn't know cigarettes were bad for you, you're lying through that hole in your trachea.
> —*Dennis Miller*

### and Kissing

They say that kissing a smoker is like licking an ash tray— which is a good thing to remember the next time you get lonely.
> —*Fred Stoller*

### and Longevity

They say if you smoke you knock off ten years. But it's the last ten. What do you miss? The drooling years?
> —*John Mendoza*

### Nonsmokers

You nonsmokers are the pissiest people. You're so demanding about your opportunity for clean air space. How can I possibly respect you? You don't have the nerve to take your own life in a horrible way, slowly and painfully, over a great number of years.
> —*Stephanie Hodge*

I don't smoke. I don't even understand what the point is. All I can tell is that these people are addicted to blowing smoke out of their faces. It's not even a good trick. If you could blow smoke out of your face without everyone knowing where it came from, that would be impressive.

—*Brad Stine*

## Nonsmoking Section

I don't let men smoke in my apartment. But if I have a woman over she can barbecue a goat.

—*Todd Barry*

I've given up booze, dope, bets, debts, cigs, sex, shopping, sugar, and anything that excites my cholesterol. Although I may be cheating on the cigarettes when I sit on the edge of the smoking section and breathe in extra deep, as I chew on my nicotine gum.

—*Katherine Griffith*

I have something to tell you nonsmokers that I know for a fact, and I feel it's my duty to pass on. Ready? Nonsmokers die every day. Enjoy your evening. See, I know that you entertain this eternal-life fantasy because you've chosen not to smoke, but let me be the first to pop that bubble and bring you hurling back to reality. You're dead, too.

—*Bill Hicks*

It's good to see people not smoking. You get dressed up, and you go out. You smoke; it gets in your clothes. You go, "What should I wear tonight, honey? How about something menthol?"

—*George Lopez*

Tobacco companies will stop at nothing to win the tobacco wars. Now their scientists are saying some of the smoking research data is no longer valid, because the rats have to step outside their mazes to smoke.

—*Dennis Miller*

**Process**

The uses of tobacco aren't obvious right off the bat. You shred it up, put it on a piece of paper, roll it up and stick it between your lips . . . and set fire to it. Then you inhale the smoke. You could stand in front of your fireplace and have the same thing going.
—*Bob Newhart*

**Quitting**

I quit smoking. I feel better. I smell better. And it's safer to drink out of old beer cans lying around the house.
—*Roseanne Barr*

I stopped smoking cigarettes, because people were always coming up to me saying, "Miss, your smoke is bothering me." So what? It's killing me.
—*Wendy Liebman*

Have you noticed that most people who give up smoking substitute something for it? Irritability.
—*Henny Youngman*

**in Restaurants**

You know what bugs me? People who smoke cigars in restaurants. That's why I always carry a water pistol filled with gasoline.
—*Paul Provenza*

**Starting**

I've taken up smoking. My doctor says I'm not getting enough tar in my diet.
—*Steve Martin*

**Tolerance**

I think we could end a lot of this intolerance in America if we all smoked cigarettes. You'd be hard-pressed to find a cigarette smoker who's prejudiced, because we smokers know something you nonsmokers don't: that we're all black on the inside.
—*John Hope*

**and Weight**

Smoking cures weight problems. Eventually.
—*Steven Wright*

**SNACKS**          See: **FOOD**

**SNEEZING**        What always staggers me is that when people blow their
                    noses, they always look into their hankies to see what came
                    out. What do they expect to find? A silver sixpence?
                    —*Billy Connolly*

                    This woman sneezed like three hundred times. She said, "There
                    must be something in the air." I said, "Yeah, your germs."
                    —*Linda Herskovic*

**SOCIETY**         I am as frustrated with society as a pyromaniac in a petrified
                    forest.
                    —*A. Whitney Brown*

**SORORITIES**      See: **COLLEGE**

**SPEECH**

Free                This country was settled by people who did not want to be
                    censored, who wanted the freedom to say what they felt.
                    That's why they came here and killed the Indians in the
                    first place.
                    —*Dennis Miller*

Public              According to most studies, people's number one fear is pub-
                    lic speaking. Death is number two. Does that seem right? That
                    means to the average person if you have to go to a funeral,
                    you're better off in the casket than doing the eulogy.
                    —*Jerry Seinfeld*

**SPERM**           My personal history: I started out as a sperm. Good swim-
                    mer. Liked eggs. Nine months, Mom kicks me out of my
                    first home. Since then, I've been living on the outside and
                    looking for similar accommodations. I find them occasion-
                    ally, but I make a mess and have to leave.
                    —*Basil White*

**SPONGES**

Sponges grow in the ocean. I wonder how much deeper the ocean would be if they didn't.
    —*Steven Wright*

**SPORTS**

See also: **EXERCISE, BASEBALL, FISHING, FOOTBALL, GOLF, HUNTING, OLYMPICS**

Athletes

I used to be quite an athlete, big chest, hard stomach. But all that's behind me now.
    —*Bob Hope*

I think sports stars make great role models, particularly if you are thinking about a career in crime.
    —*Laura Kightlinger*

I used to compete in sports, and then I realized: You can buy trophies. Now I'm good at everything.
    —*Demetri Martin*

Women play for the reason male athletes used to play: the love of the game. When I read about male professional athletes being arrested for murder, assault, rape, and theft, I agree with those who say they just can't see women competing on the same level as men anytime near in the near future.
    —*Dennis Miller*

In Russia, if a male athlete loses, he becomes a female athlete.
    —*Yakov Smirnoff*

Autoracing

Auto racing: slow minds and fast cars.
    —*George Carlin*

The fastest growing sport in the country is NASCAR. Cars going around in a circle. That's like watching your clothes spin around the dryer and thinking, "Hey, let's make a day of this!"
    —*Larry Getlen*

I want to be a racecar passenger, just a guy who bugs the driver. "Say man, can I turn on the radio? You should slow down. Why do we gotta keep going in circles? Can I put my feet outta the window? Boy, you really like Tide."
—*Mitch Hedberg*

I went to see a NASCAR race. Where did they get the name? Did two guys in North Carolina try to impress each other? "Hey Bubba, look at mah new Chevrolet." "WHOOOEEEE, Nahhhhsssss Car."
—*Dobie Maxwell*

I watched the Indy 500. And I was thinking: If they left earlier they wouldn't have to go so fast.
—*Steven Wright*

## Basketball

Shaq has gotten so big his toes look like people. Ooh, he'll get mad at me for saying that. I'll just dress like a free throw, and he'll miss me.
—*D. L. Hughley*

You know the basketball game is decided when the white guys come in.
—*Jason Love*

Women are now referees for the NBA, and they're driving some guys crazy. They don't just call a foul; they want to talk about why it happened.
—*Leslie Nesbitt*

Men own basketball teams. Every year cheerleaders' outfits get tighter and briefer, and players' shorts get baggier and longer.
—*Rita Rudner*

My parents sent me to basketball fantasy camp. I got to sleep in the same bed with Patrick Ewing. Except I like a fan, and the noise kept him awake.
            —*Adam Sandler*

Bowling            People who watch bowling: People who watch golf laugh at you.
            —*Craig Kilborn*

I like to go to the bowling alley and bring a little black marble with me, and put it inside that machine that they use to polish the balls. Then call the manager over.
            —*James Leemer*

I bowled for two years in college, because I was drunk and needed shoes.
            —*Kathleen Madigan*

You don't have to be in shape to bowl. It's the only sport where there's a way to signal for a cocktail waitress.
            —*Robin Roberts*

Boxing            Boxing gyms are still pretty much a man's domain, but now some women are stepping into the ring and onto the canvas. I don't get it. Doesn't it hurt? Damn straight it hurts. It's a man's place to pretend something doesn't hurt.
            —*Tim Allen*

How come none of these boxers seem to have a losing record?
            —*George Carlin*

Why do they interview the losing boxer after a fight? "In the third round you got knocked down. What happened?" "It's still a little hazy, but from what I could tell, that other gentleman was punching me in the face."
            —*Gary Gulman*

I love boxing. Where else do two grown men prance around in satin underwear fighting over a belt? The one who wins

gets a purse. They do it in gloves. It's the accessory connection I love.
—*John McGivern*

There's always one of my uncles who watches a boxing match with me and says "Ten million dollars. For that kind of money, I'd fight him." As if someone is going to pay $200 a ticket to see a fifty-seven-year-old carpet salesman get hit in the face once and cry.
—*Larry Miller*

Take boxing, the simplest, stupidest sport of all. It's almost as if these two guys are just desperate to compete with each other, but they couldn't think of a sport. So they said, "Why don't we just pound each other for forty-five minutes? Maybe someone will come watch that."
—*Jerry Seinfeld*

I started boxing for exercise, and on the very first day, the trainer got in the ring with me and said, "Whoever controls the breathing in the ring controls the fight." I immediately passed out.
—*Garry Shandling*

**Bungee Jumping**

You don't hear about bungee jumping as much as you used to. Did all those dumb asses die?
—*Brian Beatty*

I tried bungee jumping. They don't tell you to take the change out of your pockets.
—*Tony DePaul*

**Darts**

The world's best darts player has died at sixty-six. Cause of death was the world's worst darts player.
—*Craig Kilborn*

**Equipment**

Taking up a new sport, I have always subscribed to the rule: Whatever you lack in skill, make up for in silly accessories.

"How's your tennis game?" "Not great. But I have a hat with a tiny solar-powered fan that keeps me cool, and a racket the size of an outdoor grill."

—*Paul Reiser*

Fans

If you're not into sports, guys think you're less of a man unless you can account for time in activities equally masculine. When they ask, "Wanna go see the game?" I reply, "I can't. I gotta go put a transmission in a stripper's car."

—*Bob Nickman*

Loyalty to one sports team is hard to justify. The players are always changing; the team can move to another city, so you're actually cheering and yelling for your clothes to beat the clothes from another city. Fans love a player, but if he goes to another team, the same human being in a different shirt, they hate him now. "Boo! Different shirt!"

—*Jerry Seinfeld*

Football fans actually could be experiencing the straight man's gay pride parade. Men painting each other's faces in bright colors. Men proud to wear another man's last name on their shirt; some men wear no shirt at all. Hot wieners on every corner as you walk up to the main event. Men open up the back of their trunk for a little tailgating.

—*Wanda Sykes*

Hang-Gliding

A fellow told me he was going to hang-gliding school. He said, "I've been going for three months." I asked, "How many successful jumps do you need to make before you graduate?" He said, "All of them."

—*Red Skelton*

Hockey

An assault in hockey, or as they call it in the hood, "white-on-white crime."

—*Jay Leno*

How come women don't play ice hockey? Millions of girls played field hockey, and God knows women can skate. Maybe it's the teeth. Women have this vain silly thing about losing their front teeth.
—*Danny Liebert*

The last professional hockey player to play without a helmet announced his retirement. His actual words were, "I no play hockey never more."
—*Conan O'Brien*

Horse Racing

I went to the racetrack once in my life, and I bet on a horse called Battle Gun, and when all the horses come out, mine is the only horse in the race with training wheels.
—*Woody Allen*

I played a great horse yesterday. It took seven horses to beat him.
—*Henny Youngman*

Some people play a horse to win, some to place. I should have bet this horse to live.
—*Henny Youngman*

Ice Skating

When I was a kid I asked my dad if I could go ice skating. He told me to wait until it gets warmer.
—*Rodney Dangerfield*

I was ejected from a skating rink today. Evidently they don't allow ice fishing.
—*Kevin Nealon*

I like to skate on the other side of the ice.
—*Steven Wright*

Karate

My neighborhood is so bad I started taking karate lessons. I learned how to break my hand in half by hitting a brick.
—*David Corrado*

My brother-in-law died. He was a karate expert, then joined the army. The first time he saluted, he killed himself.

     *—Henny Youngman*

and Men

If you want a guy to do something for you, all you have to do is introduce an element of senseless danger, and it becomes a sport. "Honey, why don't you try to take out the trash—while I chase you on rollerblades with a chainsaw!"

     *—C. Lynn Mitchell*

News

I bought a newspaper the other day, and I was gonna flip to the sports section when I realized, I just don't want to read about vicious brawls, random drug testing, salary squabbles, or venomous court proceedings. For chrissakes, it's enough to make you wanna go to the front page.

     *—Dennis Miller*

Nude

The most favorite activity of nudists: volleyball. The least favorite: dodge ball.

     *—Jay Leno*

Scuba Diving

A guy buys all kinds of scuba diving equipment, $2,000 worth. He goes 150 feet down in the water, sees all the strange fish and scenery, and says to himself, "This is really worth $2,000. I'm really enjoying it." He goes down another fifty feet, sees more beautiful fish and scenery, and all of a sudden coming toward him is a fellow in just plain swimming trunks. The first guy takes out his underwater pad and pencil and writes a note to the fellow in trunks saying, "I just spent $2,000 on all this diving equipment, and here you are way down here in just a pair of trunks. What's the idea?" He hands the pad and pencil to the man, who writes back, "You idiot, I'm drowning!"

     *—Henny Youngman*

Skiing

I pay approximately $1,300 for a lift ticket, which makes me eligible for the lift chair. I don't know who invented this death machine. This is like a psycho's physics test with benches whipping by. Suddenly you're inside a math word problem.

"Estimate the velocity of a bench. . . ." Great, the one day I forgot my protractor.
—*Wayne Federman*

Skiing is too dangerous for me. The only black people who ski are the ones who went to Harvard. The rest of us ain't educated enough to like cold and pain.
—*Bernie Mac*

I say, why pay outrageous prices for ski trips, when I can just stick my face in the freezer and fall down on the kitchen floor?
—*John Wagner*

Cross-country skiing is great if you live in a small country.
—*Steven Wright*

Skydiving    I was skydiving, horizontally.
—*Steven Wright*

Snow Boarding    I went snow boarding today. Well actually, I went careening off a mountain on a giant tongue depressor.
—*Paul Provenza*

Spelunking    As soon as it's warm I plan to go spelunking with fifty million albino epileptics with tails, just to see how sperm feels.
—*Brian Beatty*

Surfing    The work people do to get to the ocean: Fight the traffic, heat, parking, hot sand, and ironically, the ocean doesn't want us. Surfing is the ocean throwing us out of itself. We try to paddle in; the ocean is a nightclub, the waves are bouncers tossing us out. The undertow is a really mean bouncer. Instead of throwing you out, he roughs you up. "You wanna come in? How about coming in twenty-five miles?"
—*Jerry Seinfeld*

**Swimming**

I can't swim, but I don't consider myself a failure. Instead, I like to think I'm fully evolved.
                —*Brian Beatty*

Swimming isn't a sport. It's just a way to keep from drowning. Riding a bus isn't a sport; so why should sailing be a sport?
                —*George Carlin*

I discovered I scream the same way whether I'm about to be devoured by a Great White or if a piece of seaweed touches my foot.
                —*Kevin James*

I always use the buddy system when I'm swimming. I use a buddy chubbier than I am, to keep the sharks away from me.
                —*Jay Leno*

If you see a shark, you don't have to swim faster than the shark. You only have to swim faster than the person you're with.
                —*Kevin Nealon*

**on Television**

I don't care what sport he's watching on TV, my husband says, "C'mon, there's only two minutes left in the game." Those are the longest two minutes in the universe. Where do you get this clock? I'd like one in my bedroom.
                —*Cory Kahaney*

My husband is so confident that when he watches sports on television, he thinks that if he concentrates he can help his team. If the team is in trouble, he coaches the players from our living room, and if they're really in trouble, I have to get off the phone in case they call him.
                —*Rita Rudner*

**Tennis**

Tennis is like marrying for money. Love has nothing to do with it.
                —*Phyllis Diller*

The Tennis Channel debuted. Which came as great news to the rich, fat, white elitists who were growing tired of the Golf Channel.

—*Mel Fine*

I play tennis, and I'm pretty good, but no matter how much I practice I'll never be as good as a wall.

—*Mitch Hedberg*

The way a man plays a game can be very revealing. I was playing tennis with a man I had been dating for a while and noticed his reluctance to keep score properly. He couldn't say, "Thirty-love." He kept saying, "Thirty, I really like you, but still have to see other people."

—*Rita Rudner*

Professional tennis. I don't understand the shushing. "Shh, shh!" Don't the players know we're there? Should we duck behind the seats so they don't see us? And that goofy scoring, win one point and you're up fifteen. Two points, thirty-love. Sounds like an English call girl. "That'll be thirty, love. And could you be quieter next time? Shhh."

—*Jerry Seinfeld*

Weightlifting      See also: **HEALTH CLUBS**

I'd lift weights, but they're so damn heavy.

—*Jason Love*

I don't believe for a second that weightlifting is a sport. They pick up a heavy thing and put it down again. To me, that's indecision.

—*Paula Poundstone*

At my gym they have free weights, so I took them.

—*Steve Smith*

Winning

Can't we silence those Christian athletes who thank Jesus whenever they win, and never mention His name when they lose? You never hear them say, "Jesus made me drop the ball." "The good Lord tripped me up behind the line of scrimmage."

—*George Carlin*

Victory goes to the player who makes the next-to-last mistake.

—*Jackie Mason*

We're a little too into sports in this country, we gotta throttle back. "We won! We won!" No, *they* won—*you* watched."

—*Jerry Seinfeld*

Wrestling

Today in America, a professional wrestler is struck down with a folding chair once every thirty-five seconds. And not one is seen by a referee.

—*Bill Maher*

If professional wrestling did not exist, could you come up with this idea? Could you envision the popularity of huge men in tiny bathing suits, pretending to fight?

—*Jerry Seinfeld*

You always know who's gonna win pro wrestling—the guy with the best nickname. "Here from Philadelphia comes the iron man, Mike the Hammer Armstrong! And he will be wrestling . . . Eugene."

—*Dan Wilson*

**STAINS**

Happiness is getting a brown gravy stain on a brown dress.

—*Totie Fields*

**STATES**

Alaska

I was in Alaska. I was there for two days and six nights. It was so cold; I saw a dog wearing a cat.

—*Wendy Liebman*

Arizona

I grew up in Tucson, Arizona, where it's 120 degrees in the summer. One day our dog burst into flames. We thought we were going have to start a backfire on the cat.
—*Garry Shandling*

California

I like California pretty much. I especially like California when it's not moving. The idea of the ground opening up and sucking me in is not my idea of a good time. I already dated someone like that.
—*Matina Bevis*

I left Los Angeles for a while. I wasn't on business; I just wanted to smoke a cigarette.
—*Richard Jeni*

If God doesn't destroy Hollywood Boulevard, he owes Sodom and Gomorrah an apology.
—*Jay Leno*

When I first moved to San Francisco it was foggy, rainy, and cold. At first I thought it's sort of romantic. I'll break up an old chair for kindling, buy a bottle of wine, and sit in front of the fire for the day. Two months later . . . a hopeless alcoholic, with no furniture.
—*Paula Poundstone*

District of Columbia

You know the difference between Washington and Las Vegas? In Las Vegas the drunks gamble with their own money.
—*Jay Leno*

Washington, D.C., is to lying what Wisconsin is to cheese.
—*Dennis Miller*

Illinois

I think that's how Chicago got started. A bunch of people in New York said, "Gee, I'm enjoying the crime and the poverty, but it just isn't cold enough. Let's go west."
—*Richard Jeni*

Louisiana

In my home state of Louisiana we bury the dead above ground so we can get them to the polls quicker.
—*Leslie Stahl*

Michigan

You think New York is bad? You ought to go to Detroit. You can go ten blocks and never leave the scene of the crime.
—*Red Skelton*

Minnesota

I was up in Minnesota last winter. It got so cold one night the lottery balls retracted into the machine.
—*Dobie Maxwell*

Nevada

August, I'm in Las Vegas, 120 degrees, but it's a dry heat. That's what they were telling me when they were putting me in the ambulance, "It's a dry heat, Mr. Pinetta."
—*Joe Pinetta*

New York

New York is an exciting town where something is happening all the time, most of it unsolved.
—*Johnny Carson*

New York: In the event of a nuclear attack, it'll look the same as it did before.
—*Billy Connolly*

New York now leads the world's great cities in the number of people around whom you shouldn't make a move.
—*David Letterman*

Utah

I was raised in Utah, and Salt Lake is very Caucasian. I was at this restaurant one time and the hostess called for "the White party." Everybody stood up.
—*Natasha Ahanin*

Wisconsin

I'm from Wisconsin. I'll watch golf on TV just to see really good weather.
—*Jeff Cesario*

**STOCKBROKERS** See also: **FINANCES** Investing

What's the latest dope on Wall Street? My son.
—*Henny Youngman*

**STORES** See also: **SHOPPING**

Candles

I remember the day the candle shop burned down.
Everyone just stood around and sang "Happy Birthday."
—*Steven Wright*

Convenience

Only in America do we shop at places with limited parking,
over-priced items, and long lines and call them convenience
stores.
—*Yakov Smirnoff*

Exclusive

I went into this one dress shop that was so exclusive, I didn't
know you had to call ahead. The saleswoman asked, "Do
you have an appointment?" I said, "No. Do the dresses have
something else to do today?"
—*Rita Rudner*

Furniture

I went to a La-Z-Boy furniture store. Not one of those jerks
got off their fat ass and helped me.
—*Auggie Cook*

General

I went into a general store. They wouldn't let me buy anything specifically.
—*Steven Wright*

Liquor

Drive-through liquor stores, that's almost a good idea. Just
the thing for that drunk driver who's constantly on the go.
"Hey, no time to go to a real bar, I've got places to go, people
to hit."
—*Drew Carey*

| | |
|---|---|
| Malls | Every town has the same two malls: the one white people go to and the one white people used to go to.<br>—*Chris Rock* |
| Mannequins | Have you ever noticed the mannequins in the store have the natural look, the bra-less look. They have a sweater on with little points. Why would I buy a sweater that can't keep a mannequin warm?<br>—*Elayne Boosler* |
| Pets | When I was a kid I got no respect. I worked in a pet store. People kept askin' how big I'd get.<br>—*Rodney Dangerfield* |
| | I used to work at a pet shop with some buddies. In our spare time, we used to braid the snakes. Then one day I got fired when I shaved all the rabbits, dipped them in chocolate, and set them in action poses.<br>—*Steven Wright* |
| Price Clubs | I shop at the Price Club. It's a big building where you can only buy things in huge industrial sizes. If you want to buy cheese, you go to the supermarket. If you want to build something out of cheese, you go to the Price Club.<br>—*Sue Murphy* |
| Target | I tried to walk into Target, but I missed.<br>—*Mitch Hedberg* |
| **STRESS** | I read this article. It said the typical symptoms of stress are eating too much, smoking too much, impulse buying, and driving too fast. Are they kidding? This is my idea of a great day!<br>—*Monica Piper* |
| | Men, your lives are less stressful. For one thing, what you are wearing now will be in style for the rest of your lives.<br>—*Carol Siskind* |

**STRIPPING**

Strippers don't like it when you tip them in quarters.
—*Bil Dwyer*

The guys in strip clubs think because they got a pocket
full of dollars they got the power, but the chicks got the
power. They spin around the pole and you guys are hypno-
tized. That's how I look at a dessert case, but at least I get
to eat mine.
—*Monique Marvez*

Strippers are supposed to be a real macho thing to go see.
I never understood this. Who was the first guy who wanted
this? Somebody sitting around reading *Playboy*? "This isn't
frustrating enough, I'd like to see some live chicks I
can't have."
—*Bob Nickman*

My friends hired a male stripper for my birthday present.
This guy starts throwing his clothes off, and asks me, "What
are you thinking, baby?" I'm thinking I've been married too
long, because I said, "You're going to pick up after yourself,
aren't you?"
—*Mary Pfeiffer*

They opened up a strip bar in my neighborhood. Big sign
out front, "Totally Nude." I thought they meant to get in.
So, I'm standing in line . . .
—*Margaret Smith*

**STUFF**

Stuff is important. You gotta take care of your stuff. That's
what life is all about: trying to find a place for your stuff.
That's all your house is: a place to keep your stuff. If you
didn't have so much stuff, you wouldn't need a house. You
could just walk around all the time.
—*George Carlin*

**STUPIDITY**          If you know the average person is stupid, then realize that half
                       are stupider than that.
                            —*George Carlin*

**STYROFOAM**          After they make Styrofoam, what do they ship it in?
                            —*Steven Wright*

**SUCCESS**            I couldn't wait for success, so I went ahead without it.
                            —*Jonathan Winters*

**SUICIDE**            See also: **THERAPY**

                       I was thinking about committing suicide, but I have a tendency
                       to procrastinate, so I just kept putting it off. They say procras-
                       tination is a bad thing, but it saved my life.
                            —*Shashi Bhatia*

                       Dr. Kevorkian is onto something. I think he's great. Because
                       suicide is our way of saying to God, "You can't fire me. I quit."
                            —*Bill Maher*

                       Sometimes I think I'd be better off dead. No, wait. Not me—you.
                            —*Emo Philips*

                       I tried to hang myself with a bungee cord. I kept almost dying.
                            —*Steven Wright*

Hotlines               I don't get no respect. I called Suicide Prevention. They tried
                       to talk me into it.
                            —*Rodney Dangerfield*

                       I used to get so depressed, I'd call Suicide Prevention.
                       A suicide hotline is where they talk to you until you don't
                       feel like killing yourself. Exactly the opposite of tele-
                       marketing.
                            —*Dana Snow*

My first job was on a suicide hotline. That was tough, because every time I tried to call in sick, my boss would talk me out of it.

—*Wally Wang*

**SUNSETS**

Today I saw a red-and-yellow sunset and thought, "How insignificant I am!" Of course, I thought that yesterday, too, and it rained.

—*Woody Allen*

**SUPERHEROS**

Batman

I liked Batman when I was growing up because he was the only realistic superhero. No superpowers, Batman just bought a bunch of cool stuff. The moral of every Batman cartoon? Rich people win. To me, that says a lot more about truth, justice, and the American way than Superman.

—*Brian Dowell*

Hulk

Did you notice when the Hulk gets big, his shirt rips off, but his pants don't? Think of the wedgie he must get.

—*Jay Leno*

Superman

I never understood Superman's clothes. We all got used to the fact that he wears his underpants over the leotard. But why do his underpants have a belt on them?

—*Jay Leno*

**SUPERSTITIONS**

A black cat crossing your path signifies that the animal is going somewhere.

—*Groucho Marx*

I busted a mirror and got seven years bad luck. But my lawyer thinks he can get me five.

—*Steven Wright*

**SUPPORT**

The most support I've gotten in my life is from support hose.

—*Janice Heiss*

**SURVEYS**

*USA Today* has come out with a new survey: Apparently three out of four people make up 75 percent of the population.
—*David Letterman*

Studies indicate that four out of five people think the fifth one is an idiot.
—*Kevin Nealon*

**TANNING**        Tanning beds are just wrong. Lying there, roasting in your
own juices. I think they should make a George Foreman tan
bed. Slightly tilted, with a drippings pan at the bottom.
        —*Mel Fine*

I fell asleep on the beach and burned my stomach. You
should see my pot roast.
        —*Henny Youngman*

**TATTOOS**        Couples who get tattooed are the most optimistic people in
the world about relationships. I don't want a former lover's
name in my phone book, much less his picture on my ass.
        —*Carol Siskind*

I've decided to get a tattoo of parsley on my inner thigh.
Because presentation is everything.
        —*Grace White*

I want to get a tattoo over my whole body, but taller.
        —*Steven Wright*

My daughter has five tattoos! And not one of them says,
"Thanks, Mom, for the wonderful job raising me. Sorry about
the C-section scar and the massive weight gain."
        —*uBu Zurub*

**TAXATION**

Audits        Worried about an audit? Always avoid what the IRS considers
to be a red flag. For example, you have some money left in
your bank account after paying taxes.
        —*Jay Leno*

Cuts        The administration says the American people want tax cuts.
Well, duh. The American people also want drive-through
nickel beer night. The American people want to lose weight by

eating ice cream. The American people love the Home
Shopping Network because it's commercial-free.
  —*Will Durst*

Forms

How many people use the E-Z tax filing form? Actually they
don't call it that anymore. It's now titled "Okay, go ahead
and screw me. I can't find my receipts."
  —*Jay Leno*

I just finished my income tax forms. Who says you can't get
wounded by a blank?
  —*Henny Youngman*

It's getting to the point where you need more brains to
make out the income tax forms than to make the income.
  —*Henny Youngman*

Paying

I wouldn't mind paying taxes, if I knew they were going to a
friendly country.
  —*Dick Gregory*

While no one likes paying taxes, we should all remember
what our taxes pay for: blowing people up.
  —*Craig Kilborn*

You don't pay taxes; they take taxes.
  —*Chris Rock*

Refunds

I just did my taxes, and I'm getting back $150,000. And
people say you can't do your own taxes.
  —*Chantel Rae*

Taxpayers

The rich keep all the money, pay none of the taxes. The
middle class pay all the taxes, do all of the work. The poor
are just there to scare the shit out of the middle class.
  —*George Carlin*

Taxpayers are people who don't have to pass civil service examinations in order to work for the government.
—*Henny Youngman*

**TEETH**    See also: **DENTISTS**

Be true to your teeth, and they won't be false to you.
—*Soupy Sales*

**TELEPHONES**

Answering
Machines

I bought my father an answering machine. He still hasn't figured out how to leave an outgoing message. You call my father's house . . . ring, ring, ring, click, "God damn it, Mary, how in the hell do you use this stupid piece of shit? Come over here and look and see if you can help me with the . . . beep!"
—*Rosie O'Donnell*

Have you ever called someone, and you're disappointed they answer? "Uh, I didn't know you were there. I just wanted to leave a message." People don't want to talk, and the phone machine is this respirator keeping marginal, brain-dead relationships alive. Because when we come home we want to see that little flashing red light, "All right, messages!" It's very important for human beings to feel they are popular amongst a large group of people they have no interest in.
—*Jerry Seinfeld*

I like to leave a message before the beep.
—*Steven Wright*

Call Waiting

Call waiting. My grandmother says, "I've got call waiting. You call and the line is busy, you wait till I get through."
—*Sinbad*

in Cars
I don't like the idea that people can call you in your car. I think there's news you shouldn't get at sixty miles per hour. "Pregnant? Whoaah!"
—*Tom Parks*

Cell
People are so obsessed with their cell phones they apparently don't want to miss a call, ever. Twice in the past week I've been in a public restroom when the stall next to me starts ringing. Followed by, "Hello?"
—*Andi Rhoads*

Collect Calls
My father always wanted to know if we were OK, but never wanted to pay for the phone call, so we had to use secret code names, "Operator, I'd like to make a collect call. From Iam Bowling, to Will B. Late."
—*Ron Richards*

Cordless
Cordless phones are great. If you can find them.
—*Glen Foster*

Functions
Personally, I'm waiting for caller IQ.
—*Sandra Bernhard*

The technological advance I wish I could get is an addition for my answering machine, a Get-to-the-Point button.
—*Alicia Brandt*

Holding
At the end of every year, I add up the time that I've spent on hold and subtract it from my age. I don't count that time as really living. Sometimes I spend what seems like hours on hold only to be mysteriously disconnected. These times are so disturbing that I feel justified in subtracting not only from my age, but also from my weight.
—*Rita Rudner*

Information        I got up one morning and couldn't find my socks, so I called
                   Information. I said, "I can't find my socks." She said, "They're
                   behind the couch." And they were!
                        —*Steven Wright*

Numbers            See also: **DATING**

                   I have a bad memory for phone numbers. But I don't think if
                   you're one digit off, you should get a whole other person. If
                   you're that close, you should at least get someone who knows
                   where they are.
                        —*Rita Rudner*

Pagers             If I had a vibrating pager, I would get a mobile phone and call
                   myself. Stand around hitting redial all day.
                        —*Dan Wilson*

Phone Sex          What's embarrassing about phone sex is that the neighbors
                   can hear me having sex, but they don't see anyone enter or
                   leave my apartment.
                        —*Sue Kolinsky*

                   Humans are the only animal who can have sex over the phone.
                        —*David Letterman*

                   Phone sex—I got an ear infection.
                        —*Richard Lewis*

                   It kills me the way they advertise phone sex: "Phone up and
                   hear a woman's secret fantasies." If there's any reality to this,
                   you'd hear stuff like, "Yeah, I'd like to be paid the same as a
                   man for the same job."
                        —*Mike MacDonald*

                   In the middle of an asthma attack, my sister got an obscene
                   phone call. The guy said, "Did I call you, or did you call me?"
                        —*John Mendoza*

There are 25,000 sex phone lines for men in the U.S. but only three for women. Apparently, when we want somebody to talk dirty and nasty to us we just go to work.
—*Felicia Michaels*

Here's my recipe for inexpensive phone sex: Call for the time of day and start shouting, "All right, slut, say it again—and add ten seconds!"
—*Jim Samuels*

Phone sex, my worst fantasy: "You're thinking dirty thoughts?" "Yeah." "Okay, your mother wants to talk to you."
—*Robert Schimmel*

I can't express my sexual need, except to strangers over the phone. Then I can go for hours, even through that loud whistle.
—*Garry Shandling*

Public

I always find money in public phones. When I bring a screwdriver along.
—*Linda Herskovic*

Telemarketing

The government has new regulations for telemarketers. Even better, the government told the telemarketers by calling them during dinner.
—*Conan O'Brien*

I hate phone solicitors. I'd rather get an obscene call—at least they work for themselves.
—*Margaret Smith*

**TELEVISION**

See also: **NEWS**, **REMOTE CONTROLS**

Imitation is the sincerest form of television.
—*Fred Allen*

So long as there's a jingle in your head, television isn't free.
—*Jason Love*

What was it with black people on TV until recent? Must have
been a conspiracy or something. Maybe white people who ran
the shows were giving them too much direction. "Mr. Jones, we
want you to come out and dance. And really shake it, like you
people do. And then fight with your girlfriend. But loud and
scary, you know, like your normal voice."
—*Bernie Mac*

The worst thing about television is that everybody you see on
television is doing something better than what you're doing.
You never see anybody on TV just sliding off the front of the
sofa, with potato chip crumbs all over their shirt.
—*Jerry Seinfeld*

Have you noticed that TV families never watch television?
—*Henny Youngman*

Bad

Watching television is like taking black spray paint to your
third eye.
—*Bill Hicks*

Bad television is three things: a bullet train to a morally bankrupt youth, a slow spiral into an intellectual void, and of
course, a complete blast to watch.
—*Dennis Miller*

Sure, most television nowadays is crap. But guess what? Most
television has always been crap. So has most film, music, painting, and literature, ever since the moment mankind started
grinding it out. I'm sure there were cave-wall drawings of dogs
playing poker.
—*Dennis Miller*

Channels

I watch the Discovery Channel, and you know what I've
discovered? I need a girlfriend. The more Discovery Channel

you watch, the less chance you ever have of meeting a
woman, because it fills your head full of odd facts that can
come out at any moment, "Hello. Did you know Hitler was
ticklish? That the sea otter has had four nipples? Don't
run away!"

    *—Dave Attell*

I don't know what's wrong with my television set. I had it on
the same station. I was getting C-Span and the Home
Shopping Network. I actually bought a congressman.

    *—Bruce Baum*

I don't like to channel surf. You guys like it don't you? You
like to change the channel. We like to change you.

    *—Wendy Liebman*

The cable TV sex channels don't expand our horizons, don't
make us better people, and don't come in clearly enough.

    *—Bill Maher*

Men flip around the television more than women. Men get
that remote control, don't know what the hell they're
watching, just keep going, "Rerun, that's stupid, he's stupid,
go, go, go!" "I think it's a documentary about your father."
"Don't care, what else is on?" Women will stop and go,
"Let's see what the show is, before I change the channel.
Maybe we work with it, help it grow into something."
Because women nest, and men hunt: That's why we watch
TV differently.

    *—Jerry Seinfeld*

Definition of

Television, a medium. So called, because it is neither rare
nor well done.

    *—Ernie Kovacs*

Educational

I find television very educational. Every time someone turns
on the set, I go into the other room and read a book.

    *—Groucho Marx*

Satellite Dishes    One night I walked home very late and fell asleep in some-body's satellite dish. My dreams were showing up on TVs all over the world.
—*Steven Wright*

Shows    I'm a huge fan of reality shows. I thought the first one, *Dukes of Hazzard*, captured white people perfectly.
—*George Lopez*

I will never understand why they cook on TV. I can't smell it, can't eat it, can't taste it. The end of the show they hold it up to the camera: "Well, here it is. You can't have any. Goodbye."
—*Jerry Seinfeld*

Stop with the reality television. If I wanted reality, I'd take the screen out of my TV and look through the box.
—*Jerry Seinfeld*

Video Games    The news is always going on about how video games are too violent. Sure, there are some video games small children shouldn't play, but I'm a grownup lady, and occasionally I need to shoot shit. And it's best if that happens fictionally.
—*Jackie Kashian*

**TEMPERATURE**    It doesn't matter what temperature a room is. It's always room temperature, right?
—*Steven Wright*

**THEATER**    I don't like movies. I like plays. This way, I can stand up and tell them it stinks.
—*Linda Herskovic*

**THERAPY**    See also: **MENTAL DISORDERS**

I'm in therapy now. I used to be in denial. Which is a lot cheaper.
—*Robin Greenspan*

Therapy is like a really easy game show where the answer to every question is: "My mom?"

—*Robin Greenspan*

for Dogs

Do you realize they have psychiatrists for dogs now? That in and of itself can screw up a dog. "Hey pal, am I allowed up on the couch, or am I not allowed up on the couch?"

—*Dennis Miller*

Fifty-Minute Hour

How come at the psychiatrist the hour is only fifty minutes? What do they do with the ten minutes that they have left? Do they just sit there going, "Boy, that guy was crazy. I couldn't believe the things he was saying. What a nut! Who's coming in next? Oh, no, another head case!"

—*Jerry Seinfeld*

Paranoia

I told my psychiatrist that everyone hates me. He said I was being ridiculous; everyone hasn't met me yet.

—*Rodney Dangerfield*

Psychiatrists

Even the best psychiatrist is like a blindfolded auto mechanic poking around under your hood with a giant foam "We're #1" finger.

—*Dennis Miller*

After twelve years of therapy my psychiatrist said something that brought tears to my eyes, "*No hablo ingles.*"

—*Ronnie Shakes*

A man goes to a psychiatrist. The doctor says, "You're crazy." The man says, "I want a second opinion!" "OK, you're ugly too!"

—*Henny Youngman*

Suicide

I told my psychiatrist I have suicidal tendencies. He told me to pay in advance.

—*Rodney Dangerfield*

Therapists

I told my mother that I was thinking about seeing a therapist. She thought that was a good idea because she heard they made a lot of money.
  —*Darlene Hunt*

If the marriage therapist irritates both of you, you can get some temporary zip back in your relationship if you team up and fight with her. That gives you some fresh sport for your money. After all, you can fight with each other for free on your own time.
  —*Sinbad*

You know you're messed up when the therapist says, "Really? You freaky, ain't you?"
  —*Sinbad*

I went to a therapist, and he said to treat every day like it's your last. So I did, I stiffed him.
  —*Bob Zany*

**THERMOMETERS**

Buy thermometers in the wintertime. They're much lower then.
  —*Soupy Sales*

**TICKETS**

See also: **DRIVING, FLYING**

I got a jaywalking ticket, which is the dumbest ticket of all. I said, "Is this going to go on my record, or can I got to Walking School and have this taken off?"
  —*Gary Shandling*

**TIME**

Someone asked me, "What's your idea of a good time?" I said "6:45."
  —*Dick Cavett*

You can measure distance by time. "How far away is it?" "Oh, about twenty minutes." But it doesn't work the other way. "When do you get off work?" "Around three miles."
  —*Jerry Seinfeld*

When I was a kid I had no watch. I used to tell time by my violin. I'd practice in the middle of the night, and the neighbors would yell, "Fine time to practice violin, 3:00 in the morning!"

—*Henny Youngman*

## TOOLS

and Men

A man's not a man until he can find his way to Sears blindfolded, and the Craftsman tool department makes his nipples rock hard.

—*Tim Allen*

My husband has to have every tool ever made. "It's an air-compressor. It shoots out air." So does your butt, use that.

—*Maryellen Hooper*

and Women

Women don't need conventional tools, we'll use anything that's handy. But when pounding a nail, don't use a shoe, shoes cost $60 a pair. A package of frozen hamburger costs $6. Use the hamburger.

—*Jeannie Dietz*

I have New Age friends who gave their little girl a toolbox of plastic tools. They were horrified later that night when they came into her room and found she was putting the hammer to bed.

—*Bob Saget*

## TORNADOS

See: **WEATHER**

## TOWNS

I hate small towns because once you've seen the cannon in the park there's nothing else to do.

—*Lenny Bruce*

**TOYS**     See also: **DOLLS**

Cardboard
Boxes

As a kid, the best toy is something you get on your own, like a cardboard box. Five years old, you get boxes like the ones refrigerators come in. When you are five years old, that's the closest you get to having your own apartment.
     —*Jerry Seinfeld*

Crayons

Remember the crayon box with the flesh-colored crayon? Little white kids, "I'm going to draw my mother and father." Black kids, "I don't know nobody looks like this. Don't throw it out, I can use it to draw the police."
     —*D. L. Hughley*

My favorite toy was the Crayola sixty-four box. It's like a child's orgasm.
     —*Cathy Ladman*

Games

I think it's wrong that only one company makes the game Monopoly.
     —*Steven Wright*

Guns

You should only use a toy gun when holding up a toy store.
     —*George Carlin*

Happy Meals

I was in McDonald's, and I saw this kid take his Happy Meal toy and throw it on the ground. His mom said, "Hey, you play with that. There are children in China manufacturing those."
     —*Laura Silverman*

Yo-Yos

I tell ya when I was a kid, all I knew was rejection. My yo-yo never came back!
     —*Rodney Dangerfield*

**TRADE
RELATIONS**

Speaking of trade relations, almost everyone would like to.
     —*Henny Youngman*

**TRANSPORTATION**    See also: **AUTOMOBILES, FLYING**

Bicycles

My nephew came over the other day, and he was wearing a helmet, shoulder pads, knee pads, gloves, and saying, "I'm a gonna ride my bike." Where? Through a minefield?
—*Wanda Sykes*

Buses

I was on the bus, and the guy in front of me went into convulsions, started swallowing his tongue, shaking, sweating, and puking. His friend was with him, and he was like, "Oh man, he was drinking for fifty-five days straight. We have to get him off the bus now." We stop, get him off the bus, and I'm thinking, "Oh great. Now who is going to drive?"
—*Kathleen Madigan*

I was on a Greyhound recently. This guy was staring at my bag wondering why it closes with a zipper and not a twist tie.
—*Tom Ryan*

The bus is the single stupidest, fattest, slowest, most despised vehicle on the road. When you get behind the bus, the back of the bus is like an eclipse. It's this huge metal ass taking up the whole windshield of your car. And when it pulls out, it even sounds like a fat uncle trying to get out of a sofa.
—*Jerry Seinfeld*

Look at all the buses that want exact change. I figure if I give them exact change, they should take me exactly where I want to go.
—*George Wallace*

Mopeds

Mopeds. It's like you're on a hair dryer. Dogs are walking faster than you're going.
—*Eddie Izzard*

Taxicabs

I saw today a cab driver take an elderly woman across the street. No, wait a minute, the word I'm looking for is . . . knock, knock her across.
—*David Letterman*

I don't like to take cabs because I don't know how much to tip the drivers. I just tip them until they don't look mad anymore.
—*Paula Poundstone*

Trains

Some people like to travel by train because it combines the slowness of a car with the cramped public exposure of an airplane.
—*Dennis Miller*

Trucks

See also: **ACCIDENTS** Vehicular

My best friend got a truck. But she didn't want to be trendy, so she got a UPS truck. Laugh, but she can park it anywhere. Worldwide.
—*Wendy Liebman*

Subways

I was on the subway sitting on a newspaper, and a guy comes over and asks, "Are you reading that?" I didn't know what to say. So I said, "Yes," stood up, turned the page, and sat down again.
—*David Brenner*

**TRANSSEXUALS**    See: **SEXUALITY**

**TRANSVESTITES**    See: **SEXUALITY**

**TRAUMAS**    I'm suffering from post-post-traumatic syndrome, and I'm going to keep talking about it until some cute guy holds me.
—*Kathy Griffin*

**TRAVEL**    See also: **VACATIONING**

Travel lets us leave behind our unrealistic prejudices about other places and the people who live there and develop new,

more realistic prejudices based on their actual deficiencies.
—*Dennis Miller*

I walked up to a tourist information booth. I asked them to tell me about a couple of people who were here last year.
—*Steven Wright*

I just got back from a pleasure trip. I drove my mother-in-law to the airport.
—*Henny Youngman*

**TRUCKS**          See: **TRANSPORTATION**

**UFOs**          The only thing that scares me more than space aliens is the idea that there aren't any space aliens. We can't be the best that creation has to offer. I pray we're not all there is. If so, we're in big trouble.
—*Ellen DeGeneres*

Only man is narcissistic enough to think that a highly evolved alien life force would travel across billions and billions of light years in spacecrafts without windows, and then upon landing on our planet, that their first impulse is to get into some hick's ass with a flashlight.
—*Dennis Miller*

When I was in the middle of the desert a UFO landed. Three one-inch-tall guys got out. They walked over to me. I said, "Are you really one inch tall?" They said, "No, we're really very far away."
—*Steven Wright*

**VACATIONING**          See also: **FAMILY**, **TRAVEL**

Beach          I was walking along the ocean. That's generally where you'll find the beach. Looking for ashtrays in their wild state.
—*Ronnie Graham*

During the summer I like to go to the beach and make sand-castles out of cement. And wait for kids to run by and try to kick them over.

> —*James Leemer*

This summer I'm going to go to the beach and bury metal objects that say "Get a life" on them.

> —*Demetri Martin*

I went to the nude beach, but they didn't like me there. You're not supposed to wear anything, and I was wearing a video camera.

> —*Dan St. Paul*

I bought a house on the beach. I thought it was a nude beach, but it turned out to be a giggle beach. When I appeared, everybody giggled.

> —*Adam Sandler*

We use a really strong sunblock when we got to the beach with the kids because we're always afraid of cancer. It's SPF 80: You squeeze the tube, and a sweater comes out.

> —*Lew Schneider*

Cruises

We took a cruise. It depends on the boat. You have to get on a good boat. They have the *Fantasy*, the *Ecstasy*. We were on the *Hysterectomy*.

> —*Rita Rudner*

Tourist Season

Why is it called tourist season if we can't shoot them?

> —*George Carlin*

**VEGETARIANS**

I tell vegetarians, "Hey, vegetables are living things too. They're just easier to catch."

> —*Kevin Brennan*

A vegetarian is someone who won't eat anything that can have children.
—*David Brenner*

I am not a vegetarian because I love animals. I am a vegetarian because I hate plants.
—*A. Whitney Brown*

There are patriotic vegetarians in the American Legion who will only eat animals that were killed in combat.
—*George Carlin*

I won't eat anything that has intelligence, but I would gladly eat a network executive or a politician.
—*Marty Feldman*

People assume that because I'm a vegetarian, I'm into other kinds of social activism. They say, "Do you care about the environment?" No, I eat the environment.
—*Myq Kaplan*

Not eating meat is a decision; eating meat is an instinct.
—*Denis Leary*

I've been on a vegetarian diet for three weeks, and never have my houseplants looked so good to me.
—*Daniel Lybra*

I was a vegetarian until I started leaning toward sunlight.
—*Rita Rudner*

I'm a vegetarian, but I'm not that hard core. I eat eggs. I have to, because I'm pro-choice.
—*Betsy Salkind*

**VENDING MACHINES**     See also: **HEALTH CLUBS**

I like vending machines, because snacks are better when they fall.
—*Mitch Hedberg*

**VENTRILOQUISM**     My mother was a ventriloquist. She could throw her voice. So for ten years I thought the dog was telling me to kill my father.
—*Wendy Liebman*

**VETERINARIANS**     I have such an expensive vet. I go to pick my dog up, and the girl behind the counter says, "$3,000." The whole waiting room looks up. A woman says, "What happened?" "Well, apparently the dog bought a car after I dropped him off."
—*Elayne Boosler*

My veterinarian has an inferiority complex: He only operates on stuffed animals.
—*Johnnye Jones Gibson*

**VIDEO GAMES**     See: **TELEVISION**

**VIRGINITY**     I don't think a woman should be a virgin before marriage. She should have had at least one other disappointing experience.
—*Maureen Murphy*

I was a virgin until I was twenty. And then again, until I was twenty-three.
—*Carrie Snow*

I used to be a virgin, but I gave it up; there was no money in it.
—*Marsha Warfield*

**WAR**

Men are brave enough to go to war, but they are not brave enough to get a bikini wax.
            —*Rita Rudner*

If women ruled the world and we all got massages, there would be no war.
            —*Carrie Snow*

**WATER**

The formula for water is $H_2O$. Is the formula for an ice cube $H_2O$ squared?
            —*Lily Tomlin*

I bought some powdered water, but I don't know what to add.
            —*Steven Wright*

I mix my water myself. Two parts H, one part O. I don't trust anybody.
            —*Steven Wright*

**WEAPONS**

Peacekeeper Missile. Doesn't that sound like Ax-Murderer Babysitter?
            —*Elayne Boosler*

The very existence of flame-throwers proves that sometime, somewhere, someone said to themselves, "You know, I want to set those people over there on fire, but I'm just not close enough to get the job done."
            —*George Carlin*

The United States has a new weapon. It destroys people but leaves buildings still standing. It's called the stock market.
            —*Jay Leno*

Countries are making nuclear weapons like there's no tomorrow. But maybe instead of trying to build newer and bigger weapons of destruction, we should be thinking about getting more use out of the ones we already have.
            —*Emo Philips*

## WEATHER

Channel

On cable TV they have a Weather Channel, twenty-four hours of weather. We had something like that where I grew up. We called it a window.
—*Dan Spencer*

Cold

It was so cold I saw a polar bear wearing a grizzly.
—*Milton Berle*

Cold weather makes it very nice for race relations. Last month, when it was fifteen below zero, I walked out of a nightclub. A drunk walked up to me and said, "Why don't you go back to Africa . . . and take me with you."
—*Dick Gregory*

It was so cold I saw a guy with a hammer trying to bust a poodle off a fire hydrant.
—*David Letterman*

It was so cold that I haven't got such a chill up my spine since I heard the words "Honey, I'm pregnant."
—*David Letterman*

A lot of people like snow. I find it to be an unnecessary freezing of water.
—*Carl Reiner*

It was so cold I saw a politician with his hands in his own pockets.
—*Henny Youngman*

Forecasts

Tonight's forecast: dark. Continuing dark throughout the night and turning to widely scattered light in the morning.
—*George Carlin*

Hot

Last night it was so damn hot at my house that I had to sleep on the air hockey table.
—*David Letterman*

How hot is it? It's so hot that I saw two palm trees fighting over a dog.
—*Rick Rockwell*

Terminology

I don't understand the terminology on TV weather reports, "The temperature today is twenty-two, but with wind chill factor, it feels like ten below." What the hell does that mean? Give me something I can use, "The temperature outside is 'Damn!' But with the wind, it feels more like 'Son-of-a-Bitch!'" I know how to dress for Son-of-a-Bitch.
—*Brian McKim*

Tornados

A tornado touched down, uprooting a large tree in the front yard, demolishing the house across the street. Dad went to the door, opened it, surveyed the damage, muttered, "Darn kids!" and closed the door.
—*Tim Conway*

**WEDDINGS**

See also: **HOMOSEXUALITY** Marriage

Bachelor
Parties

It was one of those bachelor parties where all the married men had to meet at the end and decide about what to say we did: "We got in a fight with some guys, and that's how our underwear got ripped. They ripped our underwear, and smelled good. Jimmy, you fell, and your nipple got pierced."
—*Ray Romano*

I have a friend who is about to get married. They're having the bachelor party and the bridal shower on the same day. So it's conceivable that while she's getting the lingerie, he'd be at a nude bar watching a table dancer wearing the same outfit.
—*Jerry Seinfeld*

Best Man

I was the Best Man at a wedding. I thought the title was a bit much. If I'm the Best Man, why is she marrying him?
—*Jerry Seinfeld*

Bridal Showers

When my sister got married I threw her a bridal shower. What a nifty way to spend a Sunday afternoon. My aunt bought my sister a spice rack, and thought it would be nice to individually wrap the spices. So for forty-five minutes we were going, "Oooo, paprika!"
—*Rosie O'Donnell*

What's a bridal shower if you're gay? It's the parade of gifts you'll never get because you're homosexual. "Come in and take a look at the blender, toaster, silverware you'll have to buy yourself." I hate that. I don't bring a gift anymore; I take one. I have six Cuisinarts. I don't give a shit; they owe us.
—*Suzanne Westenhoever*

Bridesmaids

I hate the saying "Always a bridesmaid, never a bride." I like to put it into perspective by thinking, "Always a pallbearer, never a corpse."
—*Laura Kightlinger*

Ceremonies

I had a civil ceremony. His mother couldn't come.
—*Phyllis Diller*

It seems like the only times they pronounce you anything in life is when they pronounce you man and wife, or dead on arrival.
—*Dennis Miller*

The divorce rate is sky-high, and I blame the vows. Why don't we just be honest? Instead of saying "till death do us part," let's just go, "I'll give it a shot." Or "I'm cool as long as he don't do nothing stupid."
—*Wanda Sykes*

What are the scariest words known to man? "Till death do us part." Why not, "Until my car breaks down"? Or "Until I run out of money"?

—*Damon Wayans*

On her wedding day, a Masai tribeswoman symbolizes her low status by putting dung on her head. American women may have to put up with a lot of bullshit, but at least we don't have to wear it.

—*Jackie Wollner*

**Dresses**

Skimp on your wedding dress. Why spend a lot of money on something you're only going to wear five or six times?

—*Charisse Savarin*

**Engagements**

That night is the most romantic we guys get. I remember when I asked my wife to marry me, I got down on my knee, and I was shaking a little stick, and I went, "Ooops, that's not the color we're looking for is it, honey?" I get teary-eyed just thinking about it.

—*Jack Coen*

Many of my friends are getting engaged and are buying diamonds for their fiancées. What better to symbolize marriage than the hardest thing known to man.

—*Mike Dugan*

My fiancée told me the rule of thumb on how much to spend on an engagement ring was two months' salary. So I moved to Haiti for a couple months, made a buck eighty. Nice plywood ring, no knots. I sanded it myself.

—*Barry Kennedy*

My father was so cheap. When my parents were engaged, he didn't give my mother a diamond ring. He gave her a lump of coal and told her to be patient.

—*Cathy Ladman*

When my fiancé proposed it was very romantic. He turned off the TV. Well, he muted it. During the commercial.
                    —*Wendy Liebman*

Before we got engaged he never farted. Now it's a second language.
                    —*Caroline Rhea*

Gifts            You know what the best part of getting married is? Opening the envelopes. That way you get to see how cheap your relatives really are.
                    —*Joey Callahan*

Honeymoons       Honeymoon night was hot. She was moaning all night in ecstasy, opening gifts. "An orange squeezer! Oh my God! A waffle maker!" Next morning the guy down the hall gave me the big thumbs-up. "Boy, you were using everything but the kitchen sink in there."
                    —*Mike Binder*

Receptions       Anything interesting in a Chicano family begins or ends in the backyard. Weddings are the best. "We're going to move all the cars out. Even that one, Rudy will get a truck from work and drag it out. We'll cut the grass—nice. The driveway, put sand on the oil, and it will be the dance floor."
                    —*George Lopez*

Rings            I like a man who wears a wedding ring. Because without it, they're like a shark without a fin. You pretty much got to know they're out there.
                    —*Brett Butler*

**WEIGHT**       See also: **DIETING**, **PHYSIQUE**

My favorite health club is the International House of Pancakes. Because no matter what you weigh, there will always be someone who weighs 150 pounds more than you.
                    —*Lewis Black*

Gaining

You know you're getting fat when you can pinch an inch on your forehead.

—*John Mendoza*

It's hard to be famous and struggle with a weight problem. I was in Baskin Robbins, just looking, and this lady said to me, "Are you Rosie O'Donnell?" I said, "Yes." "I didn't know you were pregnant." I looked at her and said, "Yes, four and a half months." She kept asking. "What are you going to name it?" "I don't know, either Ben or Jerry."

—*Rosie O'Donnell*

You reach a certain age, and your body doesn't react like it used to. Fat just jumps on your body. When you're in your twenties, you can eat a whole bag of Oreo cookies. Nothing happens. I'm now in my late thirties. I eat just one, and my butt expands while I'm chewing.

—*Sinbad*

Losing

I don't know why everybody talks about losing weight. That's an ill-conceived phrase. Fat people never lose weight. They always know right where it is. And dropping a few pounds? I dropped a few pounds last week. They landed around my knees.

—*Louie Anderson*

I had this boyfriend who told me he thought I needed to lose weight. He really hurt my feelings, but he was right. I'm proud to say I lost 173 pounds—when I dumped him. I can't tell you how much better I feel.

—*Wendy Kamenoff*

I'm trying to get back to my original weight—eight pounds, three ounces.

—*Cheril Vendetti*

**WILLS**

My wife finally convinced me to sign what's called a living will. It's a document which gives her the right to, if I become

attached to some mechanical device, terminate my life. So, yesterday, I'm on the exercise bike . . .
—*Jonathan Katz*

You can't get Mexican people to make out a will because they're all superstitious. "No, *mira, hombre*, it's like a reservation to die, *cabrón*, so you can take my things."
—*George Lopez*

A guy dies and leaves the shortest will ever. It says, "Being of sound mind, I spent my money!"
—*Henny Youngman*

**WINE**

Wine, for the very eloquent people: "I don't know whether to have the red wine with the fish or chicken." What's it matter? They're dead! The chicken's not going to reach up from the plate, and go, "The red wine!"
—*Robin Williams*

I've been making wine at home, but I'm making it out of raisins so it will be aged automatically.
—*Steven Wright*

**WIVES**

See also: **HUSBANDS, MARRIAGE**

Husbands think we should know where everything is, like the uterus is a tracking device. He asks me, "Roseanne, do we have any Cheetos left?" Like he can't go over to that sofa cushion and lift it himself.
—*Roseanne Barr*

I'm a housewife, but I prefer to be called a Domestic Goddess.
—*Roseanne Barr*

A good wife always forgives her husband when she's wrong.
—*Milton Berle*

Any husband who says, "My wife and I are completely equal partners" is talking about either a law firm or a hand of bridge.
  —*Bill Cosby*

I am not the boss of my house. I don't know when I lost it. I don't know if I ever had it. But I have seen the boss's job and I do not want it.
  —*Bill Cosby*

I met my wife in a bar. What a surprise, I thought she was home watching the kids.
  —*Ron Dentinger*

Living with my wife is like taking orders from a drill sergeant. I have to work damn hard to for a weekend pass.
  —*Irv Gilman*

When we first met my wife didn't like me all that much. Luckily, she wanted to stay in this country.
  —*Brian Kiley*

Wives are people who think it's against the law not to answer the phone when it rings.
  —*Rita Rudner*

My wife thinks I'm too nosy. At least that's what she keeps scribbling in her diary.
  —*Drake Sather*

My wife is a teacher; it's really weird to live with a teacher. I'd be on the phone, doodling on a piece of paper, leave the house, come back in two hours, and that same piece of paper is now on the refrigerator with the words "Good work!" and a big smiley face on it.
  —*Lew Schneider*

My wife is the sweetest, most tolerant, most beautiful woman in the world. This is a paid political announcement.

> —*Henny Youngman*

Take my wife . . . please.

> —*Henny Youngman*

To give you an idea how difficult my wife can be, she bought me two ties for my birthday. To please her I wore one. She hollered, "What's the matter, don't you like the other one?"

> —*Henny Youngman*

Ex-

My ex-wife, what was her name again? Oh yeah, Plaintiff.

> —*David Letterman*

and Sex

I tell ya, my wife likes to talk during sex. The other night she called me from a motel.

> —*Rodney Dangerfield*

My wife, we have no sex life. Her favorite position is back-to-back.

> —*Rodney Dangerfield*

Never tell your wife she's lousy in bed. She'll go out and get a second opinion.

> —*Rodney Dangerfield*

With my wife, I gave up. The other night, I told her, "You win, you're the boss. When it comes to sex, it'll be in your hands." She said, "You're wrong, it'll be in your hands."

> —*Rodney Dangerfield*

The other night my wife and I decided to spice things up a little. So, we switched positions. She lay on the couch with the remote, and I did the ironing.

> —*Peter Sasso*

In bed my wife sprawls out all over the mattress. I said, "I'm tired of only having two inches in this bed." She said, "Now you know how I feel."
—*Peter Sasso*

**WOMEN**    See also: **FEMINISM, GENDER DIFFERENCES, MEN, MENOPAUSE, MENSTRUATION, PREMENSTRUAL SYNDROME, SEX, WIVES**

I'm just a person trapped inside a woman's body.
—*Elayne Boosler*

in Business    A new survey shows that the more female you are physically, the harder it is to be taken seriously in business. For example, women with very large breasts have a harder time being promoted than women with penises.
—*Heidi Joyce*

Cosmetics    Why are we wearing makeup? I know a few butt-ugly guys who wouldn't be hurt by a little lip color.
—*Sue Murphy*

Femininity    People say to me, "You're not very feminine." Well, they can just suck my dick.
—*Roseanne Barr*

Intuition    Could any man ever learn that mystical thing called a woman's intuition? Which isn't mystical at all, but rather an ability to pick up and process subtle clues that men lack because we're kind of dense.
—*Bill Cosby*

Living with    Women. You can't live with them, and you can't get them to dress up in a skimpy Nazi costume and beat you with a warm squash.
—*Emo Philips*

and Men

When women are depressed they eat or go shopping. Men invade another country. It's a whole different way of thinking.
—*Elayne Boosler*

When women go off by themselves, they call it "separatism." When men go off by themselves they call it "Congress."
—*Kate Clinton*

There are countries in the world where it's the custom for the men there to cut off a woman's clitoris. This is true and very gruesome. We should be happy that this will never happen in our country, because the men here don't know where the clitoris is.
—*Janine DiTullio*

We're our own worst enemies a lot of the time, but I still blame men.
—*Janeane Garofalo*

Women might start a rumor, but not a war.
—*Marga Gomez*

All women want from men is a partner, who will share his hopes, his thoughts, his dreams. And if you don't, we're going to bitch at you until the day you die.
—*Stephanie Hodge*

Women cannot complain about men anymore until they start getting better taste in them.
—*Bill Maher*

Anyone who says he can see through women is missing a lot.
—*Groucho Marx*

I've learned about women the hard way: through books.
—*Emo Philips*

Women want food, water, and compliments. Know what men want? Food, sex, and silence.
        —*Chris Rock*

When a man says "fine," he means everything's fine. When a woman says "fine" she means, "I'm really ticked off, and you have to find out why."
        —*John Rogers*

Most women are introspective, "Am I in love? Am I emotionally and creatively fulfilled?" Most men are out-rospective, "Did my team win? How's my car?"
        —*Rita Rudner*

Women will gab at each other for fifty-seven hours, breaking down every emotional thing they're going through into nuances. A man will sit down with his buddy and his buddy will ask, "What's up with your wife?" The man will mumble, "Oh, man, she's tripping." End of analysis.
        —*Sinbad*

When I think of some of the men I've slept with . . . if they were women I wouldn't have had lunch with them.
        —*Carol Siskind*

That crazy sex drive in men is why we still have people walking around this earth. Men are baby makers, so they are always in that mode, "We gotta make more people." Women have the people, so we're like, "Wait, who's gonna take care of all these people? Get off me."
        —*Wanda Sykes*

Most women are attracted to the simple things in life. Like men.
        —*Henny Youngman*

Want

Sigmund Freud once asked, "What do women want?" The only thing I have learned in fifty-two years is that women want

men to stop asking dumb questions.
>—*Bill Cosby*

Women want men, careers, money, children, friends, luxury, comfort, independence, freedom, respect, love, and three-dollar pantyhose that won't run.
>—*Phyllis Diller*

Verbal Skills

A study in *The Washington Post* says that women have better verbal skills than men. I just want to say to the authors of that study: Duh.
>—*Conan O'Brien*

**WORK**          See: **EMPLOYMENT**

**WORLD**

Africa

I went to Africa. Now I know how white people feel in America: relaxed. Because you hear a police car coming, you know it ain't coming after your ass.
>—*Richard Pryor*

Britain

It's spring in England. I missed it last year; I was in the bathroom.
>—*Michael Flanders*

Canada

I'm Canadian. It's like American, but without the gun.
>—*Dave Foley*

I love Canada. Not a very tough country, though. They got an army; they just didn't give them guns. Look at the Canadian flag. It's not a symbol of power; it's a leaf. Don't screw with Canada. They'll dry up and blow away.
>—*Jeremy Hotz*

China          China has a population of a billion people. One billion. That
               means even if you're a one-in-a-million kind of guy, there are
               still a thousand others exactly like you.
                    —*A. Whitney Brown*

France         Boy, those French. They have a different word for everything.
                    —*Steve Martin*

               I'm French, and I agree with you, the French are rude. But they
               know how to kiss. If it wasn't for the French, you would still
               wonder, "What the hell am I supposed to do with my tongue?"
                    —*Jim Rez*

Middle East    Israel and Palestine are getting worse and worse every day.
               These people hate each other so much that they are fighting
               over a piece of land the size of a Wendy's. They're fighting
               over a piece of land so small they could only have an above-
               ground pool on it. Piece of dirt so little, that if you found it in
               your salad, you wouldn't even send it back.
                    —*Tina Fey*

               The problem in the Middle East is that the Jews and Arabs
               think they're God's chosen people. If you're God's chosen
               people, why is there nothing but war and death over there?
               Look around, you're in the desert. Have you been to
               Barbados or Hawaii? It's gorgeous over there. Maybe the
               Samoans are the chosen people. Have you thought of that?
                    —*Aron Kader*

               An investigation has been launched into pre-war Iraq: We're
               going to find out why they had our oil under their sand.
                    —*Craig Kilborn*

               Saudi Arabia is cracking down on terrorism. They've made a
               list of all known terrorists, which is basically their phonebook.
                    —*Jay Leno*

Palestine

I used to live in West Virginia, and I had this Palestinian landlady. She finds out I'm Jewish, she's like, "Your people and my people, they have a lot in common." I'm thinking: "Yeah, we both want the same land." Fortunately my landlady was willing to rent, so that's my message.
—*Norman K.*

Besides the bombs they strap to their chests, I have no idea what makes these Palestinians tick.
—*Dennis Miller*

Switzerland

The Swiss have an interesting army. Five hundred years without a war. Pretty lucky for them. Ever see that little Swiss Army knife they have to fight with? Not much of a weapon there. Corkscrews. Bottle openers. "Back off, I've got toe clippers."
—*Jerry Seinfeld*

**WRITING**

I'm a writer. I write checks. Mostly fiction.
—*Wendy Liebman*

**YOGA**

See: **EXERCISE**

**ZOOS**

Animals

When I was a kid I got no respect. My old man took me to the zoo. He told me to go over to the leopard and play connect the dots.
—*Rodney Dangerfield*

A woman in Florida got bitten on the hand at a zoo in a Shark Petting Tank. Who could have seen that coming? By the way, the Shark Petting Tank was right next to the Rattlesnake Kissing Booth.
—*Jay Leno*

There was an item in the paper today. A lion got loose in the Central Park Zoo in New York. And was severely mauled.
—*Bob Newhart*

Petting

When I was growing up, we had a petting zoo, and we had two sections. We had a petting zoo, and then we had a heavy petting zoo. For people who really liked the animals a lot.
—*Ellen DeGeneres*

A petting zoo is a great place, if you want your kid's clothes to end up inside a goat's stomach.
—*Bil Dwyer*

# ABOUT THE
# COMICS

Veteran funnyman **Joey Adams**, a syndicated comedy columnist, was the author of twenty-three humor books and hosted various radio and television programs.

**Orny Adams** can be seen yukking it up at Gotham Comedy Club. Orny's credits include Comedy Central, *Friday Night Videos*, and *Late Show with David Letterman*.

**Natasha Ahanin** is an actress and stand-up comedian who has performed at the Comedy Store in Hollywood.

**Franklin Ajaye** has appeared on numerous TV shows and in movies such as *Car Wash* and *Queen of the Damned*.

Comedian **Max Alexander** is the opening act for singer Tom Jones and was featured in the movies *Punchline* and *Roxanne*.

**Paul Alexander** has appeared on Comedy Central's *Comedy Product* and HBO's *Mr. Show*.

**Simone Alexander** is a San Francisco–based stand-up comedian and contributing writer to Laugh.com. Contact: quofacit@aol.com.

**Fred Allen** was a comedian whose career ranged from performing in vaudeville, on Broadway, and in the movies to writing for early television, including for *The Perry Como Show*.

**Gracie Allen** was a classic comedian whose career ranged from vaudeville and movies to the 1950s sitcom *Burns and Allen*.

**Marty Allen** has been part of the successful comedy duo Allen and Rossi, with singer and straight man Steve Rossi. The team rose to stardom on *The Ed Sullivan Show,* and their first album was a bestseller in 1962. Several albums later, their one movie, *The Last of the Secret Agents,* flopped, and the duo spilt until 1983, when Allen and Rossi finally reteamed to perform extensively in Las Vegas and Atlantic City.

Comedian **Tim Allen** has starred in the sitcom *Home Improvement* and movies that include *Toy Story* and *Galaxy Quest*.

**Woody Allen** is a comedian, actor, and Academy Award–winning director of films such as *Annie Hall* and *Mighty Aphrodite*.

**Rabbi Robert A. Alper** is the world's only practicing clergyman doing stand-up comedy—intentionally. Alper is also the author of *Life Doesn't Get Any Better Than This: The Holiness of Little Daily Dramas*, and the cartoon book *A Rabbi Confesses*. Web site: www.bobalper.com.

**Jeff Altman** appears regularly on *Late Show with David Letterman* and has guest-starred in dozens of network primetime shows, including *Caroline in the City*, *Land's End*, and *Baywatch*. His film credits include *Highlander II, American Hot Wax, Soul Man,* and *Easy Money*.

Musical comedian **Steve Altman** uses a sampling keyboard as his "gateway to madness." His television credits include A&E's *Evening at the Improv*, Showtime's *Comedy Club Network*, *Caroline's Comedy Hour*, MTV, VH-1, Fox's *Comic Strip Live*, and HBO.

In addition to being witty as all get out, **Tom Ammiano** has been president of the San Francisco Board of Supervisors. He ran for mayor in 2003.

**Morey Amsterdam** was a comedian best known for his role as a comedy writer on *The Dick Van Dyke Show*.

**Harry Anderson** has been a working magician for more than twenty years and ran an entertaining shell game on the streets of San Francisco when he hustled a producer from *Cheers*, which lead to his TV break. Anderson went on to star in the sitcoms *Night Court* and *Dave's World*, and currently sponsors a Sideshow shop and the magic club Oswald's Speakeasy in New Orleans.

**Louie Anderson** has been the host of NBC's *Comedy Showcase* and the new *Family Feud*, and author of the bestselling book *Dear Dad*.

**Andy Andrews** has been voted comedian of the year and entertainer of the year by the National Association of Campus Activities. His CD is titled *Andy Andrews Live, Caesar's Tahoe*.

**Jack Archey** is a CPA who decided that having a steady, well-paying job was drastically over-rated. He has since performed his comedy at the Comedy Store, the LA Comedy Cabaret, and the Hollywood Laugh Factory.

**Nick Arnette** is a comedian, speaker, master of ceremonies, and author of a popular joke book, *The Encyclopedia of Dude*.

**Tom Arnold** is a comedian and actor who has appeared in the movies *True Lies* and *Nine Months*.

**Michael Aronin** is a stand-up comedian and an accomplished motivational speaker. Web site: www.michaelaronin.com.

**Amy Ashton** is a model turned actress, who then turned comedian when she grew tired of being stereotyped as either a bimbo or a bitch.

Comedian **John Astin**'s performing career has ranged from movies *West Side Story* and *Freaky Friday* to *The Addams Family* TV show.

Comedian **Joanne Astrow** has appeared on the *Tonight Show* and in the movie *Wisecracks*. She also coproduced the movie *With Friends Like These*.

Comedian **Dave Attell** is host of Comedy Central's *Insomnia*.

Comedian **Karen Babbitt** teaches acting and stand-up at San Jose State University.

**Robin Bach** dove into the stand-up arena at the age of 40 and has since performed at Zanies in Chicago, the Funny Bone in Columbus, and the Comedy Zone in Charlotte, North Carolina, among other clubs.

**Vinny Badabing** is a writer and comedian from New Jersey. You can see more of his work at www.vinnybadabing.com.

Comedian **Michele Balan** has appeared on Comedy Central, USA Network, and Lifetime TV. Web site: www.michelebalan.com.

**Heywood Banks** has appeared on A&E's *Evening at the Improv*, MTV's *Half Hour Comedy Hour*, Showtime's *Comedy Club Network*, and HBO's *12th Annual Young Comedians Special*.

Comedian **Janette Barber** has been a staff writer for *The Rosie O'Donnell Show* and is the author of the humor book *Breaking the Rules: Last-Ditch Tactics for Landing the Man of Your Dreams*.

**Willie Barcena** has appeared on the *Tonight Show* several times.

**Arj Barker** has starred in his own Comedy Central special. Web site: www.arjbarker.com.

**Amy Barnes** has been featured on Comedy Central's *Premium Blend*.

**Roseanne Barr** is the comedian who has specialized in eponymous TV shows: the sitcom *Roseanne*, the talk show *The Roseanne Show*, and the reality show *The Real Roseanne Show*.

Comedian **Todd Barry** has appeared in his own Comedy Central special and in the movies *Road Trip* and *Pootie Tang*. Web site: www.toddbarry.com.

Comedian **Rhonda Bates** appeared on the TV shows *Vegas* and *The Love Boat*.

Comedian **Bruce Baum** has been a regular performer on ABC's *America's Funniest People* and has appeared numerous times on HBO, Showtime, and Comedy Central.

Comedian **Orson Bean** has acted in films that include *Anatomy of a Murder* and *Being John Malkovich*.

**Brian Beatty** is a writer and comedian in Minneapolis whose articles and reviews have appeared in *Blues Revue, Guitar World Acoustic, Minnesota Monthly, Publishers Weekly, The Rake*, and *Seventeen*. His jokes have appeared on the BBC comedy Web site, and he's taller than he is wide. Contact: brianbeatty@lycos.com.

**Gerry Bednob**, who likes to be known as the Turban Cowboy, is a favorite on the Vegas circuit and was an International Star Search Champion.

Comedian **Tim Bedore** headlines comedy clubs across the country, has performed comedy on HBO and Comedy Central, and has produced more than 250 episodes of his radio commentary feature *Vague but True* on public radio's *Marketplace*. Web site: www.vaguebuttrue.com.

**Joy Behar** is a comedian and actress who serves as comic relief on the ABC daytime talk show *The View*.

**Guy Bellamy** is the author of *The Comedy Hotel* and *I Have a Complaint to Make*.

**Jack Benny** was one of the first major radio personalities to make a successful transition to television. *The Jack Benny Program* aired on CBS in 1950, became one of early television's most popular shows, and ran for the next fifteen years.

**Doug Benson** is a stand-up comedian and actor whose recent television credits include *Friends* and his own Comedy Central special. He is also agent provoca-

teur of the hit off-Broadway show *The Marijuana-Logues*.

**Jon Berahya**: See Lee Curtis.

Comedian **Suzy Berger** has appeared at the Montreal Comedy Festival, and her material has been featured in the book *A Funny Time to Be Gay*.

**Karen Bergreen** has appeared on Comedy Central's *Premium Blend*.

**Milton Berle** was a comedian who popularized TV with his early 1950s comedy show. He went on to make numerous appearances on the *Ed Sullivan Show* and the *Tonight Show*, and also starred in movies such as *It's a Mad, Mad, Mad, Mad World*.

Comedian **Sandra Bernhard** has costarred on *Roseanne* and starred in a number of films including *The Kings of Comedy*.

**Matina Bevis** has performed at many women's festivals, including the Southern Women's Festival.

Comedian **Shashi Bhatia** has appeared as a host on the Sci-Fi Channel, on *Friends* and *Seinfeld*, and in the movie *Leaving Las Vegas*. Contact: ShashiBhatia@hotmail.com.

Comedian **Mike Binder** is the star and creator of the HBO series *The Mind of a Married Man*. Web site: www.mikebinder.net.

Former Rat Pack comedian **Joey Bishop** performed in movies that ranged from *The Naked and the Dead* in 1958 to *Mad Dog Time* in 1996.

In 1975, **Rob Bitter** was voted "Most-Talented Seventh-Grader" at Beck Middle School in Cherry Hill, New Jersey. Contact: thenumberthirteen@yahoo.com.

Comedian **Lewis Black** is a political correspondent and curmudgeon for *The Daily Show*. Web site: www.lewisblack.net.

**Margot Black** is a writer, producer, and stand-up whose credits include MTV's *Jenny McCarthy Show* and *Late Show with David Letterman*.

Comedian **Steve Bluestein** has appeared on Comedy Central's *Make Me Laugh*.

Comedian **Ed Bluestone** is a 1970s comedian who segued to book author. He was also known for having created the best-selling *National Lampoon* cover "Buy This Magazine or We'll Shoot This Dog."

Comedian **Stephanie Blum** took first prize in the Ladies of Laughter Funniest Female competition at Madison Square Garden. She was chosen by HBO's *U.S. Comedy Arts Festival* to be their 2003 "Breakout Performer" and was also a *Star Search* winner. Web site: www.actoneentertainment.net.

**Alonzo Bodden** has been a finalist on the second season of NBC's *Last Comic Standing*. Web site: www.alonzobodden.com.

Comedian **Joe Bolster** has performed on the *Tonight Show* and in his own HBO special, and has written for both *The Martin Short Show* and the Academy Awards.

Comedian **Buddy Bolton** has appeared on *Comic Strip Live* and in the movie *The Master of Disguise*.

Comedian **Elayne Boosler** has starred in her own HBO and Showtime specials, including *Party of One*. Web site: www.elayneboosler.com.

In the seventy years he lived in the United States, **Victor Borge**'s unique combination of classical musician and humorist was displayed on radio, films, and television. His *Comedy in Music* holds the record for the longest-running one-man show on Broadway.

**Sue Bova** is an actress, comedian, singer, and voice-over/jingle artist for films, television, Internet, radio, musical theater, and opera.

**Alicia Brandt** is a stand-up comedian and actor who has appeared in a range of roles, including on *General Hospital* and in the movie *Mousehunt*.

**Bill Braudis** has appeared on *Late Night with Conan O'Brien*, written for Comedy Central's *Dr. Katz, Professional Therapist*, and was the voice of Doug Savage on the animated series *Science Court*.

Comedian **Kevin Brennan** has appeared on NBC's *Comedy Tonight*.

Comedian **David Brenner** has had a forty-year career in comedy, which includes a record 158 appearances on the *Tonight Show*. Web site: www.davidbrenner.net.

**Steve Bridges** has been a featured guest on more than one hundred radio stations and has performed at the Ice House in Pasadena, The Comedy Store, and the Improv.

**Dylan Brody** has appeared on A&E's *Comedy on the Road* and Fox TV's *Comedy Express*, written jokes for Jay Leno's *Tonight Show* monologues, and published science fiction and fantasy novels for young adults. Web site: www.dylanbrody.com.

Comedian **Jimmy Brogan** has been a producer of the *Tonight Show*. Web site: www.jimmybroganonline.com.

**Mel Brooks** is a comedian, writer, and director of such films as *Young Frankenstein* and *Blazing Saddles*, and the Broadway musical *The Producers*.

Comedian **A. Whitney Brown** was an anchor on *Saturday Night Live*'s Weekend Update and has also been seen on Comedy Central's *The Daily Show*.

**Judy Brown** is a writer, comedy teacher, and the editor of this book, as well as editor of *Joke Soup, Joke Stew, The Funny Pages, Jokes to Go,* and *She's So Funny.* Web site: www.judybrown.info.

Comedian **Julie Brown** performed in the movies *Earth Girls Are Easy* and *Clueless,* and was the screenwriter for the Comedy Central series *Strip Mall.* Check her out at www.juliebrown.com.

**Maureen Brownsey** is a comedian and filmmaker. Her films include *True Blue.*

Comedian **Lenny Bruce** is the comedian who practically invented comedy plainspeak in the second half of the twentieth century. He produced albums that include his Carnegie Hall Concert and wrote the book *How to Talk Dirty and Influence People.*

Comedian **Steve Bruner** has performed on A&E's *Evening at the Improv* and Showtime's *Comedy Club Network.* Web site: www.stevebruner.com.

**Mike Bullard** has been the host of *Open Mike with Mike Bullard* on Canada's Comedy Network.

**Andy Bumatai** is Hawaii's favorite comedian with seven albums to his credit and appearances on TV shows that include *Baywatch.* Web site: www.andybumatai.com.

**George Burns** was a classic comedian whose career stretched from vaudeville to the *Burns and Allen* sitcom and the movie *Oh, God.*

Comedian **Brett Butler** has been the star of the sitcom *Grace Under Fire.*

Comedian **Red Buttons** won the Best Supporting Actor Golden Globe and Oscar for the film *Sayonara.*

Comedian **Joey Callahan** has performed on Comedy Central and ESPN's *Lighter Side of Sports.* Web site: www.joeycallahan.com.

**Eddie Cantor**'s career as a comedian stretched from vaudeville to Broadway and the movies, including the show *Banjo Eyes.*

**Steve Carell** is an actor and comedian, and has been a correspondent for *The Daily Show* on Comedy Central.

**Drew Carey** is, coincidentally enough, the star of *The Drew Carey Show.*

Comedian **George Carlin** has won a Grammy and a Cable Ace award, and was nominated for an Emmy for his comedy albums and HBO and network comedy specials. Web site: www.georgecarlin.com.

Comedian **Jim Carrey** is the star of films that range from *Dumb and Dumber* and *The Truman Show* to *Man on the Moon.*

**Bea Carroll** is a singer-songwriter and comedian who has performed at The Comedy Store, Upfront Comedy, and the Hollywood Grill.

British comedian **Jasper Carrott** has a series of UK gold albums to his credit, including *Beat the Carrott* and *The Mole,* as well as the popular TV series *Canned Carrott* and sitcom *The Detectives.*

**Johnny Carson** hosted NBC's the *Tonight Show* for more than thirty years. Web site: www.johnnycarson.com.

**Judy Carter** is the author of *The Comedy Bible* but bills herself as "just another Jewish lesbian comic-magician." Web site: www.judycarter.com.

Comedian **Christopher Case** has been a writer and producer for the sitcoms *Titus* and *Reba.*

**Dick Cavett** parlayed an early stand-up comedy career into his own talk shows on networks, PBS, and cable.

Comedian **Rich Ceisler** has performed on Comedy Central and HBO.

Comedian **Jeff Cesario** has won two Emmys and six Cable Ace awards for writing and producing *The Larry Sanders Show*, *Dennis Miller Live*, and his own HBO and Comedy Central stand-up specials. Web site: www.jeffcesario.com.

**Lori Chapman** has been performing stand-up comedy for the last four years all over the West Coast, from Seattle to San Diego. She's also single, and, at this point, she's willing to settle for less.

Comedian **Vernon Chapman** has appeared in the movies *Elvis Meets Nixon* and *Billy Madison*.

It stands to reason that comedian **Dave Chappelle** is the host of *Chappelle's Show* on Comedy Central.

**Margaret Cho** has won an American Comedy Award and starred in her own HBO and Comedy Central specials. Web site: www.margaretcho.com.

Comedian **Adam Christing** is the president of Clean Comedians and editor of the book *Comedy Comes Clean*.

**Louis C.K.** was featured on Comedy Central's *Young Comedians at Aspen*.

Comedian **Anthony Clark** is the star of the sitcom *Yes, Dear*.

Comedian **Blake Clark** has guest starred on *Sabrina, the Teenage Witch* as Phil the Dog and on *Spin City*, *Boy Meets World*, *The Jamie Foxx Show*, and *Home Improvement*.

Canadian comic **Bruce Clark** has been featured on the *Tonight Show*.

**Herb Clark** is a comedian from Leeds, Alabama, who has performed on the Bacardi by Night Comedy Tour and at comedy clubs including the Comedy Zone, Summit Comedy, and Comedy House Theatre. Web site: www.herbclark.com. Contact: funnynobodies3@aol.com.

**Andrew Dice Clay** was one of the crudest comedians of the 1980s—or as one reviewer put it, Clay came to the stage with a "crass, racist, misogynist attaché of gags under the guise of a stage presence, a character referred to as Diceman." Clay has also been the star of such features as *The Adventures of Ford Fairlane*.

Comedian **Paul Clay** is a TV comedy writer and producer.

Comedian **Al Cleathen** has appeared on *Evening at the Improv* and Fox's *The Sunday Comics*.

**Kate Clinton** has released a number of her own comedy albums, been a writer for *The Rosie O'Donnell Show*, and appeared on Comedy Central's *Out There II*. Web site: www.kateclinton.com.

**Jack Coen** made a dozen appearances on the *Tonight Show*, and, no fools, they made him a staff writer. He also recently starred in his own Comedy Central special.

**Brock Cohen** is a screenwriter and stand-up comedian who has performed at the Hollywood Comedy Store.

Comedian **Marty Cohen** has performed on *Evening at the Improv*.

**Myron Cohen** was a favorite comedian and storyteller on the Borscht Belt circuit and later made numerous appearances on 1950s TV, including the *Ed Sullivan Show*.

**Jane Condon** has been called "the J.Crew mother of two" by *The New York Daily News* and "an upper-crust Roseanne" by the Associated Press. Check her out at www.Janecondon.com

Scotland's favorite comedian, **Billy Connolly** has also been featured in films, including his star turn in *Her Majesty, Mrs. Brown.* Web site: www.billyconnolly.com.

**Tim Conway** is a classic comedian best known for his sketch work on *The Carol Burnett Show* and in his Dorf videos.

**Auggie Cook** is comedian from Pittsburgh who has been doing stand-up for about fourteen years and writing jokes since high school. Web site: www.auggiecook.com.

One of Britain's favorite comedians, **Tommy Cooper** made an art form of failing to perform magical tricks.

Comedian **Ronnie Corbett** was awarded the OBE (Officer of the Order of the British Empire) for, among other efforts, his participation in the film *No Sex, Please—We're British.*

Comedian **Billiam Coronel** has been a staff writer on the TV series *Men Behaving Badly* and *The Parent 'Hood.*

Comedian **David Corrado** performs throughout Los Angeles and writes for several comedians. Contact: dcorrado@ucla.edu.

After having made more than thirty national television appearances, **Rick Corso** was selected as one of Showtime's Comedy Club All-Stars and was also chosen to be on Comedy Central's *The A-List.*

The title of his first comedy album was prophetic: ***Bill Cosby** Is a Very Funny Fellow, Right?* His forty-year career includes the 1984–92 TV run of *The Cosby Show* and his books *Fatherhood* and *Time Flies.*

**Lou Costello** was one-half of the comedy team Abbott & Costello, who brought their classic vaudeville and burlesque routines—including "Who's on First"—to movies such as *Hold That Ghost* and *Abbott & Costello Meet Frankenstein.*

**Sue Costello** has appeared on *Tough Crowd with Colin Quinn* and been featured on Comedy Central's *Premium Blend.* Web site: www.suecostello.com.

**Aurora Cotsbeck** is an Australian actress and comedian who has appeared on the TV series *Stingers and Neighbors.*

**Tom Cotter** has been featured in his own Comedy Central special.

**Eileen Courtney** is a former TV technical director, comedian, and current full-time mom who is always funny, and needs to be to keep her sanity.

**David Cousin** is a comedian and juggler who has performed at Universal Studios, Dodger Stadium, and Bally's Hotel and Casino. Web site: www.jugglerdavidcousin.com.

**Mary Beth Cowan** was featured on NBC's *Last Comic Standing* and was the winner of Rhode Island's Funniest Comedian Contest.

Comedian **Barry Crimmins** is a staff writer for Air America Radio and has released two CDs, *Strange Bedfellows* on A&M and *Kill the Messenger* on Green Linnet. Web site: www.barrycrimmins.com.

**Christine Crosby** is a Canadian comedian who performs at Yuk Yuks and other venues.

**David Cross** developed and starred in HBO's *Mr. Show* and has appeared in films, including *Men in Black.* Web site: www.bobanddavid.com.

Comedian **Lance Crouther** originated the character Pootie Tang on HBO's *Chris Rock Show* and won an Emmy and Cable Ace award for his writing on that show.

Comedian **Billy Crystal** is an actor and director whose movies include *City Slickers* and *When Harry Met Sally,* and is a serial host of the Academy Awards.

**Danny Curtis**'s television appearances include *America's Funniest People* on ABC. He also entertains passengers on the Princess cruise line. Web site: www.comedy ontheroad.com/danny_curtis.html.

**Lee Curtis** and **Jon Berahya**, two up-and-coming comedians from South Florida, are the producers of their CD *Lee & Jon, Scar Your Children for Life*. Contact: LeeandJon@aol.com.

Comedian **Brent Cushman** has performed on *Evening at the Improv*.

**Sara Cytron** has been featured in the PBS lesbian and gay series *In the Life*, and in the book *Out Loud & Laughing*.

Comedian **Frank D'Amico** has played recurring characters on the sitcoms *Grounded For Life* and *Becker*.

**Bill Dana** is a classic comic of the 1950–60s best known for his comedy albums featuring Jose Jimenez, Astronaut.

**Michael Dane** has been entertaining audiences for fifteen years everywhere from Seattle to Maine as a stand-up comic and with his solo show *No Apparent Motive*. He also created the Gay and Lesbian Comedy Night at the Comedy Store.

Comedian **Rodney Dangerfield** starred in the movies *Caddyshack, Back to School,* and improbably enough, *Natural Born Killers*. He also won a Grammy for his comedy album *No Respect*. Web site: www.rodney.com.

**Ron Darian** is a voice actor and writer for the series *7th Heaven*.

Comedian **Evan Davis** has made more than forty television appearances, including as a regular performer on the *Tonight Show*. Web site: www.evandavis.tv.

**Michael Davis** is more than just a juggler. He's also a comedian who has performed on *Saturday Night Live* and the *Tonight Show*.

**Les Dawson** was a classic British comic with his own series featured on ITV and the BBC.

Comedian **JoAnn Dearing** has appeared on *Evening at the Improv*, Showtime's *Comedy Club Network*, and *Girls' Night Out*.

Comedian **Ellen DeGeneres** hosts her own talk show, was the groundbreaking star of ABC's *Ellen*, and has been featured in movies that include *Love Letters* and *Mr. Wrong*.

**Lea DeLaria** hosted Comedy Central's *Out There* and has appeared on Broadway in *On the Town* and *The Most Fabulous Story Ever Told*.

**Jessica Delfino** has been a finalist on *Good Morning America*'s Make Us Laugh All Night Long Competition and a writer for the MTV show *I Bet You Will*. Check her out at www.jessydelfino.blogspot.com.

Comedian **Ron Dentinger** was the Wisconsin winner of the *Funniest Person in America* contest.

**Tony DePaul** has been a headliner at San Francisco's famous Comedy Day.

**Tony Deyo** is a stand-up comic from High Point, North Carolina. Web site: www.tonydeyo.com.

**Sully Diaz** has appeared on the TV shows *Ellen* and *Culture Clash*, and is featured on the CD *Hot and Spicy Mamitas*.

**Kathie Dice** is a comedian, wife, mother, and hairdresser, to boot. She has also written and performed her own one-woman show, a humorous look at the life of the Virgin Mary. Web site: www.kjthedj.homestead.com/mary.html.

**Dominic Dierkes** started performing in stand-up comedy as a fifteen-year-old high school student and is currently a favorite on the college circuit. Web site: www.dominicdierkes.com.

**Jeannie Dietz** has written jokes for Joan Rivers.

**Phyllis Diller** is the groundbreaking woman comedian whose career began in the 1950s. She has appeared in a number of movies and on dozens of TV shows, including the *Tonight Show*.

**Frances Dilorinzo** has appeared on Comedy Central and in USO Tours around the world. Web site: www.francesd.com.

Comedian **Nick DiPaulo** has appeared on Comedy Central's *Comics Come Home* and *Tough Crowd with Colin Quinn*.

Comedian **Janine DiTullio** has been a staff writer for *Late Night with Conan O'Brien* and *The Jon Stewart Show*.

Comedian **Erica Doering** performs in clubs in and around Southern California. Web site: www.badcelluloid.com/erica. Contact: ericadoering@hotmail.com.

**Beth Donahue**, comedian and host of Nashville's WKDF morning radio, is also the author of the humor book, *This Is Insanity! No Dieting, No Exercising, No Counseling, No Results: Stay the Way You Look and Feel—Forever*. Web site: www.Bethdonahue.com.

**Brian Dowell** is a Los Angeles–based comedian who has been featured on the sitcom Titus.

**Tom Dressen** has performed extensively, including in Las Vegas, on the *Tonight Show*, and as an opening act for Elvis Presley. Web site: www.tomdressen.com.

Comedian **Bob Dubac** has appeared on the TV shows *Loving, Growing Pains, Life Goes On, Jack and Mike, Diff'rent Strokes*, and in his own one-man show *The Male Intellect: An Oxymoron*. Web site: www.maleintellect.com.

**Rick Duccomun** has appeared on *Evening at the Improv*, VH-1's *Spotlight*, and in the movies *Neighbors* and *Groundhog Day*.

**Mike Dugan** has appeared on the *Tonight Show with Jay Leno* and won an Emmy Award for writing on HBO's *Dennis Miller Live*. He is also the author of the one-man show *Men Fake Foreplay*. Web site: www.menfakeforeplay.com.

**Jimmy Durante** was a comedian whose career spanned vaudeville, Broadway, the movies, and 1950s TV.

Political comedian **Will Durst** hosted the award-winning PBS series *We Do the Work*, taped a *One Night Stand* for HBO, and starred in A&E's *A Year's Worth with Will Durst*, which was nominated for a Cable Ace Award. Durst also has been nominated five times for an American Comedy Award but still hasn't won, making him the Susan Lucci of stand-up. Web site: www.willdurst.com.

**Dwight** is a Los Angeles–based actor and comedian.

**Bil Dwyer** has appeared on most of the defunct stand-up shows and has had guest starring roles on *The Larry Sanders Show* and *Ally McBeal*.

**Dana Eagle** has performed at the Aspen Comedy Festival, on Showtime, the Oxygen Network, Comedy Central's *Premium Blend*, and in a bunch of commercials. Contact: dana@laughterheals.org.

**Chris Elliot** has starred in the movie *Cabin Boy* and the sitcoms *Get a Life* and *Everybody Loves Raymond*.

**Chas Elstner** has performed at hundreds of comedy clubs, opened for Gloria Estefan, and appeared on MTV and Showtime.

Comedian **Bill Engvall** has won an American Comedy Award and is a star of Comedy Central's *Blue Collar Comedy*. Web site: www.billengvall.com.

**Bob Ettinger** has appeared on *Evening at the Improv* and Showtime's *Comedy Club Network*.

Australian comedian Barry Humphries likes to dress up as **Dame Edna Everage**.

**Robin Fairbanks** is a Seattle-based stand-up comedian who has opened for comedians Ralph Harris, Sue Murphy, and Bobby Slayton. Robin is also a contributing writer and cast member of the sketch show *The Night Shift*, and has appeared in local and national commercials. Web site: www.robinfairbanks.com.

Comedian **Wayne Federman** has been featured in his own Comedy Central special, on HBO's *Curb Your Enthusiasm*, and in the movie *50 First Dates*.

**Marty Feldman** was a classic British comedian who appeared in *Young Frankenstein* and other films.

**Michael Feldman** has been featured in the book *That's Funny*.

A father of five, **Ken Ferguson** performs comedy in the Midwest: "I need to tell the world how ticked off I am, and make people laugh at the same time." Contact: Kenfergy2@aol.com.

Comedian **Adam Ferrara** has been featured on the ABC sitcom *The Job* and twice nominated for an American Comedy Award. Web site: www.adamferrara.com.

**Tina Fey** is a cohost of Weekend Update on *Saturday Night Live* and screenwriter of the movie *Mean Girls*.

**Totie Fields** was one of the top women comedians in the 1950s. Her television appearances included the *Ed Sullivan Show* and the *Tonight Show*.

**Mel Fine** is a working comedian throughout the Midwest and the winner of the Indianapolis Funniest Person Contest.

**Hugh Fink** was a writer for *Saturday Night Live* and has starred in his own Comedy Central special.

**Michael Flanders** is the British comedian who became famous for the show *At the Drop of a Hat*. He made frequent television appearances in the 1950s and 1960s, and also successfully toured the United States and Canada.

**Dave Foley** was one of the *Kids in the Hall* and then moved on to *NewsRadio*.

Comedian **Diane Ford** has received eight nominations for an American Comedy Award. Her HBO specials are classics.

**Glen Foster** has been a headliner on the Canadian comedy circuit for more than fifteen years, also performing in the United States, Great Britain, and Australia. Glen starred in his own Comedy Network Special, *That Canadian Guy*, and has appeared on numerous other TV shows including CBC's *Comics*.

Comedian **Jeff Foxworthy** is the star of Comedy Central's *Blue Collar Comedy*.

TV star turned screen actor **Jamie Foxx** first became known for his many roles on the comedy variety show *In Living Color*. Since then, Foxx has earned particular acclaim for his roles in *Any Given Sunday* and as Ray Charles in the Oscar-nominted *Ray*.

**Redd Foxx** was a stand-up comedian for more than forty years and the star of the 1970s sitcom *Sanford and Son*.

**Catherine Franco** has played leading ladies in heavy theatrical shows such as *Extremities* and *Children of a Lesser God*, played home-wrecking bitches in a dozen soap operas, and now performs in comedy clubs, including the Laugh Factory in Los Angeles. Contact: cbocaloca@aol.com.

Comedian **Al Franken** is the author of *Rush Limbaugh Is a Big Fat Idiot* and *Lies and the Lying Liars Who Tell Them: A Fair and Balanced Look at the Right*, and is a host of Air America Radio. Web site: www.airamericaradio.com.

Comedian **Stevie Ray Fromstein** has written for the sitcoms *Grace Under Fire, Two Guys and a Girl,* and *Roseanne.*

**Sir David Frost** has been on the front line of television news and entertainment for more than forty years beginning with the satirical news program *That Was the Week That Was* on the BBC in 1962. That was followed by a variety of interview programs in the UK and America, broadcast all around the world.

**Fry and Laurie** are a British comedy team best known in America for the PBS series *Jeeves.*

**Caryl Fuller**'s book and solo show, *Dueling Hearts,* is a comic tour de force about charming men and the rollercoaster ride of romance. Contact: carylfuller@aol.com.

Comedian **Jim Gaffigan** starred on the sitcoms *Ellen* and *Welcome to New York.*

**Zach Galifianakis** has been a star of the TV show *Tru Calling* and a writer for *That '70s Show.*

**Gallagher** is the giant-prop and water-melon-smashing comedian whose Showtime specials are frequently aired on Comedy Central. Web site: www.gallaghersmash.com.

Comedian **Jack Gallagher** has performed

comedy on *The Dennis Miller Show* and the *Tonight Show,* and hosted the PBS program *Money Moves.*

Comedian **Billy Garan** has appeared on Showtime and Comedy Central, and in films that include *Indecent Proposal.*

**Janeane Garofalo** is the queen of the alternative comedians and an actress who has appeared in films that include *The Truth About Cats and Dogs* and *Mystery Men.*

**Tina Georgie** has appeared on *The Late, Late Show with Craig Kilborn.*

**Larry Getlen** is a New York–based comedian, journalist, and actor who has written for *Esquire* magazine and Comedy Central's *Tough Crowd with Colin Quinn.* He has also appeared on *Chappelle's Show.* Web site: www.zhet.blogspot.com.

**Lori Gianella** is a comedian in her home-town of Pittsburgh and she masquerades by day as Assistant Director of Admission and publications coordinator at her alma mater, Carnegie Mellon University. Contact: laugh-withlori@hotmail.com.

**Johnnye Jones Gibson** works for a newspaper, freelances as a journalist, writes screen-plays, and travels the world interviewing and writing newsletters for Anthony Robbins Seminars and other events.

**Irv Gilman** is a comedian, MC, and former Council Member of Monterey Park, California.

*Last Comic Standing* contestant **Todd Glass** has appeared on numerous other TV shows, including *Home Improvement, Friends, Married with Children,* and HBO's *Mr. Show.* Web site: www.toddglass.com.

**Jackie Gleason** was a comedian and actor who starred in *The Honeymooners* and movies such as *The Hustler* and *Papa's Delicate Condition.*

Comedian **George Gobel**'s career ranged from *American Barn Dance* on radio to his own weekly television show in the 1950s to regular appearances, later, on *Hollywood Squares*.

**Lisa Goich** is a stand-up comedian, talk-radio host, award-winning copywriter, and author of the book *The Breakup Diary*.

Comedian **Judy Gold** has appeared on HBO's *Comic Relief* and the *Tonight Show*, and starred in her own Comedy Central special.

Comedian **Whoopi Goldberg** is the Oscar-winning actress of the film *Ghost*, appears on *Hollywood Squares*, is cohost of HBO's *Comic Relief*, and has hosted the Oscars.

**Bobcat Goldthwait** has starred in the movie *Scrooged* and on TV series that include *Unhappily Ever After*. He has also directed his movie *Shakes the Clown* and *Chappelle's Show* on Comedy Central.

**Marga Gomez** has appeared on HBO's *Comic Relief*, Showtime's *Latino Laugh Festival*, and Comedy Central's *Out There* special. Web site: www.margagomez.com.

**Mimi Gonzalez** produced the weekly stand-up show *Women with Balls* for six years in Los Angeles and San Francisco. Mimi has also performed comedy from Wenatchee to Biloxi to Tallahassee to Albany and counts entertaining the troops in Japan, Korea, Bosnia, and Kosovo as some of her most rewarding work. Web site: www.mimigonzalez.com.

**Reno Goodale** is a comedian, writer, and actor who has written material for Roseanne and Jay Leno, and performed as the opening act for Joan Rivers and Dana Carvey. Goodale has appeared in national commercials and on network television, and also headlines in clubs and colleges across the country.

Comedian **Doug Graham** has opened for many national acts, including Drew Carey, Kevin Meaney, Phoebe Snow, and Spyrogyra.

Classic comedian **Ronnie Graham** was a TV writer and comic songwriter of tunes that include one dedicated to Lizzie Borden, "You Can't Chop Your Mother up in Massachusetts."

Comedian **Robin Greenspan** has been featured on Comedy Central's *Out There in Hollywood*.

**Michael Greer** was an actor and comedian whose films included *Fortune and Men's Eyes*, *The Lonely Guy*, and *The Rose*.

Comedian **E. L. Greggory** is a regular at the Comedy Store in Hollywood.

**Dick Gregory** is a groundbreaking African American political comedian and civil rights activist, still active in both. Web site: www.dickgregory.com.

**David Alan Grier** has starred in the TV series *In Living Color* and *Life with Bonnie*, and in films that include *Jumanji* and *Blankman*.

Comedian **Kathy Griffin** has been featured in the sitcom *Suddenly Susan* and movies *The Cable Guy* and *Pulp Fiction*. Web site: www.kathygriffin.com.

Hailed by Backstage West as "Robin Williams's sister," **Katherine Griffith** is best known for her solo shows *Crazy Ladies* and *The Miss Pretty Hand Show*, which she has performed across the country.

Ex-Bostonian **Adam Gropman** is a Los Angeles–based stand-up comic, writer, and actor who contributes to SHECKYmagazine.com and hollywoodbadass.com.

**Mark Gross** has appeared on the *Tonight Show*.

**Mark Guido** is a San Francisco–based comedian.

Comedian **Gary Gulman** was a finalist in the second season of NBC's *Last Comic Standing*. Web site: www.garygulman.com.

Comedian **Geechy Guy** has appeared on the *Tonight Show*, MTV, and Comedy Central. Web site: www.geechyguy.com.

Comedian **Karen Haber** has been featured on *The Arsenio Hall Show* and *Evening at the Improv*, and in the video *The Girls of the Comedy Store*.

Best known for his raunchy Las Vegas routines, **Buddy Hackett** enjoyed substantial Broadway, film, and TV success with such vehicles as *The Music Man, It's a Mad, Mad, Mad, Mad World*, and *The Little Mermaid*.

Comedian **Arsenio Hall** has been the host of *Star Search* and *The Arsenio Hall Show*.

**Rich Hall** is a former *Saturday Night Live* cast member and was also a comedy anchor on *Not Necessarily the News*.

**Argus Hamilton** is a political comedian and *Tonight Show* regular.

Comedian **Rhonda Hansome** has opened for James Brown, the Pointer Sisters, and Anita Baker, and has appeared in the film *Pretty Woman*.

**Deric Harrington** is a comedian who likes his Web site, www.dericharrington.com. He also likes the taste of victory.

Comedian **Lynn Harris** has written for *The New York Times* and *Entertainment Weekly*. She's the creator of BreakupGirl.com and three resulting books, including *Breakup Girl to the Rescue!*

**Alan Havey** has hosted *Night After Night* on the nascent Comedy Channel and appeared in the movies *Internal Affairs*, *Rounders*, and *Wild Things 2*. Web site: www.allanhavey.com.

**Paula R. Hawkins** has been a semifinalist in Comedy Central's Laugh Riot Competition, and been featured as one of the Comedians to Watch on *The Jenny Jones Show*. Web site: www.artistwebsite.com/paularapage.html.

Comedian **Robert Hawkins** has been a story editor for the sitcom *Titus*, been awarded an American Comedy Award, and starred in his own Comedy Central special.

**Susan Healy** is a Los Angeles–based comedian.

Comedian **Mitch Hedberg** has performed on *That '70s Show* and in his own stand-up special on Comedy Central. Web site: www.mitchhedberg.net.

**John Heffron** was the winning comedian and last comic standing on the second season of NBC's *Last Comic Standing*. Web site: www.johnheffron.com.

**Janice Heiss** is a comedian and member of San Francisco theater group The Plutonium Players. Her writing has also appeared in the literary magazine *Passages North* and the books *Herotica 2* and *The Ecstatic Moment: The Best of Libido*.

**Kevin Hench**, TV producer and comedy writer, is supervising producer of *The Sports List* on Fox Sports Net.

**Buck Henry** has made lasting contributions to pop culture as cocreator of TV's *Get Smart*, coscripter of the film *The Graduate*, as frequent guest host on *Saturday Night Live*.

Comedian **Carol Henry** has been featured on HBO's *Women of the Night III*.

Comedian **Linda Herskovic** toured the country as one-half of the comedy team Two Consenting Adults, and she has also contributed to the literary web 'zine *Shescape*.

**Tom Hertz** has been a featured patient on Comedy Central's *Dr. Katz, Professional Therapist*.

**Trina Hess** has studied acting at Second City in Cleveland, and performed at the Cleveland Comedy Kitchen and Akron's First Night celebration.

**Old Man Heywood** is a hilarious octogenarian comedian who has performed at the Improv in Hollywood. Contact: oldmanhey@aol.com.

In the 1980s and early 1990s **Bill Hicks** made eleven appearances on *Late Show with David Letterman* and released his first concert video, *Sane Man*. Hicks recorded four comedy albums during his lifetime (including *Dangerous* and *Relentless*), and the albums *Arizona Bay* and *Rant in E-Minor*, which were issued posthumously. Web site: www.billhicks.com.

**René Hicks** has starred in her own Comedy Central special, appeared in the movie *Low Down Dirty Shame*, and has been nominated for an American Comedy Award. Web site: www.renehicks.com.

British comic **Benny Hill** was best known in America for his slapstick syndicated TV show *The Benny Hill Show*.

**Charlie Hill** is a Native American comedian from the Oneida tribe who has appeared on the *Tonight Show* and *Late Show with David Letterman*. Hill has been a staff writer for the sitcom *Roseanne* and is host of the Club Red radio program featured on National Public Radio. Web site: www.clubredwithcharliehill.com.

Comedian **Harry Hill** has appeared on *Late Show with David Letterman*.

**Stephanie Hodge** is the star of the sitcom *Unhappily Ever After*.

Comedian **Steve Hofstetter** is the author of the *Student Body Shots* series, available at bookstores everywhere. Web site: www.stevehofstetter.com.

**Daryl Hogue** is a comedian and voice-over talent whose clients include 7-Eleven, Ford, and Hewlett Packard. She performs in clubs in the L.A. area.

**Corey Holcomb** was a finalist on the second season of NBC's *Last Comic Standing*.

**Vanessa Hollingshead** has appeared on Comedy Central's *Tough Crowd with Colin Quinn* and nearly two dozen other TV shows.

Comedian **Maryellen Hooper** won an American Comedy Award. Her numerous television appearances include the *Tonight Show* and her own Comedy Central special. Web site: www.maryellenhooper.com.

**Bob Hope** was a comedian whose career ranged over seven decades from vaudeville to a series of *Road* movies with Bing Crosby to innumerable television specials.

Comedian **John Hope** has been working the circuit in clubs and colleges around the United States for many years, as "the Thinking Man's Slacker." When not providing comedy to the masses, Hope spends his spare time performing with his punk rock band and playing chess.

**Jeremy Hotz** appeared in his own half-hour Comedy Central special.

**Alex House** has appeared on *Last Comic Standing* and *The View*. She has twice won the Bud Light Ladies of Laughter contest. Web site: www.comedy.com/alexhouse.

Comedian **D. L. Hughley** is the star of the sitcom *The Hughleys* and has also appeared in the films *Inspector Gadget* and *Scary Movie*.

Comedian **Darlene Hunt** has written for the sitcom *Good Morning, Miami* and costarred on *Will & Grace*.

**Warren Hutcherson** has starred in his own HBO Half Hour Comedy special, been featured at the Aspen Comedy Festival, and been a producer of the sitcom *Living Single*.

**Eric Idle**, most famously of the Monty Python troupe and the movie *Life of Brian*, has been featured in the movies *Casper* and Terry Gilliam's *The Adventures of Baron Munchausen*. Idle's second novel, *The Road to Mars*, was published in 1999.

**Tony Invergo** is a comedian and magician who has been performing since 1988 in the United States and Europe. He is currently living in Illinois. Contact: uncent@hotmail.com.

**Dom Irrera** has starred in his own HBO specials and also appeared on TV shows such as *Everybody Loves Raymond* and *The Drew Carey Show* and in movies that include *The Big Lebowski*.

**Eddie Izzard** is the British transvestite and stand-up comedian who starred in his own 1999 HBO special and movies such as *Mystery Men*.

Comedian **A. J. Jamal** has appeared on the *Tonight Show* and *In Living Color* as well as made multiple appearances on HBO, Showtime, and A&E. Web site: www.ajjamal.com.

On his very own sitcom, comedian **Kevin James** is *King of Queens*.

**Jeff Jena** has been seen on more than forty national television shows and currently owns a comedy club in Newport, Kentucky. Contact: JeffreyTJ@aol.com.

**Jenée** has performed stand-up around the globe, including USO tours of Korea, Bosnia, and Kosovo. Jenée is also a regular contributor to *US Magazine*'s Fashion Police. Check her out at www.jenee.net.

Comedian **Richard Jeni** has been rewarded for his comic fluidity with two Cable Ace Awards and one American Comedy Award. Web site: www.richardjeni.com.

**Geri Jewell** has appeared on *Girls' Night Out* and *Comic Strip Live* and was a recurring character on the sitcom *Facts of Life*.

**Jake Johannsen** starred in his own HBO *One Night Stand* and was nominated for an American Comedy Award. Web site: www.jakethis.com.

Comedian **Chuck Johnson** has performed at the Palos Verdes Players Theater.

Comedian **Jenny Jones** was the host of *The Jenny Jones Show*. Web site: www.jennyjones.com.

Comedian **Diana Jordan** has been nominated for an American Comedy Award, has appeared in the movie *Jerry McGuire*, and is the author of the book *Women Are from Venus, Men Are from Uranus*. Web site: www.dianajordan.com.

Comedian **Heidi Joyce** is the creator, host, and executive producer of the nationally recognized *Stand Up Against Domestic Violence* CDs on Uproar Entertainment. She has also been featured on *Everybody Loves Raymond*'s "Ray Day" on CBS. Web site: www.members.aol.com/comedygrrl.

**Tere Joyce** was one of the finalists on NBC's *Last Comic Standing*.

Comedian **Norman K.** performs at clubs in the New York area. Contact: normank_comic@hotmail.com.

Palestinian-American comedian **Aron Kader** is one of the Comedy Store's Arabian Nights.

**Cory Kahaney** was a finalist of NBC's *Last Comic Standing* and has also appeared on Lifetime's *Girls' Night Out*, NBC's *Comedy Showcase*, and Comedy Central.

Comedian **Bill Kalmenson** appeared in the movie *Lethal Weapon* and is the screenwriter and director of the film *The Souler Opposite*.

**Wendy Kamenoff** is an actress, stand-up comedian, playwright, and mother of seven-year-old Griffin. Her recent TV appearances include HBO's *Curb Your Enthusiasm*, *The Bernie Mac Show*, and *National Lampoon's Funny Money*. Wendy's company, Parents with Punchlines, produces comedy fundraisers for private and public elementary schools. Contact: wendykamenoff@aol.com.

**Jackie Kannon** is a classic comedian whose albums include *Live from the Ratfink Room* and *Songs for the John*.

Stand-up comedian and actor **Gabe Kaplan** is best known for playing the title role in the television series *Welcome Back Kotter* (1975–1979).

**Myq Kaplan** performs music and comedy in the Boston area, is a regular at the Comedy Studio, and an irregular elsewhere. His CD is titled *Open Myq Night*. Web site: www.myqkaplan.com.

Comedian **Jann Karam** has appeared on *Politically Incorrect*, the *Tonight Show*, *Evening at the Improv*, and Lifetime's *Girls' Night Out*. Web site: www.jannkaram.com.

**Jackie Kashian** has appeared on A&E's *Comedy on the Road* and at HBO's U.S. Comedy Arts Festival. Check her out at www.jackiekashian.com.

Comedian **Debbie Kasper** has been a staff writer on the sitcom *Roseanne* and *The Rosie O'Donnell Show*, for which she received two Emmy nominations. Debbie is currently touring with cowriter **Sheila Kay** in *Venus Attacks*, a comedy about love, sex, and self-help. Check her out at www.venusattacks.org.

Comedian **Jonathan Katz** played doctor on Comedy Central's *Dr. Katz, Professional Therapist* and is the author of *To Do Lists of the Dead*.

**Max Kauffman** is a U.S. humorist and comedian.

**Sheila Kay**: See Debbie Kasper.

**Patrick Keane** has appeared at the Irvine Improv, the Comedy Store, Mixed Nuts, the Ha Ha Café, and other comedy venues throughout Southern California.

Comedian **Tom Kearney** is a voice-over actor for commercials and has appeared in several independent films, including *Fruit of the Vine* and *The Flipside*.

**Kelly** is a speaker/comedian residing in southeast Michigan. Contact: kelly42612003@yahoo.com.

**Eileen Kelly** is a New York–based stand-up comedian and head writer of the sketch troupe Hits Like a Girl.

**Martha Kelly** has appeared on Comedy Central and NBC's *Last Comic Standing*.

Comedian **Bobby Kelton** has appeared on the *Tonight Show* and *Late Show with David Letterman*.

Former Canadian fighter pilot and now comedian **Barry Kennedy** has appeared on A&E's *Comedy on the Road*. He is also the author of two books.

**Jen Kerwin** was one of NBC's *Last Comic Standing*.

Comedian **Joe Keyes** has appeared on the sitcoms *Seinfeld, Roseanne,* and the HBO series *Carnivàle,* written for other TV series, and is the coauthor of the long-running Los Angeles stage show *Bob's Office Party.*

Comedian **Julie Kidd** has been featured on NBC's *Power of Laughter* and on ABC's *The View,* where Joy Behar said of her, "Julie Kidd is one of the funniest housewives in America!" Web site: www.funnysinglemom.com.

In addition to being comedy's reigning Queen of Sardonica, **Laura Kightlinger** is also a writer and producer for the sitcom *Will and Grace.*

Comedian **Craig Kilborn** has been the host of CBS's *The Late Late Show.*

**Brian Kiley** is an Emmy-nominated writer who appears regularly on the *Tonight Show* and *Late Night with Conan O'Brien.*

Comedian **Karen Kilgariff** is the head writer of *The Ellen DeGeneres Show* and has appeared on HBO's *Mr. Show* and *The Drew Carey Show.*

**Andy Kindler** has appeared on *Late Show with David Letterman* and is a regular performer on *Everybody Loves Raymond.*

In his half-century comedy career, **Alan King** performed on TV, in nightclubs, on Broadway, in concerts, and in thirty films, including *Hit the Deck* and *Casino.*

Comedian **Nosmo King** is the cocreator of the Los Angeles showcase *Dreamland.*

**Bill Kirchenbauer** was featured on *Family Ties* and starred in the sitcom *Just the Ten of Us.*

**Dani Klein** is a comedian and actor who appeared on *Law and Order* and in the movie remake of *The Out-of-Towners.*

Comedian **Mark Klein** has performed on A&E's *Comedy on the Road* and Showtime's

*Comedy Club Network.* Web site: www.corpjester.com.

Comedian **Robert Klein** has segued from bestselling 1970s comedy albums to performing in a number of movies, including *The Landlord,* and a recurring role on the TV series *Sisters.* Web site: www.robertklein.com.

**Tommy Koenig** has been a mainstay on the national comedy scene since the early 1980s. He founded The Comics Studio in 1999 in New York to help a new generation of comics. Web site: www.comicsstudio.com.

**Dr. Brian Koffman** is a comedian and doctor with a family practice in southern California. He loves to laugh and joke with his patients and comedy audiences.

Comedian **Sue Kolinsky** has performed on the *Tonight Show* and her own Comedy Central special.

**Ernie Kovacs** was an innovative writer, performer, and producer of 1950s television.

Political comedian **Paul Krassner**'s CD, *We Have Ways of Making You Laugh,* was released by Mercury Records.

Comedian **Leah Krinsky** is an Emmy-award winning writer for HBO's *Dennis Miller Show.*

**Bob Kubota** has appeared on *Evening at the Improv,* MTV's *Half Hour Comedy Hour,* and *Entertainment Tonight.*

Comedian **Cathy Ladman** has appeared on the *Tonight Show* a bazillion times, played a recurring character on *Caroline in the City,* and has also appeared on *Just Shoot Me.*

**Maura Lake** is an actress and comedian who has appeared on *The Days of Our Lives* and *The Bold and the Beautiful.* She is also a graduate of the Groundlings Theater.

Known for his dry, intelligent wit and flat style of delivery, comedian **Steve**

**Landesburg** is best remembered for playing Detective Dietrich on the 1970s sitcom *Barney Miller.*

**Beth Lapides** is the creator of the Uncabaret, and has performed in and produced the Uncabaret touring company, a Comedy Central special, and CD. Check her out at www.uncabaret.com.

Ex-boxer **Rocky LaPorte** left employment as a Chicago truck driver after being shot three times and stabbed twice during robberies. LaPorte became a comedian with his own Comedy Central special.

**Lynn Lavner** has taken her original brand of music and comedy to forty-one states and seven countries. Web site: www.geocities.com/llavner.

Comedian **Denis Leary** stars in the FX network series *Rescue Me*, his own HBO specials, and a number of films, including *The Ref* and *Two If by Sea.*

Comedian **Robert G. Lee** can be seen on the religious game show *Inspiration Please* on the Faith and Values network.

**James Leemer** has appeared on Comedy Central's *Dr. Katz, Professional Therapist.*

Comedian **Thyra Lees-Smith** lives in Los Angeles and performs in many local clubs, including the Improv and the Comedy Store.

Comedian **Carol Leifer** has been a producer on *Seinfeld*, the star of her own sitcom, *Alright Already*, and a judge on the new *Star Search.*

**LeMaire** has appeared on the *Caroline Rhea Show*, the *Tonight Show*, and on Comedy Central's *Make Me Laugh.*

**Jay Leno** is host of NBC's the *Tonight Show.*

Comedian **Noodles Levenstein** performs on the Celebrity Cruise Lines.

Comedian **Emily Levine** has been a television writer for series that include *Designing Women*, and although this ain't much of a segue, a subsequent invitation to a physicists' think tank resulted in her one-woman show, *eLevine.universe*, synthesizing comedy and philosophy.

**Joe E. Lewis** was a comedian and singer in the 1920s when mobsters cut his throat. Lewis survived and returned to stand-up comedy, where he flourished in the 1940s through 1960s, appearing frequently in Las Vegas. Frank Sinatra starred in a movie based on Lewis's life, *The Joker Is Wild.*

In addition to his numerous HBO specials, comedian **Richard Lewis** has starred in the sitcom *Anything but Love* and in the Mel Brooks movie *Robin Hood: Men in Tights.* Web site: www.richardlewisonline.com.

**Danny Liebert** is a bestselling bumper sticker writer ("Jesus Is Coming—Look Busy") who has segued into performing comedy at the Comic Strip, Stand-Up NY, Caroline's, and numerous more ephemeral venues. Contact: dliebert@msn.com.

Comedian **Wendy Liebman** has won an American Comedy Award and appeared on the *Tonight Show* and in her own HBO comedy special. Web site: www.wendyliebman.com.

**Shirley Lipner** is a comedian who has also been the warm-up for the TBN shows *Rocky Road, Safe at Home*, and *Down to Earth.*

**Charlotte Lobb** is a multi-published author and stand-up comedian from Southern California. Contact: CharMaclay@aol.com.

**Penelope Lombard** tours clubs and colleges around the country, and has been seen in numerous TV appearances including on Comedy Central

Comedian **George Lopez** is the star of the *George Lopez* show on ABC. Web site: www.georgelopez.com.

**Leighann Lord** has appeared on Comedy Central's *Premium Blend*, NBC's *Comedy Showcase*, and ABC's *The View*. Leighann has won the Best Actress award in The Riant Theatre Play Festival for her one-woman show, *The Full Swanky*, and also won the New York City Black Comedy Award as the Most Thought Provoking Female Comic. Web site: www.leighannlord.com.

**Susie Loucks** has appeared on A&E's *Evening at the Improv, Caroline's Comedy Hour*, and an impressive number of other comedy shows.

**Jason Love** is a comedian whose cartoon *Snapshots* has garnered a worldwide audience through syndication in thirty-two newspapers, dozens of magazines, five hundred Web sites, and a line of greeting cards. Web site: www.jasonlove.com.

Comedian **Al Lubel** has performed on *Evening at the Improv* and *Comic Strip Live*, and has been a featured patient on Comedy Central's *Dr. Katz, Professional Therapist*.

**Tanya Luckerath** is comedian and actress who appeared in the movie *Beg, Borrow, or Steal* and the TV comedy show *Clip Joint*.

**Marla Lukofsky** is a twenty-year Canadian comedy veteran and voice-over artist.

**Mark Lundholm** has taken his "twelve-step comedy" to comedy clubs and detox centers across country. Web site: www.marklundholm.com.

**Daniel Lybra** is a Roundtable Comedy Conference award-winning comedian and comedy writer.

**Hellura Lyle** is a Los Angeles–based comedian and domestic violence peer who performs on the CD *Standup Comics Take a Stand Against Domestic Violence.*

Comedian **Paul Lynde**'s comedy roles ranged from the befuddled father in *Bye Bye Birdie* to playing Uncle Arthur in the TV show *Bewitched*. He spent more than a decade as the center square on *Hollywood Squares*.

**Moms Mabley** was one of the first woman comedians to star at the Apollo Theater in Harlem.

Comedian **Bernie Mac** has performed on TV's *Bernie Mac Show* and in movies including *Ocean's 11* and *Bad Santa*.

Comedian **Mike MacDonald** has starred in three Showtime and CBS specials, including *Mike MacDonald: On Target*.

Comedian **Norm Macdonald** has showcased his wry smirk as a stand-up anchor on *Saturday Night Live*, followed by the eponymous smirk sitcom *Norm*, and movies such as *Dirty Laundry*.

**Tracey MacDonald** is the first Canadian female stand-up comedian to become a *Star Search* Grand Champion. Web site: www.traceymacdonald.com.

Comedian **Kathleen Madigan** won an American Comedy Award for Best Female Stand-up, starred in her very own HBO *Comedy Half Hour*, and was a finalist on NBC's *Last Comic Standing II*. Web site: www.kathleenmadigan.com.

Comedian **Dexter Madison** has appeared on the TV shows *Evening at the Improv* and PBS's *Comedy Tonight*.

**Kelly Maguire** is an actress and comedian who has performed at the Comedy Store and the Improv in Hollywood. She has participated in the Aspen Comedy Festival and won a Dramalogue award for Best Actress. Her recent film credits include *Stranger in My House* for Lifetime television.

**Bill Maher** is the host of HBO's *Real Time with Bill Maher*. Who'd a thunk it?

**Meg Maly**: See **Blamo Risher**.

Comedian **Howie Mandel** has been the star of the series *St. Elsewhere*, the creator of his own animated series *Bobby's World*, and the host of *The Howie Mandel Show*. Web site: www.howiemandel.com.

Comedian **Henriette Mantel** has appeared in *The Brady Bunch Movie, A Very Brady Sequel*, and *The Animal*.

Comedian **Barry Marder** was a staff writer on *Seinfeld* and is the putative author of the *Letters from a Nut* series of books.

**Jeff Marder**, a seasoned stand-up comedian and television game show host, helped create the computer game Sklif's Attitude.

**Marilyn** is featured on the CD *Hot and Spicy Mamitas of Comedy*.

**Merrill Markoe** is the author of *What the Dogs Have Taught Me* and was the head writer for the original David Letterman show and a reporter for *Alien Nation*.

**Melissa Maroff** is a Los Angeles–based comedian and the second place winner of the Far Rockaway Trivia contest.

Comedian **Demetri Martin** tells jokes in New York City. Web site: www.demetrimartin.com.

**Steve Martin** is a comedian who has starred in, written, and directed comedy films including *The Jerk* and *Bowfinger*.

**Monique Marvez**'s signature raunchy wit and sexualized sarcasm is showcased on her CD, *Built for Comfort*.

**Groucho Marx** was a comedian who, with The Marx Brothers, made a number of the funniest films of the 1930s—including *Duck Soup*—and whose marvelous 1950s game show, *You Bet Your Life*, still deserves viewing on some cable channel smart enough to feature it.

**Jackie Mason** is a forty-year comedy veteran and the star of several one-man Broadway shows. Web site: www.jackiemason.com.

**Kate Mason** is a comedian who plays clubs and colleges everywhere.

Comedian **Sabrina Matthews** has performed at the Montreal Just for Laughs Festival and has been featured on Comedy Central's *Out There in Hollywood*, as well as in her own Comedy Central special. Web site: www.sabrinamatthews.com.

**Dobie Maxwell** has had an amazing life. His parents were bikers, and his best friend from childhood robbed a bank twice and tried to blame the second robbery on Dobie. Despite that, Dobie has survived to become a morning radio host and comedian who headlines across the United States. Web site: www.dobiemaxwell.com.

Comedian **Etta May** has appeared on Showtime's *Aspen Comedy Festival*.

**Jack Mayberry** is a political comedian who has made more than two dozen appearances on the *Tonight Show*.

Comedian **Denise McCanles** is a reporter for *LesbiaNation* and has appeared on the syndicated TV show *Night Stand*.

Comedian **Kris McGaha** cohosted 65 episodes of MTV's *Loveline*. Her other television appearances include the *Tonight Show* and HBO's *Curb Your Enthusiasm*. She also created and starred in the short mockumentary film, *Following Tildy*. Web site: www.krismcgaha.com.

**Paul McGinty** has been an actor, a comedy radio show host, a stand-up comic, and was a cut-up at the dinner table as a kid.

**John McGivern** is an actor, writer, and comedian who has appeared on HBO's *We're Funny That Way* and Comedy Central's *Out There II*. Web site: www.johnmcgivern.com.

**Brian McKim** is a writer and a stand-up comic who is also the editor and publisher of sheckymagazine.com.

**Melissa McQueen** is a regular performer at the Laugh Factory, the Improv, and the Funny Bone comedy clubs across the country. Web site: www.melissamcqueen.com.

Comedian **John Mendoza** has appeared on the *Tonight Show* and was one of Showtime's *Pair of Jokers*.

**Maria Menozzi** is a writer, actress, and stand-up comedian who performs across the country. She is also the author of an award-winning children's play, *The Poet Who Wouldn't Be King*. Web site: www.ironuterus.com.

**Felicia Michaels** has won an American Comedy Award and has released her own CD, *Lewd Awakenings*. Web site: www.feliciamichaels.com.

**Jeremy Beth Michaels** is a stand-up comedian, writer, and producer. Web site: www.abottomlesscup.com.

**Cathryn Michon** is a stand-up comedian who has been featured at the Montreal Comedy Festival. She has also written for a number of TV series and is author of the book *The Grrl Genius Guide to Life*. Web site: www.grrlgenius.com.

**Frank Miles** has appeared on HBO's *Larry Sanders Show* and is the creator of *Scared of Life*.

During a three-decade comedy career, comedian **George Miller** was a frequent guest on national television talk shows, including *Late Show with David Letterman*.

Comedian **Larry Miller** is featured in both of the *Nutty Professor* movies and played the pregnancy-obsessed father of teenagers in *Ten Things I Hate About You*.

Comedian **Stephanie Miller** survived her own *Stephanie Miller Show* on Fox to costar on an MSNBC talk show.

British comedian **Spike Milligan** is the favorite comic of Prince Charles. When presented a British Comedy award for Lifetime Achievement, Spike famously rewarded the prince by calling Charles "a groveling little bastard" on live TV.

**Anita Milner** is a lawyer, stand-up comedian, and keynote speaker who enrolled in law school in her forties, passed the California bar exam at age fifty, and celebrated her sixtieth birthday by performing stand-up comedy in Debbie Reynolds's lounge show in Las Vegas.

**C. Lynn Mitchell** has performed at the Comedy Store and the Improv in Hollywood, but recently moved from California to Oklahoma on her own personal "Grapes of Wrath" comedy tour. "Wherever there's a microphone and a drunken, semiconscious audience, I'll be there." Contact: CLynnLaugh@aol.com.

**Gene Mitchener** is a motivational speaker and self-proclaimed America's Funniest Sit-Down Comic.

Improv comedian **Colin Mocherie** is one of the inventive stars of *Whose Line Is It Anyway?*

Comedian **Jay Mohr** has starred in several films, including *Jerry Maguire* and *Paulie*, and served as host of NBC's *Last Comic Standing*.

**Kelly Monteith** has starred in his own BBC television series and appeared on numerous American television shows, including the *Tonight Show* and Comedy Central's *The Daily Show*.

Comedian **Carol Montgomery** has appeared on *Evening at the Improv*, Showtime's *Comedy Club Network*, and Showtime's *Girls' Night Out*.

**Lynda Montgomery** has appeared on VH-1's *Spotlight* but considers the highlight of her career to be her performance at the 1993 March on Washington in front of an audience of an estimated one million people.

**Mark Morfey** is a PGA Golf Professional and stand-up comedian who has performed at Funny Bone comedy clubs throughout the Midwest. Web site: www.markmorfey.com.

Comedian **Steve Moris** has been the opening act for the Beach Boys since the 1980s. He has also opened in Las Vegas for comic Louie Anderson and travels the world headlining comedy shows for Celebrity Cruise Lines. Web site: www.stevemoris.com.

**Gary Muledeer** has had a thirty-year comedy career that includes more than 250 TV appearances.

**Martin Mull** is a comedian and actor whose TV appearances range from *The Smothers Brothers Comedy Hour* and the *Tonight Show* to the role of the gay boss on *Roseanne*.

**Nancy Mura** has been the host of the Fox *Cubhouse* and has also appeared on A&E's *Evening at the Improv* and *Girls' Night Out*.

After comedian **Christy Murphy** became a finalist in Comedy Central's Don't Quit Your Day Job contest, she quit her day job.

**Maureen Murphy** has appeared on the *Tonight Show* and in the *Girls of the Comedy Store* video.

Comedian **Sue Murphy** is the star of her own Comedy Central special. Web site: www.suemurphycomedy.com.

**Robert Murray** is a software engineer and comedian who has performed in many venues throughout Southern California.

**Steve Neal** is a Los Angeles–based comedian and the writer of his critically acclaimed, one-man show *The Great White Trash Hope*. Web site: www.steveneal.net.

**Kevin Nealon** is a headlining comedian, actor, and one of the longest-running cast members on *Saturday Night Live*.

Comedian **Taylor Negron** has performed on TV shows including *Friends* and *Seinfeld*, and in movies such as *Stuart Little* and *Angels in the Outfield*.

**Rebecca Nell** is an actress, writer, and comedian who has performed at a number of Los Angeles clubs, including the Comedy Store.

**Leslie Nesbitt** says she's "a stand-up dame who won't go moxie on you," who has also contributed to Bill Maher's monologues for *Politically Incorrect* and performed on Comedy Central's *Make Me Laugh*.

**J. Chris Newberg** is a musician, comedian, and writer who lives in Detroit. He has two CDs, *Sucker 4 a Pretty Face* and *Chris Alive 2*. Web site: www.jchrisnewberg.com.

**Bob Newhart** is a comedian who has had several sitcoms named after him—and for good reason.

Comedian **Diane Nichols** has been named "a Queen of Comedy" and "the heroine of the 9 to 5 crowd" by *Newsweek*.

Comedian **Bob Nickman** has written for the TV shows *Roseanne* and *Freaks and Geeks*.

**Susan Norfleet** is a *Tonight Show* regular who has also appeared on *The Rosie O'Donnell Show* and *Ellen*.

Comedian **Matt North** has appeared on HBO's *Curb Your Enthusiasm* and in the move *Dirty Pictures*. Web site: www.GoodDrummer.com.

**Buzz Nutley** is a professional comedian who has written for the *Pittsburgh Post Gazette* and *Los Angeles Times*. He has sold material to Jay Leno and Yakov Smirnoff, and has performed as the opening act for Jon Stewart. Web site: www.buzznutley.com.

**Conan O'Brien**, a former writer for *Saturday Night Live* and *The Simpsons*, is the host of the NBC talk show, *Late Night with Conan O'Brien*.

Comedian **Cary Odes** has been a warm-up comedian for sitcoms including *Home Improvement* and *Mad About You*, and appeared on TV shows that include *Touched by an Angel* and *Melrose Place*.

**Rosie O'Donnell** hosted her own cheery talk show and has been featured in movies that include *Sleepless in Seattle* and *Exit to Eden*.

Irish comedian **Owen O'Neill** has performed at the Montreal Comedy Festival and has been a guest on *Late Night with Conan O'Brien*.

**Rob O'Reilly** is a Cleveland comedian who has played venues that include the Cleveland Improv and the Comedy Connections. Contact: rob84@bu.edu.

**Christine O'Rourke** is a screenwriter and comedian who performs at the Improv in Hollywood.

Comedian **Patton Oswalt** has been seen on *Seinfeld* and is a cast member of CBS's *King of Queens*. Web site: www.pattonoswalt.com.

**Rick Overton** has appeared on the *Tonight Show, Late Show with David Letterman, Seinfeld,* and in his own HBO *One Night Stand*. Overton's movie credits include *Mrs. Doubtfire, Groundhog Day,* and *Beverly Hills Cop.*

**Guy Owen** has been a comedian and a motivational and conference speaker for more than twenty years. He has also performed at the Comedy Store, for President and Mrs. Carter, and in commercials for Honda and Black and Decker.

Comedian **Jack Paar** (1918–2004) held the nation's rapt attention as he pioneered late-night talk on the *Tonight Show* from 1957 through 1962. He told his viewers farewell when still in his prime and headed his own NBC variety series from 1962 to 1965.

**Tom Parks** has been making people laugh for more than twenty years including on the *Tonight Show, Late Show with David Letterman*, on both HBO and Showtime, and for two seasons he was the Anchorman on HBO's *Not Necessarily the News* for which he was nominated for an ACE Award. Tom most recently hosted the Family Channel show *Wait Till You Have Kids.*

**Pat Paulsen** was a comedian featured on the groundbreaking *Smothers Brothers Show* and who ran satirically for president for three decades.

**Dave Pavone** is a stand-up comedian and comedy writer based in Phoenix, Arizona. He is the cocreator of *The Timmy Sketch Project*, a local comedy sketch show. Contact: dbpavone@yahoo.com.

**Minnie Pearl**, a member of the Grand Ole Opry cast from 1940 until her death in 1996, was country music's preeminent comedian.

Comic **Steven Pearl** has shared the stage with such well-known comedians as Sam Kinison, Robin Williams, and the man himself, Richard Pryor.

**Becky Pedigo** has appeared on Comedy Central's *Premium Blend*.

**Nancy Jo Perdue** is a stand-up comedian and Seattle-based journalist.

**Gene Perret** has written comedy material for more than thirty years for legends such as Phyllis Diller, Bob Hope, Carol Burnett, and Bill Cosby. He has won three Emmys and a Writers Guild Award for his TV comedy writing, and has published twenty-five books on humor, including *Comedy Writing Step by Step*. Web site: www.members.aol.com/geneperret.

**Tammy Pescatelli** was a finalist on the second season of NBC's *Last Comic Standing*. Web site: www.tammypescatelli.com.

**Mary Pfeiffer** is a self-described squeaky-clean comedian. Contact: MerryPfeiffer@webtv.net.

**Dat Phan** was the winning comedian and last comic standing on the first season of NBC's *Last Comic Standing*. Web site: www.datphan.com.

Comedian **Emo Philips** has appeared on numerous HBO and Showtime specials, as well as in the Weird Al Yankovich movie *UHF*. Web site: www.emophilips.com.

**Joe Pinetta** is the recipient of an American Comedy Award, has appeared on the *Tonight Show* and *Seinfeld*, and in the movies *Duets* and *Junior*. Pinette's comedy CD is titled *Show Me the Buffet*.

Comedian **Monica Piper** won a Golden Globe for her writing on the sitcom *Roseanne*. Her Showtime special *Monica, Just You* was nominated for a Cable Ace Award.

Comedian **Kevin Pollack** has starred in movies that include *A Few Good Men* and *The Usual Suspects*.

**Marty Pollio** is a juggler and stand-up comedian who has made multiple appearances on the *Tonight Show*.

**Brenda Pontiff** costarred on the sitcom *The Five Mrs. Buchanans* and has performed as a comedian at the Improvisation, the Comedy Store, and the Laugh Factory.

**Brian Posehn** has performed as a series regular on the sitcom *Just Shoot Me* and HBO's *Mr. Show*, and starred in his own Comedy Central special. Web site: brianposehn.com.

**Jennifer Post** is stand-up comedian and lawyer.

In addition to having been one of the frightfully inventive stars of Comedy Central's *Whose Line Is It Anyway?*, **Greg Proops** has been the host of their game shows *Vs* and *Rendez-View*. Web site: www.gregproops.com.

Comedian **Paul Provenza** starred on the last season of *Northern Exposure* and in his own HBO, Showtime, and Comedy Central shows and series.

Comedian **Richard Pryor** is a nearly forty-year veteran of comedy recording, movies, and TV, including the groundbreaking 1970s *Richard Pryor Show* and the movie *Silver Streak*. Web site: www.richardpryor.com.

Comedian **Paula Poundstone** has starred in a number of her own HBO comedy specials.

**Colin Quinn** is a comedian and former anchor of Weekend Update on *Saturday Night Live*. He hosts *Tough Crowd with Colin Quinn* on Comedy Central.

**Steve Race** was a BBC Radio disc jockey.

**Chantel Rae** has performed at the Comedy Store and the Laugh Factory in Los Angeles, and at the Irvine Improv.

Gay comedian **Georgia Ragsdale** has appeared at the Montreal Just for Laughs Festival and released the concert videos *Sporty Girls*, *Honey Pass That Around* and a CD, *Always Forward, Never Straight*. Web site: www.georgiaragsdale.net.

**Lewis Ramey** has appeared on Comedy Central's *Premium Blend*.

**Michael Rasky** was the featured comedian at the LA Gay Pride Festival and has performed at the Improv in Los Angeles and Las Vegas.

Comedian **Greg Ray** has been seen on *Evening at the Improv*, CNN, and *PM Magazine*. But he is perhaps best known for holding the watermelon in the Ginsu knife commercials.

**Larry Reeb** has appeared on Showtime's *Comedy Club All-Stars* and A&E's *Evening at the Improv*.

Comedian **Alex Reed** has performed on *Evening at the Improv*.

Comedian **Brian Regan** has appeared on the *Tonight Show* and in his own Comedy Central and Showtime specials. Web site: www.brianregan.com.

**Carl Reiner** is the creator and costar of *The Dick Van Dyke Show*, and director of films including *The Jerk*, *All of Me*, and *Oh, God*.

**Paul Reiser** is the star and creator of a sitcom based on his marriage, *Mad About You*.

**Melanie Reno** has appeared on Comedy Central's *Premium Blend*. Web site: www.melaniereno.com.

Comedian **Rick Reynolds**'s one-man comedy show *Only the Truth Is Funny* became a Showtime special. He has written a follow-up one-man show, *All Grown up and No Place to Go*.

**Jim Rez** is a Los Angeles–based comedian.

Comedian **Caroline Rhea** has starred on *Sabrina the Teenage Witch* and was also the host of *The Caroline Rhea Show*. Web site: www.carolinerhea.com.

**Andi Rhoads** is a Los Angeles comedian who has performed at The Improv and the Comedy Store in Hollywood. Contact: andirhoads@yahoo.com

Call out the coincidence police: **Tom Rhodes** was the star of the NBC sitcom *Mr. Rhodes*.

Comedian **Ron Richards** won an Emmy Award for his writing on *Late Show with David Letterman* and a Cable Ace Award for HBO's *Not Necessarily the News*. He has also been on the writing staff of the *Tonight Show* and *Saturday Night Live*.

Comedian **Adam Richmond** has appeared on Nickelodeon, Fox Sports Net, and in several national commercials. He has also been a staff writer for the Canadian animated series *Chilly Beach*. Contact: gunnyfuy@yahoo.com.

Comedian **Karen Ripley** has been performing as an out lesbian since 1977 and has appeared on Comedy Central's *The Daily Show*.

**Blamo Risher** and his partner Meg Maly are one of the few male-female stand-up comedy teams in America. Web site: www.funnysincebirth.com.

**Joan Rivers** is a comedian whose career stretches over four decades. She is an actress, talk show host, and bestselling author. Web site: www.joanrivers.com.

**Denise Munro Robb** has been seen on A&E, Lifetime, Comedy Central, and MTV, and is also a political activist who ran for Los Angeles City Council. Robb recently got married and came to the realization that she doesn't need a man in her life to make her happy. She can be miserable either way. Check her out at: www.denisemunrorobb.com.

**Robin Roberts** was a writer/voice performer for the nationally syndicated radio show *Rick Dee's Weekly Top 40*, and is the creator of the Los Angeles showcase, *Comedy by the Book*. Web site: www.comedyschmomedy.com.

**Johnny Robish** is a comedian whose jokes appear frequently in the Laugh Lines column of the *Los Angeles Times* and whose giglebytes are featured in the Internet radio program *Radio Free OZ*.

**Mo Rocca** is a former correspondent for Comedy Central's *The Daily Show*, a contributor to NBC's *Today Show*, and the host of Bravo's *Things I Hate About You*.

**Chris Rock** is a comedian and actor who is, natch, host of HBO's *The Chris Rock Show*. He also hosted The 2005 Academy Awards.

Comedian **Rick Rockwell** was the much-reviled bridegroom of Fox TV's *Who Wants to Marry a Millionaire?*

Comedian **Roberta Rockwell** has been featured in the Toyota Comedy Festival and the Bud Light Ladies of Laughter, and was a semifinalist in the Gilda's Club Laugh-Off. Web site: www.robertarockwell.com.

**Paul Rodriguez** has been the star of the first Hispanic sitcom on network TV, *AKA Pablo*, in the 1970s and also starred on CBS's *Trial and Error* and *Grand Slam*. He also appears in the movies *Born in East LA*, *Made in America*, and *Rough Magic*.

Comedian **Gregg Rogell** has appeared on the *Tonight Show*.

Comedian-turned-screenwriter **John Rogers** has been the head writer for the *Jackie Chan* animated series on the WB. Rogers also adapted the comic book

series, *The Mage*, and wrote the screenplay for the sci-fi movie *The Core*.

**Kenny Rogerson** has appeared on Comedy Central, MTV, and Showtime, and in the movie *There's Something About Mary*.

**Ray Romano** is the star of the CBS series *Everybody Loves Raymond* and the author of the bestselling book *Everything, and a Kite*.

**Janet Rosen** has been featured in the Marshall's Women in Comedy Festival, has written for *Glamour* and other national magazines, and lives and commits comedy in New York City.

**Flash Rosenberg** is a comedian and cartoonist who has performed at the Toyota Comedy Festival and The Joseph Papp Public Theater. She was voted Philadelphia's *Local Comedian Most Likely to Make You Laugh Until It Hurts*, and her cartoons have appeared in the *New York Times*.

Comedian **Jeffrey Ross** has both written for, and performed on, Comedy Central.

Comedian **John Ross** has appeared on TV shows that include *Coach* and *St. Elsewhere*.

Philadelphia comedian **Eric Roth** won "Philly's Last Local Comic Standing" contest. Contact: Emroth@aol.com.

Comedian **Mike Rowe** has been featured on NBC's *Comedy Showcase* and on Comedy Central's *Dr. Katz, Professional Therapist*.

Comedian **John Roy** has performed as the opening act for Steven Wright and was a semifinalist on *Star Search*.

**Bob Rubin** is a San Francisco–based comedian and author of the play *I Never Knew My Father*.

Comedian **Mike Rubin** has been a writer on Comedy Central's *Crank Yankers* and a producer of *The Bachelor*. Contact: michaeldiehard@yahoo.com.

Comedian **Rita Rudner** has appeared on *The Tonight Show*, has been featured on any number of comedy specials, including her own on HBO, and is author of the books *Naked Beneath My Clothes* and *Tickled Pink*. Web site: www.ritafunny.com.

Comedian **Tom Ryan**'s national television appearances include performances on *Late Show with David Letterman*, Showtime, A&E, and Comedy Central. He also has performed as an opening act for B. B. King, Tim Allen, and Steven Wright. Web site: www.comediantomryan.com.

Route 66 is **Terri Ryburn-LaMonte**'s personal passion. She is from Normal, Illinois, making her the only normal person represented in this book. Contact: tlrybur@ilstu.edu.

Comedian **Bob Saget** has been the star of the sitcom *Full House* and host of *America's Funniest Home Videos*.

**Mort Sahl** has been a groundbreaking political comic in the 1950s and has frequently appeared on the *Tonight Show*. He continues to provide his sardonic comments onstage.

Comedian **Dan St. Paul** has appeared on *An Evening at the Improv* and VH-1's *Stand-Up Spotlight* and in the movie *Flubber*.

In the 1960s, comedian **Soupy Sales**'s *The Soupy Sales Show* became the children's show that also made adults laugh throughout the United States, as well as in Canada, Australia, and New Zealand.

Comedian **Betsy Salkind** has been a writer for *Roseanne* and has appeared on *Arli$$* and the *Tonight Show*. Web site: www.betsysalkind.com.

**Jim Samuels** was a beloved San Francisco–based comedian who died in 1990.

**Adam Sandler** is a former cast member of *Saturday Night Live* and the star of a string of comedy movies, including *Happy Gilmore*, *The Waterboy*, and *The Wedding Singer*. Web site: www.adamsandler.com.

**Peter Sasso** performs in comedy clubs and on cruise ships. Contact: sassopeter@hotmail.com.

Comedian **Drake Sather** wrote for numerous TV shows, including *NewsRadio*, *The Dennis Miller Show*, and *Ed*. He received an Emmy nomination for his work on *The Larry Sanders Show* and cowrote the movie *Zoolander* with actor Ben Stiller.

**Dan Savage** is a writer and humorist.

Comedian **Charisse Savarin** has appeared on Fox's *The Sunday Comics*.

**Stephanie Schiern** is a lawyer and a stand-up comedian who has performed at the Comedy Store in Hollywood.

Comedian **Mark Schiff** is a regular performer on the *Tonight Show* and *Late Show with David Letterman*. He starred in his own Showtime special, *My Crummy Childhood*.

**Robert Schimmel** has been featured in his own HBO Special, and his CDs include *If You Buy This CD, I Can Buy This Car*, *Robert Schimmel Comes Clean*, and *Unprotected*. Web site: www.robertschimmel.com.

**Lew Schneider** has appeared on *Dr. Katz, Professional Therapist*.

Comedian **Jerry Seinfeld** helped rethink the sitcom with his eponymous *Seinfeld*.

**Sandi Selvi** is a wife and mother who triumphed over Multiple Sclerosis, and a comedian who performs extensively in the San Francisco area and at The Improv in San Jose. Web site: www.sandiselvi.com.

Six-time Emmy Award winner **Ross Shafer** was a host of *Match Game* and the Miss America Pageant.

**Ronnie Shakes** was a comedian and TV writer who made frequent appearances on the *Tonight Show.*

Comedian **Garry Shandling** is the star and creator of *The Larry Sanders Show.*

Comedian **Shang** has costarred on *The Jamie Foxx Show* and has been featured in the Best of the Fest on the HBO's *U.S. Comedy Arts Festival* special. Web site: www.iamshang.com.

**Craig Sharf** is a comedian and comedy writer who has sold material to professional comedians—including Joan Rivers—and to other comedy outlets such as the *Weinerville* TV show. Contact: csharf@yahoo.com.

**Jeff Shaw** is a comedian, humor columnist, and staff writer in the Alternative Cards department of Cleveland's American Greetings Corporation. Contact: Dork2Dude@aol.com.

Comedian **Allan Sherman** became a comedy writer for 1950s TV and the *Jackie Gleason Show*, and was a creator and producer of *I've Got a Secret*. While producer of the *Tonight Show* in 1962, songs Sherman had written to entertain his friends at parties were released as a comedy album, *My Son the Folk Singer*, which went to number one on the charts, and was followed by six more comedy records.

Comedian **Craig Shoemaker** has appeared on more than one hundred television shows, including HBO's *Comic Relief* and *Hollywood Squares*. His film appearances include *Scream 2* and *The Lovemaster*. Web site: www.craigshoemaker.com.

**Tricia Shore** performs at Southern California comedy venues, writes for the *Los Angeles Times* and other publications, and speaks to groups about the pleasures and pains of motherhood. Web site: www.comicmom.com.

Comedian **Will Shriner** has directed episodes of *Everybody Loves Raymond* and won a Humanitas Award for his direction of an episode of *Frasier.*

Comedian **Jimmy Shubert** was featured at the Just for Laughs Montreal Comedy Festival and in the movies *Go*, *Coyote Ugly*, and *The Italian Job*. Web site: www.jimmyshubert.com.

Comedian **Ritch Shydner** has written for the sitcom *Roseanne* and appeared on the TV shows *Married with Children* and *Designing Women*. He has also starred in films such as *Beverly Hills Cop II* and *Roxanne.*

Comedian **Jennifer Siegal** has worked as a Disneyland portrait artist, a dot.com illustrator, and a movie critic. She also writes a monthly art column in San Francisco. On weekends, she likes to go where the green lights take her.

**Laura Silverman** was the voice of the bored receptionist Laura on Comedy Central's *Dr. Katz, Professional Therapist*, and she also appeared in the movie *Half Baked.*

Comedian **Sarah Silverman** has appeared in *There's Something About Mary*, played a comedy writer on HBO's *Larry Sanders Show*, and has been a comedy writer for *Saturday Night Live.*

Comedian **Sinbad** has starred in several of his own HBO specials, including *Son of a Preacher Man*, and in a number of movies, including *House Guest* and *First Kid.*

Comedian **Carol Siskind** has appeared on *Evening at the Improv*, *Comic Strip Live*, *Girls' Night Out*, and innumerable other comedy specials.

Comedian **Daryl Sivad** has appeared on TV shows that include *The Jamie Foxx Show* and the *Tonight Show.*

**Red Skelton** started as a vaudeville performer and worked his way up to *The Red Skelton Show*, which ran for on TV for twenty years, from 1951–71.

**Traci Skene** is a stand-up comic who is also the cocreator, editor, and publisher of SHECKYmagazine.com.

Comedian **Steve Skrovan** has written for the sitcom *Seinfeld.*

**Brad Slaight** has segued from the recurring role of Izzy Adams on *The Young and the Restless* to stand-up comedy and contributing writer to the *Tonight Show.* Web site: http://members.aol.com/bisbprods.

Comedian **Bobby Slayton** has appeared in the movies *Ed Wood*, *Get Shorty*, and *Bandits*, and portrayed Joey Bishop in the HBO movie *The Rat Pack.* Web site: www.bobbyslayton.com.

Comedian **Bruce Smirnoff**'s award-winning one-man show is titled *Other Than My Health, I Have Nothing: And Today I Don't Feel So Good.*

**Yakov Smirnoff** emigrated from Russia to entertain as an American comedian from Las Vegas to the White House. Smirnoff has also appeared in movies such as *Moscow on the Hudson* and in his own TV series, *What a Country.* Web site: www.yakov.com.

**Bob Smith**, one of the first openly gay comics on TV and the *Tonight Show*, is also the author of the book *Openly Bob.* Web site: http://literati.net/Smith.

Comedian **Margaret Smith** has won an American Comedy Award, performed in her own Comedy Central special, and starred in *That '80s Show.*

Canadian comedian **Steve Smith** is also a writer, producer, and past recipient of the Banff Television Festival's Sir Peter Ustinov Comedy Network Award.

**Tracy Smith** has appeared on MTV's *Half Hour Comedy Hour* and Lifetime's *Girls' Night Out.*

**Tommy Smothers** and his brother Dick form the comedy and music duo the Smothers Brothers, most famously known for their groundbreaking 1960s comedy-variety TV show *The Smothers Brothers Comedy Show.* The Smothers Brothers continue to perform and entertain, over forty-five years into their comedy careers. Web site: www.smothersbrothers.com.

**Carrie Snow** is a stand-up comedian who has appeared on Comedy Central. She was also a writer for the first two *Roseanne* TV shows.

Comedian **David Spade** is a star of the sitcom *Just Shoot Me* and, his magnum opus, *Lost and Found.* Web site: www.davidspade.com.

**Winston Spear** has been performing in clubs for more than a decade in Canada, the United States, and as far away as the United Arab Emirates. He has been featured on CTV and The Comedy Network's *Comedy Now.*

**Spanky** has been voted "1999 Comedian of the Year" by the Campus Activities Reader's Choice Awards. Also in 1999, Spanky made his thirty-fifth television appearance on PBS's *Comics A to Z.*

**Dan Spencer** has appeared in the movie *Shakes the Clown.*

**Wendy Spero** has performed on Comedy Central's *Premium Blend.*

**Livia Squires** has appeared on Showtime. She has been a finalist in California's

Funniest Female contest and appears regularly at the Ice House in Pasadena, California. Web site: www.roadcomic.com.

**Leslie Stahl** is a correspondent and anchor of CBS's *60 Minutes.*

Comedian **Tim Steeves** has been featured at the Just for Laughs Montreal Comedy Festival.

**David Steinberg** is a comedian, writer, and director of comedy films and television.

Comedian **Skip Stephenson** was one of the hosts of the 1980s TV show *Real People.*

Comedian **Jon Stewart** is the host of Comedy Central's *Daily Show.*

**Cyndi Stiles** is a Boston-area comedian who has appeared on the bill with comedians Bill Braudis, Teddie Bergeron, and Jen Trainor. Contact: tarn707@comcast.net.

Comedian **Jeff Stilson** has been a writer for *Late Show with David Letterman* and a producer for both MTV's *The Osbournes* and HBO's *The Chris Rock Show.*

**Brad Stine** has appeared on *Evening at the Improv* and Showtime's *Comedy Club Network*, and is available from Clean Comedians booking agency.

Comedian **Fred Stoller** has written for the sitcom *Seinfeld*, has appeared on the TV shows *Everybody Loves Raymond* and *Six Feet Under*, and has appeared in the movies *Austin Powers* and *Dumb and Dumber.*

Comedian **Pam Stone** had a recurring role on the ABC sitcom *Coach*, has appeared in her own Showtime special, and is a winner of the Gracie Allen Award from the American Women in Radio and Television for her syndicated radio program *The Pam Stone Show.*

**Lisa Sunstedt** has been a featured performer in the Montreal Just for Laughs Festival and a guest star on *Tracy Takes On.*

Comedian **Glenn Super** appeared on the TV shows *Evening at the Improv, Comic Strip Live,* and *Solid Gold.*

Comedian **Wanda Sykes** is the host of Comedy Central's *Premium Blend* and star of her own sitcom *Wanda.* Web site: www.wandasykes.com.

In addition to founding her own religion (Judyism), comedian **Judy Tenuta** is a panelist on *Match Game* and star of the film *Butch Camp.* Her comedy albums include *Space Goddessy.* Web site: www.judytenuta.com.

**Mary Lou Terry** is a promising comedian from the Palos Verdes peninsula in California and is happy that she finally learned how to be funny on stage: "I made the promise, and kept it."

**Dave Thomas** is a graduate of the legendary SCTV and has since been seen all over the dial from *Grace Under Fire* to *That '70s Show.*

Comedian **Christopher Titus** was the star and executive producer of the Fox sitcom *Titus*, based on his dysfunctional family. Web site: www.christophertitus.com.

Comedian **Lily Tomlin** is an original cast member of *Laugh-In.* She has acted in films that range from *Nashville* to *Orange County*, and appeared on TV series that include *Murphy Brown.* Web site: www.lilytomlin.com.

Comedian **Paul F. Tompkins** has won an Emmy as a writer for HBO's *Mr. Show* and has also appeared on HBO's *Real Time with Bill Maher.* Web site: www.paulftompkins.com.

**Rosie Tran** is regular performer at the Laugh Factory in Los Angeles, the Ha!, the New York Comedy Club, the Boston Comedy Club, and other clubs and colleges across the United States. Web site: www.rosietran.com.

Comedian **Greg Travis** is an actor who has appeared on the TV shows *CSI: Miami* and *JAG*, and in the movies *Man on the Moon* and *Starship Troopers*.

Comedian **Stu Trivax** has appeared on the *Tonight Show*, hosted the TV series *Comic Strip Live*, and appeared in the movies *Spy Hard* and *Rebel High*.

**Aisha Tyler** has appeared on NBC's *Comedy Showcase* and hosted E! Channel's *Talk Soup*. Web site: www.aishatyler.com.

**Robin Tyler**'s 1978 comedy album *Always a Bridesmaid, Never a Groom* was her third album but her first as an openly lesbian comic. And in 1979 she became the first openly gay comedian to appear on national television.

Comedian **Jeff Valdez** is the cofounder and chairman of cable network Sí TV, and was the creator of Nickelodeon's *Brothers Garcia*.

**Jennifer Vally** has performed in comedy clubs across the United States and worked as a comedy writer and producer for the *Late, Late Show with Craig Kilborn*, the *Tonight Show*, and the Oxygen Network.

**Matt Vance** has been the morning show producer for *Mick & Allen's Freak Show* on Rock 99 radio Salt Lake City.

**Bill Vaughan** (1915–1977) was an American journalist and author.

**Cheril Vendetti** has appeared on such TV shows as A&E's *Evening at the Improv* and *Girls' Night Out*, and has played comedy clubs across the country.

**Tami Vernekoff** has appeared on Comedy Central's *Premium Blend* and is a member of

the Fashion Police for *US Magazine.*

King of the deadpan comics, **Jackie Vernon** made frequent appearances on the *Ed Sullivan Show*. His wry, sad-sack style influenced some of today's most popular comedians.

Comedian **Charlie Viracola** has had his own half-hour specials on both Showtime and Comedy Central. Web site: www.planetcharlie.com.

Comedian **Rich Voss** was a finalist on NBC's *Last Comic Standing.*

**John Wagner** is the creator of the alternative comic *Judge Dredd*.

**Lesley Wake** is a comedian and staff writer for the WB show *What I Like About You.*

Comedian **George Wallace** is a regular performer on both the *Tonight Show* and *Late Night with David Letterman*.

**Wally Wang** is a comedian and an actor who, in his latest performance on the Internet, managed to convince thousands of men that he's actually a 23-year-old blonde. He also performs in Las Vegas and has appeared on A&E's *Evening at the Improv*. He wrote the books *Visual Basic for Dummies* and *Microsoft Office for Dummies,* and publishes a computer humor column in *Boardwatch Magazine*.

Comedian **Marsha Warfield** played bailiff Roz Russell on the sitcom *Night Court* and later joined the cast of *Empty Nest*.

In addition her to stand-up and sketch comedy work, **Jayne Warren** is an actor and writer. In her spare time, Jayne worries. A lot. Web site: www.jaynewarren.com.

**Joel Warshaw** has performed for his family and friends for years, and can now also be seen performing in Los Angeles at the Comedy Store and at the LA Cabaret Comedy Club.

**Damon Wayans** was the star and one of the creators of *In Living Color*, and has starred in several movies—including *The Last Boy Scout*—and three of his own HBO specials.

Comedian **Matt Weinhold** won the Seattle Comedy Competition and has appeared on Showtime, MTV, and Comedy Central.

**Lotus Weinstock** was a beloved Los Angeles comedian whose comedy career spanned three decades, from her engagement to Lenny Bruce to appearances on the *Tonight Show, Evening at the Improv*, Lifetime's *Girls' Night Out*, and her extensive charity work.

**Cindee Weiss** has performed at the NY Comedy Club, The Comedy Cellar, Gotham Comedy Club, Stand-Up NY, and Yuk Yuk's in Toronto.

**Mercedes Wence** is a Los Angeles-based comedian.

**Sheila Wenz** has appeared on the cable channels Lifetime, A&E, and Comedy Central.

Comedian **Suzanne Westenhoefer** is the star of her own HBO special and CD entitled *Nothing in My Closet but My Clothes*. Web site: www.suzannew.com.

Comedian **Basil White** is a weird, scary man-child. Know all at www.basilwhite.com.

**Grace White** is a middle-aged hippie with a mother who loves her, a father for whom overeating is an art form, and a stand-up comedy act like no other. Web site: www.gracewhiteproductions.com.

**Slappy White** was a classic comedian whose career ranged from the Catskills to the *Ed Sullivan Show*.

Comedian **Dan Whitney**'s *Larry the Cable Guy* is featured on nearly two hundred radio stations nationwide. He has also been seen on Comedy Central's *Blue Collar Comedy*.

Comedian **Penny Wiggins** has appeared on TV's *Evening at the Improv* and with the Amazing Jonathan's live Las Vegas show.

**Harland Williams** has hosted Comedy Central's *Premium Blend* and appeared in films including *The Whole Nine Yards* and *Half-Baked*. Web site: www.harlandwilliams.com.

Comedian **Karen Williams** has performed on PBS's *In the Life*, and her material has been featured in *Out, Loud, & Laughing*.

**Robin Williams** received an Academy Award for *Good Will Hunting* and is the star of dozens of other movies including *Mrs. Doubtfire* and *Flubber*.

Comedian **Dan Wilson** has appeared on *Star Search*, A&E, MTV, and HBO.

Comedian **Flip Wilson** was the star of the 1960s television show *The Flip Wilson Show*, still running on cable.

**John Wing** has been featured at the Just for Laughs Montreal Comedy Festival.

Comedian **Lizz Winstead** is the creator of Comedy Central's *The Daily Show* and *Air America Radio*.

Comedian **Jonathan Winters** is an Emmy Award winner and has been nominated for twelve Grammy Awards. Web site: www.jonathanwinters.com.

Comedian **Anita Wise** has appeared on the *Tonight Show* and at the Just for Laughs Festival in Montreal.

Comedian **Fred Wolf** is the screenwriter responsible for the movies *Black Sheep* and *Joe Dirt*.

**Dennis Wolfberg** was a beloved 1980s comedian, a *Tonight Show* regular, and a cast member of the TV series *Quantum Leap*.

**Jackie Wollner** has been a finalist in the prestigious San Francisco Comedy Competition and is the creator of *You Animal You—A One Mammal Show*.

**Steven Wright** has appeared on numerous HBO specials, was a recurring cast member of the sitcom *Mad About You*, and received an Oscar nomination for Best Short Film. Web site: www.stevenwright.com.

Comedian **Robert Wuhl** is the protagonist and creator of the HBO sitcom *Arli$$*.

**Jim Wyatt** is a stand-up comedian and animation producer of *Garfield* and *The Twisted Tales of Felix the Cat*.

**Pamela Yager** has appeared on *Saturday Night Live* and Comedy Central's *Stand Up, Stand Up*. Web site: http://home.earthlink.net/~pyager.

**Weird Al Yankovic**'s latest CD of comedy songs, *Poodle Hat*, won a Grammy for Best Comedy Album of 2003. This is Al's third Grammy win, including Best Comedy Recording in 1984 for *Eat It* and Best Concept Video in 1988 for *Fat*. Web site: www.weirdal.com.

**Tami Yellin** teaches sitcom writing at New York University, has written sitcoms for CBS, Nickelodeon, and Disney, and is currently performing comedy all over New York and Seattle. Contact: tyf@gis.net.

**Donna Jean Young** was a comedian of the 1960s who was featured on *Laugh-In* and in her own comedy album, *Live from East McKeesport*.

**Henny Youngman** was a self-proclaimed "king of the one-liners" whose comedy career ranged from vaudeville and the Catskills to the *Tonight Show*.

**Pete Zamora** has a degree in broadcasting and theater from Columbia University in New York and has appeared in national commercials for Coca-Cola and Disneyland.

When **Kate Zannoni** isn't in a carpool, camping with the Cub Scouts, or serving pop tarts for dinner, she's a stand-up comic in Cleveland, Ohio.

Comedian **Bob Zany** has appeared on *The Drew Carey Show*, the *Tonight Show*, and in films that include *Joe Dirt*. Web site: www.bobzany.com.

**uBu (ib me) Zurub** has performed at the Hollywood Improv, Caroline's in New York, and The Cleveland Improv, among other venues. Web site: www.comics.comedy circle.com/ubu_zurub.html.